OUT THERE

Also by *Outside* magazine:
The Edge of the World
The Darkest Places

OUT THERE

THE WILDEST STORIES FROM *OUTSIDE* MAGAZINE

THE EDITORS OF *OUTSIDE* MAGAZINE

GUILFORD,
CONNECTICUT

FALCON®

An imprint of The Rowman & Littlefield Publishing Group, Inc.
4501 Forbes Blvd., Ste. 200
Lanham, MD 20706
www.rowman.com

Falcon and FalconGuides are registered trademarks and Make Adventure Your Story is a
trademark of The Rowman & Littlefield Publishing Group, Inc.

Distributed by NATIONAL BOOK NETWORK

British Library Cataloguing in Publication Information available

Library of Congress Cataloging-in-Publication Data available

ISBN 978-1-4930-4851-9 (paperback)
ISBN 978-1-4930-3082-8 (e-book)

∞™ The paper used in this publication meets the minimum requirements
of American National Standard for Information Sciences—Permanence
of Paper for Printed Library Materials, ANSI/NISO Z39.48-1992.

CONTENTS

CONSUMED

INTRODUCTION

"In my father's company, trips have a tendency to spiral into disaster," wrote Wells Tower in his 2008 *Outside* story, "Meltdown." "The mishaps are sometimes large and sometimes inconsequential, but the specter of calamity always rides in his sidecar."

Tower was recounting a family trip to Greenland gone comically sideways, but he could just as easily have been describing the essential ingredients of classic *Outside* storytelling. I could argue that the magazine, now forty years old, established its reputation in the world of literary journalism by chronicling more serious adventures, ones involving legendary explorers clashing with nature's harshest realities—frequently ending in real, not metaphorical, disasters. Examples include John Krakauer's "Into Thin Air" and Sebastian Junger's "The

Storm," both of which became bestselling books (the latter under the title *The Perfect Storm*) and Hollywood movies.

Those dark tragedies are a key part of the magazine's legacy, but longtime readers have come to understand that *Outside*'s true gift is in chronicling misadventure. That's the common thread among the stories we've selected for *Out There*, those memorable reads that begin with the promise that, even if no one's life is necessarily hanging in the balance, something may go horribly awry at any moment, and documenting that misfortune will inevitably yield rich comedic material or a surprisingly poignant moment. Or sometimes both. A woman with 700 dogs trying to fix a broken heart. A BASE jumper who can't stop himself from upping the ante. A bike advocate who cycles three-and-a-half hours—each way—to work. You get the idea.

I'll confess that I didn't always appreciate this storytelling approach. Early on in my tenure, longtime *Outside* contributing writer McKenzie Funk sent in a strange pitch about "confluence hunters," a new breed of adventurers who use GPS to tick off remote points on the globe where major points of longitude and latitude intersect. My initial reaction to these people? Get a life. There was no way *Outside* was going to endorse such a trivial pursuit. But as our wise editorial director, Alex Heard, pointed out, covering this scene didn't have to mean tacit approval of the endeavor. He convinced me that Funk would employ a deft touch; by profiling the top confluence hunter, Greg Michaels, and making an earnest effort to take him seriously, he'd deliver a hilarious story. He was right. Funk spent a week chasing far flung confluences in Bolivia with Michaels. He witnessed the absurdity, but by embracing his subject's passion, Funk experienced the best qualities of misadventure, and readers came away with a grudging respect for Michaels's obsession when they read "Because It's There. (Sort of)."

Since then, I've realized that obsession is one of several reliable catalysts for misadventure. Plenty of elite athletes obsess over goals, and we frequently chronicle them. But there are also those mere mortals among us, regular Joes with day jobs and family obligations, who get fixated on some obscure pursuit they can't let go of. Take, for example, Dallas Trombley, a young man from Albany, New York, who we profiled in 2011. Trombley had spent $200,000 of his own money to build a series of doomed watercraft aimed at taking him down the Hudson River for reasons he can't quite articulate. (You'll find him here in "Watership Down Down Down Down Down and (Alas) Down Again.") Or Brit Eaton, the man you'll encounter in "The Brotherhood of the Very Expensive Pants," a sort of postmodern 49er who scours ghost towns and abandoned barns across the West looking for vintage denim he then sells for a small fortune to fashion designers in New York. Or even one of our own, former *Outside* editor Kevin Fedarko, who chucked a magazine career to pursue his dream of being a Grand Canyon raft guide in his 40s. His memoir of that pursuit, "They Call Me Groover Boy," chronicled a tragicomic apprenticeship that required several seasons of manning the poop boat.

We've also learned to court misadventure by assigning travel stories in highly undesirable places. As a kid, I still remember the shocking headlines about the nuclear-reactor meltdown in Chernobyl in 1986. Once that disaster fell out of the news cycle, the general public largely forgot about it. So, what had happened? In 2009, we sent Henry Shukman on a tour of the abandoned city ("Chernobyl, My Primeval, Teeming, Irradiated Eden"), where he encountered a still-radioactive wasteland devoid of human life. More surprising: the quarantine zone had miraculously transformed itself into Eastern Europe's most bizarre animal sanctuary, full of wild genetic mutations.

Over the years we've sent writers to a spa offering vaginal steams, a Siberian city terrorized by bears, the Mississippi River at historic flood levels, the Australian Outback with a menacing kangaroo hunter named Cujo, and an Antarctic research station where cabin fever has driven many a scientist mad. You don't want to visit these places. Still, reading the experiences of our intrepid reporters, you find yourself exploring odd corners of the world from your armchair—and thankful for the vicarious romp.

The third leg of the misadventure stool is the world of fringe athletics. *Outside* writers have a unique ability to uncover obscure pursuits that will never reach the pages of mainstream sports sections. To report on the surprising popularity of Quidditch, an earth-bound adaptation of the sport featuring flying broomsticks in the Harry Potter series, Eric Hansen assembled his own squad and entered the World Championships in New York. (They lost, as you'll discover in "Quoosiers," but readers definitely win.) We've also covered competitive water-sliding, Mongolian horse racing, and the world championships of free diving. Unlike the others, the latter event is definitely not a source of belly laughs. In fact, it's terrifying, as demonstrated by one of my all-time favorite story introductions: "Junko Kitahama's face is pale blue, her mouth agape, her head craned back like a dead bird's," writes James Nestor. "Through her swim mask, her eyes are wide and unblinking, staring at the sun. She isn't breathing."

Acknowledging the importance of our secret ingredients for misadventure, we've used them to organize this book. In the first section, "To Hell and Back," you'll find journeys to decidedly undesirable places. This is followed by "Let the Games Begin," featuring the fringe athletes and fitness freaks. And in "Consumed," you'll meet our favorite characters haunted by ill-advised dreams.

Beyond that, what ties this collection together are the incredible voices you'll encounter. The story assignments I've described are simply raw material;

only in the hands of legendary *Outside* contributors like David Quammen, Tim Cahill, Susan Orlean, Wells Tower, Christopher Solomon, Patrick Symmes, Taffy Brodesser-Akner, Nick Paumgarten, and many others are we gifted with the alchemy that turns these subjects into literary gold. I am incredibly thankful to all our writers. Their original voices have kept us in business for forty years, and if we are to survive another forty, that's not going to change.

I must also thank my predecessors, John Rasmus, Mark Bryant, and Hal Espen. These editors established the standards of what we know as *Outside* storytelling, and their innovation and craftsmanship continue to inspire our staff each time we walk through the doors of our headquarters in Santa Fe, New Mexico. Lawrence J. Burke, our founder, chairman, and editor-in-chief, has always been rigid in his belief that longform storytelling is the backbone of our publication. His willingness to set us free to pursue our writers' passions is what makes *Outside* unique among other magazines. I am also incredibly appreciative for my colleagues Mary Turner, Alex Heard, Michael Roberts, and Elizabeth Hightower. These four long-time staffers have overseen the execution of the lion's share of the stories in this book, quietly making every assignment better with their keen observations and brilliant editing.

Finally, we wouldn't be here without our loyal readers. When an *Outside* story misses the mark, you let us know it, and for that we are seriously indebted. Your passion for great storytelling is what motivates us each month.

—Christopher Keyes, Editor of *Outside*, 2017

TO HELL
AND BACK

MELTDOWN

WELLS TOWER

After surviving cancer, Tower's father vows to see as much of the world as he can, dragging his long-feuding sons on a series of classic misadventures. Their next mission? Tour rapidly defrosting Iceland and Greenland. Bad idea? You could say that.

In the Inuit village of Tasiilaq, on Greenland's east coast, in a bar whose name, as far as I can tell, is Bar, people are enjoying themselves as though the world will end tomorrow.

There are maybe 30 folks in here, few of them women, nearly all of them catastrophically drunk. Two men who look fresh from a seal hunt are locked in a dance that is part boxer's clinch, part jailhouse waltz. One of them falls. I can feel his skull hit the floor through the soles of my boots.

I'm on vacation with my father, Ed Tower, an ebullient man of 65 with a belly that strains his parka nearly to the point of rupture. We are not handsome men, but, as a result of their near-lethal intake of Tuborg beers, the few local females (none under 50 or so) have taken a shine to us. My father is flanked by two. One looks like Ernest Borgnine; the other, Don Knotts.

A grinning elderly woman approaches me unsteadily. I hold out my hand and she falls over, bashing her face on my shin. I help her up. She thanks me, lists hard to starboard, and capsizes again.

Ernest Borgnine whispers something in Dad's ear, and his eyes go wide.

"Wells," he yells over the band, "there's a woman in here who ate her own babies."

We are in this establishment at my father's insistence. Our guidebook warned that Bar was best avoided but said nothing about an in-house cannibal. Now seems like a good time to get out, but Dad's having another close conference with Ernest. "Oh, OK," he says. "She's talking about the song they're playing."

Still, we've been in here long enough. A pair of Category 4 hangovers awaits us. But then the band lurches into an Inuit rendition of Johnny Cash's "Ring of Fire."

"Do you dance?" the woman asks Dad.

"Why not?"

I can think of several reasons, actually. One, those men by the bar are not looking at us kindly, and, it should be noted, you can buy guns in the grocery stores over here. Two, my father, survivor of an exotic strain of lymphoma, is still in delicate shape from a bone-marrow transplant a couple of years back, and I'm not eager to see him shake his fragile moneymaker on a dance floor that looks like a fourth-down blitz. Three, and most important, is the fact that, in my father's company, trips have a tendency to spiral into disaster. The mishaps are sometimes large and sometimes inconsequential, but the specter of calamity always rides in his sidecar. Here, on our ninth day, we are both still in one piece. We fly out tomorrow. The smart thing, it seems, is to quit while we're ahead.

I look at Dad and jerk my head toward the exit, but he just takes the woman's hand and makes for the dance floor.

~~~~~~

Eight and a half years ago, when the oncological bookmakers gave my father three years to live, we sat together in his hospital room and vowed that, if he survived, the two of us would take a trip each year to celebrate his outliving his expiration date by another twelvemonth. When we cooked up this scheme, I think we both privately thought we were merely following timeworn etiquette that calls for grand travel fantasies when someone is dying. (Think *Midnight Cowboy*, Joe Buck to Ratso Rizzo in extremis: "When we get to Miami . . . .") But when Dad surprised us both by beating his rogue cells into remission, it would have been a thumb in the eye of St. Christopher to go back on our vow.

Though we travel in celebration, the trips themselves rarely deliver much ecstasy. Our first, to New Zealand's Great Barrier Island, nearly killed me. This was 1999, and we picked Great Barrier because my father, a professor of economics and a man who likes value, had a friend with a jungle cabin we could hole up in for free. The "cabin" was a dank shack built of fence posts; its only furniture, a mattress unfit for a hyena, lay in shadow in a corner. To steel myself for what would be an uncomfortably intimate evening with Dad, I drank about two bottles of wine, vomited against a banana tree, and passed out beside him. When dawn broke, the evil scent in the place had intensified. Rising groggily to a sitting position, I noticed the mattress was covered in what looked like a hail of Milk Duds but which were in fact emissions from the dead and bloated jungle rat we had used for a pillow the previous night. I'm not overstating things when I tell you my heart started beating wrong that morning. When I got back to the States, a cardiologist diagnosed me with a sudden-onset heart murmur, brought about by dehydration and shock. If I keel over prematurely of an aortic aneurysm, you'll know why.

Our next odyssey, a cruise through the Galápagos Islands in 2001, nearly killed my father. He spent most of the trip suffering through a case of tropical-force Montezuma's revenge. The entire boat shook with his illness, a sound like a tuba quintet tuning up belowdecks. And I still feel guilty about what happened when he was finally well enough to go ashore. Remember the 2001 marine iguana die-offs in the Galápagos? The press blamed 200,000 gallons of petroleum spilled from a busted tanker, but I submit that one Ed Tower introduced a quantity of noxious material to the local ecology when, while skinny-dipping in a cave, he misplaced a pair of microbially "hot" Hanes briefs and some sandals you could have used for fish bait.

Other timeless moments include our 2003 trip to Istanbul, where, against my advice, Dad drank a platter of beef grease and practically went blind for 48 hours. And last year's trip through France's Loire Valley, where, out of thrift, we often shared a bed, but Dad wouldn't hear of sleeping in—please, for the love of God—his underwear, at least.

Though Dad is officially cancer-free now, he beat back a second bout two years ago and is still settling into a new immune system, thanks to the bone-marrow transplant. So for our 2007 trip, in late May and early June, we plotted an itinerary through the comparatively sterile subarctic: five days in Iceland—my older brother, Dan, would join us for that leg—and five in southeast Greenland. We also chose our destinations with a certain irony in mind. Iceland, though recovering, remains a case study of ecological disaster, a nation whose people felled nearly all of its trees centuries ago and whose topsoil, thanks to overgrazing, blows ceaselessly into the sea. To the northwest lies Greenland, whose famously decaying ice sheets make it another marquee destination on the eco-disaster trail. Some estimates predict that once the global-warming teeter-totter tips, Greenland's ice, which covers an area more than three times the size of Texas, could melt entirely within the next millennium, if not sooner, which would boost sea levels some 23 feet and drown the world's present coastlines.

As agents of human bungling par excellence, we thought it fitting to take a tour of these monuments to humanity's special gift for fucking things up.

It usually takes me at least a week of traveling with Ed Tower before I'm seized by the tantrum-pitching impulse and can barely resist the urge to punch myself again and again in the face. This time it happened in the parking lot at Baltimore/Washington International as Dad, Dan, and I readied our gear. Though my father had a brand-new rolling suitcase, he was bringing along his ancient, monstrous blue duffel, which smelled strongly of sour milk. Taking it would be akin to having a mute wino in tow.

"We could just leave this old bag," I said.

Over the years, Dad's work has carried him to all sorts of far-flung places—China, Malaysia, Croatia, Sudan. This particular duffel, he recalled, served him well years ago: "When I was in Khartoum, I was glad to have an extra bag to bring back swords and camel-hair rugs for my friends."

I got one of those swords. I was nine at the time, and thrilled to have it, until I noticed the dismaying odor. The leather grip, my father told me cheerily, had been cured in human urine. Strike a single en garde with the thing and all day you'd go around smelling like a Port Authority toilet. The rugs, purchased at something like 40 cents per, looked pretty good but turned out to be infested with a fanged Saharan flea and dyed with an unstable pigment. Every recipient got to celebrate my father's trip to Africa with a full fumigation and a costly visit from the floor refinishers.

Dad stood there with a faraway look in his eyes, visions of further souvenir bargains dancing in his head.

"I'm taking it," he said, then galumphed off for the terminal.

Just after 6 A.M., we touched down at Keflavík, in southwest Iceland, where the morning was crisp under a sky like a sheet of pressed lint.

"Oh, the joy of it," Dad said. "Off to a new adventure with my sons." He grinned a little nervously, giving us a shoulder squeeze.

Troubled as our trips may be, my brother's coming along, Dad knew, compounded the risk of disaster. At 36, Dan's a year and a half my senior. He's a dark-jawed lawyer with a lumberjack's build, and we have the sort of relationship that would make Cain and Abel move to a better neighborhood. Our parents divorced when we were in grade school, and I have no doubt that the strain of our hostilities helped provoke the split. Over the years, we've attacked each other with, among other things, fists, feet, teeth, rocks, bats, knives, bottles, a can opener, a cedar tree, a stick of butter, and a car, and we can still go from amiable to fratricidal in about three seconds.

But things went rather smoothly that morning. It was a full five minutes before we were at each other's throats.

We rented a car. Dan was keen to drive to Reykjavík, the capital, 40 minutes out of the way, to hunt up some breakfast. Dad and I were not. We had an itinerary: first the Vatnajökull, or Water Glacier, Europe's biggest, five hours to the east; then we'd double back to the black-sand beach at Vík; then tent out in the town of Thorlákshöfn for the night; then catch a morning ferry to camp on Heimaey, one of the Vestmannaeyjar, or Westman Islands, off the southern coast. We'd hit Reykjavík in three days.

"That's great," Dan snapped. "It's pretty clear you guys aren't going to listen to a goddamned thing I say."

"Oh, go to hell," I said, fists tensing.

"Ah, family vacation," our father said. "It's too bad we don't have any brownies to fling at one another."

Dad was alluding here to a fabled unbrotherly skirmish. Long ago, while in a canoe in the middle of New Hampshire's Lake Winnipesaukee, I napalmed, with hot brownie batter, the chest of a shirtless Dan, who was circling my craft in a rage in a motorboat. I later broke my forearm on the paddle he was wielding. I could feel the old fracture twinge forebodingly as we drove out of Keflavík in the early-morning drizzle.

The airport receded as I steered our rental onto the Ring Road, the two-lane highway that traces the country's perimeter. Iceland's population is a mere 302,000, spread out over a landmass a little bigger than Indiana. We were more or less alone on the narrow highway, which carried us through the desolate magnificence of the coast. To the south, undulant fields of hardened lava, flocked in mosses of a tender, watery green, sloped down to the sea. A dark palisade of mountains towered to the north, brightened here and there by silver bursts of glacial melt cascading from the peaks. Pale boulders of sheep browsed the lowlands.

"My God," said my father, gazing at the moonscape flashing past the window.

"Amazing," I said.

Dan, still fuming, was less taken. "How often do you think people kill themselves out here?" he wondered as he thumbed our travel guide. "I don't understand why people don't just start screwing like rabbits and build this place up. I mean, there's supposed to be some hotties here. They won Miss World three times. You could probably do pretty well hitting on chicks here. You've already got a great pickup line: 'I'm from America. We've got these things called trees and grass. It's killer.'"

My father leaned forward from the backseat. "Dan," he said in a tone of quiet concern. "How can we cheer you up? Is there anything we can do for you, my son?"

"I told you what you could do," Dan said darkly. "Go to Reykjavík."

A plot was taking shape against my brother, a scheme to keep him breakfastless and miserable. Dad and I were the obvious conspirators, but the nation of Iceland, where rocks and sheep had so far outnumbered breakfast buffets by about a million to zero, was not to be trusted, either. Oppressed by forces beyond his control, Dan borrowed a page from the playbooks of Gandhi and M.L. King Jr. and began a program of passive resistance in hopes of scuttling group morale beyond all reckoning.

For our first 24 hours in-country, he hung out in the car.

The protest officially got under way about an hour into the trip, shortly after Dan announced that he had to take a leak.

"That's cool—I don't need your help," he said when I offered to pull over. I looked at him in the rearview. He appeared to be eating a plastic water bottle. He chewed the bottle in half and knelt on the seat. Then, rather than set foot on Iceland's treacherous terra firma, he peed into his makeshift pissoir and pitched the contents out the window.

We soon passed a waterfall, the Seljalandsfoss, a platinum horse tail gushing from the top of a black-and-billiard-table-green parapet. We could see tiny figures in hikers' motley moving behind the cataract.

"Man, you can walk behind the falls!" Dad exclaimed.

I stood on the brakes.

"Come on, kiddo, let's go," my father said to Dan, who was sprawled in the back, ostensibly engrossed in the guidebook.

"Nah, I'll stay here," he said.

"Oh, come on, man," said Dad.

"No, thanks."

Dad and I made for the trail. The falls blew over us in a thick mist, the water electrically cold and sweet on our lips.

Walking back to the car, Dad lapsed into a coughing fit, a sound like someone blasting a blackboard with rock salt. He'd been suffering these periodic lung quakes since his last bout with chemo. It was worrisome, but he'd had his fill of doctors.

"You OK, Pops?" I asked.

"Just clearing the chest." He took a few deep breaths and gazed back at the falling water. "God, it's good to still have a pair of functional legs. God, it's good to be alive."

We trudged back to the car, where Dan was still stretched out with the guide. "What are you discovering there?" Dad asked him as I pulled back onto the road.

"Fifty-three percent of the people here believe in elves," Dan said, adding provincial occultism to the country's crimes, just behind lawlessness. Then he mumbled a synopsis of a legend about a union boss who "had relations" with an elf.

"What was that?" I asked.

"You can screw an elf."

~~~~~~

From above, Iceland's Vatnajökull, an ice cap bigger than Delaware, looks like a giant Rorschach butterfly—fitting for something steadily winging it from the earth. Doubly menaced by global warming above and active volcanoes beneath, the Vatnajökull has molted roughly 235 square miles since 1958.

It heaved into view as we rounded a curve. Spilling from between a pair of russet crags, the dirty tongue of ice had a roasted look about it, like a charred marshmallow, pallid innards oozing forth.

"Glorious," said Dad. "Let's climb the son of a bitch."

"I'll stay here," said Dan.

"But don't you want to see it before it melts?" I said.

"It isn't melting," he said, quoting an outdated and patently false passage from the guidebook, which claimed that the Vatnajökull was one of the few glaciers on the planet that was actually on the grow.

I gritted my teeth, Dad gave a glum shrug, and the two of us set off.

A sign hammered beside the path warned us that setting foot on the ice without an experienced guide might land you at the bottom of a crevasse. I paused.

"What should we do about this sign?"

"I intend to ignore it entirely," said Dad.

"Spoken like a man with diminished life expectancy," I said.

Dad began picking his way with surprising ease to a promontory atop the ice slope. He stood with his hand on his hip, looking as though he wished he had a flag to plant. I chose a path that looked less risky but twice fell to my knees.

When I'd clawed my way to Dad's side, he was staring down at the lagoons of glacial melt at the bottom of the grade. The water was a swirled gray and blue, the color of moonstone, the oddly lovely symptom of a glacier in decline.

"A century ago, this ice went on for miles, all the way to the sea," I said, paraphrasing a newspaper story I'd come across.

"It's grim to think about what'll be here a hundred years from now," said Dad. "Trailer parks, Disney World Iceland. In the grand scheme of things, this isn't the worst time to be facing one's mortality."

~~~~~~

The wind poured down off the glacier, rinsing us in the cleanest, coldest air I've ever breathed, air you could sell by the gallon in Malibu. We stood silent for a long moment, struck dumb by the wind, the ice glowing under our boots, the bright emptiness of the world around us. No planes or distant interstates sullied the silence.

"Isn't this religious?" my father said.

"It really is."

In the distant parking lot sat the car, its windows fogging up.

"Too bad Dan didn't come out," I said.

"It's a shame, a real sadness," said Dad, "but he's really doing his best to have the non-experience of a lifetime."

But Dan had done us a service: He'd become the living emblem of all that would go wrong on this trip. We stood at peace on the glacier's nose and inhaled eternity.

On the beach at Vík, which our guidebook pronounced one of the ten most beautiful in the world, my father and I walked along, stopping to cup the black sand in our palms. Then we sat at a picnic table, drinking lukewarm beers and eating beef jerky. My brother remained in the car.

Later, in the port town of Thorlákshöfn, my brother remained in the car. In the morning, we'd be catching the ferry to the island of Heimaey, so we'd fetched up at a public campsite that forever voided my grim childhood memories of car camping at franchise campgrounds whose atmosphere evoked the Okie settlements in *The Grapes of Wrath*. Not only was the place virtually free in the off-season (a boon in a country whose grottiest roadside rut-huts go for about $180 a night); the tent sites were also flat, soft as a Sealy Posturepedic, and offered views of the bay, which looked like poured chrome under the midnight sun.

This was surely the sort of place that would at last tempt my brother from his roost, but just to sweeten the arrangement, we pitched his tent for him. Dad approached the car cautiously, like a priest looking down the barrel of an especially gruesome exorcism. He opened the door.

"Tent's ready for you," he said.

"I'm sleeping here," said Dan.

My father wandered back.

"Oh, son, oh, son," he said sorrowfully, "when did this trip start going so wrong?"

I thought back to my brother angrily peeing into his water bottle.

The next morning, we stood in the parking lot, preparing to board the ferry. Dan had poorly trussed his sleeping bag to Dad's luggage, so I, having brought a duffel big enough to accommodate the golem of Prague, reached for it.

"Get the fuck off it!" Dan barked.

At least a decade had passed since we'd really laid hands on one another, but at that instant an old madness got hold of me. I felt myself spirited back to a time when I knew no greater longing than to punch my brother squarely in the face.

"Come on, bitch, let's do this!" I yelled inanely, shoving his chest.

"You want some, motherfucker?!" he bellowed, pedaling his fists. "Come here!" Dan has four inches on me and probably a good 40 pounds. If he did his worst, I'd be flying home on a gurney with my jaw wired shut. I held my ground, though my heart, still queered from that run-in with a dead New Zealand rat, beat an off-kilter paradiddle: chup-chuppity-chup.

A knot of passersby stopped in their tracks, eyes wide and eager. Dad was watching, too. In all our years of traveling together, I'd never seen his adventurer's ebullience break down. But Dan and I, in our barbarous idiocy, had finally defeated him. Confronted with his grown sons preparing to beat each other bloody over how best to stow a sleeping bag, he seemed to age years in an instant. His face sagged with exasperation and grief.

"You're embarrassing me," he said in a quiet voice, turning away.

Shame hit me in a cold wave.

We had to jog to catch him.

Once on Heimaey, we all relaxed in a green meadow in the crater of a dormant volcano, which had lost half its cone in the last eruption, centuries ago, leaving us a heart-stopping view of the sun-gilt sea. Just up from the water a golf links stretched off in emerald chromosome shapes.

"Goddamn, this place is beautiful," conceded Dan, whose mood had staged a full recovery after our abortive fistfight. Our father stretched on the grass, watching the seagulls spreeing high above.

Later, Dan and I were sitting side by side on a giant, comfy hummock, staring at the water. I broke out my stash of duty-free aquavit (Scandinavia's caraway-flavored moonshine) and offered him a drink. He knocked back a slug and made a face like a woman in labor.

"How was it?" I asked.

"Not good," he said, shuddering. "If you want me to drink more, I'll need to go eat some Tums."

Down on the course, though it was close to midnight, a few players were putting in the deathless arctic light.

"I'm so pissed at myself for not bringing my clubs," Dan said. "We could've played all night."

"I've never played golf," I said, "but I've always wanted to try."

"I'd teach you," he offered in a big-brotherly way. "Next time, I'll bring my clubs—two sets. Next time, we'll really have some fun."

My father and I found ourselves abandoned on an ice floe off Greenland shortly thereafter. It was about the size of a football field and blocked the path of the motorboat we'd booked to carry us to the mainland. Confronted with the obstruction, the boat's operators, a pair of Inuit cousins named William and Kunuck Abelson, had ordered us onto the ice—and looked to be ditching us. We stood there shivering, watching their craft move away, in reverse.

"This is a rather upsetting development," said Dad.

Dan had headed back to the States two days earlier, at the end of our Iceland tour. (In Reykjavík, by the way, he'd at last had breakfast: coffee, doughnuts, and a horrific shrimp pastry. But only after getting hauled downtown by Iceland's finest for egregiously breaching the speed limit.)

My father and I had then made for Greenland, which dwarfs Iceland but is far less inhabited. The world's largest island is almost one-fourth the size of the U.S. but home to only about 57,000 people. Its massive ice sheet, estimated at 650,000 cubic miles, covers some 85 percent of the island. Findings vary, but it appears to be sloughing around 55 cubic miles into the sea every year.

We'd decided our first stop would be the island settlement of Kulusuk, an Inuit village (pop. 300) off the southeast coast. Do not believe the old chestnut that Iceland is green and Greenland is white. Kulusuk (or "Coal Suck," as my father would not stop calling it) in late May was mostly brown. A decade and a half ago, the hotel manager told us, you could still run a dogsled this time of year, but the air was already warmer than Easter on Cape Cod, and rivulets of thaw cut deep channels in the roads. The surrounding mountains had shed their winter mantle, revealing dark structures that looked like corroded Hershey's Kisses. The village's hundreds of sled dogs, each staked in its own diameter of mud, howled ceaselessly, seeming to mourn the premature onset of the summer sabbatical. We asked a few locals whether the early thaw was part of a noticeable long-term warming trend, and they looked at us the way I imagine a Texas rancher would if asked whether he had ever heard of cows.

For two days, we ventured out a little but mostly just holed up in our room in Hotel Kulusuk, where climate change evolved in my understanding from a vague and distant crisis to a calamity of a more personal scale. I was saddened to discover that ambient temperature in Greenland in May is no longer cold enough to (a) chill a six-pack of beer dangled out a hotel window on a bootlace or (b) prevent my father from swanking around in the nude.

After 48 hours, Dad had tired of watching the island erode. "Well, son, I believe I've enjoyed about all the Coal Suck I can stand," he said. I was in bed drinking warm beer and wearing my sleep mask as a shield against the unsetting sun and the pink vista of my father's flesh.

"I'm with you there," I said. So it was decided that we'd catch a boat to the vastest metropolis on Greenland's east coast, the village of Tasiilaq (pop. 1,883).

Out at sea, the ice was plentiful. The crossing was choked with pack ice and bergs calved from the Christian IV and Steenstrup glaciers, waning north of us. As we watched the Abelson cousins' boat retreat from our floe, huge, slumping meringues of ice towered over us, their hearts glowing the otherworldly glacial blue that is somehow the equal and opposite corollary of the orange cores of live embers. The cold coming off the icebergs was a pulsing, vital thing. The wind had big teeth.

"If you fell in," my father intoned, "I don't imagine you'd have much time to reflect on the experience."

"It'd be like falling into a vat of hydrochloric acid," I said. "Glug, glug, gone."

But the cousins didn't leave us. Just as I began to really worry, William opened up the throttle and came hell-bent for leather straight at us. The boat hit the floe, leapt like a breaching whale, and slammed down hard. My father and I clutched each other, waiting for our perch to crack like a saltine.

But the ice held. The Abelsons hopped out, giggled at us, and motioned for us to start heaving on the hull.

"My God," said Dad, "we're going to man-haul the damn thing."

A hundred yards of crusty ice, full of disconcerting voids, stretched between us and open water. With each push, we'd stumble. Every fourth step, you'd sink to your thigh, praying you hadn't found the trapdoor to the blue hereafter. The work drove Dad to painful coughing jags, but he wouldn't hear of sitting on the sidelines. An hour later, we were again puttering for Tasiilaq.

~~~~~~

It took about 45 minutes to absorb the sights of eastern Greenland's grandest city—a concentration of concrete-and-plywood cottages clinging for dear life to hillsides so steep that if you lost your footing, you'd roll into the bay. We visited a staggeringly ample grocery store, which sold, among other things, badminton sets, sewing machines, and 18 kinds of rifle and shotgun. Next to the candy in the checkout lane were hardcore Danish nudie books. We roved the cemetery, where graves were marked with heaps of fake flowers, so violent a breach with the surrounding monochrome as to look like pigments splattered across a black-and-white photograph.

Before the afternoon was out, we were in a hotel, our vacation ebbing away. Despairing that we'd not yet found the proper life-affirming exploit to consecrate another year of cheating death, Dad said, "I wonder if we could bribe somebody to take us along on a hunt. Get the blood flowing." Down at the harbor, we'd seen subsistence hunters hauling in the daily catch of seals, which live here in very healthy numbers.

We asked the hotel bartender if he knew of someone who might let us tag along.

"Sure," he said. "Frederic, my father-in-law. He's old. He's been a hunter all his life."

"How old?" I asked.

"I don't know," he said. "I don't ask him things. I am very afraid of him."

We met Frederic at the public dock. He was a stoic man with a face like a dry creekbed. Though he didn't speak a word of English, Frederic made it clear that, for the privilege of accompanying him, he wanted a hundred bucks, a sum surely higher than the blue-book value of his skiff, a craft of equal parts caulk and old plywood. Dad cheerfully paid up.

Under clouds the color of wet concrete, we chuffed out into the icy rubble of the bay. A frigid hour had passed when my father spotted a dark form gliding out from behind a floe.

"Seal! Seal!" he cried.

"Right there!" I said hysterically, fluttering my hands at the aged hunter, who glanced briefly in the direction we were pointing, then went back to scanning the opposite end of the bay. When our seal revealed itself, it had transformed into somebody's skiff.

"Good thing we don't have guns," Dad observed.

Minutes later, Frederic suddenly went rapt. Fifty yards away, the dark avocado shape of a young seal's head registered above the surface of the water. Frederic squeezed off a shot. I won't go any further into the ensuing hamfisted debacle—possibly brought on by my father's proximity to the event—except to say that, before it was over, Dad winced and turned away, I let out a little shriek, and another hunter went home with our bantam quarry.

We'd clearly misguessed our appetite for bloodletting. There was nothing life-affirming about it. Ten minutes later, Dad spotted a gigantic seal turning idle laps in a lagoon between floes, and we felt only relief when it easily escaped Frederic's fusillade.

We needed a drink.

Which brings us back to bar. It's the last night of our trip, and, thankfully, no shots ring out when my father and Ernest Borgnine start to dance. The band is out of tune, Dad's boots leave muddy prints across the parquet floor, and the woman in his arms is so sozzled that her legs, like a colt's on a frozen pond, periodically scramble for purchase. He dips her, and has to strain to bring her upright, but he does so without incident, and the guys at the bar clap and smile. The smoggy air in here is like atomized creosote, and I'm worried for his lungs, but when the band rolls into a warped rendition of "Proud Mary," I'm happy to see him go another round.

Before the song ends, a middle-aged woman in thick glasses walks over and offers me her palm.

"Dance?" she asks.

"Why not?"

(Originally published April 2008)

THEY CALL ME GROOVER BOY

KEVIN FEDARKO

For anyone stubbornly holding on to a lifelong dream, here's some inspiration. Former Outside senior editor Kevin Fedarko had always fantasized about being a Grand Canyon raft guide. The first step? Quitting a stellar journalism career at age 40 and beginning his apprenticeship at the very bottom. What's it like to be captain of the "poop boat" and steering three weeks of human waste through some of America's gnarliest whitewater? Read on to find out.

It's a fiery June morning at Grapevine Camp, a spit of sand tucked along the banks of the Colorado River, deep inside the stone walls that frame the sub-basement of the Grand Canyon. From the surface of the river, the walls soar upward for more than a vertical mile, exposing geology that extends 17 million centuries into the past. During that span, the oceans have swollen and receded a dozen times, the continents have slammed together and cracked apart again, and a chain of mountains higher than the Rockies has been heaved into the sky and reduced to gravel.

Philosophically speaking, this is some heavy shit. Heavy enough to make a man perched on the bow of a humble raft at the edge of Grapevine—a man now staring at that staggering immensity of stone—scratch his head and wonder what it all might suggest about his own place in the universe.

But that doesn't last long. Any confusion about where I fit into the cosmos is vaporized by the arrival of a hefty steel box that two of the guides on this

19-day river trip are slinging onto the aluminum deck of my raft with a rude, clattering ka-thunk.

"Heads up, there, my friend," warns Bill "Bronco" Bruchak, a boatman who's built like the beer truck he used to drive in Pennsylvania. "Don't pull a muscle when you lift this thing."

"Yep," chimes in Mike "Milty" Davis, a small, cheerful guy with mischievous eyes and a snowy white beard. "That is one enormous box of poop."

I seize the handles, heft the cargo, and stagger toward the tight space between the stanchions that cradle my 12-foot-long, fiberglass-reinforced oars. Two identical canisters are already anchored on both sides of the footwell, which is where I sit when I row this barge. The top of each can is emblazoned with a strip of red electrical tape labeled FULL!!!

As I start lashing down the new can, I glance over at Monte Tillinghast, who's piloting the second baggage boat on this trip, a kitchen raft that's tied up next to mine.

"Son, you do have a load there," observes Tillinghast, whose cowboy hat and surfer shorts make him look like a maritime version of the Marlboro Man. "You know, you might want to think about girth-hitching another strap onto that there—"

Monte's suggestion, undoubtedly helpful and possibly of critical importance in how my day is about to unfold, is cut off when Andre Potochnik, the alpha boatman leading this trip, yells out, "Dories . . . ho!"

This sends Monte and me scrambling to complete our rigging and fall in behind the four dories, which, one by one, are now threading into the main current. As the last of these craft glides past my barge, the final member of our crew—a slim, deeply tanned woman named Billie Prosser—flashes a smile. "Hey, Kevin," she says sweetly. "Thanks again for doing what you do."

Her four passengers nod gamely, but their smiles are a frozen mix of polite gratitude and mild repugnance. After nearly a week on the river, these folks know exactly what's in the boxes on my boat. After all, they put it there. And although they're deeply obliged for my services, they're still trying to get a handle on who I am, what my job entails, and why in the world I agree to do it. It's a look that says, *Someone give this poor idiot some career counseling. Immediately.*

Four years ago, at age 38, I wandered through the doors of Grand Canyon Dories, an outfitter in Flagstaff, Arizona, that runs commercial expeditions on the Colorado River, and found myself staring at a tiny navy of wood-and-fiberglass rowboats. There were only about a dozen of these sleek, flat-bottomed craft inside the boathouse on that morning in March 2004. They were all painted in bold colors, and several featured flat transoms inscribed with hand-drawn scenes from the river: a bighorn sheep, a cluster of columbines, a tree frog. Each boat was graced with the simplest and loveliest lines I'd ever seen.

At the time, I had no idea that dory boats, which had been used for centuries by cod fishermen on the gale-racked combers off the Grand Banks of Newfoundland, had become legendary on the Colorado, where they are renowned for their speed and elegance. What I did know was that I was entranced. And in an impulse that defied logic and common sense, I decided—right then—that I was going to quit my job and somehow find a way to follow those boats into the water-haunted world at the bottom of the Grand Canyon.

Plenty of middle-aged men flirt with delusional schemes like this—and almost all of them wind up abandoning their fantasies once they come to their senses. For better and worse, I followed through on mine, even after I found out that becoming a guide involves a multiyear, unpaid apprenticeship in the exciting field of latrine management.

I didn't care. In fact, over the next four summers, I volunteered for extra poo-boat duty to compensate for my lack of skill in crucial areas like, say, rowing. In the course of 14 trips through the canyon, I have transported more than 7,800 pounds of excrement over a total distance of 3,400 river miles—roughly equivalent to rowing an inflatable septic tank from Tijuana, Mexico, to Point Barrow, Alaska. The price I've paid for this dubious distinction has been both humbling and steep. At 43, I find myself with no wife, no kids, no dog, and virtually no bank account. Last year, according to a nationwide survey of incomes across the U.S., I made less money than a part-time doughnut fryer in Maryland and a hospital clown in New York.

For the most part, it's been worth it—I wouldn't trade my Grand Canyon experiences for anything. My other consolation is that poo-boating, gross though it may be, is important work. Every summer, about 25,000 people opt to ride motorboats, oar rafts, or dories down all or part of the river corridor through the canyon, a route that stretches 277 miles from the eastern head, at Lees Ferry, to the western terminus, on the shores of Lake Mead. These trips usually take between one and three weeks, and because the average person will produce an ounce of excrement for every 12 pounds of body weight each and every day, the river-running industry generates more than 100,000 pounds of human waste per year. Inside a narrow canyon that receives less than nine inches of annual rainfall and endures summer daytime highs in excess of 110 degrees, it doesn't take much to imagine how ugly things could get if waste weren't handled with extreme care.

Up at park HQ, they take this business seriously indeed. The River Permit Office, on the South Rim, distributes a 45-minute video with detailed instructions on how river trips must containerize human waste, cart it out in watertight boxes, and dispose of it at a sewage-treatment plant. No trip is allowed on the river without proper education for crew and passengers and a written commitment to pack it out. It's a key component—perhaps the key component—of a complex set of rules that keep the crown jewel of the U.S. national park system as pristine as possible.

It's also something most people don't like to talk about.

If you sign on for a commercial Grand Canyon river trip, you'll learn about all sorts of fascinating things, from the Colorado's maximum depth (85 feet) and minimum width (76 feet) to the number of rock layers exposed along its length (26). The subject you won't hear discussed is the one I'm most attuned to: poop handling, and the headaches and disasters it can entail. For example, you probably won't hear about the two guides who were driving back from a river trip when their poo cans fell off the back of their truck and burst open in the middle of the road, creating a fecal slick that a bicycle tourist wiped out on. Or the unlucky boatman who had a leaky toilet transform his rubber raft into a tub of raw sewage. Or the hapless guide who tripped while setting up the lavatory, plunged his arm into the poo box, and compounded his problems by vomiting all over himself.

Mishaps like these—which are the exception, not the rule, on most whitewater trips—underscore an unsettling fact that most commercial passengers never have to confront. To wit: A river runs through your Grand Canyon fantasies, and it's not clean and sparkling. If I do my job right, you won't have to dwell on that miserable reality. In a way, I'm like Quasimodo with an oar and a toilet brush. I'm not easy to look at, but things work a whole lot better when I'm around.

A Grand Canyon oar trip usually involves 16 passengers who ride in four boats and are served by a crew of six. If it's an expedition run by Grand Canyon Dories, each guide rows an elegant 17-foot dory named after a natural wonder that was heedlessly destroyed by man—in the case of the trip we're currently on, the *Ticaboo*, the *Yampa*, the *Lava Cliff*, and the *Vale of Rhonda*.

Every trip is also supported by two inflatable rafts that boast absolutely none of the dories' seductiveness or charm. These baggage boats haul most of the gear, grub, garbage, and goop, and they're assigned names that are considerably less lyrical. The first raft, the kitchen boat, carries a tangled assortment of tables, coolers, propane tanks, rescue gear, and watertight bags containing the clients' clothing. It's usually called the *Mule*, *Ox*, or *Clydesdale*. The other boat, my boat, is called the *Jackass*.

The toilet setup aboard the *Jackass* relies on the classic "20-mil" ammunition can, a narrow metal box—14.5 inches high, 18 inches long, and 8 inches wide—originally designed to store antitank grenade rockets for the army's M1A1 bazooka. Each "rocket box" can handle approximately 50 deposits of human waste and tips the scales at about 45 pounds when full. Its key feature is a rectangular lid that creates a watertight seal to prevent spillage while locking in the odors (well, most of them). When the lid is popped open, an aluminum flange called a riser is placed on top of the box and a toilet seat is mounted on the riser. During an early river trip back in the 1970s, shortly after this system was developed, the toilet seat was accidentally left behind, the rims of the riser left telltale indentations on everyone's bums, and the box got a nickname: the groover. (Some guides also call it the duker or the unit.)

Every evening when we pull into camp, the passengers clamber out of the dories and form a "fire line" at the bow of the Mule to help Monte unload the kitchen boat. Then everyone gets out of the way while I heave the toilet components onto the front deck of the *Jackass* and, with help from a guide, lug everything to a private spot, screened by trees or rocks, away from camp. I pull the lid off the box, slap on the seat, and declare the unit open for business.

Groover etiquette follows a strict protocol that the trip leader lays out in a "poo talk" on the expedition's first night. The most dismaying moment comes when it's revealed that the rocket box is used exclusively for solid waste, while urine goes into a special five-gallon bucket placed nearby. (If everyone peed in the groover, all my rocket boxes would be full before we got halfway to Lake Mead.)

Many passengers are initially appalled by this. Here they are, each having paid $4,314 for a deluxe river experience, only to discover that their daily constitutional requires a pants-around-the-ankles shuffle between a turd box and a pee bucket shared by 21 other people. But once they get their minds around it, the clients usually come to see the unit in a radically different light. It's not affection, exactly, but you could call it grateful acceptance.

Professional poo-men help things along with an eye for aesthetics. Over the years, every camp in the canyon has acquired an established groovering spot, and many of these locations are so sublime that they've become famous in their own right. At Whitmore Camp (186 miles from Lees Ferry), we like to set up under an overhanging chunk of black lava in a spot bathed in the scent of verbena blossoms. At a place called Ledges (mile 152), you have to climb 30 feet up a stone terrace and balance on a shelf of exquisitely sculpted Muav limestone. And at mile 136, you can sit on the thunder throne while staring into the center of Deer Creek Falls, the longest and loveliest cascade on the river.

Perched on the seat, it's not unusual for passengers to take notice of things they missed during the day's excitement: the trill of a canyon wren, the sweetest-sounding bird on the river, or the whorled mysteries of sunbeams playing among the interlocking currents of an eddy. "I've had passengers repeatedly tell me that groovering spots are some of the most exquisite places they've been," says Michael Ghiglieri, another guide I work with. "The pooper is often the place for meditation—so much so that people sometimes forget why they're sitting on the thing in the first place."

We toilet wranglers take pride in our skills, and I'm pleased to report that our talents have received modest recognition. In 1997, a guide named Joe Lindsay put together a book-length homage to the trials of poo-boating called *Up Shit Creek: A Collection of Horrifyingly True Wilderness Toilet Misadventures*. In 2002, a part-time poo captain named Scott Phair—a former pig farmer from Maine who now works as a high school principal—produced a calendar called "Groovin' in Grand Canyon," which featured photographs of the finest latrine venues on the river. At the time, Phair's finances permitted him to print only about 20 copies of this landmark publishing sensation. But he's hoping his next trip through the canyon, this spring, will yield material for a more commercially ambitious redux version, due out sometime in 2009.

~~~~~~

Things were not always this organized. Back in the early 1950s, when the business of Grand Canyon river trips was just getting started, the system was simpler, but not necessarily in a good way. "Our motto was 'Go high and far, and don't forget to take a match,' " recalls 91-year-old Martin Litton, the founder of Grand Canyon Dories. "You'd go off behind a cactus or some rocks to do your business, then you'd pile a few twigs on top and burn it all up. That took care of everything."

Well, yes and no. "Often, the toilet paper would fail to burn and you'd be left with a real mess," says one of Litton's early boatmen, who prefers to remain anonymous. "Other times, you'd light those twigs and, before you realized exactly what was happening, the flames would get out of hand—at which point you'd have to start jumping up and down with your pants around your ankles, stamping out the fire and, of course, tromping all over your own poop. It became quite evident that something had to be done."

The answer was a compact toilet designed for small sailboats, which was introduced to the canyon in the early 1970s. This "marine potty" featured a detachable tank containing a chemical known as Blue Goo, which is still used in RV parks to aid in fecal decomposition. "Every morning you'd dig a hole on the beach and you'd empty out the tank," says John Blaustein, a veteran doryman. "It was grim business. The Blue Goo, which smelled like bubble gum, would splash everywhere, so afterwards you'd have to fling yourself in the river for a full-on bath. But then you'd fill the hole back up with sand, and that seemed to solve the issue. At least for a while."

The problem was volume. As river-running caught on, the number of people floating through the canyon exploded from just 205 in 1960 to 9,935 in 1970. By 1971, 21 companies had licenses to guide passengers, and almost all these outfits were burying their toilet tanks' contents on the camping beaches, the most popular of which were occupied nightly from May through September.

"With all that usage, the Goo started leaching up to the surface, so when you pulled into camp, you'd see these blue-green stains in the sand, and the first thing you'd be hit with was the smell of feces," says Brad Dimock, another veteran doryman. "There was also toilet paper all over the place, and the flies were everywhere. It was fucking hideous."

That's when Steve Carothers stepped in. A Flagstaff-based biologist, Carothers completed his first canyon trip for the Arizona Academy of Sciences in the spring of 1971. He was so horrified by what he saw that he set out to devise a better way. He quickly realized that a WWII rocket box, which could be purchased at any army surplus store for $10 to $15, offered an ideal container system. The trick was figuring out how to control the methane, a by-product of anaerobic decomposition, to prevent overheated boxes from detonating. (After cooking in direct sunlight, the expanding miasma of methane is capable of blowing the lid off the groover and enveloping an unsuspecting boatman in a blast of superheated crap. It's happened before; boatmen tremblingly refer to this phenomenon as a "pooplosion.")

Carothers performed rudimentary tests involving glass jars, pipettes, and methane-generating contributions from his office co-workers. (Don't ask.) He discovered that an ounce of formaldehyde was "extremely effective at retarding the gas production." In the fall of 1976, he published an article in Downriver Magazine called "It's Time for Change, Let's Haul It All Out!" which featured detailed instructions on the rocket-box system. In 1978, the Park Service made his technique mandatory—and, with only minor modifications, the system is still used today.

"What a tremendous difference it's made," says Carothers. "This is probably the most significant contribution I've made to science and wilderness in the last 31 years."

Carothers also discerns a philosophical dimension to his work. "In America, most of us are taught not to think much about our feces, and we're certainly taught not to talk about them," he says. "But as human beings, we all produce about a pound of poo a day, and dealing with our shit responsibly is one way for us to face our humanity. Intellectually, that's very satisfying to me. I suppose it's kind of a metaphor for life. Don't you agree?"

~~~~~~

That's hard to dispute. My only teensy gripe with Carothers's system is that it funnels most of the degrading labor onto one guy: me.

A poo captain's day is long and hard, and it usually begins at first light, when he gets up with the rest of the crew. On this particular expedition, the routine is pretty standard: While Andre, Billie, Milty, Bronco, and Monte fix breakfast and clean the dishes, I focus on my duties as the trip's turd-transport specialist.

I start by rounding up my 16 pee pails—small plastic paint cans, purchased at Home Depot, which I place in front of the passengers' tents every night so they won't have to stumble off to the groover after dark. Then I stuff whatever garbage I can scrounge into a trash bag and drench it with liquid bleach to prevent the *Jackass* from turning into a floating fly farm. Today marks the end of our first week on the river, so I also perform a quick inventory to confirm that we have an adequate supply of toilet paper (one roll per person for every five days), Clorox crystals, hand soap, air freshener, and, most important, empty rocket boxes. (I carry a total of 11 to see us through a 19-day trip, with a one-groover safety margin.) Finally, I check the day-tripper—two smaller ammo cans containing a roll of TP, a jar of hand soap, and about four pounds of Feline Pine kitty litter. This system is for clients who cannot avoid using the toilet during the day.

Around 7:30, as the crew starts dismantling the kitchen, it's time for me to encourage everyone to finish groovering. This is demeaning, but it's also a bit of a power trip. When I yell "Last call on the groover!" what I'm really telling people is "No matter how important you are, I'm about to revoke your bathroom privileges for the next eight hours." It doesn't matter that Steve sits on the board of the New York Stock Exchange or that Maureen is a highly placed official at the Commerce Department. It also doesn't matter that Ben pounds nails in Portland or that Emily, who runs a crane at the docks in Port Arthur, Texas, has been saving pennies for most of her adult life to afford this trip. In the eyes of the groover, everyone is created equal.

Everyone except me, of course. When the passengers are finished, I'm the guy who gets to grab a guide, dash up through the tamarisk trees, and break down the system.

If the groover is getting full, I lift it and drop it on the sand a time or two to "settle" things—being extremely careful not to compress the contents too tightly. (After baking in the sun for another two weeks, the contents of a compressed rocket box can cement to form what we call poo glue, which will be almost impossible to remove at the Wildcat Hill Wastewater Treatment Plant, in Flagstaff.) Then I shower the inside with a furious deluge of Clorox crystals, which helps beat back the odor. We cart the toilet seat down to the river with the riser and urine bucket, where the urine is dumped in the water and all components get a thorough scrubbing. Finally, we seal the lid and begin the Morning Poo Parade.

This can be embarrassing. As we haul our load toward the beach, the passengers spot us coming and conversation often grinds to a halt. Someone might break the silence with a remark such as "Stand back, here comes Groover Boy!" Other times, there is a subdued chuckle punctuated with a joke like "Hey, did you know that Grand Canyon poop boatmen never die—they just smell that way?"

Ha-ha, I laugh, *that's really funny*. Then I pretend to stumble, which sends everyone running down the beach screaming.

As the guides hoist the components onto my front deck, I leap aboard and start tying everything down, often rigging double and triple backups to ensure that nothing goes flying out. It's a complex operation—I use nearly 40 cam straps to properly anchor the pee bucket, the 16 pee pails, the riser, the three bags of toilet paper, the garbage, the groover seat, and the rocket boxes, plus all my Clorox and cleaning supplies.

When the lashing is done, I'm surrounded by a mountain of trash and toilet products. You're probably familiar with those wheeled carts used by folks who clean the bathrooms at airports and hospitals? Well, that's what the *Jackass* looks like, with one big difference. When I'm finished rigging, I have to row the goddamn thing through some of the biggest commercial whitewater in North America.

As the Colorado River muscles down the canyon, it stair-steps through more than 160 rapids, the largest of which can casually flip a 37-foot motor raft or smash a dory to pieces. Take Horn Creek, which is on our dance card this afternoon. It features a pair of exposed guard rocks upstream of a double hole backed by two hydraulic jumps that are sometimes called the Great Wave and the Green Guillotine.

The key to unlocking Horn Creek lies just below the right guard rock, where the current forms a shallow wave, known as a "lateral," that radiates downriver in an expanding triangle. A textbook entry starts on the far right side of the river and involves rowing—sideways and backwards—to a point just below the right guard rock. The trick is to build enough momentum so that you punch neatly through the lateral and into the calmer water inside the triangle. It's a straightforward move, but a heavily laden poop boat tends to complicate things. Imagine trying to row an outhouse, in reverse, down a wall of whitewater, and you've got some idea of what it feels like to take the *Jackass* through Horn Creek.

I watch as all four dories and Monte's Mule thread the entrance flawlessly. As several passengers raise their arms and yell "Whoo-hoo!" each boat skates across the tongue, harpoons through the lateral, and bobs merrily into the tail waves. Then it's my turn.

Among apprentice boatmen, mistakes are inevitable, and as I plow across the tongue I commit a humdinger. Instead of spearing cleanly through the lateral, I rebound off it and ricochet directly into the vortex. The top of the Great Wave surges over the front of the *Jackass*, hitting me in the face and chest with enough force to knock the lenses out of my glasses, drive me out of my sandals, and hurl me over the side of the boat, straight into the Green Guillotine.

Oh, hell.

The ordeal of being tossed into the center of a Class V rapid is referred to as "getting Maytagged." The wash cycle starts with a sharp crack to the side of my head—the blade of my right oar—as the current sucks me toward the bottom of the river.

In situations like this, veteran boatmen will tell you it's essential to remain calm. I'm in no mood to comply with this formula, however, because even though I can't see a damn thing underwater, I'm pretty sure I know exactly what's happening to the *Jackass* up on the surface. In my mind's eye, it goes like this:

As the Great Wave flips the half-ton raft upside down, the boat drifts helplessly into the maw of the Green Guillotine, which starts clawing her to pieces like a pack of ravenous hyenas disemboweling the carcass of a wildebeest. As the lashings on the aluminum frame and the nose cones give way, my toilet supplies explode in all directions. But that pales in comparison with what I'm sure is being done to my poo cans. Unable to withstand the hammering, the lids are popping off, the rocket boxes are sinking like stones, and the collective contents of all five groovers are spewing out in a giant, thundering geyser: a toxic, 250-pound plume of raw waste that will turn this stretch of the Colorado into a Superfund site. It's an appalling debacle, and surely it will spell the end of my dream of becoming a river guide . . .

Given what I'm picturing, it's actually a bit of a disappointment when Horn Creek's hydraulics, instead of drowning my sorry ass, shoot me toward the surface, where I'm squirted through the tail waves looking like a wet cat. I'm so horrified by what's happened that my best option seems to be to dive back underwater and stay there. But suddenly I see the transom of the *Vale of Rhonda*, with Miss Billie Prosser at the oars, ordering me to grab her gunwale.

"Oh, my God, Billie, the *Jackass*!" I sputter as I latch on to the side of her dory and get dragged through the water.

"No worries," she says. "The *Jackass* had a great run. Much better than you did."

And, sure enough, there she is. Despite my incompetence, my humble yellow dung barge has performed a series of deft solo moves—threading Horn Creek's maelstrom on nothing more than the shining fortitude of her own righteousness— and now she's bobbing in an eddy on the far side of the river. Beautifully upright, perfectly intact, she offers an important nuance to Steve Carothers's Philosophy of Poop:

Despite your best efforts, it is not always possible to deal with your shit responsibly. But every now and then? Your shit will just take care of itself.

It's now nine o'clock in the evening. The toilet is up; the pee pails are distributed. Down at the edge of the river, where the dories and the rafts are securely tied to each other, the crew enacts an abridged version of the bedtime ritual on The Waltons—

"G'nite, Monte . . . "

"G'nite, Kevin . . . "

I unfurl my air mattress and crawl into my sleeping bag, and you're probably wondering: So what goes through the mind of a 43-year-old man who's about to spend the night sleeping on top of six poo cans?

Well, I should probably be planning how to rearrange those groovers in the morning, so that the *Jackass* will be balanced evenly for the enormous rapids downriver. But instead I'm dwelling on how badly I screwed up my run. Not just this afternoon's bungled trip through Horn Creek, mind you, but the longer, more misguided run down the river that is my life.

During my trial-by-fire odyssey as a poo-man, I've often wrestled with the question of why I chose to do this and whether it has been an enormous mistake. Whenever I take stock of all the regrets and missed opportunities I haul around like the rocket boxes on my raft—the career I've squandered, the women I've let down—I can't help but conclude that I've conducted myself like a *jackass*. By any accurate definition, my current state of affairs looks and sounds like failure. But on a night like this, as I lie on my boat floating in an eddy at the bottom of the canyon, with Jupiter's lantern swinging in the sky, it doesn't quite feel like failure.

Granted, I have spent some truly miserable moments on the river. But those ordeals have also been leavened by moments of simple, unvarnished perfection. I have seen summer thunderstorms send dozens of waterfalls simultaneously plummeting from the rimrock to the river. I've rowed past bighorn rams battling each other on the cliffs, the sound of their head-knocks echoing off the stone. I've napped on beds of columbine and hellebore orchids, and gazed at the turquoise waters bubbling from the subterranean pool that the Hopi believe to be the wellspring of life.

Those are wondrous things, to be sure. But the real reason I don't feel like a complete loser has less to do with the gifts that I've been given and more to do with what's been taken away. By stripping most of my pride, my apprenticeship has laid bare one of the more intriguing paradoxes of the Grand Canyon: the fact that this place has the power to render a person not only profoundly diminished but also radically expanded, often in the same breath. Of the many things that the canyon and the river supposedly offer, this may be the purest of them all.

So, yes, it's true: If I keep at this baggage-boat gig for a few more years, I may someday enjoy the privilege of rowing actual passengers down the Grand Canyon. In the meantime, the *Jackass* needs a captain—a role that commands, in my experience, an unexpected dimension of dignity and even a measure of grace. It's a job whose principal dividend, I suppose, is a subdued and somewhat battered frame of mind that, as the moon prepares to rise over the rim and the night cups the river in its hands, feels almost like happiness.

(Originally published July 2008)

THESE PANTS
SAVED MY LIFE

NATASHA SINGER

Grab a pair of XXLs and head up to Talkeetna, Alaska, where Carhartts aren't just the clothes the plumber wears, and every year the populace gathers to swap tales of heroic trousers and death-defying overalls. Here's your invitation to the Carhartt Ball.

If you are the Carhartt sales representative in Alaska, you hear so many stories about how your durable, mud-brown work wear has saved people's flabby backsides from wolf fangs and grizzly-bear bites that, after a while, you stop recalling the individual anecdotes. Except during the annual Carhartt Ball in Talkeetna, a winter festival at which fans gather to celebrate another year of survival on The Last Frontier.

"One time," says Doug Tweedie, Carhartt's man in Alaska for the last 25 years, "there was this walrus attacked a guy tying his boat up to a dock somewhere in the Aleutian chain who said what saved him were the black extreme-heavy-duty Carhartts the walrus's chompers couldn't bite through." Tweedie tells me this as he busily checks the microphone onstage at the Denali Fairview Inn during a lull in the festivities. "Another time there was this couple pulled over by the side of the Alcan Highway; a grizzly bear mauled the husband, who had gotten out of the car, but our coveralls deflected the claws and saved his hide."

The Carhartt Ball is not your traditional black-tie-and-strapless-gown gala with a sit-down four-course dinner. It started in 1996 after Talkeetna's garbage-removal and snowplow magnate, Bill Stearns, came up with the idea of a Carhartt shindig as an antidote to cabin fever. Although Carhartt rarely advertises, Tweedie agreed to drive up from Anchorage to sponsor the first ball and hand out prizes in the storytelling competition, where winners take home the eponymous outerwear. Six years later, the annual event has become an occasion for area hunters, fishermen, carpenters, trappers, mountaineers, whitewater rafters, and back-to-the-land curmudgeons to don their multicolored patched chore coats, kneeless pants, and worn overalls reduced to strings, and snowmobile into the two-block-long town in the foothills of Mount McKinley to entertain one another with accounts of death-defying animal attacks and engine failures.

On December 29, festivities start early at the local VFW hall (a 60-by-80-foot log cabin), where a catwalk is set up and Talkeetnans make like Gisele Bündchen and strut down it, modeling Carhartt's upcoming spring line. Then the party moves to the Fairview Inn, where everyone crowds around the horseshoe bar wearing spanking-new carpenter pants saved just for the occasion, as well as cruddy "road-kill Carhartts"—articles of clothing that have blown off the backs of pickup trucks, gotten run over, and been rescued by passersby. With the perfectly groomed hair of a national newscaster, 51-year-old Tweedie stands out among the guests in a bespoke brown Carhartt tuxedo with black lapels. He is, after all, the master of ceremonies. So that I will blend in, Tweedie has lent me a purple jacket (brighter hues were recently introduced in the Carhartt line, to appeal to rap stars and women) festooned with battery-operated blinking lights and a gigantic hieroglyph on the back that spells out c-a-r-h-a-r-t-t in sequins and glitter.

Alaskans buy an estimated four times more Carhartt work duds per capita than their compatriots in the Lower 48, and their loyalty is not due to just the harsh weather. Up here, hair-curling adventures featuring these sturdy $40 pants and $70 jackets are what distinguish weather-beaten sourdoughs from virgin flatlanders. The company was founded in Michigan in 1889 by traveling salesman Hamilton Carhartt, who started the trend by fashioning railroad uniforms out of surplus army tent material. Today, his great-grandson Mark Valade presides over the family-owned, Dearborn-based business, which reportedly grossed $324 million in 2000. Still, what is it about this brand that has made the Carhartt survival story a phenomenon so peculiar to Alaska, a kind of currency swapped in bars late at night, over breakfast in diners, and at the state fair? As the epicenter of what could be called the Rescue-Pants Epic, Talkeetna's Carhartt Ball seems a good occasion to investigate why this extra-thick, water-repellent, 100 percent ring-spun duck cloth has become the stuff of frontier fable.

"In Alaska, you're always getting into extreme situations where everything fails but your Carhartts," Tweedie theorizes. "Then when you get out of the situation, you tell everyone about it." And they tell everyone else. All around us at the

Fairview Inn, drinking from beer steins at wooden tables, standing by the house-rules sign warning "All firearms must be checked with the bartender," villagers are one-upping each other with Carhartt war stories.

"People call every week, with animal stories, chainsaw stories, accident stories—stranded off the road in 70 below zero, skidding hundreds of feet on icy roads on tipped-over motorcycles. I've stopped writing them down," Tweedie says. Then he perks up at the thought of a humdinger. "Do you know the one about the Fairbanks policeman who was saved when an assailant's bullet ricocheted off the brass zipper of his Carhartt jacket?"

As an infamous plaque, no longer on display, put it, the winter population of Talkeetna was once "378 people and one grouch." These days it's pushing 800. If you count the tourists, the spring-summer population runs into the tens of thousands, with climbers, campers, and sightseers passing through en route to Denali National Park and Preserve. Carhartts are so prevalent here, and the villagers so vociferously loyal to them, that visitors sometimes catch Carhartt fever.

"I've had Californians and Japanese tourists, total strangers, try to buy my Carhartts right off me. Yuppies!" scoffs Ted Kundtz, a Talkeetna jack-of-all-trades, when I meet him one morning before the ball for breakfast at the town's Latitude 62° Lodge. "They called the years of wear and tear I put in them 'authentic character.'" What seems to irritate him is not that the interlopers hoped to wheedle him out of his sorry-ass jacket, but that they wanted to appropriate the adventures that came with it.

Kundtz, a no-nonsense 60-year-old with a stubbly gray beard, sits over his eggs and reindeer sausage in padded black Carhartt bibs stained with yesterday's cheeseburger juice, last night's spaghetti sauce, aviation gas, engine grease, moose turds, moose innards, and moose blood. He has just pulled an all-nighter at mile 110 of the nearby Parks Highway, helping adult students learn to carve up abandoned game for a community-ed course called Roadkill 101.

"The difference between formal and informal in Talkeetna is clean Carhartts and dirty ones," he says. "The washed ones, you wear to church. Ones as cruddy as these"—he points at various blotches on his chest and pant legs—"you clean. Preferably in someone else's washing machine."

In his varied career, Kundtz tells me, he has been a pilot, a tester of Berkley fly rods, a ski instructor, a forensic photographer, and a Green Beret. A life such as his is full of Carhartt flashbacks. On one particularly memorable night several years ago, as he drove home from Talkeetna, with the mercury hovering at minus 25 degrees, Kundtz's 700-pound snowmobile skidded off a trail by the side of the road, tumbled down a slope, and flipped on top of him. He credits the thick insulation of his jumpsuit for keeping him alive and warm during the slow, cumbersome process of digging a snow-tunnel escape route. Kundtz's story exhibits typical Alaskan sangfroid and quick-wittedness in an emergency, as well as frugality; he still has the clothes he wore that night.

"I just heard about some new high-tech, battery-operated parka," he says. "But for me, out in the remote after the batteries ran out, where would I plug it in to recharge it? A birch tree? If you live here, Carhartts are bound to save your life one time or another. Once they do save your life, you're obviously not going to throw them away. That would be like scattering diamonds on the floor."

As we head out to the restaurant parking lot, Kundtz points to his truck. In the bed is his dead Australian shepherd, Jillaroo, wrapped in . . . a beloved Carhartt. "I'm about to bury the dog in my oldest Carhartt jacket and build a spirit house over her," he says, before driving off. Even in the afterlife, Carhartts are too precious to discard.

~~~~~~

"Where is our Carhartt machete holster, honey?" computer consultant Tom Kluberton asks his girlfriend, Hobbs Butler. At the moment, Butler, a fresh-faced, red-haired 32-year-old, is too busy to help. She's occupied talking about the homemade brown Carhartt tool belt—recycled out of worn-out pants—that she is modeling for me over a pair of newish Carhartt blue jeans.

"Other people wear through the knees first; I wear through the seat," she tells me. "Then I save the waistband and the back pockets. Turn them around and you get a great tool belt you can hang a hammer on and keep nails in."

I've dropped in on Kluberton and Butler at their 1940s hunting lodge, over near Talkeetna's railroad tracks, because I heard in town that they were a repository of rescue-pants epics—not only because they have spent most of the last decade outside, rebuilding their house from the foundation up, but also because they own 12 antic sled dogs.

"Day to day, these pants will last a lifetime in someplace like Oklahoma," Kluberton says. "Up here, getting pawed, clawed, and chewed by sled dogs all day long, or being dragged along behind them through thorny devil's claw when you fall off the sled, you might get a year's wear out of them." He looks down at his raggedy, paint-stained trousers, which are five months old but could pass for antique. Kluberton, 50, is tall and loping, with a boyish face and a thick mane of graying hair. He gives me a fast-paced tour of the grounds, breezing past a retaining wall constructed by "the Sherpa that our Everest-guide neighbor, Todd Burleson, sent over to help.

"Twice now, I've had a chainsaw swing up and catch me on the leg," Kluberton continues. "That's why you wear the double-knee pants—so the chainsaw cuts off a good, long slice of your Carhartts, instead of a good, long slice of your leg. Even so, you hate to lose a pair of Carhartts. What I do is get high-temperature automotive silicon gasket sealer and glue the pants back together." When I point out that silicon gasket sealer is neon orange, he offers a more color-coordinated alternative: "You can also use duct tape as a temporary fix."

Kluberton shows me other pairs of archival trousers he has not repaired, because they serve as badges of honor. Like the pair with the black-rimmed burnt-out crotch—the pants that illustrate a kind of infallibility principle.

"What happened was, while I was driving out of the Costco parking lot in Anchorage, I was futzing with this new minitorch—the kind that will flame a cigar from 11 inches away—which I bought to melt the ice that builds up overnight in my ignition.

"I dropped the torch in my lap, and kept driving until I noticed I was feeling a bit warm. I looked down to find my crotch on fire." Kluberton holds up the gutted pants as evidence.

"The family jewels were at risk," he says. "If I'd been wearing any other kind of pants, I'd have been dead or dying, in trouble, flambé even. Instead, I pulled over to the side of the road, put myself out, and turned the lighter off. OK, they're crotchless, but they're still good Carhartts. You can wear them as long as you've got boxers on underneath."

Kluberton goes into a bedroom to change into "the pants that survived auto-da-fé" to prove it. He is right. His crotchless Carhartts don't look so bad—if you like chaps.

Fisherman John Ferrell has a story that gives new meaning to the term "fashion emergency." A 50-year-old charter-fishing-boat captain from Anchor Point, Ferrell made national headlines several years ago after his 37-foot aluminum boat, the *Irene*, capsized dramatically in Cook Inlet, south of Anchorage. I track him down by phone from Talkeetna one evening after several folks tell me he is the ultimate protagonist in the definitive Carhartt narrative.

Ferrell had taken a party out fishing when the shaft connecting the *Irene*'s engine and its transmission broke off, piercing the boat's hull and flipping it in turbulent 40-degree water. His six passengers and deckhand all clambered onto a four-person life raft. This left no space for the captain, who had to hang on to the hull of his overturned craft. The first Coast Guard helicopter on the scene pelted

Ferrell with 110-knot rotor winds as it extracted the tourists from the life raft and flew away, leaving him to await the second rescue team.

"I should have died, because I was out there for more than an hour, and generally you're a goner in 10 to 15 minutes," Ferrell recalls nonchalantly. "But I was wearing my double-knee Carhartts, which were so insulated the wind did not penetrate and I didn't get hypothermia. Sure, my arms gave out and turned to Silly Putty, but the Carhartts protected my bottom half, allowing me to keep afloat by moving my legs."

To hear him tell it—and he tells it often, since it's his best story—his boat anecdote is less about almost drowning than about clothing as miraculous as the Shroud of Turin. But behind the clothing trope, the Carhartt survival yarn is a type of Freudian talking cure: a way to get over the aftershock by retelling your life-threatening experiences to others.

"Bottom line, those pants saved my life," Ferrell says proudly. "I'm the Carhartt poster boy."

~~~~~~

The Carhartt Ball takes place on my last night in Talkeetna. And, with all due respect to John Ferrell and his pants, there are a lot of poster boys in attendance. Not to mention poster girls. Emcee Doug Tweedie makes a halfhearted attempt to be heard over the raucous crowd standing three deep at the Fairview Inn bar as he introduces the handful of contenders for the survival-story contest, while in typical anarchic Alaska fashion, the majority of survivors are loudly swapping their bios offstage. Up at the microphone, nurse Colleen Hogan describes the time she saved a car-crash victim by covering him with a warm jacket. Offering a business survival story, jam and jelly maker Laura MacDonald recounts how she once lugged 50 gallons of blueberries home in a spare jumpsuit.

The contestants are so few that all of them take home Carhartt prizes of hats and T-shirts, and their anticlimactic tales turn out to be so downright mild that I wade into the Fairview's back room, where real cliffhangers are being traded under a mounted bull buffalo. I hear some archetypal stories of Alaskan ingenuity—like the one about Donnie Elbert, the mechanic who used his overalls as a frostproof tent one night after his plane crashed in the tundra; and then there's Carl Ober, the quick-thinking river guide who saved his own life, after flipping out of his 35-horsepower boat, by tying his waxed Carhartt pants into a knot and inflating them into an emergency life vest, all while careening down the Talkeetna River.

I head across the room, where teamster Randy Brooks hoists his right leg up on a table and rolls up his pants. He has an ugly eight-inch scar on his right shin. This happened when a birch tree he was cutting for firewood fell, pinning him beneath it and bending his leg at a right angle until the fibula was shattered and the tibia broke through his flesh. Brooks says the reason he's still walking is that the thick insulation of his Carhartts kept him warm, which stopped him from going into shock during the two hours it took his two sons to dig him out from beneath the tree, call for help on a nearby radio phone, and put him in an ambulance.

"This is a true story, backed up by bills and hospital records," Brooks says, as his wife, Edie, nods. "I would have been carving a peg leg for myself out of that birch tree had I not had my Carhartts on. And I still got them. I wear them all the time."

As Brooks rhapsodizes about how his pants saved his leg, I realize that whatever permutation of Carhartt yarn you hear, it represents more than an I-lived-through-this epic or a psychological coping mechanism. It's an initiation rite, an application for citizenship. If you haven't lived through such a tale, it means either you just arrived in Alaska or you have no business being here in the first place.

And so, one last story. Even if you're born and bred Alaskan, Carhartts do more than save your hide; they can also save your love life. In 1997, Anjanette Knapp, a 26-year-old ecologist from Sheep Mountain, was trying to impress her musher boyfriend Zack Steer, 25, when she agreed to dogsled with him through a trailless stretch of backwoods in the Chugach Mountains. It was a bold move; Knapp was new to mushing. Steer would pilot the lead sled and she would follow him on her own sled. He instructed her to not let go of the dogs, no matter what.

Soon after they started, Knapp accidentally slipped off her sled into deep snow and tumbled. Steer, far ahead and oblivious to his girlfriend's predicament, sped along as she was dragged facedown, losing her boot and sock but never leaving the sled because the leg of her Carhartt trousers snagged on the brake pedal. Finally, the dogs, realizing something was amiss, reined themselves in and brought the hell ride to a halt. Needless to say, Steer was impressed by Knapp's endurance. Soon after, he ran the Iditarod with an engagement ring tied to his lead dog's collar and proposed to Knapp at the finish line.

Those pants proved not only that Knapp truly belonged in Alaska, but that she also belonged to her beloved. Reader, she married him.

(Originally published October 2002)

57 FEET AND RISING

W. HODDING CARTER

During the Great Flood of 2011, longtime contributor W. Hodding Carter pitched us on the questionable idea of floating the raging Mississippi River. The Delta native then proceeded to canoe 300 miles from Memphis to Vicksburg—surfing the crest, watching wildlife cope with the rising tide and, unbeknownst to his editors, defying government orders to stay on land.

"What's wrong?" I asked John Ruskey. He slowly closed his cell phone. Glancing toward photographer Chris LaMarca to see if he was in earshot, he gazed at the churning Mississippi. It was our second day canoeing the Great Flood of 2011, and the river was hurling us southward at a rate of almost 100 miles a day.

"My wife," John finally answered, shaking his head. "Somebody told her there's a shoot-to-kill order for anyone on the water."

This was bad news. On May 16, we had sneaked a canoe into the river in Memphis, Tennessee, setting off to paddle 300 miles downstream to Vicksburg, Mississippi. We knew, of course, that what we were doing was illegal. On May 13, Mississippi governor Haley Barbour had issued an executive order banning all non-official watercraft from the flooded areas. But we couldn't resist. Since 1998, John has worked as the only paddling outfitter on the Lower Mississippi, and I grew up in the Delta, exploring its rivers and bayous since elementary school. This was our chance to see the Old Man the way he'd been in his prime, before levees channeled the river in a controlled path around New Orleans and out to sea. Now, however, with the water raging at two million cubic feet per second—churning up football-field-size boils, countless whirlpools, and other dangers—getting shot was just one of our concerns.

Water levels like this hadn't been in the forecast for the spring of 2011. Unlike the Great Flood of 1927, the previous high-water event, this one had literally dropped out of the sky—just weeks after southern farmers had planted heavily to cash in on rising commodity prices for everything from corn to soybeans. Although there had been an impressive amount of snowmelt bulging the river in early spring, that had pretty much run its course by planting time. Then, from April 14 to 16, the storm system responsible for one of the largest tornado outbreaks in U.S. history dumped record amounts of rain in the middle and lower Mississippi River Valley, engorging the river almost overnight.

Four more systems hit in the weeks that followed, quickly producing some of the highest water levels ever recorded on the Mississippi. The river rose to 61.5 feet at Cairo, Illinois, to 47.7 in Caruthersville, Missouri, and to 47.8 in Memphis—each mark near or above local flood stages. All along the lower half of the river, in Tennessee, Arkansas, Louisiana, and Mississippi, the water was cresting at or near levee-topping heights, threatening 6.8 million acres of farmland and town after town after town.

The big question was whether the levee system would hold. After the devastating flood of 1927 submerged 27,000 square miles, killed more than 200 people, displaced 700,000, and wrought property damage estimated even then at $347 million, Congress ordered the U.S. Army Corps of Engineers to construct or improve the world's largest system of levees, dams, and floodways—including 2,300 miles of mainline levees extending from Missouri through Louisiana. The still-unfinished project was largely completed in the 1980s, but the Corps's work had never been tested like this before, and officials were doing everything possible to shore up the levees: piling on additional riprap, sheathing entire structures in plastic, and stacking up sandbags.

Since even the tiniest damage to levees can lead to river water pouring through, state and federal officials had stationed armed personnel along them to discourage anybody—terrorist or sightseer—from coming close. Back in 1927, similar armed patrols guarded the levees for hundreds of miles on both sides of the river. In *Rising Tide*, John Barry's definitive 1997 book about the '27 flood, Barry quotes an anonymous telegram sent to the governor of Louisiana and published in the press that warned river captains, "The next boat that comes down at such high speed will need two pilots, as we intend to kill the first one. Our guards are armed with Winchesters and they have orders to shoot to kill."

In the best of times, paddling a canoe on the Mississippi is considered madness, even for a professional like John, whose long dark hair, full beard, and heavy mustache seem straight out of central casting for a backwoods river god. Now 47, he first arrived in Mississippi in 1983 by riding down from Winona, Minnesota, on a raft constructed from scrap lumber and old steel oil drums; he stayed to play the blues and set up a guiding operation, the Quapaw Canoe Company in Clarksdale, in the heart of the 11,240-square-mile alluvial crescent known as the Mississippi Delta. John's canoe trips are unparalleled, but even so, people there think he's a little nuts for wanting to be out on the big river.

I know the feeling. As I learned growing up along the riverside town of Greenville, Mississippi, "good" people just don't mess around with the river. Local author David L. Cohn, who wrote about the area from the 1930s through the 1950s, once claimed that folks in the Delta fear only two things: "the wrath of God and the Mississippi River." Most people I know down there might occasionally tempt the former—but never the latter.

That's why I nearly soiled my trunks the second we saw two stubby aluminum motor-boats—the regional vessels of choice for law enforcement—racing at full speed to intercept us after they'd appeared out of nowhere 100 yards downriver. By the time we could make out that they were Bolivar County Search and Rescue, John quietly announced from the stern that a third boat was approaching from upriver.

John ever-so-casually ruddered the canoe away from them, out toward the main channel. Ignoring my pounding heart and a lifelong commitment to avoiding the law, I thwarted his escape plan, performing a hard cross-draw and aiming the bow directly toward the posse. Once we were close enough, I went into full-on good ol' boy.

"What y'all doing out here?" I asked nonchalantly. "Great day to be out on the water, idn't it?"

The five men to our right didn't even blink, but the big guy driving the downriver boat barked, "Where's y'all's license?"

"My license? In my drybag. We're out here working for *Outside* magazine, but with weather like this it sure doesn't feel like work!" Not even a smirk. Chris, with his northern accent and hipster facial hair, had wisely stayed silent, but maybe John's instinct had been wiser. The big guy asked for my license again. Stalling, I asked if he meant my driver's license.

"Naw, boy," he answered, with an exploding grin. "Your insanity licenses—'cause you boys are crazy!" Then, as if this had been their plan all along, all 15 guys started laughing and telling us we better get our asses over to the Arkansas side, where it wasn't illegal to be on the water. After I told them my mama would never forgive me if I drowned in *Arkansas,* they laughed even more, took our pictures, and sped off.

Now, at least, we knew one thing: since only a fool would be paddling this out-of-control river—and fools aren't worth shooting—we were safe. Blessed be the insane.

~~~~~~

I'd come to this misadventure honestly. I've spent much of my adult life paddling in far-flung waters—from guiding the Class V rivers of West Virginia to sailing a replica Viking ship in the Arctic Circle. But when the 2011 flood hit, I was still working on my long-term project of traveling, in broken stages, the Delta's circumference by boat. I had already paddled the Big Sunflower and Yazoo rivers, which form the region's eastern and southern boundaries. The Mississippi would just about bring me full circle to where I grew up.

It was my grandfather, the second W. Hodding Carter, who taught me to love the Delta, and in particular Greenville, which for decades was its most prominent city. He was owner and editor of the *Delta Democrat Times,* and he always called things as he saw them—which, in the immediate post–World War II era, meant arguing in favor of equal education for "Negroes." His outspoken editorials won him a Pulitzer Prize, as well as lifelong enemies like the White Citizens' Council, a bastion of militant resistance to desegregation that assailed him during the 1950s and '60s with threatening anonymous phone calls and advertiser boycotts.

His escape? The river, including Lake Ferguson, which had formed between the Mississippi and the rebuilt town of Greenville when the Corps cut off an oxbow from the main channel in the 1930s. Big, as we called my grandfather, went there to fish, once hauling up a five-foot blue catfish; to hunt deer with each of his three sons; and to net the delicate river shrimp (now in severe decline due to channelization and pollution) that were once common fare for steamboat lunches. He wrote many books about the area, but two specifically concerned the river: one, *Lower Mississippi,* a natural and human history for Farrar and Rinehart's Rivers of America series, the other a hyperbolic coffee-table book called *Man and the River.* Every page extols the river's beauty and virtues.

Although Big moved to the Delta well after the flood, he knew that his adopted town, and the entire area, owed its continued existence to the new and improved levees, especially given that, old-timers say, some of Greenville's downtown buildings were buried under Lake Ferguson. To his way of thinking, and to many in the Delta even now, the engineers and officers of the Corps could do no wrong as they turned bayous into drainage ditches, connected backwater levees to mainline levees, constructed hundreds upon hundreds of stone dikes ("wing dams") to deepen and maintain the main channel, and sliced out countless cutoffs to drain floodwaters. Everything the Corps did was OK because its ultimate goal was to protect the Delta's towns, farms, and livelihood.

But today the Delta is mostly a depleted, depressed region with a shrinking population. In Greenville, a painful number of businesses are boarded up downtown, and one-third of the population falls below the federal poverty level. Bad as these facts may sound, the river has fared even worse. As far back as I can remember, its definable features have been its muddied water and the irrepressible Mississippi funk, a suffocating mélange of rotting mud, decaying fish, fertilizer, and some unidentifiable industrial by-product that is probably best not dwelled upon, at least when you're swimming in it. Each spring the bloated river, choked with nutrient-laden agricultural runoff and channeled by levees, races straight into the Gulf of Mexico in unnatural volumes, setting off such dizzyingly fast-paced algae growth later in the summer that the plants use up all the surrounding oxygen. This process creates oxygen-free dead zones, huge swaths of lifeless ocean that first appeared in the 1970s. The record dead zone, in the summer of 2002, covered 8,500 square miles, larger than the state of New Jersey. This year's is predicted to be at least 5 to 10 percent larger.

Yet, in mid-May, as the river was predicted to crest at 65 feet and Greenville mayor Heather McTeer Hudson urged citizens to stock up on water and fill up their gas tanks, we couldn't help but be excited. The same force that led others to fight or flee the river was the same force drawing us (in Faulkner-speak) inexorably toward it. Rising dozens of feet higher than its normal level, the river simply swept over the confining wing dams and, gathering swollen tributaries under its arms, spread itself far and wide.

If we weren't defeated by massive currents or antsy levee guards, we would come closer to experiencing America's greatest river in its natural state than anyone had in 75 years.

~~~~~~

Two mornings earlier, our crew of three had been skulking around downtown Memphis in John's massive Suburban, trailing a huge wooden canoe. John was circling the same eight-block area of upscale residences on Mud Island—the tourist-friendly peninsula that juts into the Mississippi River—but failing to find the semi-secluded launching area that had been suggested by a friend. His worried look made me realize that his most recent high-water adventure, in 2008, was still bothering him.

"I guess I should tell y'all, I almost got arrested before when we tried this," he'd said on the drive up from north Mississippi. We'd met the previous night at John's headquarters in high-and-dry Clarksdale, but we didn't hit the road until around midnight. Now we were still playing catch-up at 5 A.M.

"A bunch of do-gooders tried to get us for endangering minors," John went on. "They couldn't believe we were taking my friend's two kids out on the Mississippi in a boat without a motor. As if the canoe hadn't been the preferred method of travel on the Mississippi for thousands of years! The second we backed onto the grass, this old guy, the park superintendent or something, hops out and calls the cops, saying, 'Don't you see the stay-off-the-grass signs?'"

John shoved off minutes later; "Brother" Ellis Coleman, 55, a friend of his who serves as a part-time shuttle driver, was left standing in the water, holding the trailer, when the police arrived.

"John, these policemen have some questions for you!" he shouted across the growing distance, but John just paddled on. With Brother Ellis's permanently calm demeanor, it was little surprise that no one got arrested. The lanky, implacable Delta native is brother—one of 13 siblings, thus his nickname—to popular blues musician James "Super Chikan" Johnson and the living embodiment of cool.

As John pondered where to launch this time, Ellis, again the designated shuttler, said, "What's the matter? You don't want to get arrested?"

We finally settled on an over-grown field at the peninsula's northern tip, which had been left alone thanks to its proximity to a sewage-treatment plant. We unloaded Cricket—a 24-foot bald cypress canoe, modeled after the classic Great Lakes voyageur boats, that a friend had made for John. Then we pulled on light-weight wetsuits ("Just in case!" John suggested, smiling), ate a handful of dewberries, and headed for the Mississippi.

"Hope you get arrested!" Brother E. yelled again and again, waving his straw hat as we entered the wide current.

"Are we going to see Ellis later?" Chris asked. "I'd love to go hit a juke joint or something with him."

John, who had already begun banging on the Cherokee tom-tom he plays at the start of most paddling trips, paused to say, "Not a bad idea. Ellis is known as a lady-killer on the dance floor."

It had been my idea to start in Memphis. I'd hoped to launch as close as possible to the Peabody Hotel, the folkloric northern terminus of the Delta. (Long ago, David Cohn wrote that it "begins in the lobby of the Peabody Hotel and ends on Catfish Row in Vicksburg.") But the floodwaters hadn't reached that far, so Mud Island it was. After pushing off, we paddled south, halting briefly to admire a flooded diorama of the Lower Mississippi. It had been cordoned off and pumped free of the real Mississippi River water so that clear, fresh water could be reinstalled. A little farther below Mud Island, work crews were clearing huge fields literally carpeted with garbage.

Although we were starting six days after the river had crested in Memphis at almost 48 feet, the current hadn't let up much. Judging by roadside mile markers that poked above the floodwaters, we were moving along at ten knots—11.5 miles per hour—and we weren't even paddling in sync yet.

I've ridden fast canoes, but never for more than 100 yards at a time. Consistently clocking between ten and twelve knots that first morning was a thrill, but as the day wore on, my muscles wore down. Although the river's famous counterclockwise-moving boils—formed by the powerful bottom current that spins out boat-swallowing whirlpools as it hits the surface current—had not been dramatically multiplied by the increased volume, every stroke seemed like a tug-of-war, almost as if the river didn't want us going faster than it. Chris, new to paddling, sat in the middle a few feet behind me. I could make out his every stroke and, and though I'd expected ever-increasing lily dipping, he remained solid, even keeping pace with John when I started to nod off at the end of the day. I was tempted to smack him when he said how good he felt.

"What is it about paddling a canoe, John, that seems to massage away any soreness?" he said. "I was hurting a couple of hours ago, but the repetitive motion has worked the pain right out of me. Isn't it amazing, Hodding? This is why you like it so much, right?"

"Oh yeah," I scoffed. "Incredible. I haven't gone on a 100-mile-a-day paddle in ages, but I feel better now than when we started."

Around 8 P.M., we were already far to the south—near where the river passes Clarksdale—headed for a clump of willows peeking above the water's surface.

"Camp!" John hollered out cheerfully. He had to be kidding. We'd brought hammocks for tree stringing—there'd be no land to camp on—but even I could have found better trees than these battered sticks.

"Can you camp on driftwood?" Chris asked, pointing to a 40-by-20-foot mat of woody, junky debris we'd tied up next to.

"I'm not sure," John said. "Sometimes the current packs it in tight enough to walk on, but I've never camped. I guess it will hold."

As I tied us off, John hopped "ashore," quickly walking toward the upstream edge. "I'll get a fire going so we can at least have hot coffee," he said.

Chris and I helped each other onto the nearest log and inched forward. The debris was solid, several feet thick, and littered with trash—plastic soda bottles being the most prevalent item. There was a lot of dry wood in the middle, so we started a fire on . . . an island of wood. I wolfed down a quinoa salad John's wife had made and then stumbled toward my bed—the bow of the canoe. I was deeply shimmied into a bivy sack when I suddenly bolted upright.

"Guys!" I yelled. "Can you believe this? We're camping on an island of driftwood, floating 40 feet over the nearest land!"

That wasn't the only great thing. Once we'd put the first 50 miles or so between us and Memphis, that old Mississippi River funk had vanished. In its place, a sandy, willow-sweet aroma had silently risen from the surface. Even the river's color had morphed: from ag-runoff, milk-coffee brown to a confident and glistening gray.

"Only one tugboat passed us last night. Did y'all see it?" John asked eight hours later, moments after banging a metal cup against a plate to wake me up. John had been awake since three, thanks to his unshakable sense that Driftwood Island was falling to pieces—not a big surprise given that he'd slept a mere yard from the edge. By morning's light, though, it looked a few logs bigger.

"It was the strangest thing," he continued. "Never seen a river pilot act this way. When I couldn't go back to sleep—your snoring didn't help, Hodding—I relit the fire, and it was glowing brightly when he pushed by, headed upstream. Unmissable. But he didn't shine his spotlight on us."

Having once traveled the length of the Missouri in an inflatable boat, I knew exactly what he was talking about. River pilots always soak a campsite in blinding light—for safety reasons, or amusement, or maybe just in hopes of spotting skinny-dipping women. "I think he was afraid of what he might see," John said. "'A raft of driftwood with a fire on it? Has to be some sort of apparition!' These pilots are very superstitious."

Some of them could also be a little hostile. We'd passed one headed upstream and another headed down, and neither liked sharing the river with the likes of us. We had a radio, so we could hear the downstream guy warning the upstream guy that we were in the way. He said he'd called the Coast Guard to arrest us. The other pilot signed off by hoping we'd get washed against a stand of cottonwoods and flip beneath them.

Nice. For the record, though, most of the pilots we encountered were respectful if not friendly. We would pass a dozen more tugs, and no other pilots wanted to crush us. One went so far as to call us "brave souls."

The river continued to expand in width and power throughout the second day. With each passing hour, we crept closer to the highest water—meaning we were riding the largest freshwater wave ever. In Rising Tide, Barry recalls a study in which a Mississippi flood crest was clocked traveling at almost twice the speed of the average current. "The crest, in effect, was a separate layer of water that skidded down the top of the river," he explained. Miles wide and more than 100 feet deep, these crests have been shown to move at nine miles per hour for sustained periods.

That's an incredible amount of watery momentum, and we were seeing this force live as it swept us alongside, and sometimes over, weekend homes that were flooded to the rooftops. These were hunting camps, in local parlance, but more similar in size and value to summer cottages in Maine than to bedraggled backwoods shacks. We passed one 3,000-square-foot camp with a screen porch decked out with a 36-inch flatscreen TV that faced a six-person hot tub, now three feet underwater—a fitting punishment, perhaps, for soaking with your back to the river.

As we moved downstream, we aimed west, toward the Razorback side. John measured the swollen expanse of water at 19, 22, then 35 miles wide near its confluence with the Arkansas. This was the Mississippi unbound. Gone—submerged far below and in many instances torn apart—were the wing dams, the telltale islands beloved by John and used for navigation by tug pilots, and the lowland farms cashing in on the rich alluvial plains. Other than the tugs and those three law-enforcement boats, we had the entire river to ourselves.

Well, except for the doe swimming frantically toward the shoreline. By the time we noticed her, we were blocking her crossing. We paddled downstream, angling slightly to the east, so we could get below her and herd her back on course. But not knowing our good intentions, she decided not only to hold her ground in the 15-knot current but also to head upstream. We left her alone; the "stranded" deer was probably better equipped than we were to handle the raging current.

Libby Hartfield, director of the Mississippi Museum of Natural Science, would later explain to me that, despite frenzied media stories to the contrary, the creatures indigenous to the Mississippi River's floodplains do just fine in high-water events. Fish, for example, from gar to catfish to the endangered Mississippi sturgeon, move into the calm, warm floodwaters and explode in size and number. It's true that some animals don't adapt well: individual deer, wild hogs, and nesting turkeys forced to higher ground sometimes die, along with abandoned domesticated animals, if the waters take too long to recede. But most populations thrive in the end, thanks to the regenerative effects of the flood-waters. Biologist Brad Young, who leads the Mississippi Wildlife, Fisheries and Parks Department's black bear program, told me he'd checked on radio-collared bears from the air and they were all accounted for, feasting on trapped bugs and snakes. "Bears love to swim, and they love to climb trees," Brad explained. "What's not to like about a little flooding?"

It was about then that John announced, "Time for the afternoon swim." He swims every day he's on the river, but this was the first time I actually wanted to join him. The water was cold, somewhere around 60 degrees, and refreshing.

When I looked toward shore—marked by a line of half-submerged trees—I realized we were still racing onward, us three bathers and the bobbing, headless canoe, at one with the approaching crest.

It was a great but melancholy sensation—feeling a part of this river that was now wilder than it had been in decades. It's not that we didn't lament the destruction around us. Mississippi's farms alone would suffer $250 million in damage, and it would be weeks before people in low-lying communities, like the upper Delta's Tunica Cutoff, could visit their homes, let alone begin to face the heartbreaking decision to restore, rebuild, or move on. That decision would be played out up and down the river in the coming weeks: early estimates showed close to 10,000 people displaced by the flood and $4 billion in damage to homes, businesses, infrastructure, and farms.

Clearly, given the devastation of '27, America's engineers had done right to try and make life along the Mississippi safer. But the current system's complete reliance on containing and draining had too many draw-backs. Besides the expanding dead zone in the Gulf, there were far too many natural flood basins being protected by floodgates, pumps, and levees that, at great expense to taxpayers, kept land open to only a handful of farmers. These flood basins exist all along the river, and environmental organizations like American Rivers, in conjunction with federal and state officials, Gulf of Mexico fisheries representatives, and fishing and hunting conservation groups, are promoting policies that would restore them.

Under this alternative vision, reclaimed floodplains would again support plants and animals indigenous to the area's bottomland hardwood forests, only slowly releasing runoff downstream. This would also alleviate pressure on the swamps of the Atchafalaya Basin, which were inundated by the deluge of water released in May through the Morganza Spillway northwest of New Orleans. In strategic areas, levees would be moved back or notched to reconnect the river with its floodplain.

"We need to give the river more room to move," says Andrew Fahlund, vice president of conservation for American Rivers. "Unless we restore our natural defenses, we will burden future generations with increasingly disastrous floods."

While I'd always agreed with the idea of controlling the Mississippi naturally, that was in the hopes of helping the Gulf of Mexico and the wetlands up and down its banks. Now, after experiencing the Mississippi when it was clean-smelling and free, I felt like the river itself deserved a change.

~~~~~~

That night we camped at a place on the Mississippi that I knew from childhood—one that had taught me a lifelong lesson. It was a steep, 30-foot-tall set of sandy bluffs at Leland Neck, on the Arkansas side. Always a natural beacon in the flattened Delta landscape, it was also, on the night of May 17, the only piece of dry land for miles.

In 1972, my grandfather Big died when he was only 65, worn down, perhaps, by the years of fighting his enemies—and most definitely from drinking. Who could blame him for turning to alcohol, though, when an entire state reviled him? To pay the bills and prepare the way for selling the *Delta Democrat Times*, my family and their business partner sold off some of the paper's more extraneous, high-end items. The 40-foot cabin cruiser *Mistuh Charley* went in June of '76, the year I turned 14—but not before I, in a fit of anger, liberated the 12-foot lifeboat strapped to its roof. The little dinghy was a covetable example of craftsmanship, with its sleek lines, wave-slicing V hull, and dashing teak rail. But all I cared about was that it had a temperamental little 12-and-a-half-horsepower outboard.

My parents were splitting up that summer, and my dad, who'd taken over editing the paper, was out on the campaign trail with Jimmy Carter. Back home, there were only a minimal number of rules governing our lives. Two family statutes, however, remained absolute: (1) Hodding shalt not swim anywhere near the river, and (2) Hodding shalt not be so dumb as to even think about taking that damned lifeboat onto the river. "Yes, ma'am," I told my mother in all honesty. "Not a problem. I'm not that crazy!"

The next day, my friend Martin Outzen and I motored the boat across the river to Arkansas, hauling onto the sandy beach at Leland Neck. After swimming along the shore and throwing mud at each other, one of us had the bright idea to slide down the steep bluffs. The third or fourth time we'd trudged back to the top, Martin asked, "Hey, Hodding, doesn't the boat look like it's floating away?" The scorching heat had made the air thick and wavy, but even so, I could just make out a widening patch of water between the boat and shore.

We were potentially screwed. The bridge back to Mississippi was miles away, through impenetrable woods, and even if we somehow managed to get out to the road, there was still the matter of a 20-mile walk back to Greenville, where my mother's wrath would await. "Go, go, go, go, go!" I yelled, and we slid down the hot sand as fast as possible.

It took me a few desperate seconds to mount the courage to dive in. By the time I did, the boat had drifted an eighth of a mile and was slipping into the main current. I took off and, swimming the fastest 220 yards of my life, caught up to it, scrambling over the gunwale like some gigantic marauding water bug and pulling the tiny outboard to life in a single frantic motion. I drove back to shore with the proudest grin. I didn't know it at the time, but that rule-breaking swim set me free.

I'd been telling this story to Chris and John—raving for an hour about the Neck's life-affirming, perhaps even mystical, qualities—when John announced,

"It's just around this bend." The sun hung about a foot above the trees as if ordered up by Hollywood to highlight the beauty of my steep, sandy hills. Seconds later, there they stood—in all their two-foot majesty.

"Oh right, the flood," I muttered.

Nonetheless, the former cliffs, now short, tiny islands, were awash in sunset glow, producing an immediate "Awesome" from Chris. "I can't believe we have the only bit of land all to ourselves," he sighed. "Now if I can just get far enough away from your snoring."

As we soon saw, the islands were already occupied, by a raccoon and a feral pig. The raccoon waddled into the river and swam to a stand of cottonwoods 100 feet from shore that were loudly popping and rippling like a small set of rapids. The pig, a brown, scraggly specimen, stood his ground, at least briefly, squealing at us before snorting and skipping across the shallows to the adjacent bluff island 15 feet away.

We ate cold potato soup, then sat around another driftwood fire, lingering for hours.

"John, I'm totally getting you and this river," Chris said enthusiastically. "It's definitely gotten inside my head. Making me rethink my priorities. I want more of it. . . ."

"Yeah," John replied, "It'll do that to you. I have to get out here. Alone, if possible." Then he invited Chris to come back and apprentice himself as a guide.

I slept like a stone, until, hours later, the scruffy pig returned. Perhaps attracted by my ripening river essence, he skittered over my sleeping bag, back to reclaim his turf.

The following day was just as grand, with the river thundering along at two million cubic feet per second, a volume capable of filling the Louisiana Superdome in 50 seconds. Fifteen miles south of Greenville, we tied off to a floating 40-foot willow tree fluttering with spring leaves and ended up covering ten miles during lunch. We were now less than 15 miles from Vicksburg, where the river, nearing its crest, was washing onto city streets and forcing residents to flee their homes. The main levee was holding, but what about the backwater levees and floodplains they protected? With that in mind, we canoed into the woods late that afternoon.

We were following an old river passage called Forest Home Chute. As we paddled through flooded stands of hardwoods, the trees formed a single intertwined canopy stocked with thousands upon thousands of songbirds. At times we had to repeat ourselves to override their mesmerizing, almost deafening, calls. Paul Hartfield, a local biologist with the U.S. Fish and Wildlife Service, had told me years earlier, as we canoed very near this area, that these woods depend on periodic flooding to thrive. Thick with sycamores, oaks, and sweet pecans, bottomland forests like these can then support migratory birds, from the endangered Bachman's warbler to the recovering bald eagle. Maybe the birds were celebrating the crest.

Around 6 P.M., we came upon two southern hackberry trees, their smooth white bark lit by the setting sun. They were bare of limbs for a good 15 feet above the river's surface, shielded from the main channel by hundreds of yards of swell-dampening trees and spaced a perfect ten feet apart. We strung two hammocks, one about eight feet up and another about four feet lower. John had decided to stay in the canoe, no matter how many times we pointed out the abundance of space. Once I was safely tucked in, I wanted the night to last forever. How often do you sleep with only a thin sheet of nylon and two feet of willow-scented air separating you from our largest river at its most powerful state in a century?

If the Mississippi was a little bit of heaven, then our destination six miles inland, the Yazoo Backwater Area, was surely a taste of hell. The Yazoo used to be beautiful and clear, but these days it's a muddy drainage ditch loaded with agricultural chemicals. It's also a pawn in a high-stakes battle between entrenched foes fighting over the lower Delta. For years, the Corps and its local supporters have been trying to install the world's second-largest drainage pumps in this sparsely populated 4,000-square-mile basin, even as U.S. Fish and Wildlife has been restoring tens of thousands of previously farmed acreage to wetlands. Simply put, this place is a mess.

We'd have to zigzag in, following Forest Home Chute to Paw Paw Chute and crossing a small oxbow lake to reach the Yazoo River, its flow now reversed by the surging waters of the Mississippi. From there it was just down a short canal to the backwater levees and the Steele Bayou floodgates, the last line of defense protecting these lowest of lands.

The chutes were a cinch to navigate. Telltale cottonwoods marked the submerged embankments on either side, and any culverts were way below us. Our troubles began when, after paddling down a six-foot-wide alley between trees that marked a submerged deer trail, we made it to the mainline levee only to find a shiny white SUV parked in a lookout position. This sent us sneaking back into the woods but, regrettably, not to the same deer trail. We had to resort to pulling and prying our way through dense forest. That's when the trickling current suddenly went into flash-flood mode, forced through tighter forest as it spilled over a small abandoned levee. We found ourselves immediately running a high-stakes slalom course through tightly packed, sharp-limbed trees.

"Left, left!" I called—our only option if we were going to avoid smacking into a tree and instantly turtling. I pulled hard toward our port bow, and John turned her quickly. Dead ahead there was another tree ready to take us down, then another and another: Class II–III rapids mined with trees instead of rocks. Not a good scene, especially since Chris was still standing up, taking pictures. That's when I missed a draw; we bashed sideways into two trees and started taking on water.

"Back-paddle! Back-paddle!" screamed John. Chris dropped his camera and, together, all three of us—after about ten minutes of frantic upstream ferrying, backwards—got to slower water and onto the Yazoo.

"These gates better be worth it," Chris remarked. "I've never seen John actually lose his composure."

~~~~~~

After a short paddle on the backward-flowing Yazoo, we finally reached the Steele Bayou floodgate. Built in 1969 both to drain storm water and to keep floodwaters out, it creates an unnatural confluence of the Yazoo, the Big Sunflower, and Steele Bayou. Right now the gate was closed, holding back the swollen Yazoo from the lowlands that the other two waterways flow through. It was amazing to stand on the backwater levee and compare both sides. On the Yazoo side, the water had risen to the top of the levee, where work crews had piled dirt and rocks a foot high. On the Sunflower side, the water was more than 20 feet below us.

It was impressive, frightening, and maddening. Impressive because of the skill shown by the Corps. "You've got to hand it to 'em," John admitted. "These structures are performing exactly as they were designed to." Frightening because countless vulnerable farms and nearby towns stood on ground well below us. And maddening because none of them should be there. This area was called a floodplain for a reason—it's supposed to be flooded when the rivers are high. If we would just restore enough of these traditional floodplains, then so much of the mess we're facing—increasing dead zones, endangered cities, loss of habitat all along the Mississippi River corridor, and a polluted Atchafalaya Basin—would be cleaned up naturally.

We took a shortcut back to Vicksburg, paddling across a large flooded farm and along the old flooded highway, and ended the trip near sunset, like we had the previous days. Only this time we were greeted by a crowd of onlookers—20 or 30 tourists, friends, and little kids held behind a barricade by the cops. Paul Hartfield, the biologist, had argued to the police that our ride from Memphis had been an important natural-science investigation. He must have been convincing in his uniform cap, because the police and strangers alike clapped heartily when we waded up Old Highway 61. We'd originally invited Paul to join us on our journey, but he'd had to pass due to a family illness. It was easy to see how he felt—smiling, but with a sad, wistful look in his eyes—when he shook my hand.

"You've seen the river as close to what it once was as possible," he told me a few days later. "If 1927 was the flood of the 20th century, then 2011 is the flood of the 21st. When you're an old man and the grandkids are asking Papa where he was in the Great Flood of 2011, you'll be able to tell them, 'Well, kids, I was surfin' the crest.'"

(Originally published June 2011)

PARADISE WITH AN ASTERISK

S. C. GWYNNE

Gwynne, the author of the Pulitzer-Prize finalist Empire of the Summer Moon, *is a master of historical non-fiction. That's what made him perfect for this examination of Bikini Atoll, the tiny ring of islands halfway between Hawaii and Australia that was ravaged by U.S. nuclear tests at the height of the Cold War. He returned with a tale of heaven on earth, where the vestiges of hell lie just below the surface.*

Alson Kelen is seated comfortably on the grave of his great aunt, at the far eastern end of Bikini Island in the vast, hyperblue beyond of the Pacific Ocean. He is telling a story of a lost paradise, of a life he lived on this island a long time ago.

He is 44 years old now, a short, barrel-chested man with a bald head, medium-dark skin, elaborate tattoos over much of his body, and a disarming smile. The world he describes is lush and lovely. He was ten. He and his friends played here in the coconut groves and in the brilliantly colored waters of the lagoon. They ate breadfruit and pandanus fruit. They drank coconut milk. They fashioned hooks from common nails, baited them with hermit crabs, and caught all the fish they could carry. "Every day was an adventure," Alson says. "We swam in the bluest water. We would cook the fish under the trees and eat them, and every day went like that—fishing, swimming, and cooking. It was a beautiful time."

From all appearances, this place is still an earthly paradise. Here in the Bikinian Ancestral Cemetery, with its tidy white fence and weathered graves, the 3.4-square-mile island looks exactly as Alson describes it. The sky is a deep cobalt blue; coconut palms, orange-limbed and yellow-fringed, sway in the steady trade winds. There are still breadfruit trees and pandanus trees and flame trees with brilliant red blossoms. Two hundred yards to the north, a coral reef meets the full, transparent blue violence of the Pacific.

There is just one problem, though you could stare at this palm grove for a lifetime and never see it. The soil under our feet, whitish gray in color with flecks of coral, contains a radioactive isotope called cesium 137. In high enough doses, it can burn you and kill you quickly; at lower levels, it just takes longer to do the job, eventually causing cancer. The soil itself is not dangerous to touch. The danger lies in the plant life that takes it in, and in the animal life, like the huge coconut crabs that live on the island and eat the plants. The cesium 137 is fallout, a word introduced to the world during the systematic detonation, from 1946 to 1958, of 23 nuclear weapons by the U.S. army on Bikini Atoll.

Over the course of a nuclear exile that has lasted 66 years, the Bikinian people have been relocated five times. They have nearly starved to death. They have seen their way of life vanish. They have watched as nuclear scientists swarmed over their island, trying to figure out what the bombs had done to it. They have fought the U.S. government in legal battles all the way to the Supreme Court. Alson was part of a group of three extended families who moved back to the island in the 1970s after it had been declared safe. He lived the fantasy existence he describes for me, only to be told, after the discovery of the horrifying cesium 137, that he and his people had to leave.

And still men like Alson, a former mayor of the relocated Bikinians, most of whom now live in the Marshall Islands' capital, Majuro, and on the island of Kili, want to come back to the place they believe God gave them.

Perhaps the cruelest part of exile for Bikinians like Alson is the staggering beauty of the atoll today, 54 years after the final atomic test. Just beyond the cemetery's fence, the lagoon is jumping with fish; corals are blooming; the atoll's uninhabited outer islands have become a gigantic seabird rookery; the beaches are perfect and white, the plant life lush and dense. Bikini is paradise again, but with an asterisk.

On a map, the Marshall Islands look like a large expanse of nothingness—a great, empty blue ocean dotted with flyspecks of land. That's pretty much the view from the air, too, as we sail through the cottony clouds in an old 17-seat Dornier 228 turboprop, 10,000 feet above the scrolling white waves of the equatorial Pacific. The physical dimensions of the Marshalls tell you everything about the place: 29 coral atolls and five islands that cover 70 square miles in a sea area of 750,000 square miles. It's like taking the small city of Wichita Falls, Texas, chopping it up into city-park-size pieces, and scattering it over Western Europe. One of those pieces is Bikini Atoll, which consists of a large oval-shaped reef and 23 small islands, including Bikini, occupying a total area of 230 square miles. There are some 125 miles of open ocean between it and the nearest inhabited island.

I am joined on this mid-April flight by five Bikinians, all descendants of the people who abandoned their island at the command of the U.S. government before the first atomic test in 1946. Three—Biten Leer, 49, Wilson Note, 50, and Banjo Joel, 62—are elected councilmen of the Bikini government, now located on Majuro. Jackson Laiso, 79, and Alson Kelen both grew up on Bikini Island—Laiso in the 1940s and Kelen during the aborted repatriation in the 1970s. Also with us are Japanese filmmaker Masako Sakata, who is working on a documentary about Bikini, and photographer Corey Arnold.

Our host and translator (the Bikinians speak varying degrees of English) is Jack Niedenthal, 54, American born and a larger-than-life figure in this part of Micronesia. Bearded, of medium height, and with the shoulders of the all-American swimmer he once was, Niedenthal came to the Marshall Islands as a teacher with the Peace Corps in 1981. He has lived there more than 30 years, speaks fluent Marshallese, and is married to a Bikinian woman. His intriguing title—trust liaison and representative for the people of Bikini Atoll—means that he manages the flow of trust funds from the U.S. to Bikini intended to compensate the Bikinians for their suffering and clean the place up. He is a friendly, relaxed presence; a good storyteller with a pocketful of tales spanning 30 years in the south seas.

We all met at 8 A.M. in the airport on Majuro, an island of 25,000 people that in some places is less than 300 yards wide. Our flight is taking us another 500 miles northwest. Getting to Bikini is not easy; for most people it's actually impossible. In 2010, the government-owned Air Marshall Islands, known locally as Air Maybe, had its three planes grounded for a total of 568 days for everything from compass problems to "uncommanded engine shutdown." The service to Bikini, until 2008 roughly one flight a week, is now practically nonexistent. Our temperamental Dornier was declared airworthy only at the last minute.

But it's a joyous trip for my companions. After a three-hour flight, we land on the island of Eneu, at the southern end of the atoll—a historic place, in a dark, apocalyptic sort of way. As a decaying concrete-and-steel bunker near the deserted airport attests, Eneu was once the U.S. military's staging ground for the atomic-bomb tests.

From there we board an open aluminum boat for the last eight miles to Bikini Island. As we head out into the atoll's protected lagoon, we pass buoys that mark the sites of some of the warships sunk during the bomb tests, now moldering, their cannons still intact, under 180 feet of water. Down there is the *Nagato*, the flagship of the Imperial Japanese Navy, from whose bridge Admiral Yamamoto launched the attack on Pearl Harbor. Finally, we land at the island's only dock and are greeted by some of the men who live on Bikini, part of a five-person skeletal force paid by the Bikini council to look after the remaining infrastructure.

Our rooms, which sit in the bight of an immaculate two-mile-long white-sand beach, are plain but quite decent, with running water, toilets, showers, and air-conditioning. They are relics of once successful, now defunct Bikini Atoll Divers, a commercial scuba operation that was to be an economic cornerstone of the return.

As we exit our temporary home and wade into the lagoon's 85-degree water, the only sounds I hear come from the seabirds wheeling above me and the lap-lap of waves on the sand. Sea turtles roam just offshore, near reef heads that teem with brilliantly colored fish. If there is a lovelier beach anywhere in the world, I have not been on it.

~~~~~~

Despite the natural beauty, it is impossible to walk anywhere, or look anywhere, and escape Bikini's nightmare history. Every man-made object on the island is an artifact either of the bomb tests or of some failed attempt to help the Bikinians return to their home. There are old bunkers built to shield cameras from atomic explosions; buildings put up by the U.S. Department of Energy as part of its radio-logical measuring program; houses erected by the U.S. in the 1970s for return-ing Bikinians; dump trucks, bulldozers, backhoes, semi trailers, fuel tanks, and forklifts, some decaying and covered with vegetation. There is a plywood build-ing, nearly falling apart, with a rotting sign that says King Juda Lab, which was established to provide radiation testing for repatriated Bikinians. There is a sign on the machine shop that reads WE CAN FIX EVERYTHING EXCEPT A BROKEN HEART. All of this is being reclaimed; it is all sinking back into paradise.

Operation Crossroads, the most spectacular and expensive science experiment in history, was first proposed in August 1945, a few weeks after the U.S. dropped atomic bombs on Hiroshima and Nagasaki. President Harry Truman had ordered the Army and Navy to conduct further tests of nuclear weapons. The reason, which sounds implausible if not ridiculous today, was to see if atomic bombs, when dropped on warships at sea, would sink them.

The U.S. had taken control of the Marshall Islands from the Japanese after World War II, and Bikini Atoll was chosen as ground zero. Its 167 residents, who lived in huts and fished and sailed their outriggers as they had for centuries, were persuaded to leave their homes "for the good of mankind and to end all world wars," as the local U.S. military governor put it to them. They were shipped 125 miles east to Rongerik Atoll and given a few weeks' worth of food and cheerful assurances that they could return as soon as the tests were over.

Meanwhile, Bikini Atoll became the centerpiece of a colossal military operation. By the summer of 1946, there were 42,000 military and civilian personnel in place, with 242 ships involved in the test, 156 aircraft, more than 300 cameras, and 18 tons of film. Since the whole point was to sink ships, an armada of 95 of them—the equivalent of the sixth-largest navy in the world at the time—were parked in the waters of Bikini lagoon, fully loaded with weapons and fuel. To see what the bombs might do to living things, 3,350 experimental rats, goats, and pigs were sacrificed on the decks. Servicemen sheared a number of them and put suntan lotion on their bare skin to see if that would somehow mitigate the effects of gamma radiation.

The first blast, code-named Able, was detonated on July 1 and, because the bombardier missed his target, was something of a dud. The July 25 Baker shot, however, was a monstrous success. Detonated under the ocean's surface, it drove a 2,000-foot-wide column of water high into the sky in less than a second. A few moments later, millions of tons of atomized reef and water collapsed back into the lagoon, and a giant shock wave moved out across the water, sinking the 26,000-ton, 562-foot battleship *Arkansas* and lifting the stern of the 880-foot *Saratoga* 43 feet into the air. The shock wave released massive amounts of radiation, a phenomenon that was not widely understood at the time. One hundred and twenty-five miles away, the Bikinians, newly resettled on Rongerik and already running out of food, still thought they were coming back to their atoll. Soon.

~~~~~~

There is a sense, while on Bikini Atoll, of being at the end of the world. That sense is greatly enhanced when the twin 150-horsepower outboards on your 28-foot aluminum hammer-head rig stop simultaneously in the middle of the atoll's massive shark-filled lagoon. This is precisely the situation we find ourselves in on day four: adrift, 15 miles from our lodge on Bikini, with only one day's supply of water, in a place where people without water don't last long in open boats. Though we have a radio and there are three men back on the island, our boat is the only functioning watercraft.

Our potential savior is a bandanna-wearing Filipino mechanic named Benjamin "Bai" Maloloyon, part of the five-man Bikini work-force. He is now squinting at the motors and shaking his head. Bai seems capable enough, but he speaks in a broken Marshallese-English pidgin that is hard even for the islanders to understand. Earlier that day, Jack had asked him about taking the boat to the dock, to which Bai had given a lengthy reply about preparing barbecued pig for dinner.

Up until now, today's expedition was thrilling—in the good way. After leaving the island in the morning, we ran in the lee of the big reef, out of sight of the low-lying land for long periods of time, while big turquoise waves collided around us. We had set off to explore some of the atoll's outer islands. Our main destination was the small island of Nam, about 25 miles due west of Bikini, location of one of the seminal moments in the development of thermonuclear weapons.

As we motored across the lagoon, our Bikinian travel companions, who wore shorts and baseball caps and carried throw nets and an assortment of fishing poles, explained that the atoll's outer islands were their people's traditional fishing and bird-hunting grounds. This was where they once sailed their 30-foot outrigger canoes, remarkable pieces of technology that can hit 20-plus miles per hour and amazed the first Europeans who saw them. The canoes defined the old way of life, traveling from island to island within the protected lagoon; they could also travel great distances across the open ocean.

And then, suddenly, we were there: a patch of midnight blue water in the transparent shallows of the lagoon. This was the Bravo crater, a mile wide and more than 200 feet deep, a place where imagination fails. The hydrogen bomb that was detonated on this spot on March 1, 1954, created a fireball four miles wide and raised the temperature of the lagoon water to 99,000 degrees. The blast was 1,000 times more powerful than the Hiroshima bomb and nearly three times stronger than its creators expected. It shook islands 250 miles away. It vaporized three islands in the atoll. And it killed every living thing in the air, on land, and in the sea for miles around.

Three to four hours after the blast, the 64 inhabitants of neighboring Rongelap Atoll, next door to Rongerik, watched in wonder as the snowlike ash from Bravo began to fall on their island, reaching a depth of two inches. The children played in it. People drank water saturated with it. Soon they began to experience vomiting and diarrhea; their eyes burned, and their necks, arms, and legs swelled. The Americans had not bothered to tell the Rongelapese what they were planning to do.

With these surreal thoughts in mind, we dropped fishing lines in the H-bomb crater. We spent a few hours on Nam and on neighboring Aomen island. There were seabirds everywhere, millions of them. Virtually any tree we saw contained two or three fledgling terns or boobies or frigate birds. At some point, the Bikinian men disappeared to look for food, an endeavor they took great pleasure in. Majuro, where they live, is dense and urban; food gathering is done at the supermarket. Here, there is something wild and free and timeless about it, a tradition Alson remembers from living on the atoll as a boy. "My grand-father was the leader of the community," he says. "He would call upon the men to go fishing or get birds or turtles. The basis of our culture is working together. Everyone taking part."

An hour later, the men returned from the narrow strip of jungle with broad smiles, carrying a dozen coconut crabs—large, frightening creatures that looked as though they might have been spawned by the nuclear tests. They contain cesium 137 but at a level that makes occasional consumption harmless. It was a wonderful moment: a group of men from vastly different cultures uniting to celebrate the ancient, universal human bond of a successful hunt—in this case, for radioactive crabs. The Bikinians, huge grins lingering on their faces, were already planning a feast for that evening.

But a few hours later here we are, adrift on our broken-down skiff, the indomitable Bai covered with grease and sweat and barely visible in the boat's well. We are now experiencing—I am, anyway—another universal human feeling: fear. As casually as possible, I ask Jack what Plan B is.

He smiles, surveys the giant surf crashing above the reef and the rising seas around us, and replies: "Hope."

At the helm, Edward Maddison, another member of the island's full-time crew and the former dive master for Bikini Atoll Divers, jokes: "If we had a sailing canoe, we'd be home by now."

Alson laughs and nods.

"Too bad we can't just take it to the Honda guy at Majuro," I say, joking.

"That is the Honda guy," says Jack, with a nod of his head toward Bai. I can't tell if I should be reassured by that.

Finally, an hour later, we hear one of the Honda 150s growl, and we're able to limp back across the lagoon. For me it's a harrowing reminder of what a remote place I've traveled to. For the Bikinians it seems to offer nothing more than a few placid, pleasantly existential moments.

What happened to the displaced islanders after 1946 was a tragedy of neglect. There was never enough food on Rongerik: the reef fish were poisonous; a fire damaged the island's coconut trees. There was not enough water. By 1948, they were starving to death, even though the United States had committed to taking care of them. In March of that year, the Bikinians were moved to Kwajalein Island, home to a new U.S. naval base, where they camped miserably on a small strip of grass next to the runway. A few months later they were relocated yet again, this time to the island of Kili.

This was a disaster, too, but of a different kind. Kili was a true island, which meant that there was no ring of coral, no protected lagoon, no jungle-fringed outer islands to fish and hunt, just the big waves of the Pacific crashing up against rugged shores. Fishing was nearly impossible. "It was just a small piece of rock in the middle of the ocean with some coconuts growing on it," says Alson. Once again food supplies were intermittent. At one point, the island's new inhabitants required an emergency airdrop. The Bikinian exile continued for another 20 years, long after the last bomb, code-named Fig, was detonated in August of 1958.

Then, in the late 1960s, something miraculous happened. Scientists from the Atomic Energy Commission decided that radiation levels at Bikini Atoll "do not offer a significant threat to health and safety." In June of 1968, President Lyndon Johnson announced that the 540 Bikinians living on Kili could go home, and he ordered them resettled "with all possible dispatch." Coconut, breadfruit, pandanus, and other food trees were planted on the island; debris was cleaned up. Houses were built. By the mid-1970s, more than 150 Bikinians were living on the island.

That was when the U.S. Department of the Interior began to realize that the estimates of radiation levels had been dreadfully wrong. In 1977, scientists recorded alarming increases in cesium 137 levels in the bodies of people living on the island. Now an emergency existed, and the entire population of Bikini was moved yet again, this time to Kili and Majuro. "They brought three ships and a lot of food," recalls Alson. "I was young. I saw the ships and said, 'Let's go cruising,' not knowing that this was the end of my happy life in this paradise. I was running around on the ships, but I could see that everyone else was crying. I remember they were waving and crying."

Life in exile resumed, perhaps a bit more despairingly than before. But a decade of constant research later, scientists again offered new hope. It began with radiation testing by the U.S. Department of Energy and its contractor Lawrence Livermore National Laboratory. By the mid-1980s, scientists had proven that by applying large amounts of potassium fertilizer to Bikini's soil, cesium levels could be reduced tenfold. In addition, the scientists concluded that soil excavation— simply removing the top layer of dirt—could further reduce radioactivity.

Neither of these solutions was cheap, but it was around this time that the Bikinians came into some real money. They received $75 million in damages in 1986 as part of a new Compact of Free Association with the U.S. and then, in 1988, another $90 million to be used specifically for radiological cleanup. The compact also set up a Nuclear Claims Tribunal, which meant that Bikinians' pending complaints against the U.S., dating from the early 1980s, would be heard by a new court. In 1987, a group of Bikinian elders traveled to the island to redraw old property lines; among them was Jackson Laiso, who is with us on this trip.

"You can't imagine the joy of knowing that, OK, they are finally giving us money to do this," recalls Niedenthal. "The joy of coming back with the old men was something I had never experienced."

The new attempt to return began with the cleanup of Eneu, where a small worker village was raised and the airstrip improved. Soon, a hotel was under construction on Bikini, along with new docks and roads. Generators, desalinators, and power lines were installed. All preparation for what everyone believed would be the big, definitive cleanup.

One key component of the plan was Bikini Atoll Divers, run by the Bikinians, which also offered sport fishing. The goal was to introduce the rest of the world to one of the planet's great untapped fishing and diving destinations. For divers there were the sunken warships from the Able and Baker blasts in 1946, sitting just offshore in about 180 feet of water. There were also incredible reefs. Despite atomic destruction that had blown much of the atoll to pieces, 50 years later the corals had already recovered. And with the corals came the reef fish and the fish that feed on the reef fish: 30-pound dogtooth tuna, 20-pound barracuda, and bluefin trevally as big as 50 pounds. With no human beings anywhere near the atoll to harvest them, Bikini offered sportsmen one of the most plentiful and pristine fishing environments in the world.

The first tourists arrived in 1996, and not surprisingly, the travel industry swooned. *Skin Diver, Newsweek, National Geographic,* and *Condé Nast Traveler* all proclaimed Bikini one of the best diving destinations on the planet. By 2000, Bikini Atoll Divers was attracting 250 people a year, all of whom paid roughly $4,000 for the experience—a good deal of money by the humble standards of Marshall Islands tourism and, suddenly, a real economic basis for a return to the island.

Since our boat is temperamental all week—Bai, in an effort to fix the outboards, has remachined fuel pumps that don't quite fit—we explore Bikini Island as much as we can. One afternoon we visit the world's most perfect swimming pool. Like everything else on Bikini Atoll, it has a twisted history. Back in the 1990s, an engineer had needed rock fill to build the bulkhead on the western end of the island. In keeping with Bikini's time-honored policy of blowing things up, he dynamited the reefs at the eastern end. He got his landfill but also inadvertently created a coral-banked swimming pool, three to eight feet deep, in the middle of the island's outer reef. At high tide the pool, and the reef, are invisible. When the tide goes out the reef emerges, and in the middle of it is the swimming hole. Calm and spectacularly clear, it's too shallow for sharks and excellent for snorkeling.

We arrive as the last of the water recedes and plunge in. Whatever the dynamiters did to the place is long undone: there are massive coral formations housing spectacularly colored fish. While I swim among them, Alson hunts octopus, as he did when he was a child. He has a two-foot haft with a sharp hook on the end.

He finds an octopus in a rock, and after a brief battle and several explosions of ink, Alson wins.

A while later, the tide changes and begins to rush in from the sea, where the breakers are now cresting the reef, sending powerful currents of colder water into our warm lagoon. The sharks—blacktip, whitetip, and gray reef—will soon be back, so we get out and turn our attention to fishing: the men have thrown nets, seeking mullet and mackerel.

Fish are freakishly plentiful here, and our traveling companions are obsessed with hauling them in. The day after our return from Nam, three of us fished from the lone Bikini dock. There were strikes with almost every cast. We caught several bluefin trevally and a magnificent green jobfish. On another cast, we hooked a smallish three-foot barracuda, which put up a spirited fight. A few seconds later, a school of grouper arrived and attacked the barracuda, which, now in a fight for its life, bent the pole in half. And then the sharks showed up, blacktips, probably four feet long, and the trick was to get the barracuda in before the sharks tore it to pieces. It all happened in water so clear we could see every detail of the battle.

Sharks are a constant here. The water is lovely and the reefs incomparable, but you're always looking over your shoulder. The guarantee of shark sightings was one of the diving operation's attractions, though occasionally they got more than they bargained for. "We didn't usually do night dives," says Niedenthal, who ran the operation, "but at one point the dive master decided to try one at the USS *Saratoga* with some customers who had been pestering him about it. So they loaded the boat, got their gear together, and dropped into the blackness. When they shined their lights around, all they could see was a wall of shark eyeballs glowing eerily in the sea around them. The dive lasted a total of ten minutes, never to be attempted again."

Close to the end of our trip, we were eating lunch on our boat, which now, with the jerry-rigged fuel pumps, was sucking gas at an enormous rate. Someone threw some chicken bones overboard—-inadvertently chumming the water—and a five-foot whitetip shark showed up. We watched it turn aggressively toward Corey, who was in the water putting on snorkeling gear.

"Shark!" we all shouted, then spent the next 30 seconds convincing him we weren't pulling his leg.

"I still haven't seen a shark," Corey said suspiciously, as we finally hauled him aboard.

"Oh, it was a naughty one," said Alson, who should know. "Trust me. The little ones are the crazy ones."

Just when the Bikinians' epic attempt to return lost steam is difficult to pinpoint. Niedenthal dates it from the moment, in 1995, when the council discovered that the EPA standard for radiation cleanup (15 millirems) was significantly lower than the standard the Department of Energy scientists had been using (100 millirems), thus boosting the potential cost of cleanup.

But there were other, more immediate reasons. The Bikinian world was changing. Its population, which had grown quickly (the original 167 residents now number 4,800), was poor by U.S. standards and needed a range of social services. Addressing those needs began to trump the repatriation efforts. "They had a trust fund, but it had two masters," says Niedenthal. "They had to take care of their people where they were living now: housing, food subsidies, insurance, medical plans, scholarships, health care. The other master was the cleanup of Bikini, and that just became a less important priority."

Then followed the successive market crashes in 2001 and 2008, the second of which cut their financial trusts in half. The funds recovered somewhat, now totaling a little more than $150 million. That may seem like a lot, but the trusts provide a scant $6 million to $8 million in investment income annually, which in turn allows the Bikinian government to pay out something less than $15,000 per family per year. That leaves virtually no money for the cleanup. The massive public works begun on Eneu in the early 1990s have been suspended. The worker town is now a ghost town. In 2008, Air Marshall Islands' service became so unreliable that the diving and sportfishing operations had to be canceled.

The final devastating blow came in 2010, when the Bikinians lost their largest lawsuit against the U.S. government. In 2001, the Nuclear Claims Tribunal—a body established in 1983, as part of the Compact of Free Association, to handle Marshall Islands complaints—awarded the Bikinians $563 million in compensation. But the tribunal was never adequately funded to pay a claim of that size. The Bikinians sued to force payment, but the effort failed when the Supreme Court refused to hear the case in 2010, claiming it doesn't have the right to rule over international agreements. The U.S. courts are now closed to them. "It was absolutely devastating," says Niedenthal. "We always had the idea and the hope that we were fighting for something. When we got the final rejection by the Supreme Court, that was it. We're done."

It's ironic that, even as financial woes have all but ended the Bikinians' efforts to return, the prospects for bringing radiation down to acceptable levels are better today than ever before. A March 2012 assessment from Lawrence Livermore Laboratory is strikingly upbeat. One of its recent findings is that levels of cesium 137 are dropping far faster than anyone had predicted. Though the isotope's radiological half-life is 30 years, its environmental—or actual—half-life is only nine.

"Conditions have really changed on Bikini," says Terry Hamilton, scientific director of Livermore's Marshall Islands assessments. "They are improving at an accelerated rate. By using the combined option of removing soil and adding potassium, we can get very close to the 15 millirem standard. That has been true for roughly the past ten years. So now is the time when the Bikinians, if they desired, could go back."

These findings leave Bikinians in a sort of cultural, scientific, and financial limbo. Considering the record of the U.S. government, it's hard to blame them for being skeptical. But even if they had the money for one final cleanup effort, return would be difficult. There are only 34 Bikinians still living who were born on the island. Though these and other Bikinians, like Alson, still yearn to go back to their old home, most of the young people have no such dreams. They have never been to Bikini. For them it's a myth. With 40 percent unemployment in the Marshall Islands and a 4 percent population growth rate, increasing numbers are leaving altogether for places like Salem, Oregon, and Springdale, Arkansas, where they are allowed to hold jobs based on the Marshall Islands' Compact of Free Association with the U.S.

Still, Niedenthal, who has spent the past three decades trying to help the Bikinians realize their dream, isn't ready to give up. "If somebody came and said Bikini was suddenly safe, you would not see all 4,800 people jump on a boat," he concedes. "But they view the land as a gift from God, theirs forever. They are still Bikinians and think of themselves that way. Our duty is to provide the option, so they could move back if they wanted to."

During our seven days on Bikini, our lives follow a lazy pattern: jungle walks to the north side of the island, a lunch of whatever fish we caught that day, a trip to one of the southern islands—all tempered by the wonderful freedom of having no cell-phone or Internet service.

But it always comes back to fishing. In the afternoons, the Bikinians use their throw nets, large seines with a 20-foot radius that require great skill to load and launch. I follow the men along the beach, having no idea why they are suddenly yelling and running to the water's edge. "We see the fish," says Edward Maddison during one outing, pointing to a school 15 yards offshore that I had again failed to see. "You just have to look."

In two nights, fishing with octopus-baited handlines, they catch 300 pounds of red snapper. We eat fish all the time, cooked and raw, boiled and roasted over open fires. We eat mackerel ceviche for lunch. At one point, the Bikinians catch a medium-size trevally from the beach. When I ask to see it later, they just smile. The fish was immediately consumed.

On one of our last nights, we have a cookout under the astoundingly clear skies of the central Pacific Ocean. I am talking to 79-year-old Jackson Laiso, the oldest person in our group and one of those 34 remaining Bikini natives. He speaks at length about sailing the outrigger canoes with the old men when he was a boy. Then he describes the last days in 1946. "I remember when the Americans came and they gathered the old men and explained to them what they needed," he says. "We had to move so they could test their weapon. It was a hard question, but we felt we had no choice." Our own departure will likely be the last time he sees the atoll.

A few minutes later, five Bikinian men assemble under a breadfruit tree to sing their anthem, written by Lore Kessibuki while he was experiencing the horrors of Rongerik in 1946. Soon we are listening to a sweet, sad, and hauntingly beautiful multipart harmony:

> No longer can I stay, it's true
> No longer can I live in peace and harmony
> No longer can I rest on my sleeping mat and pillow
> Because of my island and the life I once knew there
> The thought is overwhelming
> Rendering me helpless and in great despair

They are singing almost exactly on the spot where their grandparents were loaded onto those Navy boats so long ago, back in the days when paradise was something real and no one imagined, not even for a moment, that they would never come back.

(Originally published October 2012)

OVERROO'D

PAUL KVINTA

~~~~~~

Australia is home to 24 million people and roughly 60 million kangaroos. The cuddly looking creatures are still a beloved national icon, but they're also at the center of one of the world's most surprising human-animal conflicts. When we sent Paul Kvinta to investigate, he discovered a surprisingly violent struggle, epitomized by his rowdy night spent with a kangaroo sharpshooter named, fittingly, Cujo.

~~~~~~

We spot 40 kangaroos in the distance and creep toward them. "Act like they do," Don Fletcher whispers. "Put your head down, like you're grazing. Don't move straight at them." Fletcher goes full kangaroo, drooping his head, hunching his shoulders, dangling his hands from his chest and zigzagging slowly forward. He does everything but bounce and eat grass.

I follow his lead. The tactic lands us not only in the center of the mob, but 30 feet from a big male putting the moves on a feisty female. Above us, constellations glitter in the night sky. A nearby lake glows in the moonlight. In the world of wildlife biology, this is a perfect moment.

Then a car horn honks, and the moment vanishes.

Fletcher and I are standing not in the sweeping Australian Outback, with its red-rock mystery and timeless vistas. We're at the traffic circle where Fairbairn and Limestone Avenues meet, in front of the Australian War Memorial, in the middle of the city of Canberra. Traffic zooms by. Car stereos blare. Someone's dog barks. To passersby, we're a couple of downtown vagrants off our meds, pretending to be kangaroos on the memorial's manicured lawn.

The big male loses interest in the female and wanders off. "It's not mating season anyway," Fletcher says, breaking character and returning to an upright position. "I don't know what the hell he was up to." He checks his watch, and we climb back into his truck. It's 10 P.M. "Let's go."

We're prowling the dark streets of Australia's capital city in search of kangaroos, and Fletcher knows the hot spots. He works for the Australian Capital Territory, the autonomous province comprised of Canberra and vast amounts of surrounding parkland. (Think of Washington, D.C., encircled by 640 square miles of wilderness.) As one of the ACT's senior ecologists, Fletcher is tasked with helping keep Canberra's nature reserves healthy. If kangaroos weren't overrunning these public lands and spilling into city streets, ecosystem health wouldn't be an issue. But they are, and Fletcher wants to show me how acute the situation is. The war memorial backs up to Mount Ainslie Nature Reserve, and when Fletcher turns onto the street separating the two, there they are—three more kangaroos, frozen in our headlights. Two others pop out of nearby bushes. They stare at us. Then they hop off to the war memorial. More follow, one after another, a bouncy column of refugees fleeing the forest. "The grass has been devoured on Mount Ainslie," Fletcher says. "They're looking for better forage."

Each year, Fletcher has the unenviable task of calculating how many of these kangaroos to kill. The magic number for this year's citywide cull is 2,466, from an ACT population of more than 50,000. This is a thankless job, and some Australians have dedicated themselves to never letting Fletcher forget that. This morning I spoke separately to three animal-rights activists, and each referred to Fletcher as Josef Mengele, the notorious Nazi physician who chose victims for the gas chamber. A week earlier, 51 prominent Aussies, including Nobel Prize–winning author J. M. Coetzee, published a letter condemning the science behind the cull. And just a few days ago, someone registered not-so-subtle anti-cull sentiment by stuffing the bloody carcass of a baby kangaroo—known as a joey—inside Fletcher's home mailbox.

"They think I personally shoot all the kangaroos!" he says, driving. "How the fuck am I going to shoot 2,500 kangaroos?" Fletcher has a certain manic energy. At 63, he's fit and cuts a fairly dashing figure, with intense eyes and salt-and-pepper hair. He likes kangaroos, he insists. In fact, he calls them essential to conserving the Australian landscape. Grazing kangaroos create multiple levels of ground vegetation that serve as microhabitats for many plant species. If you removed kangaroos, grass would grow uniformly and other plant species would disappear. On the other hand, too many kangaroos obliterate ground vegetation and threaten smaller animal species that need healthy grass. This is the case on Canberra's reserves. Armies of kangaroos have pushed more than a dozen threatened species to the brink. It's a pretty uncharismatic bunch—the earless dragon, the striped legless lizard, the golden sun moth. Still, a "conservation cull" of a few kangaroos will save these ecosystems, Fletcher says, a fact that escapes the activists targeting him. "I see that joey in my mailbox as a rude e-mail, not a threat," he says. "Threats from activists? Give me a break."

We find kangaroos lurking everywhere. At one suburban park, several graze at the edge of a basketball court. At another, a few munch grass near a soccer goal. On the campus of Dickson College, we watch 30 of them gobble up the lawn. This particular mob—the actual term for a group of roos—had to negotiate several city blocks to get here from Mount Majura Nature Reserve, where the grass has been reduced to nubs. Running such a gauntlet reflects their desperation, Fletcher says. Ecologists call it predation-sensitive foraging, when animals living in habitats that can't support them take more risks to find food. In the wild, hungry kangaroos increase their range despite the danger of encountering predators like dingoes. In this case, the city itself becomes predator—the pavement, the lights, the cars, the dogs. The risks are innumerable.

We watch the Dickson mob in our headlights. For now these kangaroos are lucky. They've found dinner and, unlike many of their brethren across the city at this very moment, are not being shot in the head by Fletcher's colleagues.

I arrived in Canberra five weeks into the cull, and craziness was erupting all over. Polls suggested that 83 percent of Canberrans supported the cull, but a very vocal minority did not. Anti-cullers were risking $5,500 fines to disrupt government shooters, who worked at night when the roos were foraging. Wielding air horns and spotlights, the protesters were running toward gunfire, raising hell, and praying that the shooters would cease fire. On one reserve, a protester had hidden remotely operated speakers that blared the U.S. cavalry charge and "Taps" at regular intervals all night. On another, activists had allegedly destroyed a fence, resulting in the escape and injury of a farmer's horses from a neighboring paddock.

In today's Australia, the question of what kangaroos are—pest, resource, untouchable native wildlife—has become extremely contentious. The nation is home to 24 million people and an estimated 60 million kangaroos, and the relationship between man and hopping beast might be the most fraught, love-hate bond between any two species on the planet. No creature is more closely associated with one nation and its people. Kangaroos adorn Australia's coat of arms, its Olympic flag, its sports teams, and the jets of its national airline. Australians love kangaroos. Except when they hate them, which is not infrequently. Speak to a rancher in rural Queensland and a city dweller in Canberra and you'll hear the same incompatible rhetoric you might hear about wolves in the American West.

Oddly enough, I understood how kangaroos could arouse such conflicting emotions. I'm not Australian, but the animal and I go way back, for better and worse. One night, in 1987, I was camping with friends in the state of Victoria when we hit and killed a kangaroo with our truck on an isolated road. Somberly, we examined the body, only to have the head of a joey pop out of the pouch, look around, and wonder what the hell was going on. We brought it to our campsite, where it proceeded to burrow beneath my friend's sweatshirt and snooze. The next day we delivered it to park rangers. I was smitten. And then, a week later, I was abruptly unsmitten. I was doing my business in the woods, squatting, underwear around my ankles, when a large, blurry object came crashing through the bush straight at me. I wasn't wearing my glasses. Terrified, I tried to run but immediately face-planted. Sprawled on the ground, smeared in my own feces, I watched the kangaroo bounce away. I hated that fucker.

Still, most Americans would probably be shocked to learn that Australia kills three million kangaroos annually. This slaughter is possible for several reasons. First, none of the four harvested kangaroo species—eastern greys, western greys, reds, and wallaroos—are threatened in any way. Secondly, the animal is perfectly adapted to Australia's wildly fluctuating climate, so during multi-season droughts they survive by, among other things, ceasing reproduction altogether. Then, when conditions improve, roo numbers can expand rapidly, and populations are no longer managed by traditional predators like dingoes and Aboriginal hunters. The vast majority are culled as part of a commercial meat-hunting industry tied to the entrenched notion that kangaroos are pests that compete with livestock for grass. Farmers hire marksmen to thin wild kangaroos from their pastures, and the meat is exported to more than 55 countries or sold to Australian grocery stores and restaurants. (Foodies are increasingly extolling a taste that falls somewhere between venison and buffalo.) Kangaroos are not farmed, which means that, after commercial fishing, this cull is the largest for-profit slaughter of free-ranging wildlife in the world. But whether killing for meat production or to protect biodiversity, nearly all of it takes place in Australia's vast, unpopulated interior. Eighty-five percent of Australians live on the coast, while most kangaroos live inland, surrounded by a sparse human population with little interest in their cuddly charms. Last June, a town in rural Queensland began culling after kangaroos laid siege to the local elementary school and parents concluded that they might attack their children. There were no protests to speak of.

Feelings about the kangaroo slaughter in Canberra are more complicated. Located between Sydney and Melbourne, Canberra is the nation's only large inland city. Nowhere else does a highly educated, urban population of 169,000 people (390,000 if you include the entire ACT) interact daily with thousands of kangaroos. Seventy percent of the ACT is undeveloped public land, and the extensive nature reserves are prime habitat for a roo population explosion. The animals are everywhere. In 2009, Fletcher was finding kangaroo densities of 510 per square kilometer on some reserves, more than five times the desirable amount for healthy grassland ecosystems. The ACT leads the nation in car-kangaroo collisions, with an estimated 2,000 incidents each year. There are even 90 roos living on the Royal Canberra Golf Course, where, though very rare, harrowing human-kangaroo incidents do occur. In one case, a golfer jogged back to the fourth tee box to retrieve a forgotten driver head cover, only to have a startled roo chase him flat-out for 200 yards. His foursome buddies had to brandish their irons to stop the charging marsupial, but not before the terrified man vomited all over the fairway. Now the club hires a veterinarian to stalk the course with a dart gun, tranquilize the male roos, and perform in-the-field vasectomies.

In short, Australia's capital is ground zero for kangaroo mayhem. While Fletcher's cull of 2,466 is peanuts compared with the millions that are quietly killed every year in Australia's boondocks, in Canberra people notice. And they've got something to say about it.

~~~~~~

Carolyn Drew and I are sitting in her parked car at the edge of the Pinnacle Nature Reserve in northwest Canberra when we hear a gunshot. We rush to investigate, squeezing through a barbed-wire fence and trekking across a field, dodging rocks and fallen branches in the moonlight. After a while, Drew, a spokeswoman for Animal Liberation ACT, stops and scans the shadowy landscape of this 341-acre reserve. She has no clue where the shooter is. He could be on a neighboring reserve. Or he could be in a suburban backyard with a bottle of Jack Daniel's and his redneck cousins. "Shine your flashlight in the air, wave it around," she says. Shooters aren't allowed to fire if anyone else is on the reserve, and our lights are meant to signal our presence. It feels like a fairly impotent tactic, but we do it. Then we hike back to her car.

It turns out that two nights previously, when I was out stalking kangaroos with Fletcher, his men were here at Pinnacle stalking Drew. She had followed the sound of six gunshots to their source and flashed lights on the shooting crew. The crew gave chase, and Drew hid for three hours behind a gum tree. "There were no shots after that," she tells me now as we walk. "We stopped them!" Drew is lucky she didn't get nabbed. She's a squat, plodding woman, and at 60 she resembles a garden-club president more than the standard-bearer for Animal Liberation. But she's fueled by fierce conviction. She monitors Pinnacle every night during the cull. Her colleagues watch other reserves. Hunting the hunters seems like a needle-in-a-haystack strategy, given nearly 5,000 acres on nine reserves and only a handful of activists. Still, no kangaroo deserves to die, Drew insists, so she's here every night, as a witness if nothing else. "Kangaroos are sentient beings with feelings, hopes, and dreams," she says. "Do you know how they kill them?"

I do. I had discussed this with Fletcher, who insisted that the cull adheres to strict animal-welfare standards. The ACT's shooters (only one or two work each night, with support crew) must be proven marksmen, and kangaroos must be dispatched with head shots. Surviving pouch joeys are bludgeoned to death with a blow to the head. I'm pretty sure no amount of focus grouping could make this sound less brutal than it is. "This might be discomforting to humans, but we're only concerned with the joeys," Fletcher had told me. "A sharp blow to the head is recognized as the most humane approach."

After 20 minutes on the reserve, Drew and I reach her car and climb in. June is the start of winter in Australia, and it's below freezing out here. We huddle under blankets and wait for more shots. Drew doesn't mind this nightly hardship. At one point earlier in her life, she lived in a tent in the forest with her husband, two dogs, and three donkeys. She gave birth to her son in that tent. She spent her days meditating and communing with the forest animals. "Hunters would come, and we felt what the animals felt," she says. "We were sensitized to their perspective."

Drew became radicalized about kangaroos in 2008, when the Australian military conducted a cull at the decommissioned Belconnen Naval Transmission Station in north Canberra. There were 650 roos living on one square kilometer of grassland, and officials determined that they were wreaking ecological havoc. Over several days, wranglers herded them into a corral with 12-foot-high fencing, tranquilized them, and administered lethal injections. Unfortunately, this happened in broad daylight, and Canberrans stopped on their way home from work to watch. Like cats, kangaroos refuse to be herded. They ran into poles. They ran into each other. Joeys were ejected from pouches. "Lots of people are still suffering PTSD from seeing that," Drew says. "The fencing was covered with burlap bags, but we could see the shadows of the kangaroos. The big boys were trying to clear the fence. It was like this horrific shadow-puppet show." They culled 514 roos. Drew was arrested for throwing rocks. Even Fletcher conceded that it was an unfortunate event. "I don't think anyone associated with that cull would want to see it happen that way again," he said.

In 2009, the ACT government announced it would begin culling kangaroos for conservation purposes. A government report concluded that 20 percent of the ACT's native grassland sites were in "critical condition," with another 40 percent approaching that. Scientists reported that 19 threatened animal species on Canberra's reserves require healthy grass to survive. Drew and others didn't buy it. "Kangaroos have been around forever," she says. "They're a native species. They're going to drive other native species to extinction?" The government insisted this was possible, given that large urban kangaroo populations now lived hemmed in by roads and subdivisions. Officials also stressed that this cull had nothing to do with the commercial kangaroo-meat industry. Only four of Australia's eight states and territories have commercial culls, and the ACT is not one of those. No one would profit from the ACT cull. The bodies would be buried in an undisclosed pit.

In both 2013 and 2014, activists delayed the start of the cull for several weeks with legal challenges, alleging that the killing was inhumane and based on faulty science. They argued that the annual growth rate for kangaroo populations was around 5 percent, not the 40 percent Fletcher had posited. They said that roo numbers in the ACT were shrinking, not exploding. Urbanization is wiping them out. If the competing narratives presented in court were startling in their differences, they were downright hilarious when the court reviewed the population data submitted by both sides. For example, at Goorooyarroo Nature Reserve, the government counted 1,173 kangaroos; the anti-cullers counted 280. At Mount Majura, the government counted 1,242; the anti-cullers, 80. Ultimately, the court ruled for the government, which had the backing of pretty much the entire scientific establishment in Australia, and when the 2013 cull took place, 728 kangaroos were culled from Goorooyarroo, nearly three times the number that activists claimed lived there. The anti-cullers insist that even if the government's population estimate was accurate—which they refuse to concede—killing 728 out of 1,173 roos would devastate the population there.

As we shiver beneath blankets in her car, Drew admits that it's hard, year after year, tramping into the bush in freezing weather at night, risking arrest, and having little to show for it. Since 2009, the government has slaughtered more than 10,000 kangaroos. (Some 1,689 would ultimately be killed in the 2015 cull.) The legal process has achieved squat. And many of her fellow activists, Drew reckons, have simply been too traumatized to return to the fight. In 2012, for instance, in a driving rain, some visiting activists from South Australia discovered the pit where shooters had buried the bodies. Who wouldn't be disturbed seeing those soggy, bullet-ridden carcasses in the mud? "Realistically, we can't make much of a dent," Drew acknowledges. "I go out every night not necessarily to stop death but to challenge the civilization project, which is squeezing the life out of animals."

The "civilization project" in Australia began about 50,000 years ago, when Aboriginals arrived and found not only the large and small species of macropods that exist today—kangaroos, wallabies, pademelons, and others—but a subfamily of giants called sthenurines. The largest, *Procoptodon goliah,* stood ten feet tall and weighed 550 pounds. So big was this pouched monster that it was mechanically unable to hop. Instead, it ambled about upright on the hoof-like tips of its back feet and ate tree foliage. Aboriginals feasted on the sthenurines, to the point where none were left when the first British fleet of convicts, marines, officials, and their families sailed into Sydney Cove in 1788.

These first Europeans brought sheep and cattle, but they were reluctant to eat them before herds could be established, making kangaroos essential. Kangaroo grounds were designated for hunting, and wealthy families hired their own shooters. Kangaroo was a key part of convicts' rations. "They were highly valued," says Ray Mjadwesch, an ecologist who has studied the history of kangaroo—human interaction. "People didn't hate them. It took 80 years for that hatred to set in. People had immense pride in kangaroos. They sent them live back to Britain."

Once the colonies had raised sufficient livestock herds, people killed kangaroos mostly for recreation, mimicking British foxhunting. Well-dressed gunmen on horseback galloped across the countryside with dogs chasing kangaroos. Paintings of the time show frilly ladies picnicking while their men blast away.

By the second half of the 19th century, farmers began complaining that kangaroos were outcompeting their livestock for grass. An article in the *Geelong Advertiser* in 1867 argued for the "wholesale destruction" of kangaroos. Farmers resorted to battues, highly organized hunts in which lines of men drove kangaroos into a huge stockade that narrowed to a smaller corral. Edward Wakefield, a colonial official, wrote about a battue he participated in on a friend's sheep farm, where dozens of horsemen armed with clubs pushed countless kangaroos for miles toward an enclosure:

Steadily we rode after them, farther and farther into the enclosed and constantly narrowing space, until the whole surface of the ground was literally covered with kangaroos, so closely packed that they could not leap. Then, at a signal which ran rapidly along the line, all the younger and more active men charged into the mass, striking right and left with their clubs and felling a kangaroo at every blow....I got into the swing and slew and slew and slew, until my arm ached so I could not slay any more. By this time my dirty clothes and my horse were smeared and splattered with blood and we looked as if we had waded through a river of gore.

They killed 40,000 kangaroos and left the bodies to rot.

In 1876, Henry Bracker, a Queensland farmer, initiated a battue that in six weeks killed more than 17,000 kangaroos. Bracker became a folk hero in rural communities and inspired similar slaughters. His effort also prompted a resolution in the Queensland legislative assembly, calling kangaroos "an evil of such magnitude ... as to demand the immediate and earnest attention of the Government." In 1877, Queensland passed the Marsupial Destruction Act, a bounty program that by 1930 resulted in the eradication of 27 million animals, mostly kangaroos. By the 1880s, all the states in eastern Australia had bounty programs.

Somehow, despite their pest status, kangaroos still remained part of the proud Australian sense of identity. In 1908, Aussies added the kangaroo to their national coat of arms. During World War I, troops smuggled kangaroos to Europe as mascots. In World War II, they featured in propaganda campaigns. Together for Victory posters showed a boxing kangaroo and an English bulldog attacking a Japanese soldier.

But in rural Australia, the slaughter continued. By the 1950s, with advances in refrigeration, a meat trade developed. Exports supplied markets for both pet food and human consumption. At the same time, budding environmental and animal-welfare movements were materializing in the U.S. and Europe. In 1974, the U.S. banned the import of kangaroo products, citing concerns over welfare and sustainability. Australia responded by instituting strict hunting quotas and a code of conduct that required, among other things, that kangaroos be dispatched with bullets to the head. The U.S. rescinded its ban in 1981, and you can now buy kangaroo leg and loin on Amazon, although some states, like California, still prohibit the import of kangaroo products.

More recently, scientists have challenged the notion that kangaroos compete with livestock for forage, citing a lack of empirical evidence. The linkage is so squishy that no numbers exist on how much damage roos may have caused over the years. Increasingly, ecologists are viewing the kangaroo not as a pest to be managed, but as a valuable product to be conserved through a sustainable-use framework, similar to wild fish stocks. In most Australian states, kangaroo-management plans are now less about property-damage mitigation and more about maintaining healthy roo populations.

Still, as Australia has evolved into an urbanized society, the country's environmental and animal-rights movements have become stronger, more vocal, and more insistent that kangaroo culling should stop altogether. The Green Party is now the third most powerful political party in the country, and this year its branch in the state of New South Wales condemned the ACT's conservation cull. Ironically, that cull is overseen by an ACT Green, a cabinet minister named Shane Rattenbury. Rattenbury once coordinated antiwhaling campaigns for Greenpeace. Now he supervises the killing of a couple thousand roos every year in Canberra. The cull has exacerbated the split between the party's conservation and animal-welfare wings. "The conservationists look at it holistically," Rattenbury says. "We can't go back in time and undo development. We have to do what we can to conserve species. The welfare people are against killing animals." Not surprisingly, Rattenbury receives a daily barrage of Twitter hate. "It's fueled by inaccuracy," he says. "I get tweets saying, 'Stop burying joeys alive!'"

Roos rarely attack people, which is a reassuring way of saying that they sometimes do. Maybe it was bad karma, then, when Rattenbury went for a morning run in 2013 and collided with a roo rounding a hedge. The animal clawed the hell out of his legs, sending him to the hospital. Rattenbury posted photos of the wounds on social media, and images of his diced-up thighs appeared in newspapers around the world.

Politically speaking, anti-cullers have few better advocates than Steve Garlick, a retired ethics professor at the University of Technology Sydney who founded Australia's Animal Justice Party in 2009. Infuriated at the Greens, Garlick determined that "the only language these people understand is taking away votes."

I drive out to visit Garlick, who lives just over the ACT border in New South Wales, amid bucolic wine country. But when I arrive, he's flying out the front door, headed on a rescue mission. Garlick runs Possumwood Wildlife Recovery Center, and he's just learned about a kangaroo lying motionless off a dirt road in a nearby vineyard. We pile into his station wagon and take off. We find the animal sprawled beneath a tree, 30 feet from a rusty wire fence. Garlick feels along the kangaroo's flank. "Hello, boy," he says, softly. "He could have tried to hop that fence. Maybe he fractured his pelvis." Garlick injects it with a sedative and we load it into the car.

"There's not much you can do for a fractured pelvis," he says, driving. "You can give them an antipsychotic, which reduces anxiety. We'll give him physiotherapy." Garlick and his wife, Rosemary Austen, rescue about 300 animals a year, two-thirds of them kangaroos, most of them injured by run-ins with cars and fences. Except in extreme cases, they don't euthanize animals.

On Garlick's property, two modest houses stand next to each other. One he shares with his wife. The other is shared by 60 kangaroos. They're not all inside at once. Some enjoy the veranda. Others mosey about the backyard. But they come and go through the sliding-glass back door as they please. We enter the living room and find two lounging on recliners, one on the love seat, and one rummaging through the kitchen. One bedroom is occupied by a large wombat, and another serves as a treatment room, where two injured roos lie on cushions. We carefully lower the latest rescue between these two. "There you go," Garlick reassures it. "Want some water?" He offers the roo a bowl. The roo hisses.

Out on the veranda, ten roos are chilling on La-Z-Boys and piles of hay. Garlick introduces me around. Coco has two torn Achilles tendons. Sally recently had her cataracts removed. Noah is awaiting ankle surgery. Every patient has a name. I meet a wallaroo named Princess Rosalinda. Everywhere, kangaroos limp around with bandages on their legs, tails, or feet. Most will recuperate and return to the wild. The excessively hobbled will remain as pets. A small female named Cheeky sniffs my shoes. A year ago, Garlick found her tangled in a wire fence. "She was the most dehydrated, maggot-infested thing I've ever seen," he says. "Anyone else would have euthanized her." She lost her toes and now moves awkwardly in little cloth booties.

We sit in the living room to chat. It's an unusual interview. Kangaroos amble in, sniff about, and leave. One snuggles next to Garlick. Another nibbles my notebook.

In his academic career, Garlick researched the emotional lives of kangaroos. As a result of the culling, he says, those on ACT reserves exhibit anger and hypervigilance. They play less. Many suffer PTSD. If there's an overpopulation problem, they could clearly be relocated. "We've moved 3,500 kangaroos over the years," he says, referring to his rehabilitated patients. "We've got a 97 percent survival rate." (Fletcher says this solution would only "move the problem somewhere else.")

Garlick has a plan to end culling, and he's attacking on multiple fronts at once—legal, economic, and political. He calls the administrative tribunal where the ACT cull was challenged "a joke." He's assembling a Supreme Court challenge. "I've got a pro bono barrister on this," he says. "I can't stop the cull happening now, but we'll stop the next one." He also wants to shut down the larger commercial cull. In 2009, Garlick was part of a group that persuaded Russia to ban kangaroo-meat imports after testing showed elevated levels of $E. coli$. Russia was the biggest importer, providing the industry $180 million a year. Australian politicians lobbied successfully to reverse that decision in 2012, but in 2014 Russia reinstated the ban after encouragement from Garlick and others on the $E. coli$ issue. "Our worry now is the Chinese," he says. Australia has a new free-trade agreement with China, but kangaroo meat is not a part of that. Still, with market demand seriously dented by Russia's pullout, Australia is pressing China hard on the product.

The solution, ultimately, may be political. Garlick's Animal Justice Party claims a fast-growing membership of 5,000 people, and earlier this year they celebrated their first election victory, sending a candidate to the New South Wales state legislature. Soon that legislator, Mark Pearson, will travel to China to lobby officials there against importing kangaroo. The commercial cull will end when more people like Mark Pearson get elected, Garlick says. "Our leaders walk beneath our coat of arms every day and turn a blind eye," he says. "Horrific stuff is done under the cover of night, and they support it." He strokes the roo sitting next to him and adds: "It's a barbaric industry, run by thugs."

~~~~~~

I wanted to see for myself if the commercial industry is run by thugs, so I contacted David Coulton, a professional kangaroo shooter in rural Queensland who goes by Cujo. Cujo didn't seem very thuggish over e-mail. He seemed nice. In fact, he gave me some great advice that I wish I'd taken. Whatever I do, he warned, don't drive the four-hour leg from Torrens Creek to Aramac after sundown. Aramac, Cujo's hometown of 300 people, sits at the edge of the desert in the middle of nowhere. Just getting to Torrens Creek involved a four-hour flight north from Canberra to Townsville and then a three-hour drive inland. By the time I start down the road to Aramac, it's dark.

The road is sometimes paved, sometimes not. There are no towns, no lights, no cell reception. An hour in, the kangaroos appear, first the dead ones. They're scattered along the roadside—whole bodies, stray legs, stray tails, and random heaps of pulpy viscera. It's nonstop roadkill. The live roos materialize out of the blackness in midhop, springing across my tunnel of vision individually and in pairs, darting one way, then the other, making me swerve, making me slow down, near miss after near miss, for miles. I grip the wheel. I focus. Except when, for a second—less than a second—I look away, reaching for my water bottle, and *thump!* I nail a wallaby, plow right over it. Dead. The little guy wasn't two feet tall. He was innocent. I stop. Aside from the wallaby, the only damage is to my spirit. An eastern grey would have totaled my rental, so I'm lucky there. But I feel terrible.

I keep driving. The roos keep coming. In the ghostly half-light on the sides of the road, they assemble in great mobs, watching me, challenging me. I drive for two more hours, bleary-eyed, past darting roos and endless carnage. The road is death.

~~~~~~

Cujo urges me not to worry about the wallaby. We're driving the next evening to one of the properties where he's in charge of thinning the kangaroos. "Every property in this shire has a shooter," he says. "A landowner may have no kangaroos one week, but he'll have tens of thousands the next, and wallabies. They'll mow down his grass."

Kangaroos are just one of Aramac's problems. A drought has gripped central Queensland for three years, turning the landscape brown. Farms are going under. Aramac once had seven full-time sheep-shearing teams, 13 people each. Now one guy shears full-time. Then you've got dingoes eating sheep and roos stealing grass.

Ecologists may say there's no evidence that kangaroos compete with livestock for grass, but don't tell folks here that. This morning a farmer, Louellen Hannay, showed me a dusty stretch of her property and said, "We used to run cattle and sheep in that paddock, but the roos have completely flogged it."

The Queensland government conducts an annual aerial kangaroo count to determine hunting quotas. This year, Aramac is allotted 800 per week. Cujo, one of four full-time shooters here, hunts sundown to sunup, every night except Sundays and Christmas. He bags 4,000 to 6,000 roos annually. Cujo tells me that officials regularly remind shooters to avoid journalists, but he sees no reason for secrecy. "I welcome media, greenies, everyone," he says as we barrel along in his white Toyota Land Cruiser, the words OUTRIGHT CRAZY emblazoned across the top of the windshield. "I've got nothing to hide."

Indeed, Cujo is an open book. His tattoos size him up pretty well—a wild boar on his calf, two roos on his torso, and Aramac's postal code on his right biceps. He's bald, with a bushy mustache. Rather than shy away from controversy, he says the meat industry should be touting its rigorous standards. His gear is inspected regularly by the same government agency that regulates butchers and restaurants. Cujo has his own standards as well. He's allowed to kill 63 roos a night, but he typically stops at 40. "It's about sustainable harvest," he says. "I want my son to live this life." He insists that kangaroos are superior to any other animal and that the meat can all but raise you from the dead. "It's the free-range king," he says. "It's high-protein, low-fat, no-chemical, super-strength meat. You can't get cancer if you eat it."

When we arrive at the property, we lower the hinge-mounted windshield and turn on the spotlight fixed atop the cab. Motoring slowly along, Cujo steers with one hand and operates the spot with the other. A small red kangaroo bounds by. Several more appear, greys, all female. We approach some acacia trees, and a small mob hops out. Cujo stops the truck. The roos freeze in our light, 25 yards away. While still seated behind the steering wheel, he shoulders his 223 Remington and peers through the scope. *Crack!* The largest roo jerks and falls. The others scatter. We drive up and find the animal with a halo of blood expanding around its head. Cujo drags it to the back of the truck, snips off its right foot with bolt cutters, runs a hook behind the Achilles tendon, then hoists the carcass onto a horizontal bar. He runs a knife from the sternum to the crotch, opening up the roo and removing the innards. He tosses those into a bush.

On his second opportunity, a big red 100 yards off, Cujo misses. He won't miss again all night. Thirty seconds later, the big boy stops and stares at us again. *Crack!* Cujo blasts the third roo on a fence line. The fourth and fifth he drops from the same mob, in rapid succession. The sixth he nails 200 yards away. He frees his two dogs, Roxie and Ugly, to find it. Sitting next to Cujo, I soon become numb to the slaughter and transfixed by the accuracy, speed, and efficiency with which he kills. The man is presiding over his own Red Wedding on House Roo.

By 10 P.M. we have eight carcasses, and Cujo announces that it's time for a "gut-up." I'm confused. Hasn't the whole evening been one big gut-up? I quickly learn that there's a second part to the butchering process. With the bolt cutters, he goes down the row of hanging roos and prunes each left foot with a quick chop. Then, with a knife, he removes the heads and tails. We leave these amputations scattered on the ground, including the eight little heads, their eyes clotted with blood and dirt staring blankly at the stars.

Cujo is just warming up. Several dead roos later, in the middle of our second gut-up, a wild boar sprints through our idle spotlight. Roxie and Ugly tear after the pig. We give chase in the truck, and moments later anguished screams pierce the night. We find the brave mutts with their jaws locked onto the pig's face, despite its four-inch tusks. The animal is black and hairy, nearly six feet long and maybe 200 pounds. Cujo grabs its back legs, shakes off the dogs, then dives onto the back of the great beast, plunging a knife into its jugular. There's more screaming, then silence. Cujo is soaked in blood. He guts the boar and cuts out the teeth with his bolt cutters. A trophy. "Pretty nice pig," he says.

By 3 A.M., we're back in Aramac at Cujo's "chiller," a shipping container serving as a deep freeze. A hundred roos already hang in here. We add 37 more, the largest a red weighing 90 pounds. The processor's truck comes from Brisbane once a week. Cujo used to earn 45 cents per pound, but then Queensland's nine processors consolidated. Now he earns 27 cents. I need sleep, so much so that I apparently start hallucinating, or at least Cujo tells me I'm hallucinating. I thought I was looking at 37 decapitated kangaroos dangling upside down from hooks. But Cujo says I'm looking at money. "That's five, six hundred dollars," he says. "A good night."

~~~~~~

The next day, I'm leaving Aramac when I notice something more grisly than anything I'd seen here, if that's possible: five dead dingoes hanging on a barbed-wire fence outside town. Cujo mentioned this, a means of "bush communication," he called it. In this instance, the community knew that five dingoes were eating sheep on this property, and with the appearance of each carcass, folks learned that the threat level was decreasing. That may be. But as I observe the gruesome display, I have to think that the message is really meant for the greater cosmos, from a desperate people with little sway over powerful outside forces—climatic, economic, ecological. The message is that, despite everything, we are in control.

I drive east into the morning sun, distancing myself from the blood rituals of rural Australia. As I pass miles of roadkill, I think about the fluffy stuffed kangaroo I'll buy in the airport for my seven-year-old. It will no doubt have a joey in the pouch, and maybe a bush hat or a little Australian flag. It will be bloodless and meatless, and it will chomp nobody's grass. No one will hate it. Everyone will love it, especially my kid.

(Originally published November 2015)

THE BEARS WHO CAME TO TOWN AND WOULD NOT GO AWAY

SARAH TOPOL

This is the story of a place at the edge of the world, where a black bear ventured into a Russian hamlet and attacked a human. One bear became two, two became dozens, and before long no one would leave their home, and no one had any idea what to do.

The first bear appeared in town one morning in late August. It was a little after eight, and Nikolai, an elderly pensioner, had just come out to walk his cat.

He joined a neighbor on a wooden bench outside their building, which the residents of Luchegorsk, a town in far eastern Russia, call the Great Wall of China because of its expansive length. The Great Wall stands on the shore of a large man-made lake where water from the town's thermal power plant flows. In the summer, it's hard to see much of the lake for the tall green reeds that line the banks. It was from this verdant thicket that the Asian black bear ambled out, loping slowly, as if heading into town for nothing more than a leisurely stroll.

Nikolai and his neighbor stood up and gawked. The bear, seeing them, also stopped and stared. It turned around, walked back, and vanished into the reeds. That's when the dogs started barking. There are plenty of dogs in Luchegorsk, but Nikolai had never heard them make such a racket. The men turned toward the sound and noticed the bear running down the sidewalk along the side of the building.

"How did he get there? He was just in the reeds!" Nikolai exclaimed. That's when he realized: "Oh God, it's a second bear!"

The two men scurried back into the Great Wall just as Viktor Dubitsky was leaving through another entrance to take his dog out. Dubitsky had gone only two steps when he felt that something was amiss. He turned and saw the bear in mid-leap. Dubitsky was knocked to the ground. The bear swiped at his throat. Dubitsky put his arm in front of his face. The bear bit into him. He heard people shouting and felt a claw rip into his groin. He passed out. A taxi driver pulled up to the building and honked, startling the bear. It jumped off Dubitsky and ran. Passersby rushed to his aid. Neighbors threw first aid from their balconies, bottles of rubbing alcohol and bundles of gauze that ribboned to the bloody ground. Nikolai and his neighbor came back outside, surveyed the scene, and decided that they needed a drink.

An ambulance arrived around the same time as the local game warden, Anatoly Tarasenko. Luchegorsk is a few miles from Russia's taiga, a boreal forest that is home to tigers, Amur leopards, and bears, as well as some of the most valuable illegally trafficked timber in the world—primarily hardwoods like Mongolian oak and Manchurian linden. Demand is so high that vast stretches of forest have been destroyed, stressing the land and the wildlife that depends on it for survival. Tarasenko's job is primarily to stop poachers and manage hunting licenses, but he also deals with the wild animals that come into the villages that are under his jurisdiction, though they do not often frequent the relatively large settlement of Luchegorsk, population 21,000.

The bespectacled 60-year-old, with a rugged build and tidy gray beard, organized a police cordon in front of the Great Wall. He figured that the bears were in the reeds, but the vegetation was so dense that it was impossible to see inside. He called his 28-year-old deputy, Yaroslav Shishkin, and members of the local hunting association and asked them to bring hounds to sniff the bears out. The men were in the process of dividing the reeds, so the dogs could do a methodical search, when they got the next call: A man had gone into the bushes to pee across from the town's bus station, a few blocks away, and walked straight into a bear. It lunged at him, too, but he managed to get away. When Tarasenko arrived, no one could tell him where the bear went, except that it had run across the street.

Word traveled that, earlier that morning, lifeguards on the lake's beach had seen a bear swimming across the water with a cub on its back, and Tarasenko reasoned that this was the mother. A concerned mother tiger or bear is the most dangerous animal in the taiga; she will annihilate anything that stands between her and her cub. Maybe the noise of the town startled them and they'd split up. Maybe they needed to cross a road and the cub was scared off by the cars. Maybe the cub had hidden somewhere and the mother was looking for it when she stumbled across

Dubitsky. Whatever the explanation, they assumed she'd be back, searching for her cub, growing more panicked and ever more dangerous. The next day, Tarasenko received official permission from the regional government in Vladivostok: they could shoot to kill.

That was August 21. Soon there were bear spottings all around Luchegorsk—in the village itself, by the nearby coal mine, at the power plant, around summer homes on the outskirts of town, and eating from dumpsters, vegetable gardens, and the many apiaries located in the surrounding taiga. First there were a few, then a dozen, then many more—the bears were showing up around Luchegorsk at a rate of up to ten per day. They moved in elongated convoys, following each other down the same paths through open fields, like they had all locked onto the same GPS route and the coordinates led straight to Luchegorsk. Bears swam across the lake toward town and beached at the reeds in front of the Great Wall. Residents stood on their balconies to watch tiny heads bobbing in the waves. People found them in basements and gardens and saw them walking down the street.

By the end of the month, the town was besieged.

"They are everywhere," Tarasenko told one of the men who'd volunteered to help contain the animals. "What on earth are we supposed to do with them?"

Luchegorsk is about 20 miles from the Chinese border, in Primorsky, a Russian region that borders the People's Republic on one side and the Sea of Japan on the other. The town was built on swampland and suffers through sultry, mosquito-laden summers and dark, frozen winters. Luchegorsk owes its existence to the nearby coal mine, which supplies the massive thermal plant, which in turn feeds power to the entire region. Three huge chimneys tower above pastel-colored apartment blocks, belching clots of smoke the size of storm clouds into the sky at all hours. Two main roads divide the town into four neighborhoods. Where the streets intersect, there are two parks kitty-corner from one another, referred to by residents as Old Park and New Park.

The area is home to two bear species—the Asian black bear, similar to the North American black bear, and the Eurasian brown bear. The brown bears, which number approximately 3,500 in the region, can grow to more than 800 pounds and have a preference for berries, plants, and newborn animals. Asian bears are smaller, with a local population of about 4,000. Grown males weigh up to 440 pounds and have a white patch across the chest in the shape of a bat in flight. They eat mostly vegetation and are known for their climbing prowess. Both species' claws are made for digging, but when they attack humans, which happens from time to time in the wild, they wrap their arms around the person's body and swipe, often scalping them. Russians sometimes say that bears kill people by giving them a hug.

While the American species are widely studied, there are practically no bear experts in Primorsky, where I relied on hunters and park rangers to relay local lore. For example, I was told that bears love to booze. Tarasenko said that they are known to break into cellars and waddle away with containers of honey moonshine. He described them as abominable drunks. "They roll around, roar, sleep," he explained. "It looks like a pogrom. Everything is broken, thrown around."

Nikolai Agapov, a district inspector at the Land of the Leopard, one of the region's national parks, told me that he twice found a mother bear returning to the skin of a dead cub as if in mourning. Agapov related another story about how a bear stole one of his kerosene canisters, carried it 200 yards away, unscrewed it, and dumped the contents all over the ground. "That means they have to know which direction to turn the cap!" Agapov told me.

In 2015, there was a failure of every imaginable food source for the local bears—the forest was barren of Korean pine nuts, acorns, and berries. At the same time, local rangers told me, bear numbers had grown substantially; recent implementation of tighter border controls and harsher penalties for poaching and for trafficking to China had led to a spike in the population, and there were roughly 1,000 new members of each species wandering the woods. (Even so, black bears are still considered threatened, due to the demand for bile and paws in traditional medicine.) With more bears than ever competing for fewer resources, they began to migrate in search of food.

That migration led them into towns, where discarded food and summer vegetable gardens were plentiful. Bears are known for their excellent memory and sense of direction—they create mental food maps that last a lifetime. Once a new restaurant is found, it's never forgotten. When the bears discovered Luchegorsk, the options for dealing with them were limited: frighten them away, draw them to other food sources, or eliminate them. On top of that, many worried about them attacking humans. If a bear killed someone, it might decide that people were reliable prey.

"A person can be standing, gathering berries, and the bear can attack from behind. It's easy game," Agapov explained. "The bear knows that a human is dangerous. However, when it manages to kill a person once, it starts thinking: That's easy! And delicious!"

When it became apparent that the bears weren't going away, the townspeople started to demand answers: What was being done to protect the people? Children were playing at the lake. How could the government let bears wander around town? Pensioners needed to harvest their vegetable gardens before winter came. Why weren't the authorities shooting the beasts?

Tarasenko scrambled to assemble a 14-person response team, made up of park rangers and hunters, to patrol the town in shifts. Residents would call emergency services, which would direct the call to Tarasenko, who would then dispatch his team to chase the bears away. There were other precautions: for example, they decided to block access to manholes and basements where bears could hide. Someone suggested it would be best to cut the reeds down, too, but so many pipes and electrical wires ran through the thicket that the plan stalled.

Tarasenko wrote up a list of instructions for what to do in the event of a bear sighting, to be distributed to the community and published in the local paper:

When in the forest or in places where predators are present, safety precautions need to be taken. One needs to rustle; talk loudly! If the bear shows interest in you or aggression, one should speak loudly to mark one's species affinity—that one is a human. One can raise one's arms, pretending to be a large animal. A woman's hysterical cries will provoke it. One shouldn't scream—that is aggressive—but speak with a loud and clear voice. At every stage of contact, whether it is approaching or not, one shouldn't run, and one shouldn't turn one's back toward it. It is necessary to carefully step back, talking loudly, without screaming in panic!

Parents were told to escort their children to and from day care. Police cars drove around with sirens blaring. A team of four used the hose from a fire truck to spray the reeds in front of the Great Wall to push the bears out.

At around 9 P.M. on August 26, Tarasenko's measures were put to the test by one of the primary volunteers. Alexander Zhdanov, a stocky 43-year-old with a buzz cut, operates the train that moves coal from the mine to the plant. He is known around town for his enthusiasm for hunting, unearthing World War II relics, and backcountry snowboarding. Zhdanov had just finished dinner and settled down to Russia's version of Facebook when a friend—a policeman—called to tell him that two bears had been spotted. Officers had injured one with a handgun.

Zhdanov grabbed his Saiga hunting rifle and ran out of the house. He drove to the intersection where the police had parked and got into their van. "We shot him, but we couldn't do more. What if he attacked us? We just have a pistol," one of the policemen told Zhdanov.

As they scanned for activity in the shadows, people began running out of Old Park screaming: "Bears! Bears!" Zhdanov saw a dark mass careening across the sidewalk. He jumped out of the van and sprinted after it. The police followed in the vehicle, illuminating the street with the headlights.

"Run! Get out of here! There's an injured bear!" Zhdanov shouted to anyone who could hear him—children, women, elderly people, all out enjoying the summer night. The bear was hampered by its injury but still running, moaning, jumping into the metal fence and ricocheting off. Then it disappeared into a residential block with a playground in the middle of a courtyard.

Zhdanov stopped and listened. Silence. *I can't shoot. There are people everywhere,* he thought. He turned to the right and saw the bear mid-crouch, a mere six feet away. He fired. The bear fell backward and moaned. Zhdanov shot twice more. The bear scraped its claws against the sidewalk and whined.

People poured out of the surrounding buildings to get a better look. Cars pulled up with their headlights on and watched. It took the bear ten minutes to die.

An autopsy revealed that the bear was a four-year-old female, small for its age. It had been lactating and looked to be the same size and shape as the bear that had attacked Dubitsky. (The taxi that startled it away had a dash-cam recording of the attack.) Tarasenko surmised that it was the mother bear, looking for her cub.

"Maybe it wasn't her. We can't say for sure. You have a bear. What can we say about a bear that is running? It has no cap, hat, or handkerchief, right?" he told me. "It had to be her," he decided. They would find what they presumed was her cub, drowned, a few days later.

But like so many of the details in this story, no one could be truly sure—not citizens, not hunters, and certainly not government officials. Maybe a bear arrived on Monday, or perhaps Wednesday. There were five of them, or just one. The summer onslaught bled together. Timelines were nonexistent, as if everyone had been too busy chasing too many bears to remember.

One thing was sure: by mid-September, the bears seemed to have settled in for good. Taxi drivers prospered, called to take people the few blocks they would normally walk. Children played a new game: "Let's make you a bear, and we'll surround you!" Teenagers dared each other to go looking for bears at night; they wandered around town in packs, hooting with nervous laughter at every shadow. Two bears feasted on watermelon rinds in the dumpster across from the Great Wall so many nights in a row that locals parked their cars nearby and waited for them to appear, hoping to make home movies.

Outside Luchegorsk, apiaries were torn apart. Beekeepers went on nightly patrols into the forest, rifles at the ready. The sound of gunfire echoed through the trees. They shot in the air, they shot overhead, and then they just shot directly at the bears. They didn't even bother to properly hide the carcasses. Zhdanov estimated that 100 bears were extrajudicially killed outside Luchegorsk alone. In all of Primorsky that fall, there were around 60 documented cases of bears coming into villages, approximately 18 cases of conflict with bears, and four or five human deaths. Bears injured hunters, grandmothers, and children.

"I felt unfairness, anger, and joy," Tarasenko explained when I met him at his office. "Unfairness because there are many villages, why are they coming to ours? Second, why are there so many of them? Third, why do people stick their noses where they shouldn't, obstructing our work? If officials are already doing their job chasing the bears away, half the town shouldn't be running behind them, taking pictures, screaming, and giving advice. This made me angry."

Then he paused, adding, "That there are bears left, especially the Asian black bears, this was joy."

The problem spread. In the neighboring province of Khabarovsk, it landed squarely on the shoulders of Yury Kolpak, the 54-year-old director of wildlife protection for the entire region.

Kolpak is short and trim, with salt-and-pepper hair and a wide face. I met him for tea at a road stop along the highway that connects Luchegorsk to the city of Khabarovsk (population 550,000), outside the small town of Bikin, where bears had run rampant. A pregnant woman was among the injured; locals told me she survived because she bit back. Four bears had been shot in Bikin alone, and another three were hit by cars as they traveled the roads.

That fall, Kolpak got a call anytime something fluttered. Kids who didn't want to go to school conjured bears. A woman reported that she'd been attacked by a bear when actually she'd run into a wire fence while escaping one, injuring herself in the confusion. One bear made frequent appearances at a cemetery, digging up graves. But the incident that Kolpak said almost broke him occurred in Sergeevka, a village on the outskirts of Khabarovsk.

It was a Sunday, around 9 A.M., when he responded to a report that a bear had been living in the basement of an apartment building for several days. Kolpak estimated that some 200 people gathered to watch him deal with the situation. While he was waiting for backup, he was repeatedly asked if the bear would be tranquilized instead of killed.

"Just put him to sleep," onlookers advised.

"OK, does anyone want to come with me to sing lullabies?" Kolpak joked.

He tried to explain that there was no way to tranquilize the bear, because in the basement's darkness they had no idea where it was, how big it was, or how much tranquilizer to use. Tranquilizer darts need to hit the right place on the body, and they need time to work—an animal can run around for ten minutes until the drugs take effect. But some weren't swayed. Onlookers crowded balconies and called down: "You murderer!" From another balcony came the reply: "Go down there yourself and go in the basement!" Meanwhile, one policeman even hinted to Kolpak that they might actually be better off trying to tranquilize it.

When Kolpak finally went in, it didn't take long. The bear was chuffing. Kolpak turned his flashlight on the animal and fired. Not everyone was grateful. Even two months later, Kolpak was sensitive. He told me that he had done everything he could to warn the population about how to avoid bears. He asked people to clean out their gardens and to gather fallen fruit, especially pears. "When it starts rotting, it gives off the smell of alcohol. For them it's a drug. They walk toward it and don't react to anything," Kolpak told me. "You catch a bear, drive it to the taiga, and he will come back in two days because he remembers there are still pears. It's a worthless enterprise. And to risk people's lives, especially children—no one would do this. The only right decision is to shoot them." But Kolpak and others who had done so were constantly forced to justify their position, particularly after a bear crashed into a shopping mall in Khabarovsk city and was shot by law enforcement.

Kolpak showed me a photograph of a fisherman who was torn apart by a bear earlier in the year. The body was beheaded and quartered—it looked like something out of the *Game of Thrones* special-effects department. "And you tell us it's inhumane to kill a bear in a city," Kolpak said, his voice rising. "So probably we should have waited until this happened."

~~~~~~

As the number of bears killed grew—many of them in plain view of citizens— public opinion crescendoed. Rumors spread. Conspiracy theories abounded. Some were convinced that the first bear killed in Luchegorsk was actually a cub, and its mother had been killed later. They didn't think it was right to kill a baby. Some didn't think it was right to kill any bear at all. Some thought the bears had all come from a bile factory over the border in China, so the animals were used to human contact, and that the officials were killing bears left and right because they were irresponsible, or that somehow someone was profiting from all this.

Zhdanov was either a murderer or he was a savior. Tarasenko had done his job admirably or he had completely failed. The two men tried to explain that they couldn't just put up a sign on the road asking bears to walk around the town. Tarasenko told people not to run toward the bears, not to take pictures, and, for God's sake, not to take selfies, but not everyone listened.

The problem was that most of the bears that came to Luchegorsk were black bears, which are unbearably cute. With shiny black fur and perfectly round ears, they look like walking illustrations from a children's book. When Tarasenko explained that they were hungry, a few elderly women began feeding them.

Zhdanov once admitted to me, tearfully, mid-cognac, that he was thinking about giving up hunting—it had all grown too sad. He operated by a code of honor with the God of the Hunt, to whom he left an offering each time he went out. He appreciated hunting as a fair game between him and his prey. Yet after the recent killing, he wasn't sure how he felt. He was tired. The forest was being clear-cut, and the taiga's inhabitants were suffering for it. He had begun feeling something more for them these days.

Bears are the spirit animals of the nation—the symbol of Mother Russia. They feature prominently in everything from classic folklore to a viral cartoon series called *Masha and the Bear*. President Vladimir Putin's ruling party, United Russia, features a bear on its flag. Putin himself has evoked the bear to explain Russia's foreign policy. Perhaps there was more symbolism than people let on.

At the Luchegorsk bus station cafeteria, I met a drunk taxi driver named Kolya and his slightly less inebriated dinner companion, Dasha, who had two fluffy Pekingese tethered to their table. They decided to explain the bear situation to me: "They shot every single one that came into the city. They made it look like they were chasing them out, but actually they fucking killed them! They didn't take them anywhere," Kolya said.

"How do you know?" I asked.

"I'm a local resident!" he exclaimed. This tirade continued for a while, until they pressured an unsuspecting man waiting in line to join the conversation. "There's a girl here collecting opinions about bears—did they suffer needlessly, or were they attacking people?" Dasha asked.

"There was a migration from China," the man, named Sanya, said.

"Right, and they just killed them stupidly," Kolya said.

"No, they were harming people. They did it to make the situation safer," Sanya tried to explain.

"But did people suffer?" Dasha cut him off.

"Of course," Sanya said.

"How many?" Kolya pressed.

"A lot, a little, it doesn't matter," Sanya answered.

"Did you personally suffer?" Kolya asked.

"What difference does it make how many?" Sanya retorted. "If even one person suffered."

"Because one person was injured, they killed thirty bears?" Dasha asked.

"It's enough if even one person suffered!" Sanya said. "Why should we put people at risk for the sake of bears?"

"It would be better if you suffered than forty bears and my dog," Kolya announced.

"I think it would be better if forty people suffered than forty bears," Dasha said.

"Forty bears [suffering] is better than one person," Sanya retorted.

"Sarah, don't pay attention to him!" Kolya exclaimed, ending the conversation.

~~~~~~

However people felt about it, there were concrete repercussions to shooting so many bears: orphaned cubs wandering the forest. The lucky ones made it to the Wildlife Rehabilitation Center Utyos, in the southern part of Khabarovsk. (The center was founded in 1991 by a famous tiger catcher named Vladimir Kruglov, who hog-tied more than 40 live tigers before his death. It's now run by his daughter and son.)

Though the sanctuary is far from state-of-the-art, it has released more than 300 orphaned cubs into the wild over the past 20 years. A large administrative house and a wooden lodge for visitors sit below the tiger enclosure and a rusted bear cage. A 12-acre bear enclosure has been under construction for the past several years. When I visited, they were still waiting for the last part: heavy wire from Belarus. It was due to arrive the following week.

In 2015, the sanctuary had taken in eight cubs. It had turned down 30 more. The center's veterinarian, Yana Panova, took me to see the cubs one morning. They were sleeping in a pile on one side of a divided cage. Panova placed bread, carrots, and apples on the other side. When she opened the slot, a few cubs eagerly rushed out and began to munch.

They were puffy black balls with tiny ears and deep brown eyes. They pulled the apples toward them with their front paws and chewed with their mouths open. I badly wanted to pet one. Inadvertently, I stepped on a twig, and the crunch sent a few of them charging at me, bashing into the metal frame. I sprang back and laughed nervously. I could see Tarasenko's predicament.

By October, Tarasenko had caught three orphaned cubs, and a fourth had been heard crying outside Luchegorsk for days. Natalia Prodan, a 41-year-old former journalist, learned about it from an acquaintance and joined a group of volunteers who fed it. As the days grew colder, they decided that they needed to get the cub somewhere safe for the winter, so Prodan contacted a former zookeeper in Ussuriysk, a town 260 miles away, who agreed to find a home for the cub.

It was three weeks before the proper documentation came through. During that time, Prodan and her friend Natalia Kargina took turns leaving apples, carrots, condensed milk, and meat for the cub. They began calling it "our Mishka," the diminutive form of cub. The pair didn't actually see Mishka with their own eyes until Kargina watched a video of the cub sitting in a tree that Zhdanov had posted online. Kargina showed the clip to Prodan, and the women grew concerned—why was the cub sitting motionless in the tree for so long? They contacted Zhdanov, who agreed that the cub looked sick. They needed to catch her immediately.

Prodan runs an extracurricular media program, and she decided to let two students come along the next day to produce a segment about the cub's rescue. The two girls, Irina Katsuyta, 15, and Sonya Shtyarova, 16, were so excited the night before that they couldn't sleep.

The small group arrived a little before noon. It was Irina's first time on camera. In the segment, the petite blonde kneels excitedly in front of the empty den, speculating on what Mishka has been eating. Dogs start barking. "It could be the sign of attack," Zhdanov announces and crashes into the forest, his handgun drawn, to look for the cub. He manages to scare off the dogs and chases Mishka into a muddy ditch. Still filming, the girls run to the spot. Mishka peeps out of the water-logged ditch and whimpers. The cub is soaked, her round ears sticking out.

When Tarasenko arrived, the men captured the cub in a blanket and brought her to a nearby barn for the night. They had rescued the bear. The girls and Prodan were ecstatic. They filmed the end to the happy tale as the bear was driven to safety.

But the next morning, Prodan got a call: Mishka had died from injuries overnight. An autopsy revealed a rubber bullet in her body. Someone had probably shot her while she was sitting in the tree.

Mishka was the last bear seen in Luchegorsk. Soon after she died on October 7, the others seemed to disappear. They weren't wandering around town, they weren't sitting in the reeds, and they weren't terrorizing the townspeople. Some thought they had migrated farther south in search of food or perhaps had retreated to the region's ridges to build their winter dens.

While I was in Khabarovsk, the first big snow of the season fell. The taiga's golden autumn hues disappeared under a blanket of snow so white it was blinding. Pine and Mongolian oak trees drooped under its weight, like a ballet frozen mid-dance. This was the moment when bears were supposed to begin hibernating. People told me it was likely that many that survived the shootings would die over the winter for lack of fat, shrinking the population the following year and restoring the natural order.

But many locals and hunters worried that some of the animals would be too malnourished to sleep. Such bears are called shatuns, dangerous insomniacs that no longer fear anything in their fight for survival. According to legend, they are vicious predators, undeterred by any of the usual defenses, fervently eager for human flesh. And so the hunters remained vigilant, watching for signs of their return.

(Originally published June 2016)

OUR LADY OF STRAYS

BOB SHACOCHIS

*Shacochis has a home in the mountains near our Santa Fe headquarters, and as any
Outside editor who has visited can tell you, the man is crazy about his dogs. When
we heard about a no-kill sanctuary in Costa Rica, where hundreds of canines run
wild, we knew we had an assignment he couldn't pass up.*

For many years, hundreds of years, in Costa Rica's central valley and its lush
surrounding highlands, one well-respected family has been known for one
enduring distinction—not for its great wealth or political influence or cultural
prowess, but for the extraordinary beauty of its women. Lya Battle, who looks
like a petite, auburn-haired heroine on *Game of Thrones,* is living proof of the
Barrantes family's legacy, and 49 years of being put through the wringer hasn't
really dented that firepower.

Yet any true story about Lya plays out between the opposite poles of what is
beautiful and most desired in the world and what is ugly and unwanted. In the
emotional heartlands between those two realms, Lya became famous, not just in
Costa Rica but around the globe, for her undying devotion to ugly—not just plain
old ugly, but *fugly* ("fucking ugly"), a word you often hear in one of her favorite
sentences, "Oh, my love, you're so fugly, give me a kiss"—and her generous kisses
make her perhaps the most promiscuous woman on earth, with hundreds of panting, downtrodden lovers, most of them with four legs, if not three, and wildly
scrambled pedigree.

One could be forgiven for thinking that as a dog lover (or "dog slut," as she
laughingly describes herself), Lya Battle is out of control. But out of control is

a matter of perspective. Especially considering how it was that Lya became renowned as the Mother Teresa of Mutts, the mistress of a place called Territorio de Zaguates (roughly translated as "kingdom of strays"), a situation that might never have happened the way it did if one day her father, who she adored, had not shot her mother, who she did not.

~~~~~~

The journey to the Territorio is so cartographically challenging that somewhere along the way, you begin to believe that the place is imaginary, a mythical Dogtopia of endless, drooly love. It seems impossible to get there, and yet eventually you do, zig-zagging through the provincial capital of Alajuela's maze of avenues and alleys, winding your way up into the mountains through a puzzle of villages and coffee plantations, frowning at your cell phone as its Waze app tells you to turn on routes that bear no markings. Somewhere ahead is the town of Carrizal, and beyond that the Poás volcano, and in between, the dogs.

Past Carrizal's parish church, you turn up a narrow potholed lane that climbs the mountainside, passing through a neighborhood of ramshackle houses, scowling old men in tank tops sitting on their stoops, guys washing their cars on the street. Nobody waves back, and although the vibe is not exactly hostile, it's certainly not welcoming, either. In fact, Lya and the community are at war, she claims.

Beyond the last houses, the lane goes up and up through dense jungle until it is blocked by the Territorio's massive gate, flanked by high walls that vanish into the bush. Here, rain or shine, in the middle of the road, sits an extraordinary white dog, Yiya, less of a guard than a self-appointed greeter, a solitary figure separated from everybody else by another quarter-mile of driveway. Yiya telegraphs the message "I'm a born outlier but an essential part of the operation." He'll leave his station at feeding time, go up the hill to eat, and then return to duty at the gate, not a fellow with an identity crisis.

The drive carves around a grassy slope, arriving at a small plateau and the first signs of spreading chaos, punctuated with tail-wagging clusters of bedlam. On the plateau, and in the pastures above the central compound, there's a mad flow, like English soccer fans or swarming bees.

I don't know who counted them, but reportedly there are one billion dogs on earth. One-fourth are pets, which means 750 million are *zaguates*—strays, mutts, mongrels, village dogs, scavengers, pariahs, or whatever endearment or insult you wish to assign them. The Territorio's fluctuating population is six or seven or eight hundred, Lya is never quite sure, although there's a continuous effort with pro bono vets to vaccinate, neuter, and tattoo them all.

My wife and I arrive on volunteer day. The visitors seem to be just playmates, each with his or her own pack of admirers dotted across the terrain, which is exactly what Lya hoped for when she invited regional businesses and organizations to donate their employees' time. There are also weekend events, hours-long hikes that sometimes attract hundreds of people from down in the capital, San José, which sprawls all the way to Alajuela. When I ask Lya the size of the Territorio de Zaguates, her smile is uncertain and she gestures up the mountainside into the clouds; later she'll explain that the dogs run on about ten acres of her family's 142-acre farm.

From the moment we park, we are a magnet for dozens of barking dogs, half-suspicious, half-delighted, a subgroup best categorized as *Who's There!?* Not everybody cares. The majority group, clearly, belongs to *Let's Go Somewhere!*, a prevailing sentiment with an irresistible appeal for those so inclined, no matter their mobility or lack of it. But other spirits are determined to hunker down and can't be budged, the sick or the slothful looking on from the sidelines, the paranoid or obsessively territorial glued in place.

There is something so fantastical, and a bit freakish, about Lya's vision, that its actual existence blends naturally into magical realism. Dogs gaze at us from within sections of concrete culverts, or stare over the top of individual foxholes they've burrowed into the red soil, or follow us with sleepy eyes from the shady bushes. I expect to see them up in the trees as well and am not surprised when we reach the main building, part storehouse, part bunkhouse, and find dogs head-high up on the supply shelves, peering out from the shadows like barn owls. They're under the shelves, too, and huddled into open closets, and sprawled on every inch of the veranda not already occupied by a row of donated baby strollers, each containing a partially paralyzed dog or, less charmingly, a muttering furball who refuses to be evicted.

Incredibly, every dog has a name. Everybody's different, clownish and hilarious: fuzzy splats of happiness, skeletal shells of wincing eagerness, buoyant lumps of grinning muscle, the faltering and the withered, the robust and the dignified, dogs like pieces of frayed rope with legs and head, senatorial dogs like Boris, old and wise and reposed, a seeming mix of corgi and Bernese mountain dog that resembles the 30-pound butt of a half-smoked cigar. Blanquita is a dirty-white floor mop who has betrothed herself to Ronney, one of the workers, and cries inconsolably from the minute he leaves the compound until his return the next morning. There's a sweet little dog I of course call Stumpy, his right front leg hacked off with a machete by his owner after a long night drinking at the cantina. And there's Milu, one of the precious cohort Lya calls her "walking dead," who came to her with distemper a couple of years after she opened the Territorio in 2008. To save a dog from distemper is no small task, and now Milu, in his dotage, weighs less than a fart and walks like a drunken tarantula.

Behind the building are the holding pens for a handful of seriously bad kids— Lya declares that they made their own hell and now they can live in it—and the newbies, who take days or months to assimilate. Today's newcomers are, unfortunately, typical—a teat-swollen, wailing mother dropped off without her litter, a handsome Rottweiler abandoned because he jumped on people to greet them, and an enormous slobbery bulldog-mastiff mix, who only Lya can approach because he's learned to hate men. His owner drove up in an expensive SUV with a large sack of food, a rifle, and the dog. Take him or I'll shoot him, said the man, who wrongly claimed that the dog was deaf and therefore worthless.

Down the length of this terrace of pens and outbuildings stretches a long, gutter-like cement trough where a trio of Nicaraguan workers lay down hundreds of pounds of kibble each morning, igniting a quasi-orderly hierarchy of eating, a four-wave sequence based on personality types, until everybody has snarfed their fill.

Watching over it all in black rubber boots, khaki pants, and a white T-shirt is the imposing figure of Alvaro Saumet, 47, the Territorio's seemingly gruff alpha commander of the *perros*. Alvaro is a Colombian, and you can readily imagine him in a military uniform, leading his men on a raid of a guerrilla hideout. He is also Lya's husband and the former lingerie king of Costa Rica. Connecting the dots between bras and bulldogs is fairly complicated.

It's easy to forget or overlook that beauty has a price, sometimes extracted from its source yet often paid by its admirers. Lya has, like an alchemist, transformed something ugly into something beautiful, and that would also be the story of her family, except in reverse. Decades ago, the Territorio was the farm of Lya's maternal grandfather, a short, dark-skinned man—part indigenous Indian, he claimed— praised for his nobility and goodness, who became one of the first pharmacists in Costa Rica. He married Lya's famously pretty grandmother, who everybody said looked like a movie star, yet she shared a more problematic trait with the other Barrantes women—a cold, closed heart. Lya's grandfather loved German shepherds, but his wife, who hated them, would poison her husband's dogs. Together, Lya thinks, they must have screwed up her own beautiful mother's brain.

Lya's mother, Maria Barrantes, was an exceptional student, and her father sent her to the University of Toronto, where she met Matthew Battle Murphy, Lya's father, whose family had immigrated to Canada from England after World War II. Matthew was a biologist, Maria an educator. When Lya was five, her homesick mother decided to return to Costa Rica. Lya and her younger brother, Steven, grew up in an old, affluent neighborhood in San José, in a house with a father who always looked at life positively and a mother who only saw the dark side of everyone and everything. Her overprotective parents would not allow Lya to have a boyfriend until she turned 15. Nor were they role models of any healthy exchange of affection. Lya, meanwhile, had inherited her father's fascination and tenderness toward the nonhuman world.

"Who isn't loved? Snakes?" she says. "Then I love snakes. Who isn't loved? Toads? Then I love toads. These are the things that keep you going. I'm the kind of person who says it hurts to see cattle or pigs or chickens in trucks. All I knew about animals is how much I loved them."

Seriously afflicted with attention deficit disorder, Lya struggled through school. She studied preschool education in college, then allowed herself to be prematurely talked into marriage with a perfect gentleman from one of San José's best families. She was 22 when they divorced.

Then she met Alvaro, who, though younger than Lya, was more mature than the society bons vivants she'd been dating. Alvaro was an entrepreneur with an eyebrow-raising profession—he smuggled high-end women's underwear from Colombia to Costa Rica and sold it on the black market. He told her he couldn't guarantee her the life of a princess, but they moved in together and he went legit, opening the first Touché lingerie franchise in Costa Rica, then two more. Lya spent her days working as a tutor, helping high school kids with their college applications, which she still does.

At the same time, however, Lya's younger brother decided to become an operator in Costa Rica's booming travel industry, packaging cruise tours, and lured the family into the mess he eventually created. As his project slid into bankruptcy, Lya and Alvaro's business began a slow tumble, and Steven's foibles inflamed their parents' already volatile relationship. What happened next, as Lya tells it:

And one day there comes a time when a kind man has finally had enough— Dad just shot her. This is a man who couldn't squash a fly. They were arguing about Steven. My dad always carried a pistol in his car, because every week he had to drive into the mountains to pay the workers at the farm in cash. So this day he picked my mother up after her exercise class in the city and told her he wanted to drive up to the farm to get a weed whacker, and they started arguing, and he stopped at a vacant lot and shot her, dragged her body out into the lot in full view of people in the area, and drove on to the farm, where he cleaned off the seat, picked up the weed whacker, drove home, and acted like nothing happened.

That was in 2000, and her father went to jail the next year, where he remains today, at age 83. After the murder, her brother tried to seize the farm; after eight years in court, Lya and her father got it back.

By this time, Alvaro and Lya were facing a radical restructuring. "We were going to make our life simple," says Lya, which in retrospect sounds like a cosmic joke. Unable to afford their suburban home in the hills, they moved into a smaller place in town. Previously, Lya had kept a dog, abandoned by a construction worker, and a pet pig. The new place, however, had a backyard, and that's how her dog love took over.

"We started picking up strays, taking them to vets," Lya remembers. "I started thinking, What happens to the dogs you rescue but can't keep? So I started keeping them."

A year passed, and then another, and Lya had about 30 dogs. At first it wasn't really a problem—there were no neighbors—but then someone built on the lot behind them. By this time, Alvaro's shrugging tolerance for Lya's passion had transformed into his own big-hearted love for the dogs, yet the situation quickly became untenable. They married on 8/8/2008 (the only date Lya was certain she would not forget), the farm emerged from litigation, and Alvaro suggested that they move the dogs there. The idea was to hire a family to take care of them, but that never worked out. So Lya and Alvaro commute 45 minutes to the farm most days.

By 2009, they had about 120 dogs. Then one day they heard that a large shelter in the capital was closing and had decided to euthanize its 80 dogs, so Lya and Alvaro took them, and two years later simply stole the same shelter's dogs when, infuriated, she learned it had never actually closed. "We kind of did know that we were crazy," she says, "and now we had 300 dogs, but still nobody knew about us. And we couldn't afford to buy another grain of kibble."

The first guardian angel to appear on Lya's doorstep was a young woman named Marcella Castro Wedel, pushing a doll carriage with Puppy inside, a diminutive pit bull with paralyzed hindquarters. A solitary go-it-alone dog rescuer, Marcella started coming over to photograph Lya's dogs to post on Facebook. "We were enjoying the dogs and not really worried about what was going on outside," Lya says, "but Marcella changed that." She convinced Lya that the farm needed its own Facebook page.

As the Territorio's profile began to blossom on social media, one of Costa Rica's biggest advertising agencies, Garnier BBDO, decided to launch a public-service campaign aimed at animal welfare; to Lya's astonishment, it chose the Territorio as its centerpiece. The agency created a brilliant, joyful video celebrating what it promoted as the unique, one-of-a-kind breed of every individual mutt—the Bernese mountain corgi, for instance, or the golden doodle terrier and the German Staffordshire retriever. Highway billboards advertised the mutts, television stations broadcast features, and Lya and her dogs began to garner media attention around the world. Then Superperro, Costa Rica's biggest dog-food manufacturer, stepped in to the campaign, donating kibble for every Facebook like.

"We never wanted to grow," says Lya. "It happened because it happened, and now people from all over the place were dumping dogs at our gate. We just wanted the dogs to have a better life and for people to get that shit out of their heads about mutts." Generally, in Central and South America, strays are accepted as an unappreciated part of the landscape by everyone except private rescue agencies and compassionate individuals. Now people were showing off their mutts and competing for the most eclectic "breeds" as status symbols. "But the campaign caused more problems," says Lya.

A popular Costa Rican joke describes a man selling lobsters from two baskets, one basket labeled imported, with a lid on it, and the other basket lidless, labeled local. When asked about the difference, he explains that you don't need to put a lid on the Costa Rican lobsters, because if one tries to crawl out, the others will drag it back in.

"This is very true of our society, people pulling down anybody who tries to rise above the bottom," she says. "I don't mind having a shitty car, living in a little house—my happiness is with the dogs." Four years ago, she alleges, "there was this former volunteer who managed to hack our Facebook page and shut it down, 84,000 followers just disappeared, and we had to start over from scratch."

Some organizations were angry about Lya's loud criticisms of shelters and their shabbiness. Others still feel the Territorio is overpopulated. "My personal opinion is that they have too many animals," Lilian Schnog, manager of the Animal Shelter Costa Rica, told *Outside* in an e-mail. "I never visited them, but we get a lot of last year's vet students at our shelter; they were in tears and said all the animals have ehrlichiosis. I do not believe that a shelter can run properly without a vet present." To this Lya replies that the tick-borne disease is indeed a problem in Costa Rica, but a veterinarian from the National Animal Health Service (Senasa) does visit the Territorio monthly to certify that the animals are in decent health.

The ongoing battles with neighbors are particularly disheartening. The boundaries of the Territorio are porous, and occasionally a dog will wander downhill into town and end up poisoned. Vandals have smashed irrigation pipes to deprive the dogs of water. Recently, Alvaro and his crew noticed vultures circling above one of the high meadows and hiked up to find five of the farm's eight horses had been butchered by poachers to sell the meat to illegal sausage makers.

Inevitably, there are the issues with waste and sanitation. (Not to change the subject: after our first visit, my wife retrieved her cell phone from her handbag to discover, inexplicably, a mysterious dollop of poop on its screen.) Disposal is a Sisyphean chore usually handled by the Nicaraguan laborers, who shovel the excrement into empty dog-food bags. The bags are hauled to the municipal dump, and Lya is given a receipt to verify the transaction.

The neighbors, she says, claim "we contaminate the land with our shit, the underground water supply with our urine. Oh, I say, do your cows not piss in the fields? But now I had to get legal proof. It costs thousands of dollars to get scientific proof to satisfy Senasa. And here, you're guilty until proven otherwise. But we always find angels in the darkest moments."

One day an elderly woman who followed the Territorio's Facebook page contacted Lya, offering the free services of her daughter, an environmental engineer. The daughter was able to certify that the mountain's aquifer was clean. "There's nothing our neighbors can do," says Lya. "They've tried everything. And now it's traffic—they say we're damaging the road." True or not, the narrow road through the neighborhood leading to the farm becomes impassable on days when the Territorio opens its gates to the public. "When people say, 'Why do you go through all this shit?' I say because what we're doing is right, and conventional shelters are not the solution."

Indisputably, there's an overload of sadness and pathos and loneliness out there in Shelterland. Cue the lugubrious ASPCA commercials back in the States, the wretched images and bereaved voice-over so depressing you want to shoot yourself. In the Territorio, though, you're always smiling.

~~~~~~

We're hiking up the mountain with the dogs, through pastures and bush and canopy, hoping the afternoon rains hold off for another hour. My wife is ahead with Alvaro and Daniel, one of the local employees, while Lya and I dawdle behind with the main pack, scores of mavericks spread out on our flanks, a river of raucous fur flowing euphorically up the slope, a sight every bit as marvelous, even in its reduced magnitude, as the wildebeests on the Serengeti plains. Unless, of course, you don't like dogs.

"If you can hold on to your problems while you hold on to a dog," Lya believes, "you have bigger problems than you think. We have to go through hell with our dogs, but it's how we grow. If you can't connect with a dog, then there's something really wrong with you."

From Lya's perspective, nobody's more dangerous than someone who would hurt an animal. It's a subject that invites diatribes from her about Costa Rica's success at living off the fame of being eco-progressive while its toothless animal-welfare law doesn't seem to care how you treat an animal as long as you pick up its shit. Noncompliance benefits everyone from the meat industry to cockfighters to hunters who poach sloths in the rainforest. "It's illegal to have dogfights, and what's the punishment? Nothing," she says. "We call it the Ley de Mierda—the shit law. We printed the actual law on dog-poop bags, and put turds inside the bags and took them to the government in protest." Finally, after years of promised reform, the national legislature is close to passing a referendum meant to toughen enforcement.

As we ascend the mountainside, Alvaro and his local muchachos, in front of us and racing toward the clouds, qualify not only as extreme athletes but as some of the world's best anger-management specialists. Back at the compound a thousand feet below, which sometimes has the anticipatory feeling of a crowded open-air bus terminal where all the passengers are excited dogs, bubbles of tension form regularly, and a visitor quickly realizes that to be employed at the Territorio, you have to have a big, authoritative voice. Somebody's always bellowing, "Don't do that!" When the tension turns into a scuffle, Alvaro or the nearest available muchacho jumps into action, hollering *"Vamos vamos vamos!"* and sprinting up the slope. The incipient brawl dissolves into thin air, dogs by the dozens peeling off from the rumble to gallop after them.

About 500 feet above us, Alvaro and Daniel and my wife and 300 of their best friends have paused to rest, and above them rolling thunder echoes off the Poás volcano as storm clouds gather darkly. Lya and I don't hear the command to turn around, but suddenly the pack reverses course and cascades down toward our own pack of 200, and in a few minutes they merge riotously. Daniel, approaching us, has the impulse to throw himself flat on the ground, and within seconds he's invisible under a smothering tsunami of dog love.

Every dog is determined to lick Daniel's laughing face. Every dog cannot lick Daniel's face. Ergo, a fight erupts, and Lya and I watch speechless as a little brown and black punk, a min pin, a dwarf Doberman, flies out of the heap like a rocket-propelled grenade and bites my wife on the calf, then flies away in guilty glee. "You little shit!" Lya and my wife both shriek in outrage, but the attack was so cartoonish in its ridiculous lack of motivation that we had to stop ourselves from laughing. After all these years, Lya has been bit so many times that she claims she's no longer impressed.

No matter what, no matter how badly the dogs have been mistreated before they arrive here, no matter that they're a mangy mess, they still want to be around people, which is why Lya and Alvaro started the public walks, and the dogs, even the malefactors, are infectiously exuberant as communal beings. In fact, their happiness raises a question that doesn't seem to have a perfect answer.

Before word of Territorio de Zaguates began to spread, Lya and Alvaro would adopt out three dogs a month, a rate that's since quadrupled, the running count to about 130 dogs, with 10 to 15 new dogs arriving weekly. Superperro has developed a DogMates app, which helps match people with strays in need of a home, but Lya and Alvaro are particular about who can have their dogs. Before they agree to an adoption, they want to meet the potential owners and follow up with a phone call a month later.

On our first day visiting the *zaguates,* we met Amanda, a young woman from San Francisco searching the hordes with her mother-in-law, who on a previous trip had fallen for a dog she wanted to take home. Trying to imagine the arc of that dog's destiny seemed impossible, but Lya is full of stories with happy endings. She takes out her phone and shows me a photo of one of her dogs, Chifrigo, lolling around Miami with a pair of cats and a bichon frise. A vicious chow mix known as El Chapo, after the notorious narcotrafficker, is now Kate. She has become adorable.

But the likelihood that the hundreds of other dogs will ever be adopted is zero, which raises the eternal existential question: So what? The difference between shelter dogs quivering in a kennel and Lya's *zaguates* scampering through the idyllic meadows of a canine paradise is profound and, ultimately, irreconcilable. "You don't have to adopt them," Lya says, "but at least you can be nice to them," a philosophy that applies to all refugees, human and nonhuman, from an insecure life, and in this case only Lya and Alvaro know the real cost of that kindness. "Yesterday," says Alvaro, "I promised I wasn't going to take any more dogs. I'm so tired. But you find out the horrible things that happened to them, and you can't tolerate it." Sometimes there's no money to pay their workers at the end of the month.

Only man, says Lya, can domesticate an animal and then ignore it. The *zaguates* are never asked to be not-dogs. The dogs are provided food and companionship without any inclination to compromise their freedom. It's hard to say if, without the proper funding, the Territorio can provide a sustainable model on its own terms, or one that can be reproduced in other countries by other rescuers. Regardless, the Kingdom of Strays exists as a realized, functioning vision of a better, more humane world.

The day before we arrived, we'd spent the night at an isolated resort on Costa Rica's magnificent Pacific coast. At dinner that evening in the resort's outdoor restaurant, I watched as a little black dog stopped at a table where a young couple were dining and waited patiently for a handout that never came. Perhaps the dog sensed my disapproval of her lousy people judgment, and she finally gave up and approached our table, where she hit the moocher's jackpot. My wife wondered what her name was, and I said she must be Negrita—little black one. The waitress stopped by and indeed confirmed her name—Negra, black but not so little, because the staff, when they sit down to eat their own meals, always fix Negra a plate as well. She comes and goes as she wants, said the waitress, but most nights she follows guests back to their rooms, and sometimes they invite her in and she sleeps with them. And so it was in the morning. I woke up to find Negra lying on the sofa, my wife feeding her cold cuts.

We had found the only *zaguate* in Costa Rica who had no need for Lya and Alvaro and the embrace of their boundless, sheltering love. Still, I couldn't help but think that Negra was missing out on all the fun.

(Originally published February 2017)

NO CANNIBAL
JOKES PLEASE

TIM CAHILL

Cahill, a founding editor at Outside, *had the cover story in the debut issue of the magazine, which premiered as an insert inside a 1977 issue of* Rolling Stone. *He made his name chronicling serious adventures with an irreverent tone, an effervescent mix that helped define the voice of the magazine. Here, he takes on the controversial topic of cannibalism—and as usual, tests the limits of appropriate humor.*

It was, I suppose, a single piece of ineptly executed and cynically fashioned art that sent me fleeing five hundred miles upriver, back into time, and deep into the material heart of the swamp. The people I wanted to meet—it was only later that I would come to know them as Karowai—lived a Stone Age life and knew almost nothing of the outside world. They were, some said, headhunters, cannibals, savages. If so, they still owned their own lives.

Which didn't seem to be the case with the people who lived in the administrative center located at the mouth of the great river that drained the swamp. It was only my second night in the town Agats, and it was raining, again, here on the southern coast of Indonesian Irian Jaya, the western half of the island of New Guinea. Torrential rain hissed into the Arafura Sea, and it pounded down onto the slick brown tidal mudflats. This area, known as the Asmat, is named after the region's most famous inhabitants and is the world's largest swampland.

The electricity in the town dimmed, sputtered, and died. It was 100 degrees at eight in the evening, and the wooden boardwalk, set fifteen feet above mudflats, was slick and treacherous as I followed a man who called himself Rudy past darkened and shuttered clapboard buildings. There were fine things Rudy thought I needed to see. Artifacts I should buy.

Rudy's aboriginal art shop was another clapboard affair, and rain thundered down on the galvanized-tin roof of the place. The electricity in the town blinked on for a second—a flash of sickly orange—then coughed piteously and died for the night.

This was not unexpected, and Rudy carried a flashlight. He was an Indonesian but not a native inhabitant of Agats; Rudy came from Java, the capital island of the Indonesian archipelago. He was a short, slender man with burnished golden skin and straight black hair. He wore a lime-green polo shirt with an alligator over the place where his heart might have been, and his shirt was open to display a small gold Playboy bunny hanging from a thin chain around his neck.

Rudy was in the business of selling native Asmat art. The Asmat are Papuans, sturdy black people related to Australian aboriginals and thought to be linked to the "Java Man" who lived over half a million years ago. The word "Papuan" derives from a Malay word, *papuwah*, meaning "frizzy-haired."

Throughout the whole of recorded time—and as recently as the 1960s—the Asmat people were the most feared cannibals in the southern swamps. Head-hunting formed the core of a complex system of survival designed to appease various malevolent spirits. Art was essential to that life, and the Asmat were master carvers. Their ancestral columns—which look a bit like totem poles as envisioned by Giacometti—were delicate, flowing poems of war and revenge. Asmat carvings, coveted by collectors, are included in the permanent collections of the Museum of Primitive Art and the Metropolitan Museum in New York.

By the 1990s, tribal warfare was very nearly a thing of the past, and the spiritual impetus that fashioned Asmat art had been degraded. Javanese sharpies like Rudy hired villagers to hack out sad, uninspired pieces that could be sold to unwary visitors, most of whom came off adventure cruise ships.

Rudy's darkened shop was filled with carvings piled one atop the other and marked with tags that read SHIP, PRICE, CABIN NUMBER. Broken pieces lay in a pile and occupied a corner of the shop. The replications of ancestral carvings, the bis poles, had been fashioned quickly, out of soft wood—not the traditional ironwood—and the spirits did not dwell in them.

Rudy sensed my growing irritation and turned the yellowing beam of his flashlight onto a squat wooden carving he imagined I might be inclined to purchase. I stared at a blocky chunk of wood, coarsely chiseled to represent a man and a woman locked in a carnal embrace. The soulless figure was as crude as something scrawled on a bathroom wall and had nothing to do with the delicacy of traditional carving that did, indeed, sometimes encompass copulatory scenes. Rudy's dying light illuminated the clunky travesty and lingered on splotches of black paint meant to represent pubic hair.

"Sexy," he whispered.

I thought for a moment of Michael Rockefeller, who had visited the Asmat in 1961 as part of a Harvard Peabody expedition, and returned soon after to purchase art for an exhibition in the United States. Rockefeller planned to visit some of the more remote villages near Agats, but his boat capsized in a fierce tide and was driven out into the Arafura Sea. His two guides swam to shore where they summoned help. Rockefeller and a Dutch art expert, Rene Wassing, stayed with the overturned boat. The next morning, Rockefeller, tired of waiting, left Wassing with the boat and began to swim toward shore, which was four to seven miles away. He was never seen again.

Rockefeller was a good swimmer, and he had rigged up a flotation devise out of two empty jerricans. There are sharks in those waters, as well as man-eating crocodiles. The tide was also very heavy.

Nevertheless, at least one local missionary believes Rockefeller was a victim of ritual cannibalism. Had he made it to shore, Rockefeller would have washed up near the village of Otsjanep. At the time Irian Java was a Dutch colony, and some years earlier Dutch police investigating a head-hunting incident at Otsjanep had killed the local chief and four others. The Asmat believe that a man killed in war will not rest until avenged by the death of an enemy. Rockefeller, naked and defenseless, would have been seen as a representative of the "white tribe."

Whatever the truth of the matter, it can be argued that Michael Rockefeller died for art.

Rudy moved in close to the sad, sorry copulation figure, trained his light on the genitals, and said again, "Sexy."

It was not a piece to die for.

"Rudy," I said. "I gotta get out of here."

I wanted to go up river. Back in time.

The boat was a forty-foot long dugout, no more than three feet wide, and powered by a forty horsepower kerosene Yamaha engine. My traveling companion, photographer Chris Ranier, had wanted to get out of Agats very badly. He is best known for his documentation of endangered and disappearing cultures, and Agats was a town where you went to the Asmat museum because traditional culture was, as they say, history.

We had no radio in the big dugout, only a bit of rice, one spare propeller, and two burlap bags full of trade goods. Our guide, William Rumbarar, was a Papuan from the nearby island of Biak, and it was William who hired two local Asmat boatmen to accompany us: Conrados Kamua was a slender, clever man, good with engines, and Stef Metemeo was a short, muscular gentleman with an infectious smile, who functioned as the Minister of Morale for our trip back in time.

There were plenty of Javanese guides available in Agats, but the native Papuans seemed to distrust all the Javanese out of hand, reason enough to choose a Papuan guide. And William, for his part, knew the stuff. One recent book on the Asmat, for instance, suggested that there were Neolithic peoples living in tree houses only a few hundred miles upriver and that these Stone Age tribes were friendly and welcomed visitors. William had been there.

"Gone," he told us. "All modern now." By which he meant that the people had come down out of the trees and that they now lived in clapboard houses with tin roofs. The children all went to school, the adults went to church, and everyone wore missionary-clothing-drive T-shirts and shorts. It wasn't that my book was incorrect: All this had happened in the five years since it was published. "Change is very fast now," William said.

That change—the homogenization of humanity—seems to be the direction of history. There is a certain sad inevitability about it all. For the upriver people in the Asmat, it happens like this: Missionaries come, followed by the government in the form of soldiers and policemen and bureaucrats. And then the multinational developers arrive, hard on the heels of government, and they promise a better life to anyone who wants to log the forest and farm the waste. Perhaps the development would involve mining or petrochemical exploration, but the result has always been the same. Everywhere. The living culture is entombed within museums.

Still, William explained, if we wanted to go farther upriver, deeper into the swamp, he knew of some people who still lived in the trees, people who used stone tools and were largely ignorant of the outside world. If this was, in fact, the case— the irony wasn't lost on me—I would be an agent of the changes that offended my romantic notions of human diversity. I would personally entomb some of the living culture in prose, and Chris would document it on film. Perhaps, several generations down the line, young people in the Asmat would study his photographs in an attempt to understand what had happened to them.

"How far upriver are these people?" I wanted to know.

"Past Senggo."

Senggo? Where had I read about Senggo? I paged through the best and most recent guidebook I had been able to find, *Irian Jaya,* by Kal Muller (Periplus Edition, Berkeley, California). The book, published in 1990, said "some unacculturated ethnic groups live in the jungles upriver from Senggo." Very good. However: "Cannibalism is frequently reported and surely practiced here."

"Who are these people you know upriver?" I asked William.

He said, "Care-oh-eye." Karowai.

Muller's book didn't have a lot of encouraging things to say about Karowai hospitality. It said, in fact, that they were cannibals. The Dutch Reformed Church has been proselytizing among the estimated 3,000 or so Karowai for ten years and has yet to celebrate a single baptism. One missionary, the Reverend Gert van Enk, calls Karowai country "the hell of the south." van Enk himself, according to Muller, "is not allowed into most of the tribal territory, and if caught there would be pincushioned with arrow." Confirming other sources, van Enk says that cannibalism is still common among the Karowai. A death is believed to be caused by witchcraft, and a culprit (or scapegoat) must be found, killed, and eaten by the relatives in revenge. This leads to a never-ending cycle of cannibalism.

"You sure this is, uh, safe?" I asked.

William said, "Oh, yes, very safe, no problems, don't worry." And then his body was shaken by a sneezelike convulsion followed by a series of helpless, high-pitched wails. It was, I understood after thirty seconds or so, the way William laughed.

The rivers of the Asmat, seen from the air, are milky brown, the color of cafe au lait, and they meander drunkenly through varying shades of green in great loops and horseshoes. The water comes from the central highlands of New Guinea. It flows from glacier-clad peaks 15,000 feet high, and plunges through great canyons into the flatland swamps, where it forms dozens of interconnected waterways that empty into the Arafura Sea.

The Asuwetz River (also called the Baliem) is a mile wide near Agats, on the coast, and at low tide the banks are a sloping wall of slick brown mud twenty feet high. Mangrove trees, buttressed by high exposed roots, brace themselves against flood tide.

Women in long, thin dugout canoes that were the same gray-brown color as the river stood to paddle against the flow of the river. Thirty years ago, the handle of a paddle would be carved in the visage of an ancestor's face. That ancestor would have died in war and the paddle would have served to remind everyone of the necessity for revenge. None of the paddles I saw were carved in this way. Such artwork is now against the law, part of the Indonesian government's push to finally end head-hunting.

Upriver villages consisted of several poor huts set on stilts above the swampy ground. Some of the villages were arranged around rectangular houses 150 feet or more long, called yews. There were doors evenly spaced along the length of the yews, one for each family group, though only men are allowed inside. In past times, head-hunting raids were planned in the yews, and the Indonesian government sent soldiers to burn most of them down years ago. The upriver longhouses, however, were too remote to attack and exist much as they must have centuries ago.

At the Asmat village of Kaima, we pulled into the beach fronting the yew. Mean, slinking, little dogs battled pigs loudly for garbage under the yew. Women and children sat on the porch, weaving string bags made from orchid fibers.

One of the men issued a sort of command, a grunting hiss. Instantly the women and children were gone, clambering six feet down notched poles to the ground. Suddenly there were several dozen men standing on the porch. They wore shorts in varying degrees of repair, and some of the men sported T-shirts with such cryptic messages as JEAN-CLAUDE VAN DAMME—KARATE. A few of the men stood with their arms crossed over their chests, a defiant and aggressive stance in this culture.

We stopped because the chief here was said to possess five human skulls. We wanted to talk with him about the skulls, about the old ways, about the time before missionaries. The men of Kaima, for their part, saw three strange Papuans, expensively dressed (shoes!), and two white men. It was unlikely that much good could come of such a visit.

There was an uncomfortable aura of suspicion and distrust. Conrados talked with the chief, a powerful-looking man of about thirty-five with fine, regular features and wary eyes. The chief was wearing yellow shorts and dried rattan strips around his considerable biceps.

I hunkered down by one of the dozen hearths in the yew. There were beautifully carved spears against one wall, some polished black ironwood bows, a variety of arrows with different bone points for different pray, and at least one polished by uncarved drum near each fire. All the woodwork was finer by far than any of the carvings I had seen in the boardwalk shops of Agats.

Conrados squatted by my side and explained that the chief might, in fact, have one skull. The chief didn't know for sure. Because of the missionaries and the government, he didn't know. For 20,000 rupiah (about $10) he could look.

"Tell him it's twenty thousand rupees only if he finds the skulls."

The chief disappeared. The rest of the men stood around silently. They didn't talk with Conrados. I glanced over at the finely carved weapons. It was all very uncomfortable. We seemed to frighten the men of Kaima just about as much as they frightened us.

Presently, the chief returned with the improbable information that he couldn't find his skulls. Misplaced the pesky buggers. There were, he told Conrados, too many people around for him to be able to find his skulls. The missionaries. The government.

We had already seen an illegal Asmat skull outside of Agats, in the village of Syuru. It was a twenty-minute walk from town over a wide, well-maintained boardwalk set variously five and fifteen feet above the boggy ground. After about ten minutes, the wooden walkway began to deteriorate precipitously.

There were missing planks, rotted planks, broken planks, and then no planks at all, only a few sticks. One of these broke under my weight, and I grabbed at something that held and then swung there for a moment. Like a kid on the monkey bars.

Syuru was a small, traditional village of thatched-roofed huts on stilts. There were no boardwalks in the village itself, only a series of half-submerged bark walkways. As I wobbled my way over the narrow tree trunks—small children took my hand to steady me in this process—a humming, murmurous sound I had been hearing for some time began to separate itself into individual moans and wails.

An important man had died the day before. Now the women had covered their bodies with ashes and soot. They would mourn in this fashion for seven days. The sounds were coming from several houses at once. Wailing and moaning would build to crescendo and then subside for a moment. Suddenly, a loud voice from one of the houses—sometimes it was a man's voice; sometimes, a woman's—would shout out a hoarse, anguished speech in Asmat. I had no translator, but I imagined the words were something like: "He was a good man; he worshipped ancestors, he fed his family, and now he's gone." And the moaning and wailing and shrieking would start all over again.

In the swamplands of the Asmat, all the dead returned as ghosts, but those improperly mourned can be malevolent. They can make a living relative's life hell. A cranky ancestor strews banana peels across the path of life. Literally. People in the Asmat don't fall down without a reason.

When someone dies, a proper show of grief makes a favorable impression on the recently deceased, who can then protect his descendants from all those evil spirits that populate the netherworld.

The yew at Syuru was separated from the village proper by the boardwalk. The night before, Conrados, a local Asmat, had spoken to the men of Syuru. Here the men were expecting us, and there were no women on the porch in front of the dozen doorways. It was 9:00 A.M. and most of the children were in school. It was a good time to talk heads with the guys.

The yew was two hundred feet long, at a guess, with high rafters, and there were at least fifteen fires, all set in a row, in the center of the structure and neatly spaced along the length of the floor. Only a few of the older men were present, and when a couple of schoolchildren stopped on the boardwalk to see what was going on, a thin, muscular man in threadbare gray shorts ducked through the door. He stood on the porch and said "Scram" in Asmat. The sound, the same one I heard in Kaima, is a grunting hiss. The children hurried off down the boardwalk without looking back.

The men squatting around the fires in the yew wore shorts, and they smoked clove-scented Indonesian cigarettes called kreteks. This smell mingled with the odor of woodsmoke and singed pig fat. No doubt human flesh—locally called "long pig"—had been cooked over these fires in past generations.

An older man in faded beige shorts smeared his face and chest with white ashes. He put on a feathered headdress made of bird-of-paradise feathers and produced a fire-blackened human skull from the bag. It was all very surreptitious, and there was a good deal of looking around, because we were engaged in something everyone knew was illegal. The sounds of mourning, across the way in the small huts, rose to another tormented crescendo.

I noticed that the skull lacked the lower jaw, which meant it was the trophy of a head-hunting raid. The skulls of powerful ancestors, sometimes kept as safeguards against evil spirits, are invariably intact, the lower jaw lashed to the skull with strands of rattan. Head-hunting trophies, on the other hand, are invariably missing the lower jaws, which are detached and worn on a necklace: a fearsome emblem of proficiency in war. The man with the skull—no names: the missionaries; the government—demonstrated the value of the powerful skull. He rolled out a palm mat and law down with his head balanced atop the blackened skull. It did not look like a comfortable way to nap.

During sleep, I had read, a man is most vulnerable to the evil influence of the spirit world. Therefore it is wise to keep a skull nearby during sleep. Men formerly slept in the yew using the powerful skulls of their ancestors, or their enemies, as pillows. Across the rotting boardwalk, a man's rich baritone voice called out a long, sing-song lament. And then, from twenty houses, the sobs and shrieks and wails began anew. I stared at the man on the mat, whose eyes were closed and who might have actually been asleep. He seemed perfectly serene.

~~~~~~

We were well above Kaima and had been motoring against the current for ten hours. Here, about 250 miles upriver, the villages generally consisted of a yew and four or five huts. They were separated, one from the other, by twenty or thirty or fifty miles. There had been two short afternoon rainstorms, tropical downpours accompanied by rumbling, ominous thunder. The sky was all rainbows and brushed Wagnerian clouds. The forecast overhung the river and it seemed to me, in my ignorance, all of a piece: unvariegated greenery.

The river was flowing down to the now distant sea at about three or four miles an hour, but it looked sluggish, weighted down with brown silt, and its surface was a viscous brown mirror reflecting the overhanging greenery and the operatic sky. Yellow leaves, like flowers, floated among the reflected clouds. A swirling mass of neon-bright blue butterflies swept across our bow in a psychedelic haze. The world felt like the inside of a greenhouse, and the air was heavy with moisture and the fragrance of orchids.

A snowy egret kept pace with the boat, and blue-gray herons, looking vaguely prehistoric, rose from the banks of the river in a series of horrid strangled croaks. In the forest, cockatoos screeched loudly enough to be hear over the laboring of our kerosene engine. The cockatoos bickered among themselves: ridiculous, self-important dandies with their white feathers and marching-band topknots.

Chris and I bickered with a good deal more dignity, I thought. He likes to sing, and has a completely monotonous voice, which is entirely beside the point. The point is—and this can't be stressed too strongly—*Chris Ranier gets the words wrong.*

"Wooly wooly, bully bully . . ."

"Chris."

"What?"

"It's Wooly bully, wooly bully."

"That's what I was singing."

"You weren't. You were singing, 'Wooly wooly, bully bully.'"

"'Wooly wooly, bully bully?'"

"Yeah. 'Wooly wooly, bully bully.' Not 'Wooly bully, wooly bully.'"

In the midst of this perfectly asinine conversation, William erupted in a convulsive sneezing snort, followed by a series of high pitched wails. And then Stef and Conrados buried their heads in their hands and wailed, as if in helpless grief.

"Bully bully," Chris sang. "wooly wooly."

I moved to the bow of the boat and sat sulking about this insult to Sam the Sham when what appeared to be the soggy brown remnant of some flood-filled tree suddenly disappeared from the surface of the river with a faint splash, and a swirl of bubbles.

Crocodiles were once plentiful in these rivers, and local people considered them something of a bother. One famous beasty took up residence near the Asmat village of Piramat and killed fifty-five human beings before it, in turn, was killed in 1970. The animal was twenty-three feet long.

These days, crocs are seldom seen in the larger rivers. They were hunted for their hides in the late 1970s, and now, William said, they are usually found only in narrow backwaters, deep in the swamp.

Just before sunset we passed a village where a thin, attenuated man who might have been painted by El Greco paddled out to sell William some fish in exchange for a quarter-pound of tobacco. It cost another quarter pound of the stuff to buy a large black bird with a blue mane like a stiff doily that ran from just above its eyes to the black of its neck. The bird was about the size of a large duck. It had bright red eyes with black pupils. William said the bird was mambruk and that it was going to be our dinner. I thought: I can't eat this. It would be like chomping down on the goddamn *Mona Lisa*.

The water took on the impressionistic pinks and yellows of a pastel sunset, so the reflected greenery on its surface was alive with color. Our wake, in the pink-yellow water, was for a moment bloodred.

There was a half moon already rising in the pastel sky. A huge bat, the size of a goose, passed overhead and was silhouetted against the moon. These mammals, sometimes called flying foxes, are nothing like the horrors in Grandma's attic. They're actually kind of cute, with velvety foxlike faces, and they fly in straight lines or great curving swoops, beating their wings slowly, with eerie deliberation, like pelicans. I caught the acrid stench of ammonia bat droppings—and guessed that the fly foxes probably roosted in some nearby trees. And then there were hundreds more of them, passing across the moon, in the final dying of the light.

~~~~~~

The river was milky in the moonlight, incredibly bright against the black forest that blotted out the sky to either side. Stef knelt in the bow of the boat, watching for floating logs and fallen trees. It seemed to me that some of the logs simply swam away, though the rippling lunar ribbon that stretched out ahead of us set the mind whirling through various fandangos of fancied dread.

Senggo, the only upriver settlement marked on most maps, was a neatly arranged village of about twenty houses positioned face-to-face across a muddy raised-grass track flanked by irrigation ditches on both sides. The place was quite "modern" by William's definition: clapboard houses; tin roofs; a two-story residence; two homes with glass windows; latrines built over deeply dug trenches; large, adequately drained agricultural projects; a resident missionary; and even a policeman available to stamp and sign our *surat jalan* (literally: "travel letter") in exchange for only a very minor bribe.

No one seemed particularly concerned when I told them we were going up-river to see the Karowai, though nuances of meaning were a bit difficult to discern with my Indonesian vocabulary of about a hundred words.

"*Karowai bagus orang-orang?*"

No, they're not good.

"*Karowai tidak bagus orang-orang?*"

No, they're not bad.

"*Apa?*"

They're Karowai.

The storekeeper—he stocked bottled water, Lux soap, canned corned beef, sardines, margarine, T-shirts, towels, and shorts—welcomed us into his home, where we slept, sweating, on rattan mats as clouds of mosquitoes had their bloody way with us.

A goodly number of roosters spent the entire evening practicing for the dawn, so we were up before first light and back out onto the river at sunrise. A horde of schoolchildren stood on the dock and shouted good-byes. We had spent almost twelve hours in the company of dozens of people. The Stone Age was only a few more days upriver.

William spent several hours teaching me to finally see the swamp. The tall trees? The ones over there that grow from a single white-barked trunk and have elephant ear size leaves? Those are called sukun, and the Karowai eat fruit, which is a little like coconut.

Stands of bamboo often grew on the banks of the river, in a green starburst pattern that arched out over the water. Banana trees also grew in a starburst pattern of wide, flat leaves. They reached heights of seven or eight feet, and yielded small three-and four-inch-long bananas.

Rattan, a long, tough vine used to lash homes together, to string bows, or to tie off anything that needed tying—the local equivalent of duct-tape—was identifiable as a slender, leafless branch, generally towering up out of a mass of greenery like an antenna.

Sago, the staple food, was a kind of palm tree that grew twenty to thirty feet high, in a series of multiple stems that erupted out of a central base in another starburst pattern. The leaves were shaped like the arching banana leaves but were arranged in fronds.

When sago trees are cut, William explained, the trunks are split open and an ironwood stick is used to pry out the pith, which is forced through a fiber screen to separate the fibrous material from the sappy juice. The juice is a stick blue-gray starchy fluid, about the consistency of library glue, and the Karowai eat it every day of their lives.

The pith is pounded into a starchy extract that looks like a ball of chalk. It can be baked into a kind of doughy bread. A single sago tree yields about seventy pounds of starch. Karowai villages are located near large stands of sago.

So—sukum, rattan, bamboo, banana, sago—the forest was no longer a mass of unvariegated green. Naming things allowed me to see them, to differentiate one area of the swamp from another. I found myself confirming my newfound knowledge at every bend in the river. "Banana, banana," I informed everyone. "Sukum, sago, sago, rattan, sago, bamboo . . ."

William, like any good teacher, seemed proud enough of my accomplishment for the first half hour or so, then the process began to wear on him. I was like some five-year-old on a drive in the country, pointing out every cow in the pasture to his weary parents.

~~~~~~

A river lunch: one nice hot sun-baked tin of dog-food-like corned beef with a rather mournful-looking cow on the label, a little of last night's rice, a couple of pygmy bananas. Mash it all up in a bowl, and watch the egret above, impossibly white against the blue of the sky and the green of the sago. When the outboard began to splutter, Conrados stopped abruptly, in midriver and began to tinker. It was unbearably hot, well over 100 degrees, and I broached the idea of a brief swim. The possible presence of crocodiles was debated. I reminded William that there were hardly any left. He reminded me that we had seen at least one the day before. Stef, standing on the gunwale of the boat, settled the debate with a front flip into the silt-laded brown water, and then, somehow, we were all in the river, splashing each other like children, surely immortal (it couldn't happen to *me*), and secure in the knowledge that the resident crocs would take someone else, a fact that would certainly sadden those of us who survived. And besides, it was *incredibly hot*.

Sometime later that afternoon, after Conrados cured the Yamaha, we traded a length of fishing line and a dozen hooks for what William assured us was *the* culinary treat: two pounds of fat sago beetle larvae wrapped in sago leaves and secured with a thin strip of rattan. The maggoty-looking creatures were white, with brown heads, and about the size of my little finger to the second knuckle. William mimed popping one into his mouth, nodded, made a yummy-yummy sort of face, and sneezed out his good-natured laugh.

He apparently thought I'd be horrified at the idea of eating bugs. In point of fact, I'd rather eat bugs than that damn beautiful bird we had devoured the night before.

We passed men standing on the rafts of five or six large logs, stripped of the branches and peeled of their bark. The logs were roped together with thick strands rattan. Further upriver, the rafts were larger: twenty or thirty or even eighty logs. Sometimes there was a small A-frame shelter made of sukun sticks and sago leaves on the rafts.

The logs, I learned, were floated down the Senggo from here—one man said it would take about four days—where they were purchased by "men from the Java" for 5,000 rupees apiece, about $2.50.

At the next raft, one of the larger ones, William had Conrados turn back, and we picked up one of the loggers, a thin young man named Agus. He was wearing a gray-tattered T-shirt and shorts. He was, William explained, one of his Karowai friends and our local contact.

~~~~~~

The Karowai village, situated on a bend of the river, was a miniature Senggo: just a few houses on stilts facing one another across a raised path, and a flooded-out field of yams where a few men with metal shovels were digging drainage ditches. It occurred to me that cannibals aren't generally interested in yams. A blackboard in one of the open-sided buildings probably functioned as a community center and school. The men, about a dozen of them, wore shorts, and the women wore knee length grass skirts. There were no tree houses in evidence. It seemed, all in all, a fairly civilized sort of place here in the hell of the south.

And the people, once they learned we had tobacco to trade for a place to sleep, welcomed us as brothers. Chris and I were assigned a private room in the men's house, but I felt like wandering around a bit. I saw Agus chattering urgently with a local man who wore an earring fashioned from the silver pull-tab from a softdrink can. The pull-tab glittered in the slanting light of the late afternoon sun. The man nodded several times, then dashed off, at a dead run, into the forest. The entire encounter had looked vaguely conspiratorial.

Stef cooked a dinner of fried catfish, along with a healthy portion of sago beetle. The larvae were fried brown in the pan. They were crisp and sort of fish-tasting on the outside, probably because they had been sautéed in fish oil. Inside, the larvae were the color and consistency of custard. They were unlike anything I'd ever eaten before, and the closest I can come to describing the taste is to say creamy snail.

The people in this village, I told William after dinner, weren't the Karowai I had read about in Muller's book.

"Change is very quick now," William reminded me. Two years earlier, just after Muller published his book, the government had instituted a program designed to stop ritual warfare among the Karowai and to get people to stop eating each other. They had summoned all the Karowai chiefs and provided transportation down the Senggo, where everyone could see the tangible benefits of civilization, like canned corned beef and Batman T-shirts. If the chiefs would agree to end their deadly feuds, the government would help them. It would provide agricultural experts, and it would help the people build grand towns like Senggo. We were, William explained, staying in one such town.

There were, however, still people who lived in trees. They built their houses deep in the swampy forest, well away from the river, which meant well away from the government and well away from the missionaries. Tomorrow we'd take a nice little stroll through the swamp and meet them. William said that Agus lived there, in one of the tree houses. When he wasn't logging.

"Where?" I asked. "Which way?"

William pointed off in the direction that the pull-tab man had taken. And it became clear to me that Agus wanted his relatives to know that we were coming. The message was probably something like: "Yo, we got honkies; hide the heads."

We didn't actually stroll through the swamp; the forest floor was a mass of knee-high grasses, spongy marsh, and low bushes. The understory hid an uneven surface, full of brackish potholes and unexpected tussocks. The exposed roots of larger trees humped up out of the ground in a series of ankle-breaking traps. It was much easier, all in all, to walk on fallen trees that happened to point in the right general direction, and it was not easy to walk on the fallen trees at all. The larger ones were slippery with moss and the smaller ones tended to crumble under my weight.

I thought, as soon as we get through this shit, we'll be on the trail. About an hour later it occurred to me that this shit *was* the trail. Fallen trees were the equivalent of Agat's wooden walkways.

William cut me a good walking stick, which was helpful. I like the stick and thought of it as a scepter, a symbol of my dignity: Behold, it is Tripod, Mighty Jungle Walker. Prolonged log walking is a bit like riding a bicycle: Speed equals stability. And I was, in fact, moving pretty fast on a large mossy log that spanned the narrowest section of a deep, foul-smelling scummy black pond when William and Stef and Conrados and Agus all began screaming, "Sago, sago, sago!"

"I see it," I called back. The sago tree was at the end of my log, on the bank of the bond, and I leaned out to grab it, because I was going just a little too fast.

"*Tidak!*" No!

The trunk of the sago palm, I discovered to my regret is the vegetable equivalent of a porcupine. They are thorny sons of bitches, sago, palms, extremely uncomfortable to grab for stability on mossy logs, and I had to listen to William sneeze about this prickly lesson, on and off, for over an hour.

And, of course, it rained on us. And then we could see the arc of a rainbow through the trees, and then it rained again, and suddenly we were in a large clearing surrounded by tall white-barked trees 150 feet high. In the middle of the clearing, fifty feet in the air, was a house with open sides and a thatched roof. The main support, set directly in the middle of the floor, was one of the white-barked giants that had been cut off at the fifty-foot level. The corners of the house were supported by convenient smaller trees and stout bamboo poles. The floor, I could see, was made of crossed sticks of sukun, and the thatch was sago frond.

There was a bamboo ladder up to about the twenty-five-foot level and that gave way to a thick rounded pole with notches for steps. Agus shouted some words in Karowai. Someone shouted back from above. There seemed to be a bit of negotiation going on. Mosquitoes in thick clouds attacked those of us on the ground. They were very naughty, and probably malarial.

And then I was clambering up the bamboo ladder and making my careful way up the notched pole. There were nine people sitting on the platform: two-infants, two nursing mothers in knee length grass skirts, two little boys about three and four, one boy about nine, and two naked men, each of whom had a leaf tied tightly around his penis. There was no one who might have been a grandmother or grandfather. Anthropologists who have studied tree dwellers on the nearby Brazza River figure the average life expectancy of these semi-nomadic hunters and gatherers is about thirty-five years.

One of the men, Samu, wore a ring of bamboo in his nasal septum and a double ring of rattan through the sides of his nostrils. He was, William said, the chief of this house. Three families lived here, and each of the three men had two wives.

The tree-house platform was rectangular: about twenty feet by twenty-five. The bones of several small fish hung from the ceiling, secured by rattan strings. I saw no human skulls, but there were dozens of arrows fitted into the ceiling and piled in the corners. There were two fires—a men's fire and a women's fire—and both were built on bed of small rocks over a reinforced triple-thick area of flooring. The children sat with the women, around the women's fire.

Agus and William continued to negotiate with the Karowai men. We were not the first white people these tree dwellers had ever seen. The year before, William had brought in two European groups, seven people, though no one ever stayed for more than a few hours. We wanted to hang out for a day or so, stay the night, shoot the shit. Which complicated matters.

In his two previous visits, William had learned precisely what the Karowai require in terms of trade goods. The swamp here does not yield good stone, and in the very near past, the Karowai had had to trade with outside tribes for stone axes. We had steel axes for them (I could see another steel ax set in a corner of the platform, next to an ironwood bow with a rattan pull-string and a set of arrows made from reeds and tipped with sharpened bone).

Aside from the axes, the Karowai were pleased to accept fishing line, metal hooks, salt, matches, rice, and tobacco. These were acceptable gifts, much admired and appreciated. We were welcomed to stay the night. They didn't accept credit cards here at the Karowai Hilton.

Samu, as headman, got first crack at our tobacco. He packed the rough-cut leaf into the end of a narrow bamboo tube, which fit into a wider tube that was etched in geometric red-and-white designs. He put the wide tube in his mouth, placed the narrow end against a hot rock, inhaled, then rocked back onto his heels. His face was beatific.

One of the women, Pya, reached up into a string bag hanging from the roof of the house, fished around a bit, and came up with a white ball of sago pith, which she dropped onto the embers of her fire. After a short time, I was offered a piece the size of a tennis ball. The food had the consistency of doughy bread and was very nearly tasteless. The term "half-baked" kept clattering through my mind, but I smiled and complimented Pya on her culinary skills. I used one of the few words of Karowai that I knew.

"Manontrohan." Very good.

It was the first word I had uttered in the tree house, and as soon as it tumbled out of my mouth, I wanted to call it back, because it was, of course, a lie. The older of the two men, Samu, stared at me. His expression was that of a man whose intelligence had been insulted. Sago? Good? People eat this soggy crap every day. All the time. They do not sit down for regular meals, but eat only when they have to, because there is no pleasure in the taste of sago. They eat it because there is nothing else. Good? It's not good, you imbecile. It's sago.

I felt chastened and reluctant to say anything else, maybe for the rest of my life. It was better to just sit there and pull sago thorns out of my hand with my teeth.

The Karowai exchanged a few words. There was a failed attempt to remain dispassionate, and then all of them were laughing. The laughter was aimed at Chris and me. This familiar teasing and testing of strangers seems to be a universal human trait, and Chris, in his many travels, has learned to defuse it by laughing right along with everyone else. My strategy exactly. Soon enough the laughter became genuine, and we were all giggling and poking one another in the hilarity of the mutual insecurity.

There was a nice breeze fifty feet above the ground, and no mosquitoes at all. Chris asked William if the Karowai live in trees to avoid mosquitoes. William transferred the question to Agus, who was learning Indonesian, and Agus—although he knew the answer—respectfully asked Samu. Samu nodded and said a single word in Karowai.

And the answer came back—Karowai to Indonesian to English: "Yes."

There was a very long silence.

Samu finally added that it was also safer in the tree, by which he meant, I think, that in this boggy flatland the tree house had the military significance of being high ground. A single man with a bow and a sufficient supply of arrows could hold the fort against any number of similarly equipped attackers. There were even strategic holes in the floor, places where a skilled archer could pick off anyone foolish enough to try to hack down the columns that support the house.

"So there's still war?" I asked.

Samu's reaction might have been a case study for Psychology 101: Here, students, is a man about to tell a lie. The chief shifted his gaze, he stared at the ground, he coughed lightly and occupied himself for some time bringing up a great gob of phlegmy spit that he lofted off into the forest below.

"No," he said finally. No more war.

William took a hit of tobacco from Samu's pipe and attempted to defuse the situation with what he took to be an innocuous question. Where did Samu get his penis leaves? There was a strong bag full of them hanging from the roof.

Samu fidgeted uncomfortably, stared at the ground, coughed again, spat again, and finally allowed that he didn't actually recall where he got the leaves.

I thought: God knows, Samu, your secret would be safe with us. The pure hard fact of the matter was that Samu would likely lose his leaves to one of the massive timbering operations now just cranking up in the Asmat. Indeed, only three years earlier, Agus had lived in this very tree house. Now he had given up his penis leaf for shorts and a T-shirt that read PIECE. It was a simple, sad irony: Agus, having encountered civilization in the person of William two years ago, was now cutting down the forest that had fed him and his people for centuries.

Agus used the money he made to buy steel axes. Generally, the Karowai move every two years, after they have exhausted the local sago. It takes about a month to build a new tree house. With a steel ax, the process takes only two weeks.

The Karowai didn't like coffee or tea, but they craved tobacco. Traditionally, they had smoked dry bark.

And rice! When William fixed Agus his first bowl of rice, the Karowai had burst into tears, it was so good. It was William who had brought him all these things, awakened him to the world as it existed beyond his village: showed him steel axes and rice and matches and canned corned beef. And though Agus and William were about the same age, Agus called his benefactor Father. He was a sweet man, Agus, ambitious and bewildered at the same time. He wept every time William had to go away.

"I get the leaves," Samu said by way of accommodation to the question that had been asked some time ago, "from the trees." He nodded out toward the forest.

And then there was another long silence. Several hours' worth of it. The Karowai seemed perfectly comfortable just sitting around, smoking, enjoying their company in a haze of tobacco smoke and self-contained neolithic composure. I, on the other hand, felt constrained to fill up the fleeting hours with productive activity. To that end, I spent a good deal of time scribbling in my notebook:

- Karowai culture
  - Inappropriate comments
    - Eat me
    - Sago is good
  - Inappropriate questions
    - Been in any wars lately?
    - Where you guys get those dick leaves?
  - Inappropriate subject matter
    - Cannibal jokes
  - Appropriate behavior
    - Sitting in a hunkering squat
    - Smoking
    - Spitting
    - Being silent
    - Keeping the fire going
    - Tending to the fussy child or infant
    - Smiling dreamily for no particular reason

About midafternoon, unable to sit still any longer, Chris and William and I took a walk through the swamp to visit one of Samu's neighbors. It was another hour or so to a second clearing, where there was another tree house, which was probably only thirty-five or forty feet high. Our host was named Romas, and he had a pair of what appeared to be red toothpicks sticking out of the top of his nose. The toothpicks were, in fact, bones from the wing of a flying fox, colored reddish brown in the smoke from the fire.

There were fish bones hanging from the ceiling, as in the first Karowai house, along with a turtle shell and a number of pig jaws hanging from a rattan rope. We had a long conversation about these trophies, which seemed a little anemic to me. The fish looked like ten-inchers, little guys, but the Karowai-to-English translation suggested that they were, in fact, the remnants of memorable meals. When Samu came to visit, Romas said, his neighbor always noticed a new set of bones. And the needlelike bones, going dark red in the smoke from the fires, became an occasion to engage in hunting stories. They were, these pathetic remains, conversation pieces. Interior decorating.

Against one wall was a war shield, four feet high, decorated in geometric designs, colored white and red. Next to the shield were several bows and several bunches of arrows, all of which were unnotched and unfeathered, so that when Romas allowed me to fire one off into the forest, it began to wobble after only fifty feet or so. The arrows do not fly true for very long, which is probably not much of a problem in the forest, where there are no long vistas. Some of the arrows were tipped with cassowary bones. Cassowary are ostrichlike birds whose powerful legs end in claws that are capable of disemboweling a man. Next to the armaments were several seven-foot-long tubes of bamboo that contained drinking water.

The men in the tree house assured me that we were not disrupting them in the least and that they were doing what they ordinarily would be doing, which was precisely what everyone in Samu's house was doing. Romas reached into the embers of his fire and pulled out a bug that looked a good deal like a large iridescent grasshopper. He stripped off the wings and popped it into his mouth, like a piece of candy.

I was given a wooden bowl of the blue-gray glue that is sago sap. Sago, in fact, was all I'd had to eat over the past twenty hours. It wasn't unpleasant, just tasteless, and I fully understood why a man who had eaten nothing else in his life would burst into tears over a bowl of rice.

Romas said he hunted wild pig and cassowary. He also ate bananas, cassowary eggs, insects, and small lizards. The only sure thing to eat, however, the only dependable crop, was sago. Sago sap. Sago pulp. An endless diet of sago.

It rained three times that afternoon, and each downpour lasted about half an hour. In the forest there was usually a large-leafed banana tree with sheltering leaves where everyone could sit out the rain in bitter communion with the local mosquitoes.

Just at twilight, back in Samu's house, where everyone was sitting around eating what everyone always ate, a strong breeze began to rattle the leaves of the larger trees. The wind came whistling through the house, and it brought more rain, cooling rain, so that, for the first time that day, I stopped sweating. My fingers looked pruney, as if I had been in the bath too long.

Samu squatted on his haunches, his testicles inches off the floor. The other man, Gehi, sat with his back to the wall, his gnarled callused feet almost in the fire. It was very pleasant, and no one had anything to say.

After the rain, as the setting sun colored the sky, I heard a gentle cooing from the forest: mambruk. The sky was still light, but the forest was already dark.

Hundreds of fireflies were moving rapidly through the trees.

William rigged up a plastic tarp so the Karowai could have some privacy. Chris and I could hear him chatting with Samu and Gehi. They were talking about tobacco and salt, about steel axes and visitors.

Chris said, "I don't want them to change."

We watched the fireflies below. They were blinking in unison now, dozens on a single tree.

"Do you think that's paternalistic?" he asked. "Some new politically correct form of imperialism?"

"I don't know," I said.

But I thought about it. I thought about it all night long. When you suspect that your hosts have eaten human flesh in the very recent past, sleep does not come easily. It seemed to me that I was out of the loop here, not a part of the cycle of war and revenge, which was all just as well. I had expected to meet self-sufficient hunter-gatherers, and the Karowai were all of that, but they wanted more. They wanted steel axes, for instance, and did not equate drudgery with any kind of nobility.

I tried to imagine myself in an analogous situation. What would I want?

What if some alien life force materialized on earth with a superior medical technology, for instance? They have the cure for AIDS, for cancer, but they feel it is best that we go on as we have. They admire the spiritual values we derive from our suffering; they are inspired by our courage, our primitive dignity. In such a case, I think I'd do everything in my power to obtain that technology—and the hell with my primitive dignity.

I thought about Asmat art and what is left in the world that is worth dying for. I thought about Agus, who wept over his first bowl of rice and whose first contact with the outside world set him up in the business of cutting down the forest that had fed him all his life.

I thought about the butterfly I had caught when I was a child. My grandmother told me never to do it again. She said that butterflies have a kind of powder on their wings and that when you touch them, the powder comes off in your hand and the butterfly can't fly anymore. She said that when you touch a butterfly, you kill it.

Butterfly; Karowai.

Sometime just before dawn, I heard a stirring from the Karowai side of the house. Samu moved out from behind the plastic tarp and blew on the embers of his fire. Gehi joined him. The two naked men squatted on their haunches, silent, warming themselves against the coolest part of the forest day. Presently, the stars faded and the eastern sky brightened with the ghostly light of false dawn.

A mist roped up off the forest floor, a riotous floral scent rising with it, so I had a sense that it was the fragrance itself that tinged this mist with the faint colors of forest flowers. The mist seemed the stuff of time itself, and time smelled of orchids.

As the first hints of yellow and pink touched the sky, I saw Samu and Gehi in silhouette: two men, squatting by their fire, waiting for the dawn.

(Originally published October 1992)

CHERNOBYL, MY PRIMEVAL, TEEMING, IRRADIATED EDEN

HENRY SHUKMAN

When the Chernobyl nuclear plant melted down in 1986, it drove 60,000 people from their homes in the Ukraine. Twenty-five years later, we sent Shukman to report on the surprising rebirth taking place inside the exclusion zone, an enchanted post-apocalyptic forest from which entirely new species may soon emerge.

The wild boar is standing 30 or 40 yards away, at the bottom of a grassy bank, staring right at me. Even from this distance I can see its outrageously long snout, its giant pointed ears, and the spiny bristles along its back. It looks part porcupine, a number of shades of ocher and gray. And it's far bigger than I expected, maybe chest-high to a man. The boar is like some minor forest god straight from the wilderness, gazing wild-eyed at the strange spectacle of a human being. For a moment it seems to consider charging me, then thinks better of it. When it trots away, it moves powerfully, smoothly, on spindly, graceful legs twice as long as a pig's, and vanishes into the trees.

I climb back into our VW van, tingling all over. The sighting bodes well. I've come to what is being dubbed Europe's largest wildlife refuge in early July, when I knew spotting animals wouldn't be so easy. (Winter, with its scarcity of food and lack of foliage, makes them more visible.) And within a couple of hours I've ticked a wild boar off the list. Maybe luck is on our side.

But luck isn't our only obstacle to wildlife spotting here. This is northern Ukraine's Chernobyl Exclusion Zone, a huge area, some 60 miles across in places, that's been off-limits to human habitation since 1986. Even now, 19 years after the collapse of the USSR, nothing happens in this former Soviet republic without sheets of paper typed and stamped in quintuplicate. It took months of e-mails and phone calls to get permission to spend a few days here. Yes, we're only a couple of foreign vagabonds—photographer Rory Carnegie is an old travel buddy of mine from England—but we have cameras and a telephoto lens, and my notepad has lines in it: obviously we're spies. The Soviet Union may have died, but the Soviet mind-set has not.

At the Chernobyl Center, a kind of makeshift reception building in the heart of the old town, I had to hand over a solid nine inches of local bills—hryvnia, pronounced approximately like the sound of a cardsharp riffling a deck—sign a stack of agreements, compliances, and receipts, and then get checked on an Austin Powers–style Geiger counter made out of chrome. Finally, under the protection of a guide, a driver, and an interpreter, we were free to set off into the zone—as long as we did exactly what our guide said.

A handful of dilapidated roads cross the zone, half-overgrown with weeds and grasses, and the whole area is littered with pockets of intense radiation, but nature doesn't seem to mind. All nature seems to care about is that the people, along with their domestic animals, are for the most part gone. The zone is reverting to one big, untamed forest, and it all sounds like a fantastic success story for nature: remove the humans and the wilderness bounces right back. Lured by tales of mammals unknown in Europe since the Dark Ages, we're setting out on an atomic safari.

It was soon after 1 A.M. on the night of April 26, 1986, that one of the world's nightmare scenarios unfolded. Reactor 4 in the huge Chernobyl power station blew up. The causes are still the subject of debate, but it was some combination of a design flaw involving the control rods that regulate reactor power levels, a poorly trained engineering crew, a test that required a power-down of the reactor, and a dogged old-style Soviet boss who refused to believe anything major could be wrong. At any rate, it was spectacular. Eight-hundred-pound cubes of lead were tossed around like popcorn. The 1,000-ton sealing cap was blown clear off the reactor. A stream of raspberry-colored light shone up into the night sky—ionized air, so beautiful that inhabitants of the nearby city of Pripyat came out to stare. When it was all over, estimates former deputy chief engineer Grigori Medvedev, the radioactive release was ten times that of Hiroshima.

Chernobyl had been a mostly peaceful settlement for 1,000 years and a predominantly Jewish town for the past three centuries, famous for its dynasty of Hasidic sages. Since the Russian Revolution, the Jews have thinned a lot, but even today there are two shrines to the Hasidim where once a year devotees come to light candles and pray. It's incredible what survives a disaster. As Emily Dickinson said, "How much can come and much can go, and yet abide the world."

In 1970, nine miles from the town, the Soviet Union started building what they hoped would become Europe's largest nuclear power station. (Only four of the planned eight reactors had been completed when disaster struck.) To go with it, they erected a brand-new concrete city, Pripyat, whose 50,000 inhabitants greatly outnumbered the 12,000 living in Chernobyl. The nuclear industry fell under the military complex, and the traditional Soviet culture of secrecy was all over it. Radiation is bad enough, but compound it with Soviet pride and paranoia and you have a potent mix of Kafka and Ray Bradbury.

The first the rest of the world knew of the Chernobyl disaster was when workers at a Swedish power station more than 1,000 miles away reported for work two days later, checked themselves with a Geiger counter, and found they were highly radioactive. By the following day, April 29, radioactive clouds had been carried by prevailing winds right across Western Europe and into Scandinavia, and *The New York Times* ran a front-page story about the catastrophe. The Soviet newspaper *Pravda* devoted a full eight lines to the "accident" that day—on its third page. It wasn't till May 15, three weeks later, that General Secretary Mikhail Gorbachev finally announced what had happened.

Thirty people died on the night of the explosion or soon after. Two days later, a convoy of 1,100 buses shipped out all the inhabitants of Pripyat, turning it into a ghost city overnight. The vast might of the Soviet Union went into overdrive with a massive cleanup operation involving 600,000 workers. A layer of topsoil was removed for miles around the site. (The government has not said where it went, but many believe it was dumped in the nearby Dnieper River, where silt would have buried it.) Hundreds of thousands of trees were planted, to bind the ground and reduce the spread of radioactive dust.

But the cleanup turned out to be even more lethal than the explosion itself. Soldiers were offered two years off their service in exchange for just two minutes shoveling nuclear waste. Thousands of people won medals for bravery and were declared Heroes of the Soviet Union but at the same time picked up cancer and thyroid problems that would dog them for the rest of their lives. Thousands of evacuated locals and cleanup workers are said to have died in the ensuing years from radiation doses, and it's reckoned that some 2.7 million people alive today in Ukraine, Belarus, and Russia have been directly affected by it.

In the following weeks, bureaucrats in Moscow designated an 1,100-square-mile Exclusion Zone—roughly the size of Yosemite—reasoning that the farther from Chernobyl people were, the better. This is mostly true: almost all of the crew working at the reactor when it blew died within a few weeks, as did several of the firemen who arrived on the scene minutes later, but the backup laborers who got there later mostly survived, albeit with dire health problems.

In all, two towns and an estimated 91 villages were emptied. But radiation doesn't travel consistently or evenly. If radioactive dust is picked up by a cloud, it will fall where the rain falls. There are still parts of Wales where the sheep farmers can't sell their meat, and last summer thousands of wild boars hunted in Germany were declared dangerously radioactive.

Today, around 5,000 people work in the Exclusion Zone, which over the years has grown to an area of 1,660 square miles. For one thing, you can't just switch off a nuclear power plant. Even decommissioned, it requires maintenance, as does the new nuclear-waste storage facility on site. The workers come in for two-week shifts and receive three times normal pay. Any sign of disease at the annual medical, however, and they lose their jobs.

There are also some 300 people living in the zone: villagers who've been coming home to their old farming lands since not long after the disaster and teams of radioecologists from around the world who've come to study the effects of radioactive fallout on plants and animals. They've effectively turned the zone into a giant radiation lab, a place where the animals are mostly undisturbed, living amid a preindustrial number of humans and a postapocalyptic amount of radioactive strontium and cesium. On the outside the fauna seems to be thriving: there have been huge resurgences in the numbers of large mammals, including gray wolves, brown bears, elk, roe deer, and wild boar present in quantities not recorded for more than a century. The question scientists are trying to answer is what's happening on the inside: in their bones, and in their very DNA.

Once you enter the Zone, the quiet is a shock. It would be eerie were it not so lovely. The abandoned backstreets of Chernobyl are so overgrown, you can hardly see it's a town. They've turned into dark-green tunnels buzzing with bees, filled with an orchestral score of birdsong, the lanes so narrow that the van pushes aside weeds on both sides as it creeps down them, passing house after house enshrined in forest. Red admirals, peacock butterflies, and some velvety brown lepidoptera are fluttering all over the vegetation. It looks like something out of an old Russian fairy tale.

Ukraine officially opened Chernobyl up to tourism in January 2011, but small groups have been able to visit the zone for the past few years. There are small tour operators based in Kiev that take visitors on day trips. You don't need Geiger counters or special suits; you just have to stay with the tour, pass through several checkpoints, and get tested for radiation on your way out. The tours will shuttle you around some of the main sites—the deserted city of Pripyat, a small park filled with old Soviet army vehicles used in the cleanup, various concrete memorials to the fire crews who lost their lives after the blast. Visitors are strictly confined to areas the authorities have scanned and declared safe.

Staying longer than a day is more complicated. The Chernobyl Center has a guesthouse where nonofficial visitors like us can stay and be fed delicious if over-priced Ukrainian stews and escalopes. At sundown each evening there's a curfew. Walk to the nearby shop where the local workers buy their beer and bread and you could get yourself arrested.

Chaperoning Rory and me at the center and on our daily excursions is our guide, Sergey. He lives in a town near Kiev, but for the past ten years he's been spending two weeks out of every four in the zone, showing visiting scientists and the odd tourist around. Sergey is a tough, taciturn guy who looks like an old sergeant major, with a silver mustache and a head of cropped white hair. Our plan is to explore the forest, the old town of Chernobyl, the nearby rivers, the empty city of Pripyat, and some villages where a few peasants are still living. One of the papers we had to sign when we entered was an agreement that if we stepped any-where Sergey hadn't told us to, we wouldn't hold the authorities responsible for any health issues.

So far, the only visible sign of radiation has been a digital readout on the mostly deserted post-office building in Chernobyl. Instead of telling the time and tem-perature, it shows the microroentgen levels in different sectors of the zone, which fluctuate according to changes in background radiation and the weather.

The most contaminated of the villages were bulldozed and buried soon after the explosion, with only a few mounds and ridges left to show they were ever there. The meadows are mostly gone, replaced by forest. Russia is a land of forests, but the true forest, the primeval untouched forest that human eyes may never even have seen, is called pushcha—which roughly translates as "dense forest." This is what has been reestablishing itself at Chernobyl, regenerating at an unprecedented rate.

At the edge of Chernobyl, we stop by the half-mile-wide Pripyat River. It's unbelievably peaceful. A black dog, which knows Sergey, slumps down in the grass beside us. A handful of long, stoved-in rowboats moored at the shore take me back to the punts of my Oxford childhood. They're stamped with the initials of the local KGB and must have been moldering here since Soviet times. Frogs plop into the water, boatmen skedaddle across the surface, dragonflies hover—it's like a weight has been lifted from the world. A sparrowhawk turns in lazy circles; a pair of ducks race by, low down, necks stretched, and make it to a willow on the far bank with a clatter of relief.

We pass two brick sheds with padlocks on their doors: the shrines of zaddiks, Jewish wise men.

"Why locked?" I ask Sergey.

Not missing a beat, he says, "Many people don't like Jews." (Something else that survived the apocalypse.)

We meander along the sleepy brown river. The main sounds are the different shades of hissing of wind in the trees: high nearby, deeper and steadier farther away. Occasionally the wind picks up, flicks a ripple along the surface. This must be what life was like 1,000 years ago, when the entire human population of the globe was roughly 250 million. There's space for everyone, time for everything.

On our way down off the bridge, we spot a slender roe deer 200 yards up the road. It stands still a moment, head cocked, then like a sylph it slips into the trees, so swiftly I don't even see it go. A little farther on, we spot an elk between two bushes. He looks at us, head lifted, then strolls out of sight.

The van drops us off at a dark footpath that winds up through the woods, past a chain of collapsed wooden houses. Inside, their floors are littered with clothes, bottles, stuffing from mattresses. Pieces of gutted insulation lie strewn like corpses under the trees. It's not so much a town with trees in it as a forest with an old town falling to pieces within it.

Sergey tells us about the herds of boar he has seen, 50 strong, rampaging through the forest. And about a starving wolf pack that surrounded a scientist friend of his in a wood one winter day. He had to shoot every last one to get away.

It's not just the forest that's come back but all its creatures. It's the land of Baba Yaga, the old witch of Russian folktales. Is this the world before humanity? Or after? Is there a difference?

~~~~~~

Traveling in Ukraine can be quite a party. The Ukrainians prefer not to engage in talk on its own. It's better with a bucket of vodka and a carton of cigarettes.

It's three in the afternoon of our second day when seven of us settle at a make-shift table beneath a spreading mulberry tree in the luscious garden of Ivan Nikola-yevich's home. Officially, no one is supposed to live here, but within a few months of the disaster, several hundred farmers, families like this one, returned to their ancestral homes and have been quietly living here ever since, tolerated by the government and apparently free of any unusual health problems.

We're in the tiny village of Upachich, deep in the zone. There's Ivan himself, dressed in a sleeveless shirt with only one button and a pair of trousers that have seen so much yardwork, he could be a man from any of the past few centuries. When we met him half an hour ago, he had just finished gathering up his small field of hay with a pitchfork, building the kind of hayrick Monet and Van Gogh loved to paint. There's Ivan Ivanovich, his son, who was helping him, with designer stubble and a wristwatch that place him somewhere in the past few decades. The two of them are still dripping and red-faced from their labors. And there's young Ivan's mother, Dasha, wearing a timeless Russian babushka headscarf and a subtle, sublime smile.

It feels like we haven't walked into a home so much as a story by Gogol. Corn-cobs are drying on a line. Indoors, there's a big stove with a built-in shelf on top for sleeping on in winter, buckets of potatoes standing on the floor, scraps for the hens, a basin with its own cistern you fill up from the well.

Ivan the son is busy wiping down the table, spreading out sheets of newspaper for all the foodstuffs: eggs from chickens pecking under our feet, tomatoes from the garden, bread, a bowl of tiny forest raspberries, a whole dried river fish, crystallized and orange from its time smoking in a homemade stove. It's all local and it all looks great, but most tempting of all are the mulberries hanging above my head. They resemble elongated blackberries, and there's something about the way they're growing among the elegant oval leaves of the tree that makes them irresistible. I'm dying to reach up and grab one, but they frighten me. We're only ten miles from the power station.

Whatever you do, friends advised before we came, don't eat anything that grows there.

The older Ivan comes out of the house carrying a glass jar full of clear fluid in his trembling hand.

"Vodka," someone declares appreciatively.

That'll be safe, I think to myself: shop-bought.

"No, no. Samogon," Sergey explains, eyeing the jar with a gleeful twinkle. "Better than vodka."

Samogon?

"Homemade."

My heart sinks. The local moonshine. But before I can ask if it's really safe to drink, we're clinking glasses, wetting our fingers, and I cautiously take a sip.

"You're not exactly drinking as you should," Sergey notes, suggesting that I chug.

"Clean—it must be clean!" declares one of the Ivans.

Sergey is already slamming down his empty glass. What can I do but oblige?

Conversation begins to flow. Sergey starts expatiating on the advantages of village life. "When you want make business, make networking, you live in the city. But here, there is natural food, for example this samogon, it is so good for you."

I'm far from sure, but the dad gets up and shows me round the garden. He wants me to see where the tomatoes grow, and the grapes and vegetables, and where he finds the root he uses in his special medicinal vodka. Swaying, puffing, he pulls up a little plant, then lumbers off to the pond to rinse it: a lump of ginseng.

A couple of samogon shots later, my fears have abated and I'm tucking in like the rest. The fish is so smoky my eyes water, and soon my hands are stained bloodred from all the mulberries I've eaten. A bird starts singing. Flakes of sunshine shift over us. The hay is in, there's a pig fattening for Easter, and the oats are almost ready for the scythe. If this isn't rustic life at its timeless, bibulous best, what is?

***

Most everyone in Chernobyl displays a predictable bravado about living with radiation. In the relative cool of the evening, the workers on their two-week shifts gather outside the guesthouse to sit on tree stumps and chew the fat, drink beer, smoke cigarettes. With a line of dark chestnut trees nearby and the pale night sky overhead, amid the silence and stillness of the deep forest, it's a lovely scene, even with the insistent black mosquitoes that bob around our faces.

"Radiation is good for you," one of them tells me. "Every year I get younger," says another. And another: "I work here so when I come home glowing my wife will think I'm a god."

A particularly hearty-looking man who works as a janitor asks me, "How old do you think I am?"

"Sixty," he answers himself. A preposterous answer: he looks not a day past 30. The best decontamination? "A bottle of vodka."

But radiation is scary. It's particularly scary because it's mostly undetectable to the senses. If you feel sleepy and have a chemical taste in your mouth, it might be because of radiation. If you're able to see it, in the form of purple ionized air—as they did that night in April—or, worse, feel it in the form of instant-tanning heat, it's probably too late for you.

Still, it's a fact of life. We all live under constant radioactive bombardment: there's solar radiation, terrestrial radiation, there's even radiation in our food, since all living things contain radioactive potassium-40 and our food consists mostly of once-living things. There are different units of measurement—like dps, or disintegration per second, and curies, grays, sieverts, rads, rems, roentgens, and so on. The average terrestrial dose is three microrems per hour—but in some parts of the world this goes as high as 100 microrems, with no perceptible ill effects. (In fact, there's some evidence that cancer rates are lower in these areas; perhaps mild stress to the immune system makes it work better.)

A dangerous dose is hard to pin down. Worldwide, for most people, those daily microrems add up to about 360 millirems per year. Scientists agree that humans can safely handle 1,000 a year. Astronauts on the International Space Station receive 18,000 millirems of cosmic radiation over six months—but it's once in a lifetime, so it's seen as an acceptable, voluntary risk. But edge that up to 30,000 millirems and you're looking at what caused increased cancer rates among the blast survivors of Hiroshima and Nagasaki. And yet animals can handle even more than this: large mammals and birds are generally safe with 36,000 per year, small ones with even higher doses, and reptiles with higher still. The more complex the animal, the more sensitive it is.

Nuclear power involves various radioactive substances that differ from the hydrogen isotopes in a modern thermonuclear weapon. There are the fissile materials (which make the reaction happen) like plutonium and uranium, and the fission products (which result from it) like radioactive iodine, cesium-137, and strontium-90. It's these last two, along with some plutonium, that mostly contaminate Chernobyl today. Some emit alpha or beta particles, some gamma rays. Alpha particles have a short range: in air, one to two inches; in skin, one to two thousandths of an inch. So if they're coming from outside you, they can't penetrate your skin. But if inside—if you've eaten something contaminated, for example—they're nasty. Their short range means they're more likely to deposit their energy within a small area—small enough to attack both strands of a DNA molecule, possibly causing cancer. Beta particles, meanwhile, can travel about 20 feet through air and a quarter of an inch through skin; they can't reach internal organs from outside the body. Gamma rays are essentially X rays. They can be more or less penetrating, depending on strength.

The half-lives of radioactive materials vary, too. Cesium's and strontium's are around 30 years, plutonium's is 88 years, but with uranium-238—the base product used to create plutonium—it's more than four billion years. A long half-life means the substance remains radioactive much longer but gives off its radiation more slowly. The half-life of radioactive iodine is only one week, which means it gives off a lot of radiation quickly—another reason the Soviet authorities were so irresponsible in not announcing the Chernobyl disaster sooner: a lot of lethal, iodine-contaminated food got eaten those first few days after the explosion.

All through our trip, Sergey has been telling us how healthy he is, in spite of ten years in the zone. Only at the end will he reveal that he can't run anymore because of pains in his legs. Too much "strontsy," he says. But he's fine, he adds, because the strontsy is only in his muscles, not the bones. Not yet anyway.

One of the workers tells me he doesn't drink, not even beer. "I do sports, so I cannot drink," he says, lighting up another cigarette.

"But what about the radiation?" I ask him.

He shrugs. "Life itself is dangerous, my friend."

~~~~~~

The world beyond the apocalypse may not be so great for humans, but for the other denizens of the planet it looks like a bonanza. Today there are around 5,000 adult wild boars in the Chernobyl Zone. In 1995 there were many more, but they suffered an epidemic and have now stabilized. There are 25 to 30 wolf packs, a total of maybe 180 adults. Many more lynx live here than before, along with foxes, barsuks (a Ukrainian badger), hundreds of red deer, and thousands of roe deer and elk. Out of the disaster comes a paradise of wildlife. The Garden of Eden is regenerating.

But it's not so straightforward.

For 17 years, biologist Igor Chizhevsky has been studying how animals metabolize cesium and strontium. He works with the Chernobyl Radio-Ecological Center and is a friendly, serious, broad-faced man. He has made Chernobyl his career. When he comes to talk with us in the guesthouse, he sits stolidly in an armchair, barely moving at all for an hour, while telling us in a doleful Slavic voice about how things are really going down here for the animals.

When humans abandoned the zone, he says, it wasn't just they and their domestic animals—including 135,000 cattle—that left. The "synanthropic" species that live around humans—pigeons, swallows, rats, and the like—also left the territory in large numbers, leaving it free for a wild ecosystem to reestablish itself.

"Structure of entire fauna system change," Igor says.

House mice, which thrived on grains no longer grown here, have been replaced by forest and field mice. Likewise with the bird species. But it's the larger mammals we're interested in.

On the surface, Igor says, the wildlife seems to be thriving, but under the fur and hide, the DNA of most species has become unstable. They've eaten a lot of food contaminated with cesium and strontium. Even though the animals look fine, there are differences at the chromosomal level in every generation, as yet mostly invisible. But some have started to show: there are bird populations with freakishly high levels of albinism, with 20 percent higher levels of asymmetry in their feathers, and higher cancer rates. There are strains of mice with resistance to radioactivity—meaning they've developed heritable systems to repair damaged cells. Covered in radioactive particles after the disaster, one large pine forest turned from green to red: seedlings from this Red Forest placed in their own plantation have grown up with various genetic abnormalities. They have unusually long needles, and some grow not as trees but as bushes. The same has happened with some birch trees, which have grown in the shape of large, bushy feathers, without a recognizable trunk at all.

"Genomes, er, unpredictable," says Igor. "Genome not exactly same from generation to generation. They change."

This is not good for a species. Genomes are supposed to stay the same. That's what holds a species together. No one knows what these changes could result in.

"Soon or late," Igor says, "new species will evolve."

In other words, new animals could actually be in the making here. The area has become a laboratory of microevolution—"very rapid evolution," says Igor—but no one knows what will emerge or when.

One Stanford scientist I spoke to later had a terse summary: if there are genetic changes, and if these pass down to the next generation, and if they survive natural selection, then it's reasonable to talk of evolution. There are two theories about why this may happen. In classic Darwinism, random genetic changes that help an organism survive in its environment are naturally selected through generations, because the individuals with those characteristics do better. But "mutagenesis," an alternate theory, posits that organisms deliberately adapt to their surroundings. The process is not accidental. For example, in Chernobyl, if mice are developing radiation resistance by passing down cell-repair systems, is that because some individuals just happened to develop this attribute and to fare better, or is it because the species deliberately developed this capacity in response to the environment?

Sergey takes us to a real-life laboratory nearby: just an old house, but inside it's been gutted, and the walls are lined with shelves of cages, each one full of scurrying white mice. A rank stench hits us as soon as we walk in.

The white-coated lab technician—yet another Ivan—notices my grimace and smiles. "Yes," he says. "And we just cleaned the place this morning."

He explains that they're studying the effect on the mice of the radioactive spectrum here in the Chernobyl Zone. They took probes from the Red Forest and re-created the conditions here at the lab, then started giving the mice food laced with cesium and strontium.

Why here? I ask.

"This is already a contaminated area. So we don't risk spreading radiation elsewhere." In other words, the zone has become a kind of refuge for radiation research.

He and his team are studying the mice to understand their resistance to radioactivity. They've found sensitivity to ionization, which results in certain tumors, and some of this passes down through the genes. But they're also finding heritable radiation resistance—which could perhaps be beneficial to humans someday.

In spite of being a clearheaded scientist, Ivan gives us a surprise when asked if he's OK being photographed. He starts laughing nervously. "I'm afraid of American shamans and what they may do to me," he confesses. Apparently, some old-time beliefs are still being inherited around here too, even in a science lab. The Ukrainians are complex people: part Soviet, part soulful Slav, part subsistence farmer. Even this lab has its own vegetable patch out front.

On our last morning I wake up early, and as I lie in my bed at the dorm I hear, quite distinctly, a wolf howling. It holds its note a long time before reaching for a higher one, then a still higher one. It sounds like a healthy howl. But no biologist has yet been able to study these wolves in sufficient numbers to have a clear idea of their genetic health. They know what their bellies are full of, but the meat has its own genetic instability. These wolves may have a vast untracked forest to roam, but what is happening deep in their DNA no one knows. Will there be new species in a few generations? There may already be, out in the forest, and we wouldn't even know.

Later that morning, on our way to the ghost city of Pripyat, we see a fox darting across the road—nothing more than a black silhouette, curiously low to the ground. Or perhaps it was a small wolf, says Sergey. Then a big bird, which turns out to be an eagle, is suddenly ahead of us, grappling with a sapling it has attempted to land on, bending it down low, then letting the young tree spring back up again as it rides away on giant brown wings.

Sergey tells us that Pripyat used to be the most beautiful, spacious city he ever saw. More roses grew there than anywhere else he ever knew. There were never any shortages, and you could get fine clothes, Czech-made shoes. It was a model of what Communism was supposed to have been.

It's weirdly distressing to be here. As a human, it's like staring down the barrel of our likely fate. We may wipe ourselves out with a nuclear holocaust, or with carbon and methane, or some other way we can't yet conceive of. Or nature may do it for us. When it happens, trees may or may not mind. Cyanobacteria poisoned their own atmosphere two and a half billion years ago by releasing vast quantities of a gas that was poisonous to them—oxygen—and in the process created an atmosphere suited to higher forms of land life. Who knows what creatures may adapt to a high-carbon, high-methane atmosphere if we keep going the way we are? They may include us, or not.

From Pripyat we drive on to the old power station itself. It's a large area of vast concrete buildings. One of them is the stricken Reactor 4, some 200 feet tall, with a giant chimney still rising out of it. For almost 25 years it's stood encased in a "sarcophagus" of cement, but the seal is far from perfect, and it leaks dangerously. We park 200 yards away to look at it but stay only a few minutes. A new steel sarcophagus is slowly being built; when finished, it will be the world's largest movable structure.

There are canals threading through the giant buildings, which provided water for the old coolant system, and in one of them the catfish have grown to prodigious sizes. We stop on a metal bridge and gaze down into the brown water. Suddenly the monsters rise to the surface, some of them a good ten feet long, black, whiskered, curling around as they hunt for the bread people feed them.

They're not big because of radiation, Sergey insists. It's just that they haven't been fished for a quarter of a century.

The whole area is like this: fecund, scary. Later Sergey takes us to an army barracks where some soldier friends of his keep a few wild pets. From the dark doorway of one of the sheds issues a terrific subterranean grunt, and a moment later, as if in a hurry, out trots another wild boar. It comes straight at the fence, presses against it with the weird, wet sucker of its long, long nose, then raises its bristly head and eyeballs me as if I'm something from another planet.

In a pen next door there's another forest sprite—the barsuk, a very close relative of our badger. When it comes out of its kennel, it runs up a woodpile, turns at the top, and proceeds to stare right into me with deeply strange eyes. Something in me seems to recognize something in it, and I feel a pang of longing. Is it for the deep forest, the pushcha? For the trees, the smell of autumn leaves, of mushrooms and mold? For the freedom to live our own way, far from society?

Crouching and staring, the barsuk doesn't move a muscle. It could be a stuffed animal, with eyes of glass. Or perhaps a new species, staring at the world with new eyes.

(Originally published February 2011)

HUMBLE IS THE PREY

DAVID QUAMMEN

David Quammen began writing his "Natural Acts" column in Outside *in the 1980s. It became a reader favorite, in large part due to the author's unique ability to reveal the complexity of the natural world with prose that never feels like homework. Take this story. You might be familiar with Komodo dragons, but you've never before read an account of their super-predator abilities like this one.*

The carcass of a freshly killed goat flies through the air, cartwheeling upward and outward over the heads of a phalanx of tourists. Ninety pounds of inert protein, it ascends toward its apogee bearing the weight of a ponderous question: Is there a place in our world for the great flesh-eating predators that make no distinction between goat, deer, and human?

It rises through the hot tropical air above a deep gully, and my attention, until now diverted elsewhere, shifts to fix on it. "The goat," says a voice in my brain. "I didn't realize that they'd *throw* it." Spotlighted by shafts of sunlight penetrating the tamarind trees, it floats through a backward somersault. For an instant it hangs. We tourists, all seventy-some, gape. On one level, what's being offered is just bait. On another, it's a proxy for ourselves. And then the goat falls. It lands with a meaty wallop on bare dirt.

Nine giant reptiles pile onto it like NFL linemen.

Nine giant reptiles snarf and gobble. They chomp. They gorge. They thrash, they scuffle, they tug and twist. They stir up one hellacious ruckus. The goat, or whatever's left of it after a minute of this, is invisible now, and the reptiles have composed themselves into a neat radial pattern, jaw-locked side by side, tails swinging, like a monstrous nine-pointed starfish. Their round-snouted faces, which looked amiable as old work boots until just a moment ago, have gone smeary with blood. When the goat rips in half, they split into two mobs and the tussling continues. They have each seized a mouthful, but the mouthfuls are still held together, barely, by a battered skeleton. They wrestle. They lunge for new jaw-grips and clamp down, straining greedily against the tensile limits of goat bone and sinew. It all happens fast. The lucky ones snatch away big gobbets, swallow hastily, and dive back for more. They climb over one another; foot to face, elbow to eyeball, for second helpings. Their teeth are terrible little knives, serrated along the cutting edge, perfectly suited for slicing out great whonks of meat, yet despite the wild scramble they manage somehow to avoid mutilating one another. They compete madly, but they don't fight. They ignore the five dozen Nikons and Minoltas that crackle above them like Chinese firecrackers. They polish off the goat–flesh and offal, skull and backbone, hide and hooves–as thoroughly as if it were a hamburger. Only about twelve minutes pass, maybe fifteen, until two of the more tenacious animals are scuffling over a last slimy bone. The others splay onto their bellies, relaxing on the bare cool dirt of the gully in patches of shade. They rest and digest.

These aren't crocodilians. They're something more extraordinary: dry-land reptilian predators that lurk in savanna forest within one small region of eastern Indonesia, where they reign at the top of the food chain, eating any and every sort of red-blooded victim that's reckless enough to give them a chance. They are the largest and most fearsome of all lizards, cartoonishly notorious, almost legendary, though not well or widely comprehended in their herpetological actuality. What I mean by that: Everybody's heard of them, but nobody's heard much. Truth is, they're even more astonishing, in the flesh, in the wild than their reputation would seem to promise.

It's Sunday on the island of Komodo, and I've come here to ask the ponderous question: Can humanity live with dragons?

Can we live without them? What will we lose from the wild places on Earth–from our sense of the word *wild* itself–when we lose all prospect of being devoured by homicidal beasts?

In the local dialect, Mangarrai, their name is *ora*. Mangarrat speakers don't call them Komodo dragons–no more than do English-speaking biologists. Science knows them as *Varanus komodoensis*, grandest of all living representatives of the varanid family of tropical lizards. Varanids in general are far-flung throughout the Asian and African tropics, but this particular giant is confined within a very small range. Isolated for millennia, adapted to certain special circumstances, it's a species almost synonymous with a single locale. Within the towns and villages of the region, a slang usage seems to have supplanted the traditional Mangarrai word, and nowadays people call them, simply, Komodos.

Komodo itself is a tiny island of sharp volcanic peaks, grassy hillsides, and forested valleys, a place that at first sight looks ordinary. Less than 200 square miles in area, it's smaller than Oahu, but larger than Alcatraz. It lies in a gap of shallow tropical ocean between the islands of Sumbawa and Flores, north of another big island called Sumba, about halfway out along the great Indonesia archipelago that stretches from Sumatra to New Guinea. Unlike Sumbawa to the west, Sumba to the south, or Flores to the east, Komodo catches scant rainfall and holds few permanent sources of fresh water. Lontar palms mark the high ridges, sparsely, like candles on a lake. The hillside savannas are interrupted in some spots by igneous bluffs, big brows of rough gray rock looming out over the slopes. The valley forests are dry and deciduous, dominated by tamarinds and a few other trees. Tall piles of bare dirt and compost, shoveled up by mound-building birds of the species *Megapodius freycinet* for incubating their eggs, bulge from the forest floor like giant anthills. Sulphur-crested cockatoos, beautiful but hopelessly unmusical, skrawk in the treetops. Wild pigs and rusa deer forage through the understory and roam upward on faint trails into the savanna. On the east coast is one fishing village, made possible there by grace of a rare, precious well. Fortunately for the giant lizards, Komodo's scarcity of water has always discouraged human settlement. Farther north along the coast, in a forested valley called Loh Liang, is another small cluster of buildings. This is where the tourists step ashore.

Twenty years ago, Loh Liang was the main research site during the first thorough study of the ecology and behavior of *V. komodoensis*, conducted by an American herpetologist named Walter Auffenberg. Nowadays it's the site of a visitors' camp (simple cabins, an office, an open-air cafeteria) that serves as headquarters for Komodo National Park. Since the island has no airstrip and no roads, the Loh Liang compound is reachable only by boat. A public ferry, running between Sumbawa and Flores, stops here several times each week. Old wooden cargo boats stand ready to cruise over from Flores whenever an impatient traveler (like me) cares to charter one.

Loh Liang is slightly atypical of Komodo as a whole. Half-tame deer stroll on the beach and loiter between the buildings, accustomed to the handouts. For several hours each evening, the cabin rooms are lit by electricity. Bottled water is available at the cafeteria. And twice every week, Sundays and Wednesdays, at a chain-link corral overlooking a gully less than two miles' walk from the compound, park officials offer the dragons a dead goat.

To some people that sacrificed goat might seem deplorably artificial–or barbaric–but in fact it's a sensible management compromise, done at the imperative of ecotourism, which is crucial to the conservation of this otherwise inconvenient, expendable species. And it certainly makes for good public spectacle: reliable, vivid, photogenic, safe. It allows modestly adventuresome travelers to glimpse the behavior and the anatomical tools that make *V. komodoensis* one of the most formidable predators on the planet. No zoo visit, no nature film seen on PBS is adequate substitute for the artificial but very real event.

The tourists and the park rangers gather *inside* the corral, from which the dead goat is heaved *out*. That arrangement is nicely symbolic of who owns the forest, who doesn't, but it's also quite practical. The Komodos emerge from their secret retreats, evidently alerted by the tempting goat smell and the general human hubbub. One animal appears, then another. Then, by God, a whole gang of them. The largest are ten feet long and weigh 200 pounds, big as adolescent alligators. Unlike alligators, they walk high on their legs with a steady, surging stride. They surround the corral. Expectant but calm, they pose obligingly for everyone's camera. They nose up to the fence, almost like puppies. Their tongues, which are bile yellow, forked, thick as Polish sausages, flap out languidly and then withdraw, tasting the air for aromas. The goat flies, with no warning, and suddenly these lummoxy reptiles become very damn quick and scary.

That's been the scenario this morning: another Sunday, another goat. They've attacked, performing all those Komodoesque verbs you've already read. The calm has returned almost as abruptly as it left.

The Komodos rest briefly while the tourists, sated by spectacle, drift away. The corral empties. The mob scene is over, the Fujichrome has been shot, and I've got the overlook to myself. After another few minutes the Komodos too wander away, all except one placid individual who continues basking. Finally, a pair of rangers approach to pry my hands off the chain-link fence. They inform me in polite Indonesian that the show has ended. They want to finish their morning's work by escorting me back to camp: They carry forked staffs, a nice low-tech precaution against any lingering Komodos that might come lurching out of the brush.

Most of the tourists depart on the next boat. Kamp Komodo becomes blessedly deserted, except for the rangers, myself, the cafeteria workers, four English kids disconsolate at have missed their ferry, and my own pal Nyoman the Balinese Tailor, whom I've hornswoggled into making this trip as a translator. No, we can't leave yet, I tell Nyoman. We've only begun to address the ponderous question.

A Komodo hatchling is just a foot long, cute as a chipmunk, and no danger to anybody. Walter Auffenberg found that the hatchlings eat insects and small lizards, for which they forage beneath the loose bark of dead trees. They also hunt grasshoppers in the savanna. The grasshoppers, Auffenberg wrote, "are captured by stealth." Smallish and medium-sized Komodos feed mainly on rodents (several species of which have invaded the island along with humanity) and on native birds that feed or nest on the ground. As Komodos grow larger–so much larger–the identity and size of their prey changes, while their hunting strategy becomes more refined. Too big for arboreal foraging, too big for a prolonged chase, they specialize in the lurking ambush. Adult Komodos are patient predators, slow-moving over medium distances, lacking the stamina for pursuit, but godawful quick on the first lunge. Also, they're strong. They're deadly effective at close quarters. A full-grown Komodo, according to Auffenberg, often feeds on animals as large as or larger than itself. These prey "are obtained through both stealth and surprise," he wrote, with eloquent redundancy. A favorite Komodo trick is to hide in thick brush at the edge of a trail, waiting for some unsuspecting creature to pass.

Their ambush technique yields the larger Komodos an occasional dog, an occasional civet, an occasional goat. They eat carrion, too, and sometimes they cannibalize another Komodo. Their primary food items, as reported by Auffenberg, are wild pig and rusa deer. They have also been known to kill horses and to wait brazenly near a mare in labor, ready to scarf up the newborn foal. They have been known to kill and eat water buffalo. They have been known, yes, to kill and eat humans.

If these dietary proclivities sound ambitious, consider one other: elephants.

Five years ago, in the journal *Nature*, a scientist named Jared Diamond published a short article titled "Did Komodo Dragons Evolve to Eat Pygmy Elephants?" They did indeed, Diamond argued. Auffenberg himself had first suggested the possibility, based on paleontological evidence of two now-extinct elephant species that had inhabited the island of Flores (and probably also Komodo) during the Pleistocene. The smaller of those two elephants, *Stegodon sompoensis*, may have stood only five feet high and weighed no more than a buffalo. Diamond reasoned that Komodo dragon ancestors must have fed on the pygmy elephants during their own evolutionary progress toward gigantism, because there were no other big animals available within the reptile's native range. Buffalo, rusa deer, and wild pigs probably didn't reach Komodo and Flores until shipped in by humans, just a few thousand years ago. That was many millennia too late for the evolution of *V. komodoensis*.

Why did the ancestral Komodos evolve into giants? Those dainty and succulent elephants may have furnished a necessary condition, but not a sufficient one. Why didn't the varanids of Komodo remain small, subsisting comfortably on a diet of insects and geckos and ground birds? If they were destined to enlarge, why didn't they enlarge only so much as their cousin species, such as *Varanus indicus* and

Varanus mertensi, which are big but not gigantic lizards that would never dream of attacking a horse?

"That size is related to predation is obvious," Auffenberg wrote. "In almost all organisms, optimal predator size is largely determined by the interaction of both the abundance of different prey size classes and the relative energy extractable from them by predators of a given size." Roughly translated: Evolution enforces efficiency, so if larger body size allows a predator to victimize large-bodied prey and to do that more efficiently than it could victimize small-bodied prey as a small-bodied predator, then evolution may well produce gigantism.

Two other variables can't be ignored, not even in this breezy summary. The first is competition. If the large-predator niches are already filled by other species, then a flesh-eating varanid lizard is not likely to find an advantage in gigantism. Better to stay small, in that situation, living efficiently at the scale where competitors are abundant but prey is more abundant still. Within the insular ecosystem of Komodo, however, to the good fortune of *V. komodoensis*, there are no big native predators offering competition. Tigers and leopards didn't make it this far out into the Indonesian archipelago because tigers and leopards, unlike varanid lizards, unlike elephants, are reluctant to swim across ocean gaps.

The other variable is hunting strategy. Does a given predator spend its time and its energy chasing one potential victim to the point of exhaustion? Or does the predator spend more time, and less energy per unit of time, waiting in an ambush? Auffenberg cited a study of hunting behavior among spiders–spiders, yes, and it's not such a far-fetched comparison as it seems. Spiders are all predators, diverse and successful enough as a group to have explored a huge variety of life-history strategies. The study, by an arachnophilic ecologist named Frank Enders, featured the Salticidae family, commonly known as the jumping spiders. Salticids don't catch their prey in webs; they rely instead on stalking and sudden attack. Enders's paper included a wide-ranging discussion of other predator groups and suggested to Auffenberg that "ambush and surprise behavior tended to increase the size of the prey taken." If that's true for salticid spiders, it might also be true for varanid lizards.

Whether it is true, or just plausible, this is how I prefer to see *V. komodoensis* based on the best (or at least the most interesting) scientific work available: as a flesh-eating lizard, grown huge on a diet of elephants, that behaves like the world's largest jumping spider.

Ho ho, we're in luck. Midafternoon Sunday now, and Nyoman has scored us an invitation to hike over the mountains with a backcountry ranger and explore a more remote valley. On that side of the pass there will be no contrived spectacles, no chain-link fences, no tourists, and plenty of Komodos. The ranger is a friendly young Floresian named David Hau, and the valley is called Loh Sabita. Within an hour, having stuffed our packs with malt biscuits and sardines and bottled water from the cafeteria, we start walking. For reasons of safety, we want to reach Loh Sabita before dusk.

Not far from the feeding corral, we leave the main trail and turn north on a much fainter track. The brush is thick on both sides of us. "Good cover for an ambush," says the voice in my brain. "If I were a Komodo, this is where I'd be, waiting for witless Americans." When we move into the forest, where the understory is sparse and the sight lines are longer, I feel slightly more comfortable. We cross a dry streambed, in the dust of which we see tracks: the sinuous mark of a dragging tail, with clawed footprints along each side. The stance is narrow, the stride short.

"Komodo?"

"Ya," David says.

"Kecil?"

"Ya, ya."

In Indonesia, *kecil* means small. In Komodo specifically, it means too small to bite off your leg. We pause to watch cockatoos. We sample the serikaya fruit, cobbled green globes filled with sweet pulp like vanilla yogurt. We pass the tall earthen hump of a mound-builder's nest. The nest is defunct, dug open by some egg-robbing predator.

"Komodo?"

"Ya," David says.

"Kecil?"

No answer. Maybe he didn't hear me.

We climb out of the forest onto a grassy slope and follow the trail upward, toward a mountain saddle between two valleys. It's not a long climb, but the sun is blastingly hot. My shirt is soaked, and Nyoman, a city boy, looks ill. At the crest, we pause for breath and water, savoring the view back toward Loh Liang. A white wooden cross stands here, propped with a cairn. The plaque on it says:

IN MEMORY OF
BARON RUDOLF VON REDING BIBEREGG
BORN IN SWITZERLAND THE 8 AUGUST 1895
AND DISAPPEARED ON THIS ISLAND
THE 18 JULY 1974
"HE LOVED NATURE THROUGHOUT
HIS LIFE."

And nature, in the end, had a gustatory fondness for him. I've read about the Baron. He stopped for a breather hereabouts while the rest of his party hiked on; two hours later, when the others came back, there was nothing left but a Hasselblad with a broken strap.

We top over the saddle and descend through savanna, into the valley called Loh Sabita, where the deer are not tame, the water is not bottled, goat carcasses don't fall from the sky, and the Komodos still live by their skill as hunters.

There's a select category of animal that cuts across phylogenetic groupings to encompass the following: *Panthera tigris, Carcharodon carcharias, Ursus maritimus, Crocodylus niloticus, Ursus arctos, Galeocerdo cuvieri, Carcharias gangeticus, Crocodylus porosus, Panthera leo*. More familiarly: the tiger, the great white shark, the polar bear, the Nile crocodile, the brown bear (including those subspecies known as grizzlies), the tiger shark, the Ganges river shark, the saltwater crocodile, the lion. Reptiles, fish, bears, cats—what's the common link? They're all solitary predators that are big enough, fierce enough, hungry and indiscriminate enough, to kill and eat a human.

Elephants have committed many lethal tramplings, but elephants don't feed on the victim. Buffalo and rhino can be as dangerous as runaway trucks, but they aren't carnivorous. Buzzards eat human flesh, but they don't kill for it. Hyenas have been reported to kill and eat humans, but hyenas are pack hunters, not solitary predators. The leopard might qualify, and several additional species of shark, and possibly the anaconda or the reticulated python, but precious few other living creatures belong to this category. *V. komodoensis* does.

Beyond the sheer luridness, this list has a special potency. The capacity for treating *Homo sapiens* as prey has given at least some of these ultimate predators a mythic status, a transcendent sort of mojo, and that mythic dimension has arguably played a significant role throughout the dawning of human self-consciousness, as our species deduced–and later defined–its position in the world.

Folk beliefs from all across Southeast Asia portray the tiger as a preternatural beast of humanlike motives and magical powers. The crocodile was once considered a water divinity by the Dayaks of Borneo, exempt from killing by Dayak hunters except in very particular circumstances of revenge. The brown bear has held great prominence in the rituals and legends of native peoples across Asia and North America, from the Bear Mother story as told by the Utes, to the bear festival celebrated by the Ainu on Hokkaido. The prospect of that mythic dimension is part of what drew me to the Komodo.

I didn't aspire to any serious anthropological study of local beliefs and legends. My chief purpose was simply to see *V. komodoensis* as a real animal within its ecosystem. What did it eat, where did it hide, how did it hunt? But I was curious, too, about its transcendent mojo.

~~~~~~

The ranger post at Loh Sabita consists of two thatch-roofed cabins on stilts, an outdoor kitchen, a rough wooden table, and a kerosene lamp. Nearby is a spring. In front of the cabins, a broad estuarine mud flat stretches off toward a fringe of mangroves along the beach. We arrive just before dusk, with the distant tree line beginning to go dark and the cockatoos, as they move toward their roosts, looking grayish pink. Loh Sabita is a lovely place. I can understand why David seems glad to be back.

His three colleagues—Ismail, Johannes, the avuncular Dominikus—greet us warmly and insist on sharing their dinner. Dried fish and rice have never tasted better. Then Dominikus serves tea, a mosquito coil is lit, and they roll all clove cigarettes and sit back to talk. I follow as best I can with my thirty-word Indonesian vocabulary. It emerges that a friend of Ismail's was attacked just two weeks ago by a Komodo. Yes, the man survived. He's in a hospital on Flores, Ismail says.

Such attacks are uncommon, but they happen. Auffenberg mentioned a handful, including the case of a fourteen-year-old boy who met an especially bad-tempered Komodo in the forest. Auffenberg got his account from the victim's father. The boy, trying to run away, had tangled himself in a vine. "The vine stopped the youngster for just a moment, and the ora bit him very severely in the buttocks, tearing away much flesh. Bleeding was profuse, and the young man apparently bled to death in less than one-half hour." In other cases death may be less prompt, caused by a massive infection of pathogenic bacteria, which Komodos carry like a form of toxic halitosis.

David tells of another. This one occurred seven years ago at a village called Pasarpanjang, not on Komodo itself but on Rinca, a smaller island nearby that also harbors *V. komodoensis*. It was noontime, a family had just finished lunch, a six-year-old sprang up from the table and ran down the outside steps. A Komodo had skulked into the village and hidden itself under those steps. It stopped the child somehow, maybe with a swat of its tail, and then pounced. It had the child half swallowed by the time help arrived. The whole village turned out. They pried open the animal's jaws, got the child free, killed the Komodo. But the child, David says, was already dead.

After a halcyon night at Loh Sabita, I hear still another. Some fishing people have beach nearby to take on fresh water from the rangers' spring, and in thanks for this hospitality the women among them are fixing us lunch. One of the women has a Komodo-attack story, but she's too shy to tell it to an American journalist. Her name is Saugi. She wears an orange sarong and an acerbic, self-conscious grin. While Saugi cleans and fries fish, hiding herself back by the fire, gentle Dominikus teases the narrative out of her, to be translated in fragments by Nyoman. It all happened to Saugi's mother.

Her mother was cutting thatch. "Suddenly, the Komodo come from the hill." A puppy was playing nearby, and Saugi's mother thought that the Komodo would eat it. "But dog is too quick. Komodo is get there, and maybe angry or disappoint." So instead, switching targets abruptly, it struck the woman. Clamped its jaw onto her arm and held. She struggled. "Is like a dance," reports Nyoman. In a far corner of the kitchen, Saugi works vehemently on a fish. She mumbles. "The mouth of the Komodo is already bite, and stop, and just stay there," Nyoman says. Saugi's mother pushed a sarong over the animal's eyes (which must have seemed horribly near, gazing up into hers) and attempted to wrench free. The jaws wouldn't unlock. She tried to pull herself up into a tree. "And she is, *swooosh*, like this"–Nyoman sweeps back his arm, as though pulling a rabbit from a hat, and glares at me wide-eyed. Why must we torment this woman? asks his sensitive Balinese heart. "And the meat of mother is already in mouth of Komodo." Half the flesh of her arm had been stripped away. But Saugi's mother was luckier than some others; she survived. She spent a month in the hospital, managed to keep her arm, and even recovered the use of it, more or less.

Saugi goes silent. The cold-minded stranger with the notebook, namely me, gapes demandingly at his translator. "Now is still can see . . .," says Nyoman, hesitating. "Still can see . . . how you say? Spots? If you cut, and can see later?" Scars, I say. Saugi finishes her task, washes her hands, wraps an end of her sarong onto her head like a turban, and stalks away.

~~~~~~

Later that day, David and I hike out into the habitat. We follow a set of Komodo tracks along a dry streambed through the forest. We come to a wall of lava, the vertical face of a volcanic bluff rising far above us and out over the treetops. At the wall's base, David shows me several small caves where Komodos have denned. He shows me a pile of Komodo dung. The pale grayish white color indicates a high concentration of digested bone. Other dung piles nearby, more than a few, suggest that this is a well-favored piece of terrain. We circle around the wall, coming out of the forest into sunlit savanna, and then we climb up to a flat spot atop the bluff. Here we find bleached bones. They look to be fragments of femur or humerus, dry as tinder and light as balsa, half crushed by mastication. "Deer. Komodo is here one time. David lifts a piece. "He can eat all."

From this quiet moment, events surge forward rapidly.

As I inspect bone fragments, David glasses the opposite slope of the valley with my binoculars. "Ah, Komodo!" he chirps. "Komodo!" With his guidance, yes, I can barely spot it: an elongated form, dark, almost a half-mile away, on a light patch of dirt. It doesn't budge. It's basking. Or maybe I've trained the binoculars on a Komodo-shaped log. "All right," says the voice in my head. "Better than nothing. Can't expect the same artificial immediacy as produced by a dead goat. We climb off the rock and ascend toward another large bluff. There's a commotion just ahead of us in the brush. And then a full-grown Komodo breaks into view, spooked by our noise, scrambling straight up the face of vertical lava. Lumps of rock crumble and all. My jaw drops like the lid of a dumpster.

This animal is as big as any I saw at the feeding, but for God's sake it's climbing a cliff. Think of an alligator galloping up the side of a four-story building, and you have roughly the image. I get my binoculars up just in time to see the Komodo summit. It pauses there, a giant reptilian silhouette against the bright sky. Then it tops over, disappearing from view. At that moment, I hear David scream . . . as another full-grown Komodo charges out of its hiding place, ten feet behind us, and makes a split-second decision against carving six pounds of flesh either from David's buttocks of from mine. Yaaaggh. We whirl.

Too late for defense, but we've been spared.

Through our carelessness and its own stealth, this animal got exactly the opportunity for which all hungry Komodos reportedly yearn: ambush advantage against walking meat. But it chose not to capitalize. Instead, it has peeled a sharp turn and set off downslope toward the forest. It moves as discreetly as a rhinoceros. It seems even more badly startled than we are. David and I run after it. We see it plunge down a gully. We give chase for fifty yards at precisely the right pace to ensure that we won't catch up.

When my breath is coming normally again, I'm aware of mixed feelings about this encounter. The thrill value has been high. But I really don't want to check into some Flores hospital with a massive leg wound, blood loss, and bacteremia, and I'd sworn that I was going to be faultlessly cautious. The lesson, I suppose, is an obvious one: that these animals are good at what they do and that what they do, though spectacular, can be risky to humans.

We return to search for the other Komodo, the cliff-climber. No sign of it on top of the bluff, except for some large claw marks carved into the brow of the rock. We scout the area timidly. Then we work our way down off the savanna. At the head of another dry streambed, near the forest edge, David stops.

He picks up a bone. This one is tacky with dried blood and saliva. Again he grows excited. "Too late!" he says. "Late one day. Eating in the night. Maybe yesterday." It's the site of a fresh kill, he means, and the Komodo has only just finished its meal.

Or maybe it hasn't quite finished. A strong, sweet, bad smell floats in the afternoon air.

Twenty steps on, we find the head and neck of a three-point rusa stag, attended by a million hysterical flies. The deer's upper ribs dangle raggedly from a stub of spine. Its eyes are sticky and black. It looks like it was hit by a train.

He can eat all, I remember David saying. We abandon the deer head to its flies–and to its other claimants, wherever they lurk–and we get the hell out.

I collect one further account of Komodo predation against humans. For this story, though, I'm obliged to leave Loh Sabita, leave Komodo altogether, and sail back to Flores.

It's a fact generally unknown to those who have heard of this animal, but who haven't heard much, that Komodo dragons aren't native only to the island of Komodo. They also inhabit Rinca (where the six-year-old child was killed, where Saugi's mother was injured) and a tinier island named Gilimotang and some forested areas of western Flores. The total population is roughly 4,000. Indonesian officials estimate that the island of Komodo itself supports about 2,500; Rinca, about 800; Gilimotang, maybe 100: and in western Flores is a wildlife refuge, Wae Wuul, where the latest census found 129. The species is protected by law, but it's still perilously rare.

The Wae Wuul area includes several villages. The local people are obliged to share their forest trails and their meadows, and sometimes their chickens and their buffalo, with the local Komodos. Three years ago, a man from one of those villages was mauled.

Wae Wuul is unreachable by road, so Nyoman and I come by boat and hike in from the coast. We walk up a small mountain, down again, then along a narrow bushy trail through a verdant valley. At the Wae Wuul ranger post we find more than I'd hoped for: the typewritten original of an incident report, composed and signed by the village chief one day after that latest mauling.

The report tells of a man named Don Lamu, who strolled in one afternoon to move his buffalo onto the pasture and (as translated from careful Indonesian into imperfect, but vivid English) "got attack from Komodo which caused a very serious pain which needed a very long cure." The date was September 1, 1989. Don Lamu and a friend were fetching the buffalo from a wallow. They heard a dog bark insistently. They went to look, assuming that the dog had cornered a wild pig. No pig. For a moment they were distracted and unwary–like Saugi's mother, like the child who dashed down the steps, like David and me at the Loh Sabita bluffs. "Suddenly," says the report, "a Komodo appeared between the two people. One of them run away, but Don Lamu couldn't do anything because the distance between Don Lamu and Komodo about six inches." Six inches sounds odd, but the essence is that this animal appeared from nowhere and struck at short range. Don Lamu tried to kick, but the Komodo "fall upon back of Don Lamu's knee until it serious injured." He kicked with the other leg. "But the animal gave respond by its teeth so that his left leg was also torn by the Komodo's teeth." With its second lunge, the Komodo had seized hold. Here the report adds a sentence that hints at the lonely intimacy between predator and prey: "Then Don Lamu sat down and held the Komodo's mouth while he was shouting asking for help."

His friend returned with a chopping knife and whacked at the animal until its jaws opened. He moved Don Lamu some yards away. But the Komodo came at them again. "Don Lamu's friend was angry and a fight happened," says the report. The unnamed friend plays a heroic role, no doubt partly because Don Lamu himself was in serious condition when the report was composed and the friend, as sole witness, supplied the narrative. With only his chopping knife, the friend stood off the Komodo. He killed it.

This story raises several questions. Among them, though not at the top in humanitarian terms: Should we mourn that dead animal?

V. komodoensis is, to my mind, one of the most magnificent species on Earth. That only 4,000 individuals exist, and that many of those 4,000 live at the outskirts of villages on Rinca and Flores–where they face multiple risk and eventual doom in the unequal battle between humans and nature–is a sorry circumstance. "Problem" dragons, like "problem" grizzly bears, will be disposed of, though the real problem is an elementary conflict between the species. The Komodos of Rinca and of Flores may suffer total extirpation within a decade of two, by habitat loss if not by chopping knife. The tiny population on Gilimotang could disappear at any time. When the species is eliminated from these three other locations and confined solely to the island of Komodo, it will face additional sorts of jeopardy related to catastrophe theory and genetics. And we will have arrived, to my mind, at the threshold of another sad diminishment of the vitality and charm of our planet. But then again, my mind has the luxury of inhabiting a body that's not obliged to move water buffalos or raise children in the meadows near Wae Wuul.

Cold as it may be, my mind can't forget the measured but poignant plea in the village chief's closing statement. *Demikia hal ini Kami sampaikan dihadapan Bapak untuk bersama memikirkanya.* "That's our report. We hoped that everyone would try to find out the way how to overcome the problem."

~~~~~~

Before visiting Komodo, I harbored the notion that large predators have played an important role, over the past 20 or 30 millennia, in shaping the way *Homo sapiens* thinks of itself as an inhabitant of the biosphere. I still harbor that notion. Have tigers and lions and bears made the forests and savannas scary? They have indeed, and that's probably been a good thing. Have crocodiles and sharks committed ugly, horrific acts of homicide and anthropophagy? They have indeed, and by doing so they have probably helped us to keep ourselves in perspective. Humans are part of the natural world. We've arisen from it, as the giraffe and emu have, and we live even now as part of it, though God knows we've cut it and burned it and shoveled it away from us on all sides as far as possible. We are part of the natural world, but we are not–though we tend to presume otherwise–its divinely anointed proprietor, nor its evolutionary culmination. One reminder of our real status, one corrective to our presumption, is that human beings, sometimes, within some landscapes, have served as a middling link in the food chain. We have been treated as prey by animals that are bigger and more fierce.

Those times and those landscapes are becoming rare. Large predators face higher jeopardy of extinction than most other categories of species. Large predators that are native only to small zones of circumscribed habitat face the highest jeopardy of all, and many among that group–the Bali tiger, the Japanese wolf, the Newfoundland white wolf, the warrah, the Barbary lion, the Kamchatkan bear, the thylacine of Tasmania–are already extinct. The Komodo dragon is an exception, so far.

As we continue losing those large predators, I suspect, we'll lose something else too: the important spiritual influence that they have exerted, throughout thousands of years of human history, toward keeping us humble. When we lose what remains of that, we'll sashay toward new dimensions of hubris.

Spiritual influence, transcendence mogo: same thing in different words. What I'm referring to is the heightened appreciation bestowed on an animal as it turns up in rituals, legends, cave paintings, creature masks, tall tales, totem poles, festivals, epic poems, amulets, medicinal recipes, and scripture. The 41st chapter of the Book of Job, for instance, contains a wonderful paean to the leviathan, the fire-sneezing monster with armored skin, heart firm as stone, eyes like the eyelids of the morning. The leviathan is a mythical creature, maybe part whale, maybe part reptile, that was conjured up for spiritual purposes from materials of psychological and zoological reality. It's mentioned at several points in the Bible, but Job 41 is its résumé.

When he raiseth up himself, the mighty are afraid; by reason of breakings they purify themselves.
The sword of him that layeth at him cannot hold; the spear, the dart, nor the habergeon.
He esteemeth iron as straw, and brass as rotten wood.
The arrow cannot make him flee: slingshots are turned with him into stubble.

The speaker is God, lecturing Job on the terrible majesty of this beast. The lecturer's purpose, at least initially, is to deepen Job's humility and his reverence toward his Creator:

None is so fierce that dare stir him up: who then is able to stand before me?

But God, to His credit, gets carried away, rambling on into a celebration of the leviathan for its own sake:

Darts are counted as stubble; he laugheth at the shaking of a spear.
Sharp stones are under him: he spreadeth sharp pointed things upon the mire.
He maketh the deep boil like a pot; he maketh the sea like a pot of ointment.
He maketh a path to shine after him: one would think the deep to be hoary.
Upon earth there is not his like, who is made without fear.
He beholdeth all high things: he is king over all the children of pride.

The leviathan of the Old Testament was invented to keep humans humble. Meanwhile, real animals with big teeth and long claws and hungry bellies were prowling the forests and savannas, making the dark waters boil like ointment, and accomplishing a similar function.

What's the transcendent mojo of a giant lizard that eats deer, pigs, goats, horses, pygmy elephants, men, women, and children? What's the mythic importance of *V. komodoensis* among those rural Indonesian folks who suffer its terrors? To this question, I've got no answer. Walter Auffenberg couldn't find one either, and his inquiry was more thorough than mine. "A search of all the old literature on tribal customs and beliefs of inhabitants of Sumba, Sumbawa, and Flores did not disclose any legends or myths reporting the ora," he wrote, "nor did the missionaries with whom I talked on Flores know of any." Maybe the animal has no mythic role in that culture. Or maybe the written sources are incomplete and anthropologists haven't yet done justice to the oral traditions of the region. But if the people of Komodo, Flores, and Rinca venerate their dragon with the same imaginative ambivalence as addressed elsewhere to tigers and bears, I won't be surprised to hear it.

Still, there's another perspective on large predators. It's directly opposed to what I've just offered. This other view was well expressed by a biologist named Alistair Graham in a wonderfully garish book titled *Eyelids of Morning*, about the mingled destinies of crocodiles and humans:

> So long as one is constantly threatened by savage brutes
> one is to some extent bound in barbarism; they hold you
> down. For this reason there is in man a cultural instinct to
> separate himself from and destroy wild beasts such as
> crocodiles. It is only after a period of civilization free of
> wild animals that man again turns his attention on them,
> seeking in them qualities to cherish.

Graham is right. But his truth, I persist in believing, isn't the sole and complete truth.

It's late afternoon in Komodoland. Nyoman and I have a boat to catch. Tomorrow morning we'll return to the world of airports, taxis, hotels, genteel gardens within stone courtyards, goldfish and ferns and tiny geckos–and to the privileged situation of cherishing *V. komodoensis* from afar. But first we've got to hike back down the narrow trail from Wae Wuul, through miles of prime habitat. I'll be acutely aware of blind corners, bearing Don Lamu's story in my notebook, and hoping for some piece of reconciling wisdom to come jumping out of the bushes.

(Originally published October 1992)

EXTREME WELLNESS

TAFFY BRODESSER-AKNER

We've had a lot of great opening lines over the last four decades, but I'm certain there's never been one quite as memorable as this one. I'll let Taffy Brodesser-Akner take it from here.

One's vagina should be steamed in the upright position. In a room that's lined wall-to-wall with real, actual jade, a woman (OK, me) dressed in a satiny, royal purple sheath that attaches just under the armpits—like the world's least flattering strapless gown—sits atop a throne. The throne is wood and looks like a toilet, with a deep, dark hole in the middle. The gown goes over the body and the throne, creating a little biodome. Once you're seated, steam from a container of mugwort tea and herbs rises and slithers up to its target. Meanwhile, infrared light is shot up at said same target (the vagina, in case you forgot), and it is those two things, the tea and the light, that combine to allegedly—big fat allegedly here—regulate hormones and "disinfect" the area. When you're done, your nether region should feel new, like you just unwrapped it for the first time.

The V-steam gained popularity when Gwyneth Paltrow featured it on her website, Goop, calling it "the real golden ticket." It's all the rage now, say the people at Tikkun Holistic Spa, meaning that everyone knows about steaming, even though, in the U.S., it mostly exists in this one underground facility in Santa Monica—Santa Monica being the Capitol of Panem for spa treatments. But it's actually an old treatment, they say. Cleopatra did it, though there's no word on where she got infrared light.

I asked my handler if I was supposed to feel different, and she told me, Oh yes, absolutely, that since she started receiving V-steams on the regular, for maybe five months now, she's been in harmony with the world, like she's gotten in touch with her power, like she just woke up to what she's capable of after all these years.

By this point, such talk wasn't so crazy to me. I'd been on what people in the detox industry call *a journey*. I'd had hot rocks put on my body in an effort to stimulate my lymph system and drain me of toxins, part of a procedure called the Bartholomew Method. I'd stood on Santa Monica Boulevard and psyched myself up to get a vitamin infusion in a juice shop, where you sit in one of those chemo-therapy chairs and hook up to an IV. (Reader, I couldn't do it.) And now this steam thing, all in an attempt to reach optimal health through innovative treatments, or at least figure out what their appeal is. Don't get me wrong: The Bartholomew Method featured the best massage I've ever had. The steam itself was awkward but OK. But there was a juice fast and a colonic-palooza coming in a few days, and I was kind of dreading it.

~~~~~~

Wellness is a big, active, growing sector in the health and fitness market. The spa industry, formerly known for massages, pedicures, and facials, has mutated to become a $16.3 billion giant that offers a dizzying array of options. There are now more than 21,000 spas in the U.S., with eager customers (most of them women) racking up 179 million visits annually. When the International Spa Association conducted its survey, spokespeople at four out of five spas polled said they would be adding new, more out-there treatments to their menus, things like energy work and breath work and snail facials and cupping and, yes, V-steams.

And here we get into questions of philosophy. My V-steam cost $50, which is a lot to pay for sitting over hot vapor. Is your money well spent on this stuff? It depends on what you're looking for. It also depends on how much money you have and how you define wellness. Is a massage only supposed to feel good, or is it supposed to lead to a tangible state of bliss? Is it a pleasure of the now or an invest-ment in tomorrow? At Tikkun, a woman who was getting her V steamed before I did asked, loudly enough for everybody in the waiting room to hear, "How do I know if it's working?" It struck me as the wisest thing that anyone had said in days.

I know what people think about detox—that it's a way to deal with an ultra-toxic world. Even so, the true impetus for it seems to be something a little more subtle and even a bit nefarious: on Planet Wellness, despite all the oohs and ahhs about the glories of nature, there's a general mistrust of the way the human body actually works, with natural systems getting overridden so that nutrients and herbs and tea and light and wishes can get inside you through avenues that weren't necessarily meant to accommodate those things. It seems that the further we go with fancy and intricate treatments, the more we're engaging in a ritual effort to make ourselves pure again. And this is something that has a lot of implications for how we feel about ourselves as women, particularly as we age. I don't mean how our bodies look and work differently as we get older, but how we think of ourselves as whole people who have a history, people who have made mistakes, people who have eaten a cheeseburger on occasion, people who have loved the wrong people and have been imperfect in a way that feels unforgivable. In my journey through detoxification, I didn't find that these treatments were just attempts to be young again. No, they were attempts to be new.

~~~~~~

Let me back up. In the waning days of 2016, post-election and pre- any sign of hope or healing, I, jittery like a Chihuahua with anxiety and stress, accepted a story assignment to travel deep into the underbelly of spa territory, Los Angeles, to learn why a good old massage-and-cocktails afternoon no longer did the trick. In truth I maybe *Secret*-ed the whole thing. I'd been working so hard and traveling so much that the only way I could rationalize leaving my family again for something this indulgent was to take a paid gig.

And well, maybe I *was* toxic. Maybe we all are and that's the problem. "On average, a human will have between 80 and 120 known toxic chemicals in their body," says Bruce Lourie, coauthor with Rick Smith of the bestselling *Slow Death by Rubber Duck*, a book about the poisons that seep into our everyday life. Lourie and Smith write about new science focused on the mechanics of endocrine-disrupting chemicals, which are insidious and can lead to thyroid and reproductive problems and birth defects. These chemicals come at us from just about everywhere, in low levels that accumulate to become high levels, from our plastic coffee cups, our flame-retardant pajamas, our nonstick pans, not to mention what we eat and drink.

After reading Lourie and Smith's excellent book, I could feel the toxins creeping through my system and promising me a life of compromised health. If you're less neurotic than I am, you should at least consider that lasting health is in no way guaranteed to you, that the lottery of illness is nothing that can be predicted, at least not absolutely. "It's like cancer," Lourie told me. "Some people smoke all their life and never get lung cancer; some people never smoke and they get lung cancer. But we still know that smoking causes cancer."

As I came to learn, there are different tiers of opt-in health. There's regular health, which is like, say, me feeling OK when I wake up and also feeling lucky each week that I don't pick up a virus or get diagnosed with a chronic or fatal disease. There's maintained health, where you get regular checkups and do now mainstream things like acupuncture and herbs and supplemental vitamin D. Then there's poor health. In this category, there are some people with the means to seek ultrahealth as the antidote to their poor health in hopes of getting back to regular health. If it works, they quickly become people who seek ultrahealth as their status quo—why wouldn't they?

And that is the ugliest part of this whole detox business. It forces you to ask yourself who has the right to feel good and happy and healed and whole, and who can actually afford it. That's the worst part.

The rest is not so bad.

~~~~~~

After the Bartholomew Method, after the steam, after the aborted IV attempt, I made a pilgrimage 100 miles east to We Care Spa, in Desert Hot Springs. According to lore, We Care was founded by a woman who had an illness and no support network. She tried all the medicines and nothing helped, so she did what she observed animals do, which is: she went into the woods and she fasted and she healed. Only her woods were her very nice house, where the spa is still located, and she added colonics to the mix—a lot of them.

I first read about We Care five years ago, in a book about an anti-inflammatory cleanse called *Clean*, by cardiologist Alejandro Junger. Junger and other doctors, like bestselling author Joel Fuhrman, believe that our intestinal tract, where up to 70 percent of our immune system is located, is overworked and tired from breaking down all the food and chemicals we're ingesting. Their theory is that fasting—consuming only a liquid diet for a certain amount of time—gives your intestines a rest, allowing your immune system to go about healing other things in your body. Many elite athletes and trainers have embraced something called intermittent fasting—eating only one meal a day, for instance—which they say forces the body to burn up stored fat to fuel performance.

As paleo and other popular diets seek to re-create the physical dynamism of our ancestors (who lived to about 35, FYI), holding steady on that whole thing about food not being readily available, the trend has become extremely and ridiculously profitable.

I had never really tried it, but the spa that Junger described set off a fantasy in my head: a place to hit the old reset button on all your organs and your life, which you'd do with a liquid diet, an aggressive series of colonics, plus various other treatments, and then more colonics. I would think about the spa from time to time with a certain kind of yearning. Finally, I was going.

I pulled up to We Care on the morning of December 23, finding an actual oasis in the desert. There were rock formations and saunas and infrared saunas and floating outdoor beds and meditation pyramids and statues of all the gods you can imagine, including jaunty elephants. There were winding paths and a meditative labyrinth.

I arrived under a cloud of headache and dysphoria from We Care's strongly suggested three-day prefast precleanse program, which puts you off sugar, caffeine, and many other substances. I was immediately sent to a yoga class, which was just starting, and let me tell you, there is no yoga like yoga for people on a liquid diet. It's so gentle and caring. We did a chakra meditation! We talked about our hips! I don't think we did one standing pose.

Afterward I was shown how to make two different drinks out of mixes, one green and one brown. The green was for energy or something and it was not terrible. The other drink, the detox drink, was made with brown powder, cinnamon, olive oil, and alkaline water. You have to down the brown drink quickly or it turns into a very literal sludge. If you are even a little slow, it solidifies into a swamp thing and you have to start all over. Once the sludge is in your colon it can bind to all the crap in there and bring it on out. It's useful but gross.

Later, at the orientation, we were told how the place works, particularly how our many, many colonics would work. The recommendation is to have one per day, unless you're staying for a month, in which case maybe skip a day or two. Wikipedia describes colonics as water therapy used "to remove nonspecific toxins from the colon and intestinal tract," but that definition does not do justice to the reality. A colonic is the act of getting a hose shoved up your ass to flood your colon with water, so that when the water comes out, so will the poop lodged in your colon. That's how indulgent a spa We Care is. You don't even have to poop on your own. They send soldiers in to liberate it. Sit back, relax, we got you.

At We Care, eating is not one of the attractions. You get by on a fast, consuming about 100 ounces of liquid per day—juice, teas like Blood Purifier and Liver and Kidney Detox, a very thin vegetable puree at night—because, we're told, we all came in drastically, alarmingly dehydrated. You take some supplements. You select from a few à la carte treatments. And you spend all your waking moments obeying orders—showing up for the treatments on time, preparing the drinks, urinating endlessly, and trying the sauna, which will help you sweat out toxins. There are classes on nutrition; there are classes on intention and mindfulness; there are stretching classes and sleeping classes; there is a fire ceremony (no, really); and there is a very practical and useful smoothie class, where you get a sample of the smoothie made, which, let me tell you, by day three is the satisfaction equivalent of pizza and a margarita.

And then there was the considerable, ridiculous amount of time we spent talking about poop. We used words like *eliminate* and *release*. We referred to the poop itself as *matter,* which, sure, but isn't everything matter? We talked about our colonics and we talked about ways to move them along a little better, to *facilitate* them. There were three separate machines in the main gathering area that helped facilitate the poop. A couple of them would shake you like a martini until it was jostled free. There was also a machine that you used by lying on the floor and putting your feet into slots. It dragged you from side to side, also to liberate the poop.

I don't think I met a single woman who was there for the first time. There were two women in their early thirties who said they come regularly. "Detox is my way of life," one told me. "And it works. Do you see how I'm not sick? I never get sick!" I told her that she was 30, that she had a lot to look forward to.

But most of the women were older and looked like they had a strong familiarity with maintenance protocols like foot Botox and dermal fillers. People were usually there for eight days. Some stayed longer—a woman in her sixties or seventies or eighties told me that she and her husband come for two weeks every year. I met a few women who came because they'd just gone through a divorce and needed the clock to stop for a minute while they considered their lives. One woman was there for the fourth time—she'd woken up with a bad taste in her mouth a year or so ago, and she'd been to all these doctors for testing and no one could tell her what was wrong. I heard a rumor that another woman, who was there for a week but had been there in August for a month, had an entire colonic room installed in her apartment.

On the second morning, I saw the woman in her sixties or seventies or eighties take a big tablespoon of castor oil from the refrigerator, swallow it, and chase it with a frozen lemon she sucked on.

"Have you tried the castor oil?" she said. I told her I hadn't. "You should. It really moves things along." The woman who led my orientation had warned us that at some point, someone would suggest we take castor oil to "move things along." She said we should not, under any circumstances, consider doing this. We should only take the castor oil if our colon hydrotherapist suggested it. So I asked my new friend, politely, "Did your colon hydrotherapist suggest this?" She rolled her eyes and said no, indicating that I was some kind of baby for even suggesting that she, an adult, needed permission to take castor oil. I could smell the lemon on her breath as she said, "Are you here to eliminate or aren't you?"

And somehow, by that point, I was. Maybe it was the fact that I finally had a moment to think. Maybe it was because I was filled with hope and resolve in a way

I hadn't been in years. Maybe it was because there is only so much being taken care of that you can experience before you feel like you actually *are* being taken care of. Which is a long way of saying: I took the castor oil.

I have a doctor friend who's heard me out on all this and thinks I'm nuts.

"Where is any study substantiating anything that they've said?" says Albert Fuchs, an internist in Beverly Hills and a person I rely on for stone-cold medical opinions. I'd told him what I'd learned at the We Care digestive class, that allergies often happen because we don't chew our food well enough. The teacher said we have to chew down to the consistency of baby food, because food particles can exit the stomach through the lining, a phenomenon known as leaky gut, and once the food enters the bloodstream, a healthy immune system will attack it as a foreign substance and create an allergy. See? I say to my doctor friend. That makes sense to me.

"So this hypothesis somehow has escaped our greatest allergists?" he says. Then he sighs. The thing missing from every claim I'd heard at the spa, he says, was observation, meaning a controlled study.

"There are lots of things that feel good that don't have medical benefits," Fuchs says. "I like to refer to those things as entertainment, and I don't say that mockingly." His example: movies. "Movies don't have a medical benefit. They might relax you a little when you're stressed, but I think movies are great." He doesn't understand why some things can't just be fun or feel good without having to have a health benefit attached to it.

In a way, what Fuchs thinks or has proof of is beside the point. Alternative therapies exist on the far side of what he represents, and many people believe that's fine.

And the medical establishment, well, it's wrong a lot of the time—studies mislead or new wisdom becomes apparent. When people can't find a cure through traditional means, they can often find different answers with alternative therapists and a different kind of reception. It's important to realize that no one here is actually lying. In fact, this could be the only context in which the phrase *alternative facts* actually works.

"Certain alternative remedies give back control of suffering to patients, provide more intimate-human connections, and in some cases produce more visible effects, lending credibility to the therapy," says Travis A. Weisse, a science historian at the University of Wisconsin. "The doctor-patient relationship has been slowly eroding, not only with specialization and the fact that people now see panels of doctors, but because emergency rooms are slammed, there are insurance-coverage problems, et cetera. It can make a patient feel devalued."

Science is fallible; science doesn't know everything. Weisse cites an example: how the American Medical Association dismissed organic food and vegetarianism for years, despite growing data that showed concerns about pesticides and health problems from eating meat. People are warier of the medical establishment. As Weisse puts it, "It is possible, easy, and very common to both see a doctor and do a detox or other alternative remedy and hold both of those in your mind at the same time."

I spent a lot of time trying to find quantifiable outcomes that would impress my friend Dr. Fuchs, or hard medical facts that would call out the alternative therapists. Bruce Lourie and Rick Smith did a series of experiments on themselves for their research, like testing their sweat for BPA and their urine for heavy metals. They tested their blood and urine before and after and found some of the detox treatments to be effective, including cleanses. But all a cleanse really involves, Lourie will tell you, is restricting intake and pushing through a lot more water than you think you need. I asked both Lourie and Fuchs about fasting. Lourie thinks it's OK if you don't do it too often; Fuchs basically rolls his eyes. "There are no proven health benefits from fasting," he says. "There is also no long-term weight loss after fasts."

But I no longer cared about the truth. I understood the magic of the colonic. I knew what it was like to feel empty now, and empty is a great way to think of yourself if you want to feel new and unsullied. I was through the looking glass. I had seen the promise of ultrahealth, all these women telling me over and over how their lives were changed by their relationship with We Care, and who can resist the idea that the small things wrong in your life have nothing to do with bad decisions or the way you can be unlucky sometimes? Who can resist the theory that it was a literal backup of poop in my colon that was keeping me down? Other cultures call aging wisdom. But we don't want wisdom. We want fresh starts.

So yes, I went all in. I had a treatment in which my skin was brushed all over and rubbed down with magnesium, which is an anti-inflammatory, then wrapped in a burrito of the same material that Superman's parents sent him to Earth in while I sweated out all my toxins. I was oiled and broiled and roasted and flipped and dredged. I was rinsed and scrubbed; I was coated and steamed. I was exfoliated as if I was the subject of an archaeological dig. I was moisturized to within an inch of my life. I was wrung out like a dirty washcloth till the water ran clear.

And then I took the castor oil again. I booked a reflexology session, and the man jabbed his finger into the bottom of my left foot and told me my colon was blocked up, and he went to work on it through my feet. He said it was like there was a marble in there, and I screamed—and in my scream I could feel it all start to work, like progress was being made. I doubled my resolve and sat on that vibrating machine and upped it to level 20, the highest level, which is an earthquake for your innards, and I did a guided meditation in which I could see the poop running from me, and in my poop I imagined that everything bad in my life was being expelled: politics, deadlines, carpools, my father moving to Florida, my mother's arthritis, my mortgage, all of it, everything was coming out.

I imagined that all my stress would bind to the crap inside me and I could shit out everything that troubled me and maybe I'd emerge from it a clean slate, a version of myself that had not ever eaten a hamburger or drank too much. Maybe all my mistakes would be wiped clean. Maybe underneath the poisons that had invaded my skin I was someone who could do life better—it wasn't too late, it couldn't be too late. I could wake up very early and meditate. I could be faster and more efficient and check Twitter less often. I could exercise regularly and floss every day, twice even. I could learn to say "take care" instead of "buh-bye" at the end of a phone call. I could read the books that everyone else seems to be ahead of me in. I could never yell at my children and always be romantic and sexually available with my husband. I could have glowing skin and a poop routine that put all these people to shame. I would be new; everything could be forgiven. I would finally be new again and I could find a way to forgive myself for being human.

Because that's what we were here for, right? We were here to *eliminate,* as the lemon lady said. We were here to hide in the woods while we got better. We were here to let it all out so we could start over. So we gathered and made this our full-time job. We shat out our sadness and our loneliness and our fears of what was happening in the world outside the spa. We shat out the fact that we don't know why our marriages fail, why our bodies fail, why we rarely achieve the things we are supposed to. We shat out aging and uncertainty and the very many parts of life that are hard and we waited to see if it was working. But where did all this get us? I went home and was overdue on two assignments. It turns out that you can leave all your poop in the desert, but wherever you go, there you are.

~~~~~~

On my last day at We Care, everyone I encountered did a double take. They told me I was glowing, and I ran to the bathroom to look and oh my God they were right. I looked beautiful and young. I had started thinking I was getting old and ugly, but now it was clear to me: it was just the poisons I ingested. In the cab ride after I left the spa, I thought of all the ways I would keep up my protocol, how I would not let this beauty and health leave me again. But I got to the airport and I was hungry and there was no plethora of vegetable juice or detox tea. There were only nachos and cheeseburgers, and I felt my glow draining from my face just being in the same dimension as those things. I got on my flight and the flight attendants were rude, and I got home and my husband said I looked beautiful and there was pizza waiting, and then a few days later I looked into the mirror and it was all gone. And suddenly I was back across the looking glass, back to being me, wanting to return to the spa and angrier than ever before that none of this had ever truly been mine.

But now I've been home for a while, trying to recalibrate myself into someone who could tell this story the way I was meant to, which is as an outsider: what it was like to be there, but also what it was like to never have truly been there, not really. But I haven't been able to summon that.

Instead I find myself thinking about the people I met. I think about one friend I made, who was on her fifth visit, who braided my hair like hers when I told her how much I liked it and who told me that she was considering LSD microdosing. I think about the woman who did my digestive release, how she kneaded my abdomen, listening carefully for movement. I think about the colon hydrotherapist who put her hand on my head and told me to close my eyes and breathe. I think about the man who did my reflexology, how he was determined to stay until that marble was out—and when it was, I let rip a stream of gas that brought to mind the Hindenburg, and we both laughed as he shouted to the heavens, "Better out than in!" I think of the woman who stood over me during my V-steam. Once I was seated, she had said to me, "I want to tell you something while you're here. I want to tell you that your life could be good now. I want to tell you that you don't have to make it through your problems in order for your life to be good now. I want you to know that you have a power within you that is unique, and that is only yours, and that when you learn how to harness it, you are going to make a real difference in the world. You are really going to change the world, Taffy." Can I tell you that when she said that, I sat there in my regal strapless gown, light and tea being flown through my lower orifices, and I cried?

~~~~~~

I also think of the woman who conducted the fire ceremony on the night I left We Care, how she was just coming from a solstice ceremony and her car had been robbed of all her neat instruments and how she showed up anyway with a smile on her face to help us get through it all, even though it was still hard to think of those of us who could afford a few days here as the people with problems.

That night we all wrote those problems on small pieces of paper and we set them on fire and they disappeared into the air, poof, like they never existed. The woman stood over me with a rattle and she chanted, and I cried then, too. I cried for all of it, and I cried because whatever you think of detox and the people who sell it, they are mostly people who care very much for you and who know how fragile happiness and health are and who want you to have a good life. I cried because I wished the women at the spa with me, the visitors, would emerge from this place and they would have a good life, too, and that we could all forgive ourselves for being human and for having gathered experience. I cried because I knew that we interpreted our life's worth of experience to be a kind of sullying, and that the men in our lives would never think that of themselves; the men in our lives aren't capable of hating themselves the way we are. I cried because it was so sad to me that we have such little faith in systems that we couldn't even trust the ones that were still working. But mostly I cried because it was time to go, and I had no mechanism for keeping this place close to my heart. I knew that I'd leave and never return, and that as empty as I felt then, I'd soon screw it up by getting full on the wrong things, and as time went on I'd revert to the person I've always been and return to seeing these vision quests as mostly silly and hilarious. And that is a shame, because I'm two months out now, and I can still tell you they're not.

(Originally published May 2017)

LET THE
GAMES BEGIN

THE HELL ON EARTH
FITNESS PLAN

NICK HEIL

Nick Heil has covered the outer edges of fitness science for Outside *for more than a decade, reporting on everything from alpinists using Viagra for altitude acclimatization to the training habits of ultrarunning star Rory Bosio. In 2008, he heard about Gym Jones, a back-to-basics workout center with a (very) tough love ethos run by former climbing star Mark Twight. We're still somewhat surprised Nick lived to tell the story.*

I heard about Gym Jones the way you hear about a secret trout stream or an all-night rave—through word of mouth and friends of friends. To me, gyms tend to come in two varieties, neither particularly appealing. Option A: the Fitness Super-centers, with their overcrowded cardio dens and cucumber-scented saunas. And Option B: the Iron Grottoes, run by mulleted muscleheads in Metallica T-shirts. Gym Jones, the rumor went, was something else entirely—a new type of facility devoted to a mutant strain of fitness that combines elements of powerlifting, gymnastics, endurance sports, and military-style calisthenics. Insiders insisted that this odd hybrid was building bombproof athletes of all types and ages, and that the movement had acquired a devoted following in places from Washington, D.C., to Vancouver, B.C.

Gym Jones is located in Salt Lake City, where it was created by Mark Twight, a world-class alpinist who chiseled a career on walls of rock and ice so dangerous that, in some instances, he had only about a 50 percent chance of survival. Twight retired from climbing in 2001—at least from the suicidal stuff—and recommitted himself to the art and science of physical conditioning. His expertise attracted an elite cross section of clients—mountaineers, military special ops, cage fighters—but the gym, the origins of which date back to 2003, remained a largely underground phenomenon until 2007, when it was publicized that Twight had trained the British actors who portrayed Spartan soldiers in the war-porn fantasy film "300." Over the course of a few months, he'd turned the doughy troupe into a phalanx of freshly waxed Chippendales models, with marbled arms and abs like giant tortoiseshells. The superbods inspired a viral buzz that catapulted traffic on the Gym Jones Web site from a million hits a month to more than 11 million.

Like its owner, the gym took on a mystical, slightly nightmarish quality: part martial-arts dojo, part smash lab, part medieval dungeon, all intended to facilitate the arduous process of mental and physical transformation. When I checked out the Web site, I was greeted by a skull and crossbones and a warning: "Gym Jones is not a cozy place. There are no televisions, no machines, no comfortable spot to sit. Effort and pain may not be avoided. Physical and psychological breakdowns occur."

The routines were said to be so intense, so blindingly debilitating, that they brought even the hardest men to their knees, whimpering in slicks of their own sweat. "The first time I went through one of those workouts, my legs swelled up like balloons. I couldn't walk for a week," says Rob "Maximus" MacDonald, a world-champion mixed-martial-arts fighter who now helps Twight run the gym.

OK, I thought, that which does not kill me, and then I e-mailed Twight, asking if I could come out to give it a try. His response was swift and dismissive. Who the hell was I? Did I have any idea what I was getting myself into? "Many of our guys worked out for a year before they started meaningful training," he wrote. "I'm not interested in having someone take a shallow look. A quick peek is a waste of time."

I told him I was hoping for more than a quick peek. As a 41-year-old amateur athlete, I was acutely aware of the encroaching infirmities of middle age, but I hardly felt like my days on skis, a bike, or a soccer field were anywhere close to being over. I might be slipping, but I still felt strong and capable. With a little help, I figured, I could unleash whatever whup-ass was left.

Twight agreed to let me attend one of his two-day introductory seminars, provided I came prepared. That meant I had to "pretrain," so he put me in touch with one of his handpicked disciples, Carolyn Parker, a 39-year-old mountain guide based in Albuquerque, New Mexico, not far from my home.

Once a week for the next two months, I drove to a grassy field where Parker, a stunning physical specimen with a fondness for climbing waterfall ice in designer leather pants, schooled me in "the Gym Jones way." The first day, she threw a medicine ball so hard that it knocked the wind out of me. Other sessions involved dizzying combinations of dead lifts, squats, lunges, strange ballet-like kettlebell routines, and various other exercises of sadistic invention.

One day, we did something called "30-30s." Parker giggled maniacally as she handed me two 20-pound dumbbells. She told me to raise them to my shoulders and push them above my head as many times as I could in 30 seconds. Then I had to hold the weights up, arms locked, for 30 more seconds, and repeat until I'd finished four one-minute sets without a rest. By the last set, I could manage only a few reps, my arms noodling while I emitted a snorting sound, like a warthog. At the end, I fell into the grass, soaking wet. Parker stood next to me with her hands on her hips. "I think you're ready," she said.

And so, like some sad pilgrim seeking redemption through his own suffering, I arrived at an unmarked warehouse in Salt Lake City on a blistering June day, armed with just enough knowledge to stir a deeply nauseating realization: What I was about to experience was really, really going to hurt.

Gym Jones was conceived in a windowless room in a decommissioned bread factory in downtown Salt Lake. The name was bestowed by Twight's wife, Lisa, a martial-arts student who sometimes carries knives hidden in her boots and who told me wryly that she has "a knack for marketing." Mostly, Twight used the space to train friends and himself. He was still climbing hard enough that he wanted a dedicated space in which to keep in shape, and mainstream facilities didn't cut it.

"We wanted to do stuff they wouldn't put up with," he says. "Throwing medicine balls, dropping weights on the ground, working genuinely hard, and creating something with our own spirit, especially the music."

Ah, yes, the music. Few things had fueled Twight's angst-ridden ride as a climber more than punk rock's Sturm und Drang: Sisters of Mercy, the Damned, Skinny Puppy, and a trove of others, spliced together on mix tapes that he blasted into his ears while hacking up some heinous frozen cliff. His 2001 collection of climbing essays, *Kiss or Kill: Confessions of a Serial Climber*, contains stories with titles cribbed from song lyrics, like "Glitter and Despair" and "House of Pain." Twight's worldview could be so nihilistic that one friend nicknamed him Dr. Doom.

Twight made money in various ways—from sponsorships, from training elite soldiers in alpine fitness and survival techniques, and from serving as a distributor for Grivel, an Italian climbing-gear company. His interest in starting his own gym evolved in part from experiences he'd had with a then-fledgling program called

CrossFit, developed by Greg Glassman, now 52, a charismatic former gymnast from Santa Cruz, California, whom everyone simply called Coach.

CrossFit emphasized old-school exercises and movements like squatting, jumping, pulling, pushing, and so on. Glassman had a gym in Santa Cruz but mainly shopped his product through daily workouts posted on crossfit.com, the Web site he launched in 2001. He contended that CrossFit was all most athletes really needed, because it had the remarkable ability to develop strength and endurance simultaneously. It relied on weight-loaded drills combined with "natural movements" performed with grueling intensity. The circuits were christened with colorful names, like Fight Gone Bad, or after Navy SEAL CrossFitters killed in action. Glassman even created a mascot, Pukie the Clown, a Bozo-like character with a cascade of vomit flowing from his mouth.

Twight first tried CrossFit in December 2003, when Glassman invited him to Santa Cruz to attend a certification seminar. He was plenty fit—he could run up 2,000 vertical feet in 45 minutes—but not compared with other workshop participants. They competed against each other in Fight Gone Bad—a three-lap, five-station circuit involving rowing, dead lifts, box jumps, overhead dumbbell presses, and medicine-ball throwing—and Twight finished dead last. "There wasn't enough oxygen in the state of California for me," he said.

Both humiliated and fired up, Twight flung himself into a CrossFit regimen for the next four months, then tested its effectiveness at a Utah ski-mountaineering race called the Powder Keg. He finished in a satisfying 11th place, against a tough field of experts. Convinced that Glassman's style of training was a genuine secret weapon, he became a CrossFit "affiliate"—not exactly a franchisee but a booster for the CrossFit mantra.

After a couple of years, however, Twight says he began to grow disillusioned with the program. CrossFit thrived on a regimen of unstructured daily workouts, but Twight discovered that, while this bolstered his overall fitness foundation, it came at a cost in terms of sport-specific performance. Twight soon found that his power output had increased in certain arenas but his long-range endurance had faltered. He noticed the same thing surfacing among his athletes.

"In December 2006, I gave a test to guys who were training with me that I thought was indicative of their progress," Twight says. "They underperformed to a degree that made me say, OK, everybody's benched for two weeks. I'm gonna go home and figure this out. That's when I realized that we weren't making progress because we weren't planning our training to make progress." CrossFit, he said, conditioned people for CrossFit. "But the gym is not our sport," he says. "Everyone here trains for something else."

Twight recommitted himself to the concept of periodization—modulating volume and intensity over the course of multi-month training cycles. "The biggest disappointment with CrossFit came from treating training as competition (stopwatch, posting comments, etc.)," he wrote to me later. "Our intensity declined, form degraded, and our attitude turned negative as shit got hard, because the training was not designed to support athletic performance outside of the gym. Now we build in recovery periods to assure proper intensity and form. We insist on progressively harder intervals (the last should be the fastest). We don't train to failure. We mimic work/rest intervals common to the sport-specific task."

Twight still relied on CrossFit-style circuits for the foundation-building phase of his training, and when videos of his work on 300 emerged, showing the actors performing the familiar circuits, Coach blew a gasket. Not only had Twight split from the tribe; he was cashing in on his newfound knowledge. Commercially, CrossFit was doing much better than Gym Jones. (It's on track to earn more than $13 million this year. Twight, whose operations remain private, earns roughly $200,000 a year with Gym Jones.) But Coach remained bitter, angered that so much attention followed the film training, and he accused Twight of pilfering copyrighted CrossFit material for his military seminars.

"Here's proof of the authenticity of Mark Twight's program," Glassman wrote in an e-mail. "Mark was caught stealing my work, re-copyrighting it and selling it to the Navy. Gym Jones is an excellent program. I am its author/inventor/developer."

Twight laughed when I told him this, though he acknowledges using some of the CrossFit teachings. "Is what we do derivative?" he said. "Of course it is. Everything is. C'mon, we're just picking shit up and putting it down. I won't let my personal falling-out alter my respect for what Greg's done and what he's taught me . . . but it wasn't the end-all, be-all. My mistake when I separated was not separating fully enough. I was lazy and I fucked up. But what I do now comes from a lot of places—his material, my material, and many others."

By the time I arrived at the June seminar, Gym Jones had just moved into its fourth and, Twight hoped, last location—a 6,000-square-foot garage full of black rubber floor mats, barbells, squat racks, and other torture-chamber accoutrements. As promised, the only mirror was in the bathroom, and the block walls featured just two decorations: an American flag and a sign, cribbed from Fight Club, that read in part, "Every word you read of this useless fine print is another second off your life. Don't you have other things to do? Get out of your apartment. Meet a member of the opposite sex. Stop the excessive shopping and masturbation. Quit your job. Start a fight. Prove you're alive."

If I wasn't the weakest person there, I was pretty far down in the pecking order. The group included an Ironman triathlete from California; a couple of ski mountaineers from Boulder; a jujitsu fighter from Australia; and a New Orleans–based former SWAT commander with a full sleeve of tattoos. A few rows of metal chairs had been set up in front of a whiteboard. I sat in the back near several guys who looked to be more my speed: T.J., a recent college grad who'd come at his parents' urging; John, an engineer and aspiring marathoner from Ontario; and Andy, a paunchy father of two from New York who was trying to get back in shape. Twight, who looked like Sgt. Rock with his jutting chin and shorn, graying hair, passed out three-ring binders, along with a copy of *Kiss or Kill*. Promptly at nine, we dove in.

The whiteboard session lasted most of the morning, and I tried to absorb it all despite a persistent sense of dread about the looming workouts. At last we retired to the mats and warmed up. Our first circuit was called Tail Pipe. It involves rowing 250 meters on a Concept2 machine as fast as you can while a partner stands in front of you, holding two 53-pound kettlebells at the top of his chest until you finish. As soon as you're done rowing, you switch places until you've done both exercises three times, without a break. I teamed up with Andy, and we grunted through the drill in just over nine minutes. The fittest guys in the class finished in about half that time.

"Why do you call it Tail Pipe?" I asked one of the coaches, still doubled over and wheezing like an asthmatic.

"Because," he said chirpily, "it's like sucking air out of a car's tailpipe!"

The afternoon wasn't much better. I struggled to complete the Kettlebell Complex—a series of awkward lifts and swings—and dropped out of Nothing But Pull-Ups altogether. Sunday followed a similar program and, much to my dismay, got even harder, since it involved dead lifts. The dead lift is a straightforward exercise that involves standing in front of a loaded barbell, squatting down, and then hoisting the weight to your thighs. The more weight you add, the more it feels as if your spine is going to splinter like a celery stalk. Lifting twice one's body weight is considered a respectable benchmark. The world record is a little over 1,000 pounds.

I got up to 315, about 85 pounds shy of my double-body-weight fantasy, before throwing in the towel. I had been trading turns with John, the marathoner, who I thought had stopped because he was worried about an old back injury. But then I noticed him walking in circles in the corner of the gym, listening to his iPod, clenching and unclenching his fists. At 45 years old and 158 pounds, John was both the oldest and smallest guy in the class, and everyone gathered around as he fought all the way up to 325 pounds, dropping the bar with a theatrical grunt, followed by a round of cheers. I asked him later what he'd been listening to.

"The Strokes," he said. "I love music. It gets me so pumped. Before that last lift, I could feel the hairs on my neck standing up."

The day concluded with the Jones Crawl, a two-exercise ordeal in which you're supposed to dead-lift 115 percent of your body weight ten times, then complete 25 two-footed jumps onto a 24-inch-high box—three sets, as fast as you can. Even the tougher seminarians seemed nervous. As we took our places, one of them cried out, "Spartans, prepare for glory!"

I tried to do 200 pounds, but it was too heavy. I barely completed the required ten dead lifts in the first round and had to sit, huffing, before I could contemplate the box jumps. Twight allowed me to reduce the weight, but only slightly. By my second set, I could no longer speak. During my third round of box jumps, I caught my toe and wiped out, raking my shin against the box's wooden edge and removing a strip of flesh. I looked at Twight, who I assumed would let me quit, since a bright red rivulet was now running down my leg. "Bloodsport," by New Model Army, thundered from the boom box. "Last round," Twight said, expressionless. "Let's go."

The whole thing lasted about eight minutes, though it felt like eight days. The only person with a slower time than mine was T.J., the college kid, but he'd lifted more weight.

That night, I staggered back to my room, haunted by a December 2005 story in *The New York Times* called "Getting Fit, Even If It Kills You," which dwelled on rhabdomyolysis. "Rhabdo," as gym rats call it, is a condition brought on when muscle tissue is so severely damaged that it releases myoglobin and other harmful substances into the blood, triggering kidney failure. Rhabdo has been linked to high-voltage electric shock, car accidents, physical torture, drug abuse—and, in a few cases, high-intensity workouts.

I was OK, just whipped. Before I finally crawled into bed, I stood shivering in an ice-cold shower, because we were told it would help reduce muscle swelling.

~~~~~~

The gut-busting circuits seemed to have served their purpose: By Monday I was so sore I could barely move, and it forced me to contemplate some deep questions: What the hell was this, and why was I doing it anyway?

To be fair, the Gym Jones seminar wasn't simply an opportunity to bathe in the geyser of testosterone that erupts when brawny men gather in a room full of heavy weights. In fact, if anything, I came away from the weekend impressed by Twight's holistic approach, his invocation of restraint, his belief that less really can be more. He encouraged honest self-assessment and rigorous attention to the bigger picture: nutrition, recovery, goal-setting. Of our 20-plus hours in the gym, at least two-thirds had been spent in front of the whiteboard. "I don't want to give a man a fish," Twight told me afterwards. "I want to teach him to fish."

There was a lot to learn, not much of it comforting. For starters, my diet was a mess. Beginning my day with a softball-size blueberry muffin and a triple cappuccino, as I'd done for, oh, the past 15 years, apparently didn't cut it. Training was important, but nutrition was the true foundation, because it was the engine of transformation at the molecular level. Twight pushed a Zone-like strategy of roughly equal parts carbs, protein, and fat. The rules were vaguely familiar: more protein, more fiber, more healthy fats like fish oil, and so on; way fewer processed carbohydrates, a daunting challenge when you realize just how much of the American food supply is created from corn and sugar.

"Want to lose weight fast?" Twight said. "Try not drinking alcohol for a month." These were the facts, he insisted; whether we chose to accept them was up to us.

As fascinating (if discouraging) as I found the dietary discussion, I was even more caught up in the Gym Jones weight-lifting philosophy. Since I was sticking around for a few days, Twight took me to meet Dan John, a strength-training czar who lives in Murray, a suburb of Salt Lake. "Dan is the master of simplification," Twight said on the drive out. "I've probably learned more from him than nearly any other individual."

John, 51, runs the Murray Institute for Lifelong Fitness, or, as he likes to call it, MILF. The way Twight talked about it, I expected MILF to occupy some gleaming hilltop campus, but in fact it's shoehorned into John's two-car garage, between his Mazda 6 and a refrigerator full of soda, beer, and bottled water. A rusty squat rack is pushed up against one wall, and two deep furrows have been worn into the concrete floor where the barbell plates repeatedly land. MILF also has an annex, a weedy alley that parallels an irrigation canal behind the house. When John and his jocks aren't swinging kettlebells or performing squats in the garage, they can often be found out back, dragging a weighted sled up and down the dirt lane.

John spent the afternoon sharing his 25 years of accumulated knowledge about strength and performance. Weight lifting, properly deployed, will serve any athlete at any level because it develops power, he told us, and power is the one thing central to almost every sport. Most of what I knew about weight training I'd learned in high school, where I mimicked routines that had originated in competitive bodybuilding. The strategy entailed isolating muscles and working them until they failed—curls, bench presses, triceps extensions, etc.—and then moving on to the next muscle group. After a while, your muscles got bigger, and, naturally, everyone assumed that a bigger muscle was a stronger muscle.

But that isn't always the case. In fact, exercise physiologists discovered that muscle isolation is often counterproductive when it comes to executing more complex natural movements, where muscles are required to work in concert. Hence the value of Olympic lifting, with its expanded range of motion. Physiologists also discovered that only certain types of lifting make muscles grow larger—specifically, doing eight to 15 reps in sets that end in complete exhaustion. In contrast, slightly modified approaches, like fewer reps with heavier weights, build stronger muscles without making them bigger—particularly appealing to endurance athletes, for whom increased size is considered a liability.

There's legitimate science behind the high-intensity work, too, and both John and Twight believe that, done right, it produces rapid and profound results. The most convincing studies have been done by a Japanese physiologist named Izumi Tabata. In 1996, Dr. Tabata discovered that short-duration, high-intensity training enhances anaerobic capacity while simultaneously increasing aerobic endurance. This allows you to shed more fat than with moderate-intensity aerobic exercise, and it also produces a metabolic afterburn as the body works to repair itself. Circuits like those we did at Gym Jones are sometimes referred to in the weight-lifting community simply as "Tabatas."

"Strength is the glass," John called out as Twight and I walked down the driveway at MILF late that day. "All your other training is the liquid."

Before I left Utah, I joined Twight for a bike ride. He was training under the guidance of Dr. Massimo Testa, a sports physician whose résumé includes work with Miguel Indurain, Lance Armstrong, and a peloton's worth of other pros. Testa was helping Twight get ready for the Tour of Park City, a 170-mile race with 9,000 feet of elevation gain. I felt slightly ridiculous when Twight showed up on his carbon-fiber rig, decked out in full race kit, since I was winging it on a rented touring bike and wearing hiking shorts, running shoes, and a T-shirt. But anything was better than following him into the dark recesses of his pain cave, even if it meant chasing him around the mountains outside Salt Lake.

Thankfully, this was a recovery day for him, and we spun along a winding canyon road at a pace I could manage. Twight likes to describe himself as a "control enthusiast," and he told me that, as much as Gym Jones seemed poised for bigger things, he was willing to grow the business only if he could do so without compromise. He'd hired a business coach at the end of 2007 to help him sort out the process, and a few things were already in the works. He planned to increase the number of seminars, which routinely sell out despite costing $1,500 per person, from four to 12 times a year. A set of training DVDs (working title: *Unfuck Your Head*) was in production. He had six part-time trainers and 30 paying clients and would bring on more as demand warranted. At night, or early in the mornings, he was chipping away at a book, a comprehensive philosophy behind his training methods. And he's currently finishing a dimension of the Web site that will cater exclusively to paying members, who will be able to interact with Twight and other coaches, exchange ideas, and create the kind of virtual community that will mirror the real ones beginning to materialize all around him.

The trickiest part, he said, is communicating the essence of his project. Changing your body is just mechanics; it's changing your mind that presents the real challenge.

"If the mind is not first trained to enjoy hard work, to relish suffering, to address the unknown, then no program, no amount of training can be effective," he told us during the seminar. "The muscle we are interested in training is inside the skull."

For all the clanking iron and sweaty caterwauling, what Twight has created at Gym Jones is not a place where its denizens are guaranteed to succeed but an environment in which they're allowed to fail—sometimes catastrophically. "The risk of failure, social or physical, is paramount, because failure and dissatisfaction are the parents of thought," he said. "Success and fulfillment do not inspire or require introspection."

We reached the top of a high pass. Twight wanted to keep going down the other side, but I told him I was too spent from the weekend. "Fair enough," he said as we about-faced.

I wondered if the world is ready for what he has to offer, if people are prepared for such serious commitment. Clearly, at least a few are. No-frills outfits created in the spirit of Gym Jones are beginning to sprout everywhere—Mountain Athlete, in Jackson, Project Deliverance, in St. Louis—places devoted to helping us endure the kind of flogging that training like this entails. Twight had told me about a young climber from France who'd found out about him on the Web, flown to Salt Lake, slept in a city park, and showed up at Twight's house the next day. No e-mails. No phone calls. "I want to train at Gym Jones," he told Twight, who was so impressed he invited him to stay for the next three months.

What Twight rails against is mediocrity—not in terms of output, but effort—and, for him, too much of what fitness has become in America engenders exactly that. He's matured considerably since his days as a tortured alpinist, but he hasn't relinquished his rebellious inner punk, pushing back against so much of what we're told and sold every day. Fitness for him will never be a program, because, by definition, it has to be a perpetual and ever-evolving process—individually crafted and constantly reevaluated and revised. "It's easy to be hard, but it's hard to be smart," he wrote to me, quoting an old Marine saying, but it was cold comfort, since such insight implies that the progression never gets any easier.

Worse, perhaps, was my gathering awareness that I'd bought it. Gym Jones had introduced me to the whole picture: How to create a rock-solid foundation and how to build off that to achieve my specific athletic goals. What that might be I wasn't quite sure, but I'd lost five pounds since I started training with Carolyn Parker, and despite the beating I'd taken in Salt Lake, I already felt stronger. I realized I'd drunk generously from Twight's rancid punch and, in a strange, masochistic way, looked forward to returning to the grassy field in Albuquerque, where Parker would continue doling out the punishment.

I tried to keep Twight in sight as we descended, whooshing past a few other cyclists grimacing through their long grind up the canyon. I couldn't remember the last time I'd gone so fast on a bike, and it was exhilarating and terrifying at once—hunched over the handlebars, swooping around the switchbacks, hurtling toward a future in which I imagined that what we were doing and what we were capable of doing had somehow, suddenly, become the same thing.

(Originally published December 2008)

HOCHSTGESCHWINDIGKEIT!*

JOSHUA FOER

One year, in the New Yorker's *annual travel-themed Journeys issue, there was a story about elevators. I loved the broad interpretation of an elevator ride as a journey, so a few years later, when we were compiling stories for a special issue on the theme of water, I wanted to find an entry that would be similarly unexpected. We found that story in Germany, where competitive water sliding is apparently a thing, and Joshua Foer was game to enter the chute.*

The fastest speed ever achieved on a water slide is 57 miles per hour.

It was clocked in 2009 on the Kilimanjaro, a 164-foot-high, 50-degree plummet at Águas Quentes, a water park outside of Rio de Janeiro, by Jens Scherer, a German advertising executive. Scherer, 30, the reigning champion of competitive "speed chuting," also holds four Guinness world records in the sport, including the one-day distance record, for chuting 94 miles on a slide near Munich. That's like traveling all the way from New York to Philadelphia on the bare skin of your back. During those 24 hours, he slept for just an hour and a half and climbed 30,000 vertical feet worth of steps, the equivalent of hiking from sea level to the summit of Mount Everest.

Approaching 60 miles an hour on a water slide is not simply a matter of leaping and letting gravity do its thing. Speed chuting is a skill. An art. And there are people who take it very, very seriously. Almost all of them are German, and there are more of them every year. They compete on teams with names like Slide Fast,

---

*"Maximum speed!"

Die Young and regularly travel many hours to weekend tournaments sponsored by water parks across their country.

"Speed chuting," like "skiing," is a catchall term that encapsulates a range of events, from simple top-to-bottom timed runs to sliding marathons (fastest to cover 26.2 horizontal miles). For the moment, it remains an exclusively German sport whose place in the national athletic firmament perhaps best resembles paintball in the U.S. Those who compete are crazed; those who don't find it odd and maybe even a little scary.

When I first heard about speed chuting, this past winter, it didn't sound scary to me. It sounded freaking sweet. So in February I called up Scherer to find out how I could get in on the action. My timing couldn't have been better, Scherer told me. In late March, the German National Speed Chuting Championship, the Kentucky Derby of the sport's yearlong circuit, would be held in the Baltic Sea resort town of Scharbeutz. To my surprise, Scherer noted that the contest was open to anyone. Even more tantalizing, no American had ever competed in speed chuting, meaning the title of American champion was unclaimed. I decided I ought to do something about that.

"If you come a few days early, I would be happy to teach you my techniques," Scherer graciously offered. "You can crash on my couch."

Let me be frank: Nobody would ever mistake me for someone who belongs in a major athletic competition. My daily exercise regimen consists of a half-mile shuffle to the coffee shop to pick up a pair of banana-oat mini-muffins. Fortunately, Scherer hadn't seemed fazed when I noted my lack of fitness. He gave me some basic advice to start prepping for what he described as "rocking the tube."

Training for speed chuting, he explained, is sort of like powerlifting. All I had to do was isolate a couple of core muscles and work them until they were rock solid. "So long as your back and stomach are strong, you don't especially have to worry about the rest of the body," he said. He also wanted me to find a local water slide and take some practice runs. Easier said than done when you live in New England and it's winter. Ultimately, I committed to doing 50 sit-ups and 10 pull-ups each morning—a routine I remained fanatically devoted to for exactly eight days.

Still, I allowed myself visions of glory as I flew into Zurich and took a train across the German border to Hattingen, the tiny town where Scherer lives with his girlfriend, Sandra Westhoff, southern Germany's female speed-chuting champion. Scherer picked me up at the train station and drove us straight to the Aquasol water center, in nearby Rottweil. Facilities like Aquasol are quite popular in Germany, where long winters have people seeking out indoor exercise. Inside, there were saunas, hot tubs, lap pools, and a wicked four-story water slide Scherer called "the Black Hole." Added in 2003, it features a 394-foot tube, the longest in southern Germany. The interior is made entirely of black fiberglass and is illuminated with trippy flashing lights. As in any competition-ready chute, at each end there was a pair of laser triggers measuring times down to the millisecond.

Scherer, five-eight and lanky, toured me around wearing goggles and a snug, dark-blue Speedo-style suit tagged with the URL of Miller Ice Power, a nanotechnology company that had given him some experimental racewear. He had earrings in his left ear and a Celtic tattoo on his right calf. A marathon runner and fitness fiend, he got into speed chuting the year Aquasol opened its slide, when his mother pointed out an announcement for southern Germany's first championship in the newspaper. Scherer entered and won, as he has every year since. After capturing his first national title, in 2003, he has gone on to become a minor celebrity, appearing on German TV to teach Playboy Bunnies to speed-chute or to demonstrate how to somersault down a slide.

Despite his frequent use of *Point Break*–style bro slang, Scherer goes about chuting with a Teutonic seriousness. He sat me down in a plastic deck chair at the foot of the Black Hole and attempted to elucidate the physics of chuting. "It's all about the friction, dude," he said, rubbing his palms together. To go fast, I needed to minimize the surface area of skin and suit making contact with the slide. Basic speed-chuting position involves crossing your ankles, tensing your core, and arching your back so that there are only three points of contact with the slide: the shoulder blades and a single heel. Scherer lay down on the tiled floor and showed me how he throws his arms up behind him, clenching his triceps against his ears to keep his head up.

On the slide, the trick is to know when to maximize speed and when to dial it back. When Scherer comes around curves, his body is sometimes so far up the tube walls that he's looking down on the channel of water below. But if you ride too high in the wrong spot, you can stall, crashing onto your stomach and killing your run, if not sending you to the ER for stitches on your forehead. You also have to know how to manage the last 30 or so feet of the tube, when you reach top speed and even the most refined chuter tends to be out of control. Then there's the landing pool, which you want to enter with your legs tightly crossed. Hit it at 50-plus miles per hour and you'll be lucky if a nasal enema and a mouthful of snot are the worst of it.

Even when they do everything right, hard-bodied athletes aren't always the fastest chuters. Sometimes it's the cannonballs, 250-plus-pound behemoths like six-time national champ Christoph Feiden and perpetual runner-up Andreas Köhnke, whom Scherer refers to, with a hint of derision, as "the old-schoolers." They have bellies that drape over their Speedos, and they hurl themselves down slides with a single muscular heave. "They have no technique, just stomachs," says Scherer.

Finally, there's a third group of sliders, to which I belong: the freaks. On my first ride down the Black Hole, I clocked a 22.39, a middling time some four seconds slower than Scherer's. Still, I was moving surprisingly fast, about 30 miles per hour by the end. By my tenth go, once I'd gotten a handle on how to arch my back, I was clearing the bottom laser in 20.35, a fairly decent time that had Scherer raising his eyebrows.

It turns out that my most substantial bodily flaws make me perfectly suited to speed chuting. My slightly hunched posture causes my shoulder blades to comfortably pop out like bobsled runners. My flat ass is easily suspended off the fiberglass. My bird legs cut a tight hydrodynamic profile. Even my love handles turn out to be an asset in a sport where having a little meat on the bones translates to faster times.

I had just one physical disadvantage: the continuous tract of Semitic fur that runs from my lower back to my toes. After an especially dismal run of 21.71, I asked Scherer if my hirsuteness was slowing me down.

He bent over and took a close look at my thighs. "If you want to increase the speed, we'll need to make a shaving session this evening," he said. I chuckled uncomfortably. He didn't. "But, truly, if you keep your ass off the slide, it shouldn't matter," he added. For the sake of saving a few milliseconds, some of the most ambitious competitors shave or wax, but Scherer finds them needlessly vain.

My biggest problem was my baggy swimsuit. "You know, you're not going to win in those," he said, examining my trunks. In his quest for speed, Scherer has experimented with just about every possible form of swimwear, including the sharkskin-like unitards favored by Olympic swimmers and a type of low-friction foil he wrapped around his entire body. He's also coated his skin in soaps, oils, waxes, hydrophobic gels, and a kind of cream used to tenderize the udders of dairy cows—all of which are officially verboten in competition. But no matter: "There is simply nothing faster than bare skin," he says.

Even a few square inches of Speedo can cause unnecessary drag. As I stood behind him before a run late in our session at the Black Hole, he reached back and jacked the rear triangle up his crack like a G-string. "I'll see you at the bottom, man," he said. Then he dried his hands on a towel, leapt into the tube with an exaggerated mule kick, and slid down on nothing but flesh.

The water slide is such an obvious idea that it's hard to believe it was actually invented, like the lightbulb or the telephone, by a single individual in a single burst of inspiration. Even harder to believe is that it didn't happen until 1971. That was the year a California campground owner named Dick Croul, on vacation in Hawaii, rode a natural flume and decided he'd be the first person to build his own. He returned to Placerville, California, dug out a five-acre lake at his campground in the Sierra foothills, built a mound out of all the surplus dirt, and covered it with Gunite, the cement-and-sand mixture that lines swimming pools. Visitors to the campground rode the 350-foot slide on inch-thick gym mats.

From Northern California, Croul's invention spread rapidly to other campgrounds. All those early slides were made of Gunite, which meant they ripped up the back and could be ridden only on mats. Then, in 1976, Disney introduced the world's first commercial fiberglass slide, at Disney World's River Country, in Orlando. The year after that, Wet 'n Wild, the world's first water park, opened in Orlando.

The fiberglass slides—smooth, lightweight, modular—created an entirely new form of thrill: the body ride. Just man, water, and gravity. The late seventies and early eighties saw an explosion of highly questionable designs up and down both coasts. Infamously, Action Park, in Vernon, New Jersey, made the first attempt at a vertical loop-de-loop, with a long, straight tube that ended in a comically tight curlicue. A trapdoor had to be built into the top of the loop to rescue stuck sliders. Those who did make it around the bend sometimes had broken noses and other injuries to show for it, earning the place the nickname "Traction Park." The tube stayed open for exactly one month before it was shut down by the New Jersey Carnival Amusement Ride Safety Board. Likewise, in Singapore, a multi-lane racing slide sent riders several feet in the air as they crested a hill. Riders often landed on top of one another in the wrong lanes, and it was eventually closed.

The early slides were "basically bunny runs," says Rick Hunter, a former member of the Canadian national ski team, whose Ottawa-based company, ProSlide, is a global leader in the water-slide industry. "Now we understand compounding curves," he says. "It's like driving a race car. If you're going into a curve, you don't rip on the wheel; you turn slowly. We put you on the wall, shorten the radius, and hold you there."

ProSlide and its competitors have produced a number of stunning slides in recent years, the most expensive of which cost about $4 million to erect. At the Summit Plummet, a 12-story drop at Disney World's Blizzard Beach, even an unskilled chuter can top 50 miles per hour thanks to a 66-degree slope. Others, like the Wildebeest, at Holiday World in Santa Claus, Indiana, add features but require the use of inflatable rafts. The Wildebeest, the world's longest "water coaster," at 1,710 feet in length, includes sections in which riders are carried uphill with magnets. At the Blue Bayou Water Park in Baton Rouge, Louisiana, the Azuka, the largest "tornado" slide, drops riders 80 feet into a 70-foot-wide funnel, where they swing like a pendulum, experiencing weightlessness.

Of course, none of these slides was created with competitive chuters in mind. Hunter told me he'd never heard of German speed chuting. "Sounds pretty wild," he said.

Scherer dismisses most of the elaborate twisters crafted for the water-park masses. "I'm not terribly impressed by any of them," he says. Still, when a new slide opens anywhere in Europe, he's often called in to act as a test pilot. The week before I showed up, he had been at the Wave, near Innsbruck, Austria, trying out Wild Pig, the world's first double-loop slide. (The loops are tilted 45 degrees off vertical to prevent stalling.) The park's management sent him down with a box strapped to his stomach to measure G-forces on turns. In order to gain the approval of the TüV, a government-affiliated German safety organization, riders can't exceed 2.6 G's. Scherer says he topped out at nearly 6. "But since the people from the government can't go as fast as me, the slide is still considered legal," he explained.

Meanwhile, Scherer and other chuters have started building slides of their own. Recently, Scherer hired a carpenter to construct a small, perfectly vertical loop-de-loop, the first since Action Park's. His grand dream is to build a 900-foot kamikaze—taller than most Manhattan skyscrapers. He and his partner in the project, Rolf Allerdissen, another chuter, have been in talks with the government of Namibia about building the slide into the side of a major sand dune.

Last year, Scherer and his team built a mock-up of their Namibian kamikaze on a smaller industrial sandpile in Bavaria. After digging a trench down the 360-foot hill and lining it with plastic Slip 'n Slides, they brought in a local fire engine to pump water to the top. The first slider, a TV stuntwoman named Funda Vanroy, ended up flipping end over end and landing face-first at the bottom, bruised and with a bloody nose, having just missed getting decapitated by the boom of a video camera.

~~~~~~

Scherer had to go to work on my second day in Germany, so he sent me to the local sporting-goods store with Westhoff to buy a Speedo. He'd offered to let me borrow one of his own banana hammocks, but after witnessing his self-wedgie technique, I politely declined. Either way, he seemed deaf to the erotic undertones of my shopping for minimal-coverage swimwear with his girlfriend. But, having never worn tighty-whiteys, much less a Speedo, I needed the help.

After sorting through racks of dangling nylon suits, I selected a blue-and-white number and retreated behind a fitting-room curtain to tug it on. When I shyly pulled back the curtain, I asked Westhoff if I should maybe go up a size. She had me do a 360, pausing without humor to eyeball my junk, and shook her head.

That afternoon, Scherer and I went back to Aquasol. In my new suit I was immediately a full second faster than I'd been the previous evening, and my times dropped by a few milliseconds on each successive run. After two hours at the slide, our heels and shoulder blades raw, Scherer and I retired to the heated salt-water pool. "I want to show you something," he said as we relaxed amid a group of elderly women doing Aquarobics. He swam out into the middle of the pool, floated for a moment on his back, then began sinking.

"I don't float," he said, standing up again. "I can't explain it. I never have."

"Is that why you're so fast?" I asked.

"I really don't know why I'm the best. I often wonder," he said. "I mean, I use the same technique as all the others. I guess maybe it's my dense bones."

The next day, we took an eight-hour train ride across the country to Scharbeutz. The championship was being hosted by the Ostsee Resort and Spa, a five-star beachfront hotel. We checked in and hit the slide for practice runs.

Everything about the Ostsee tube was world-class. The curves were tight and nicely timed, the changes in grade were surprising, and the drop-off near the end was exhilarating. A technician had spent the week before the competition caulking every fiberglass seam with silicone to make it extra-smooth. Video cameras were installed in the ceiling of the tube so that a gallery of spectators could watch the chuters negotiate several of the course's more difficult turns on a bank of six screens.

For all that effort, I was pretty sure that about half the 117 competitors who'd shown up were there only because it sounded like a fun way to spend a weekend afternoon. The age range was impressive: The youngest entrant was eight; the oldest, 74.

Then there were the real competitors. Like golfers studying the greens before a major championship, we wanted to know those curves and banks intuitively. We kept anxious eyes on each other's times. "Let your butt hit the slide a bit," Scherer advised me. "You don't want the others to know your true speed."

There was a group of particularly amped guys whom Scherer kept referring to as the Weirdos. "It's OK to take water sliding seriously, but for these guys it's the meaning of their life," he told me. "The Weirdos are always saying, 'That guy is cheating!' or 'That guy oils his back!' They don't have jobs or educations. One of them is mentally disabled."

The Weirdos were easy to pick out. They were the ones hollering obnoxiously after good times and slapping the water with their palms and yelling "Scheisse!" after bad ones. One of them, on a practice run just before me, stepped up to the start position, dropped the back of his suit around his thighs, and launched his completely bare ass down the slide.

There had been bad blood between Scherer and the Weirdos ever since the group banded together to oust one of Scherer's close friends from the presidency of the German Race Sliding Federation, amid accusations of financial impropriety. Scherer countered by accusing one of the Weirdos of pedophilia. (The guy had e-mailed Scherer asking for pictures of some of the younger competitors.) Scherer tried, and failed, to have him banned for life from national competitions. He pointed him out as we waited in line at the top of the slide. "Stay away from that guy," he said. "He's Weirdo Number One."

In speed chuting, too much training can be counterproductive, because the more you slide, the more likely you are to bruise your points of contact with the fiberglass. When we went back to our hotel, I examined my damage in the bathroom mirror. I had a pair of red bull's-eyes on my upper back, surrounded by blue clouds of bruising. Scherer smirked when I showed him. "White skin, red cuts, blue bruises: very American," he said. His own left elbow was bleeding from a bang-up coming down off a high turn. Ralf May, one of Scherer's friends from Aquasol, had a hip so bruised he could barely walk.

Over beers at a traditional northern-German restaurant, I asked Scherer whether he thought I had any chance in the championship. "I'm not going to tell you you're going to win," he said. "I just can't do that. But it's possible you could make the finals."

He shrugged. "Anything is possible."

The event was split into three divisions: Women competed in their own group, and the men were put into welterweight and heavyweight classes, with the dividing line at 70 kilograms, or about 155 pounds. I swear that under normal circumstances my five-eight frame would be a fair distance south of that, but I'd spent the better part of the winter holed up with the shingles and overdoing the minimuffins. At the official weigh-in, the digital scale put me at 66.7 kilos (147 pounds), which meant I was going to be one of the heaviest competitors in the welterweight class—a certain advantage. Even better, of the 17 competitors who'd registered as welterweights, three came in overweight and had been bumped up. My competition was 13 lanky teenage boys and an eight-year-old.

The morning consisted of three time trials. The ten competitors with the lowest combined time would then advance to the finals in the afternoon, where two more runs would decide the medal rankings. When Scherer's name was announced over the loudspeaker for his first slide of the day, the official timekeeper—a man wearing camouflage hunting pants hiked above his ankles, fluorescent orange suspenders, a cowboy hat, and aviator sunglasses—introduced him as "the most famous water-slider in the world." The crowd of three dozen spectators, arrayed on plastic deck chairs at the foot of the landing pool, hooted and clapped in rhythm.

My own introduction a few minutes later was no less raucous. As I stepped up to the slide, a German techno remix of John Denver singing, "Take me home, country roads . . ." blared through the sound system, a respectful if slightly confused nod to my home country.

After our three morning runs, Scherer was in first place in the heavyweight division and I was on my way to making my country proud, ahead of all the teenagers but one, a 17-year-old from Team Wedel named Jannik Ahrens, who weighed in a kilo heavier than me. At the top of the slide, as we prepared for our two deciding afternoon runs, I asked Ahrens if he thought that extra kilo accounted for the 18 hundredths of a second that separated us.

"I think it's this," he said, turning around. He popped his shoulder blades out. They protruded like a third pair of limbs. You could have hung a hat on each of them. He was a freak like me.

I got into position for my first run, looking over my shoulder at the line of welterweights waiting behind me, then up at the camera looking down at me. I took a deep breath. If I'd come all this way to Germany, I might as well go for it. I reached back, twisted the seat of my Speedo into a tight little rope, yanked it up my tush, then flung myself down the slide.

Halfway down, the water was spraying so hard up my nose that I couldn't breathe. My shoulder blades were burning. My ass was so far off the slide I could feel a breeze between my cheeks. Then, on the third-to-last turn, catastrophe struck. My momentum carried me so high up the wall that I flipped and fell several feet before landing face-first on the tube, banging my arm on the way down. I rode the last two turns on my stomach before I was able to right myself. When I got out at the bottom, I looked up at my time: 22.51, a full second slower than Ahrens's slowest run.

Scherer, whose own gold was secure after a blazing first run of 18.54, was waiting at the landing-pool steps. He put his arms on my shoulders. "You need to relax your body more as you go around the curves. From now on there are no more errors. Rock the tube, Josh! Relax and rock the tube!"

As I climbed back up the steps to the top of the slide, those words rang in my head. I went G-string again, but this time I let my body go limp around the turns, and I could feel myself accelerating even faster than on my previous run. Just as I was about to flip on the same turn that had done me in, I spread my legs slightly and managed to stay upright. At the end of the tunnel, there was a moment of quiet, then I hit the pool and German techno exploded in my ears. When I climbed out, my legs were shaking. I looked up at Scherer, who flashed me a pair of shockers and pointed excitedly up at my time: 21.93 seconds. Still second place behind Ahrens but a righteous finish. I wrapped a towel around my waist and pumped my fist for the cheering crowd.

A podium was brought out. Cameras flashed. A middle-aged blonde in pantyhose and flip-flops hoisted a plastic chalice emblazoned with the logo of the Ostsee Resort and Spa and handed me a certificate. For my second-place finish, I received a snack basket filled with German delicacies: herring fillets in tomato sauce, a box of muesli, a jar of pickles, pea stew, and bockwurst sausages. I left them in my hotel room, along with my wet Speedo.

(Originally published July 2010)

THE UNDISPUTED KING OF DOGSLED TOURISM

STEPHANIE PEARSON

It's not easy building a tourism business in Norway's frigid north. Don't tell that to Kenth Fjellborg, who built a dogsled-touring empire that attracts 5,000 would-be mushers a year to a frozen patch of tundra 100 miles north of the Arctic Circle. And he's not afraid to yell at the customers.

The sky is gunmetal gray, a shade somewhere between inviting and malicious. We're 40 miles due east of Tromsø, Norway, a city that sits on the Norwegian Sea more than 180 miles north of the Arctic Circle. Yesterday, kiteboarders were ripping across the frigid late-April water propelled by gusty winds, a testament to the commonly held belief that of the three Scandinavian bloodlines—Norwegian, Danish, and Swedish—Norwegians are the most hardcore. The proponents of that stereotype, however, have yet to meet Kenth Fjellborg, Arctic Swede.

"Get dressed! Put your boots on!" Fjellborg shouts to jolt us out of the heated van. "When we get going, we're not going to stop! The sun is hiding in the sky, but we're going to go right into the white! Men, you do the number one outside. The outhouse is not for gentlemen. But I hate it when pee is spread over the snow."

It's the first morning of our journey, and the marching—or, rather, mushing—orders have begun. Six of us, all neophytes, will be guided by Fjellborg on one of his most rigorous Arctic dogsledding adventures. We're lined up like a United Nations train: Fjellborg is in front; the three American, one British, and two Swedish sledding rookies are in the middle; and 26-year-old Norwegian-Scottish guide

Amanda Calder, who wears two knives at all times—one for dogs and one for humans—brings up the rear.

We'll each lead a team of five or six dogs on a five-day, 160-mile journey from the old Rognli homestead, which sits in the Signal Valley, on a historic backcountry "highway" between Norway and Sweden. We'll climb 2,400 feet into the Arctic tundra, then travel southeast along frozen waterways that will lead us to Fjellborg's home in the Swedish village of Poikkijärvi. Poikkijärvi is on the banks of the Torne River, directly across the water from Jukkasjärvi, the village Fjellborg's ancestors first inhabited in 1690. Nine generations of Fjellborgs have lived within a 25-mile radius of Jukkasjärvi ever since.

But first, a dose of äkta svensk gästfrihet—genuine Swedish hospitality. Cooking over an open fire, Fjellborg and his pit crew of two, who helped transport our 46 dogs and will leave us here, have set out a small smorgasbord of reindeer stew, lingonberry jam, and mashed potatoes, along with that staple of the Swedish backcountry diet, polar bread—a whole wheat pita topped with butter and cheese.

The hearty brunch, inspired by the Sami, who have herded reindeer in the northern latitudes for 8,000 years, will fuel us until we reach Pältsa, the Swedish Tourist Association's northernmost mountain hut, which will be our home our first night and sits across the border in Sweden, about 20 miles from here, at 68.8 degrees north latitude. The hut was used during World War II as a base for Norwegian resistance fighters. Farther along the trail, we'll stay at a Sami run fishing camp, then at the residence of an old Swedish family who've lived here almost as long as the Fjellborg clan, and, finally, at Sevuvuoma, an ancestral Fjellborg homestead, which Fjellborg bought from a distant cousin and has recently renovated. From there we'll mush roughly 20 miles to his house in Poikkijärvi.

"Do you know the Sami word for 'vegetarian'?" Fjellborg asks. "Poor hunter!" Then he gets down to business.

"Ladies and gentlemen, we've been talking and eating, and now we are going to go," says the 42-year-old musher. Fjellborg is blond, strong, and five foot ten—a relatively modest height that he blames on a lack of leafy greens in his childhood diet. His blue eyes have been scanning the darkening sky since we arrived, so he hurries us through a truncated version of dogsledding 101.

"If you don't work the brake, you will have difficulty steering the sled," he says. "Have pressure in the lines, and put your lead dog in first. And don't let the team go. If you do, I will scream at you in bad words!" One more thing, he adds: "Don't scream at your dogs. They are all trying their best."

"Do they speak English?" asks Todd Fairbairn, a 43-year-old entrepreneur from New York City.

"Just don't speak German to them," says Fjellborg. "They don't like that."

My team of honey-colored Alaskan huskies, with Morris and Trista in front, Meyra in the middle, and Nelson and Whopper in back, are small but feisty. Whopper is nipping at Nelson, Nelson is baying like a treed lion, and Morris is pooping on the pure white snow.

By now the dogs are going ballistic, yelping and straining at their collars. Fjellborg releases his brake, which unleashes a chain reaction of howling beasts that charge into the white abyss.

There are many time-honored Scandinavian traditions. Dogsledding is not one of them. In Jukkasjärvi, the sport goes back only 50 years. When the Sami, who preceded Fjellborg's family by a few millennia, needed transportation, they hitched their reindeer to a sled or skied. A carbon-dated ski fragment found in Russian Lapland predates the invention of the wheel.

Today, however, the human-to-dog-ratio in Jukkasjärvi is 519 to 1,000. The influx of dogs is thanks to Fjellborg and a few local kennels, but it's also the result of an increasing worldwide fascination with harnessing the power of man's best friend. In the Scandinavian countries, especially Norway, the number of competitive mushers has grown exponentially in the past decade.

"Either you gotta be tough or you gotta be stupid," Fjellborg likes to say about making a living 124 miles north of the Arctic Circle. It seems he's the former. In the past 25 years, he has created what amounts to a Swedish dogsledding dynasty, and he now has 125 selectively bred Alaskan huskies he keeps in immaculate kennels in his vast yard.

"I breed the best," Fjellborg says. "If you're interested in motorcycles, you like a good motorcycle. If you're interested in dogs, you like a good dog."

In addition to the kennels, Fjellborg's home base includes a house, a separate suite of rooms with a sauna for guests, a garage full of winter toys—from skis to kid-size Arctic Cat snowmobiles—and, of course, the ubiquitous Volvo station wagon. He shares the compound with his wife, Ann, 42, a lithe, blond skier from southern Sweden, and their three towheaded little girls, Klara, 9, Elina, 7, and Amanda, 4. Occasionally, Fjellborg's unofficially adopted son, a 56-year-old Sami reindeer herder named Nils Anders Blindh, who jokingly calls Fjellborg Dad, shows up at the house to make the morning coffee. Fjellborg's father, a retired cop, and mother, who still bakes the family bread in a massive wood-fired oven, live next door.

Fjellborg is an anomaly in a country where the national ethos is *logom*, an old Viking term derived from the words *laget om,* which literally mean "team wise" but refer to the mandatory sharing of booze after pilfering it from enemies.

Today the term suggests approaching everything in life, including entrepreneurship, in moderation.

"When I was 16, I wanted to be like Onassis. Do you know him?" Fjellborg asks me during a lunch break a few days into the trip. "I heard he had lots of chicks. So I got a big wooden boat to take tourists up the Torne River."

After saving money from his tour-boat operation, Fjellborg began working with dogs at a kennel near his village. In 1989, he won the first dogsled race he entered, Sweden's Nordic Marathon, which inspired him to fax a letter to Alaskan Joe Runyan, that year's Iditarod champion, to ask if he could work for him.

"I was really into racing and wanted to see how the big boys were doing it," says Fjellborg.

When Runyan responded with a yes, Fjellborg moved to Alaska to learn the competitive side of dogsledding. He was 19.

"Kenth was a lively guy," says Runyan, now 63. "I had a five-mile hill that I used to run. Every once in a while, I'd sucker him into going with me. I don't remember if he ever beat me, but he definitely could keep up. That was part of the job description: tough-guy musher trying to win the race. Kenth bought into that."

In 1990, Fjellborg returned to Sweden to complete a then mandatory ten-month stint in the Swedish army, joining the Arctic Rangers, soldiers trained to survive the most extreme cold and operate behind enemy lines. That same year, he bought his first Alaskan husky, a female named Derby, for $3,500. By 1994, Fjellborg had bred, bought, or borrowed enough dogs from Runyan to assemble a strong team that nabbed a top-20 finish at the 1,150-mile Iditarod; he wears the medal, a brass belt buckle, to hold up his pants. Since 1995, when he started his dogsledding business, Fjellborg Arctic Journeys, he has taught Lauren Hutton how to mush; wrangled dogs for a Van Halen video; guided Monaco's Prince Albert II on his successful 2006 expedition to the North Pole; produced an Arctic leg of the 2010 Amazing Race; and hosted Crown Princess Victoria of Sweden at the renovated family homestead in Sevuvuoma. He runs trips 120 days a year, from longer, expedition-style adventures to shorter outings.

Fjellborg's reputation has spread thanks to his connection with the Ice Hotel, the 59,000-square-foot snow palace in Jukkasjärvi that attracts 50,000 visitors annually. For the past 21 years, carefully selected artists have created what look like real-time renderings of their best psychedelic dreams using only snow, ice, and sneece (a combination of ice and snow) mined from the Torne. A 2011 favorite was the Bubblesuite, a whimsical bedroom straight out of a James Bond film with reindeer skins on the bed and curvy ice-bubble walls, created by two Dutch artists.

Fjellborg oversees the hotel's sled-dog experiences for guests. He also provides authentic Swedish resourcefulness to clients who use the Ice Hotel's surreal backdrop for ad campaigns. Two years ago, the creative director from Hermès flew from Paris with 21 employees for a fashion shoot. Fjellborg's job was to scout the perfect location for an image of a dog team rounding a bend in the woods. That one shot took three days.

All told, Fjellborg and his staff take out upwards of 5,000 clients a year. "What is stimulating to me is that I live 100 miles north of the Arctic Circle, and I don't have to go anywhere to meet people. They all come to me," he says. "Yet I can still take part in what my ancestors have done—catching game, hunting, and fishing."

"I may not be street-smart," says Fjellborg, who ranks driving through Milan as the most terrifying experience of his life. "But I know my way around the woods."

Hopefully, Fjellborg knows his way around the open tundra. It's day two of the expedition, and last night, right after we were greeted at Pältsa by the caretaker and two Finnish skiers who were thawing out in the communal kitchen, the weather went bonkers. The wind was so strong that the snow was falling horizontally.

Pältsa sleeps 22 guests in two huts, in rooms lined with bunk beds, and is situated in one of the most beautiful locations on the trail, which makes it a popular stop on the Arctic snowmobile circuit. But today it's just a couple of brave Finns on skis and us.

Fourteen hours later the wind and snow haven't let up, but Fjellborg is cracking jokes at breakfast.

"If you want to learn Swedish, listen to me, not them," he tells the non-Swedes as we eat our oatmeal. "One hundred years ago, people spoke Finnish, not Swedish, up here, so we've learned a more correct language."

Fjellborg is comparing his Swedish with that of Andrea Westerlind, 30, and Martin Berling, 35, the two other Swedes in our group, who moved from Stockholm to New York City to introduce Sweden's premier outdoor-clothing brand, Fjällräven, into the U.S. market. Fjellborg has been a guide, organizer, and logistics man for many of the company's product-development and testing expeditions for more than 20 years.

"Kenth, did you know the original people came from Africa and not Sweden?" says Berling, who, at well over six feet tall and with a full red beard, looks like a 21st-century hipster Viking.

After breakfast I suit up in a Fjellborg-issued snowsuit, a fur-lined bomber hat, and custom-made polar boots. The temperature is in the mid-twenties, and the dogs are almost buried in snow. A few of us try to coax them out of the fetal position with a mixture of chicken, lamb, and beef that Calder has spent the past hour hacking into bite-size pieces and mixing with water into a cold doggie stew.

After the dogs are fed and the sleds are loaded, the clouds part and a small patch of blue appears in the sky. The wind, however, is so strong that I can't walk in a straight line. We have at least 30 miles to travel today, so it's time to mush. When all goes well, we cover approximately ten miles an hour. We harness the dogs, and then Fjellborg gives us two rules.

Rule number one: Stay close.

Rule number two: Don't lose your gloves.

We set off on an unnamed trail, marked every 50 feet or so by a five-foot wooden pole with a red cross on top. The scenery is supposedly breathtaking, a wide-open range of low, rounded 800-foot peaks combined with *palsas*—giant weather-sculpted frost heaves that push up in frozen waves. But we're in a universe of howling white nothing. The snow is blowing so low, fast, and hard that what little I can see looks straight out of one of those cheesy movies depicting heaven, if heaven had 50 mile-per-hour winds. I'm not cold, but the white-on-white void induces vertigo, and the pelting snow is relentless. Luckily, the musher in front of me—Raan Parton, a 30-year-old cofounder of Apolis, an apparel company in Los Angeles—is wearing bright red snow pants. It's the only marker keeping me on track.

We bounce up and down on the sleds like bobbleheads for a few hours until Fjellborg stops, sets his sled's claw brake, and starts trudging back toward Calder at the end of the line, where they huddle over what looks like a GPS unit.

Ten minutes later, Fjellborg backtracks on foot along the route we just traveled and is immediately out of sight. After a few minutes, he reappears and returns to his sled.

"Follow me, and kick a little bit!" he commands as he turns the train around.

How far off track are we? I don't ask. Now is not the time to question. I release the brake and mush.

Dogsledding is not difficult, but it does require prolonged focus. During distance events like the Iditarod, hallucinations are common. Operating on too little sleep, Fjellborg once conjured up an old Swedish barn while mushing on Alaskan sea ice, and Calder kept seeing ghost bridges during one endurance-mushing escapade. The bridge mirage, common among mushers, has something to do with the way their hat brims block their line of sight.

I'm not hallucinating, but I am having trouble controlling my sled. My team, which has been charging hard since the start, keeps veering dangerously close to the wooden markers. To weave around the signposts, I throw my weight in the opposite direction, but, finally, the inevitable happens: the dogs swerve, and I smash into a pylon, which gets firmly lodged under the sled. Despite 50 pounds of added resistance, the dogs don't stop, and I can't brake because the pylon is between the brake jaw and the ground. Besides, if I stop, I'll be lost. So I push on, brakeless, until the pylon works its way out from under the sled about a mile later.

We eventually find camp—a cluster of Sami-owned fishing cabins nestled on the shore of a massive lake that we can't see. Once again, two Finns—a different duo from the pair we met at Pältsa—have arrived before us, this time by snowmobile, and they reek of liquor.

"Where are you from?" they ask. "We are from Finland!"

That night, over a dinner of arctic char, sauerkraut, and potatoes that Fjellborg whips up in his cabin's tiny kitchen, Westerlind uses her iPhone calculator to confirm that the wind speed was at least 50 mph. Someone else asks Fjellborg how lost we were.

"You don't have to know exactly where you are, just the neighborhood," he responds. "It's much better not to think about it too much."

The next morning, we wake up to an alternate universe, the Arctic of expedition dreams, in which there are no clouds and it's so bright and clear that I can see the silhouette of a lone reindeer, head bent in search of lichen, on top of a low hill a mile away. After a few hours, we descend below the tree line and pass a white ptarmigan in the brush hiding from the dogs. Our objective is to reach Fjellborg's home in Poikkijärvi by Thursday, which gives us two and a half days to cover 100 miles.

The first night, we stop in the village of Kattuvuoma. Oddly, there are cars here but only 12 miles of road. The closest road that connects to anything is 16 miles away. People tow the cars into the tiny settlement over the ice in the winter and use them only in the summer.

We're staying at the yellow farmhouse of Sven-Erik Stöckel, a 76-year-old descendant of a bear hunter. His grandfather's traps, along with fishing nets, skis, spears, saws, scythes, and a long wooden contraption that turns out to be a sheep castrator, are still in the barn out back, which he calls his museum. "This is what your wife is going to do with you when you get home," says Fjellborg to James Bishop, 41, a Brit whose wife gave birth four months ago, as he makes a giant chopping motion with the castrator.

Later that evening, Stöckel explains that during World War II, this area, known only as North of Tornetrask Lake, was a popular corridor for Russians, Poles, and Germans trying to escape the Nazis. His parents harbored them, along with Norwegian resistance fighters, who had a base atop an unnamed peak nearby.

"Sven-Erik's mom and dad saved a lot of lives," Westerlind tells me as she translates his story from Swedish.

The next day, we mush across a string of iced-over lakes, whipping snowballs at each other. In some places, the turquoise water is exposed. The dogs seem to have a sixth sense for the holes, some of which I narrowly avoid.

By late afternoon, we've reached what looks like a brand new red farmhouse and low-slung barn amid several neglected log buildings. It's the homestead in the village of Sevuvuoma that Fjellborg bought from a distant cousin and renovated. He fortified the farmhouse's original interior log structure, and his wife decorated it with Swedish antiques they hauled in by boat. Black-and-white photos of Fjellborg's ancestors hang on the log walls, and a scrapbook contains photos of Princess Victoria having a picnic on the lawn. It's all very Ralph Lauren meets Scandinavian country chic. Fjellborg gives us a tour, then schools us with a family-history lesson.

"My distant cousins were very good hunters and always had a big stack of moose meat they hid under the frozen woodpile," he tells us. "They didn't want to show everybody how much meat they had because at that time there was not much moose around, and hunting times were limited."

Almost 100 years later, the Fjellborgs still live large. Just because we're deep in the Arctic doesn't mean we're deprived of luxury. Later, by candlelight, we drink cabernet sauvignon out of long-stemmed crystal glasses, eat curried arctic char (which Fjellborg has produced in a galley kitchen with no running water), and laugh over Westerlind's gutsy tackle of a runaway dogsled team earlier in the day. The next morning, we mush to Poik kijärvi, where Fjellborg's three daughters, dressed in snowsuits and flower-print rubber boots, rush out to hug their dad, while the rest of us bid a melancholy goodbye to our worn-out dogs.

But before we go our separate ways, for our final night, Fjellborg breaks out a celebratory bottle of Minttu peppermint schnapps for a toast in preparation for the most sacred Scandinavian ritual of all.

"*Minttu* is Finnish for 'cold on the outside, warm on the inside,'" he says as he raises his glass. "And now we're going to have one hell of a sauna."

(Originally published December 2012)

TWIN FREAKS

NICK PAUMGARTEN

"High-altitude skiing is an eccentric and thinly populated outpost in the extreme-skiing/ski-mountaineering galaxy," writes Paumgarten. "It has a herky-jerk history and a lineage of larks." That description gives you a good sense of the appropriate skepticism he brought to this story on the Marolts, twin brothers from Aspen trying to make a name for themselves in a fringe sport.

If there's anything that high-altitude skiers agree on, it's that skiing in or near the so-called Death Zone is rarely, if ever, anything but awful. The snow, when it's not Coke-bottle ice, stinks; the higher you go, the worse it gets. The thin air cottons your mind, deadens your legs, and makes each turn a brutal chore in a place where a sloppy one can be fatal. The Swedish ski mountaineer Fredrik Ericsson—who, in an attempt at a first descent on K2 last year, watched his partner, Michele Fait, fall to his death—has said that making four or five turns at that altitude is as hard on the legs and lungs as skiing a continuous pitch of 1,000 vertical meters in the Alps. That's if you're fortunate enough actually to ski; Himalayan expeditions, expensive and time-consuming on a good day, are as likely to end in storm-siege, retreat, or worse as they are in anything resembling success. It can take a month or more to bag a single run.

Which may be why so few people do it. High-altitude skiing is an eccentric and thinly populated outpost in the extreme-skiing/ski-mountaineering galaxy. It has a herky-jerk history and a lineage of larks. To most people, the idea of skiing down Everest, for example, still evokes the 1970 footage of Yuichiro Miura, the so-called Man Who Skied Down Everest, hurtling over the ice on his ass, skis spinning in the air, parachute trailing uselessly behind. Since then, others have had cleaner runs. Hans Kammerlander, Reinhold Messner's old climbing partner and the man whom many consider to be the most accomplished Himalayan skier of them all, skied off Everest's summit via the Northeast Ridge in 1996, after a high-speed ascent without the use of supplemental oxygen or Sherpas. But he had to downclimb some of the way, due to a lack of snow, and so his achievement, towering as it was, earned an asterisk. In 2000, a Slovenian named Davo Karnicar skied from the summit (which he reached using oxygen and Sherpas) down to Base Camp by way of the standard Southeast Ridge climbing route—passing, along the way, a corpse that had been lying there for four years. Over the past few decades, there have been dozens of successful descents of the 14 Himalayan peaks over 8,000 meters, for the most part by Europeans. Still, when you consider the thousands of climbers who've summited those peaks in that time, it's surprising how few of them chose to go down even part of the way on skis.

So why is it that Mike and Steve Marolt, middle-aged certified public accountants and identical twins, spend nearly every minute that they aren't preparing tax returns lugging skis toward the Death Zone or training to get back up there? The Marolts, 45, live in Aspen and are North America's most dogged and single-minded practitioners of high-altitude skiing. They are fourth-generation Aspenites from a distinguished ski-racing family. They are also, strictly speaking, weekend warriors. The term "adventure athlete," so widely applied these days to those who make some kind of a living or name doing bold, marketable stuff out of doors, does not suit them. They are just strong skiers who happen to have devoted most of their free time, over the past two decades, to skiing at high altitude. Not least among their achievements is the curious fact that they actually enjoy the skiing up there.

Ten years ago, they became the first Americans (or, as Mike Marolt sometimes says, the first skiers from the Western Hemisphere) to ski from above 8,000 meters. The awkward wording of the claim requires explanation. The mountain was Tibet's 26,289-foot Shishapangma, the 14th-highest peak in the world. It was the Marolts' first trip to the Himalayas with skis. In October 1999, seven months before the Marolts went, an expedition of elite American alpinists had gone to Shishapangma to ski a new route down the southwest face. During the ascent, a gigantic avalanche tumbled down from a glacier and killed two of them: Alex Lowe, one of the world's top mountaineers, and Dave Bridges, a cameraman from Aspen. The attempt was abandoned.

In April 2000, the Marolts, not nearly as experienced as Lowe and his mates, went to Tibet to climb and ski the more traditional route, to and from the Central Summit, which is about 50 feet lower and much more accessible than the Main

Summit. An Austrian named Oswald Gassler had been the first to ski from it, in 1985, and since then a few others had done so, but no Americans.

The Marolts had been told it was an easy eight-thousander. They were accompanied by a photographer and a childhood friend with whom they'd been going on ski expeditions for more than ten years. They were alone on the mountain. On their way up, as they acclimatized with some mid-mountain skiing, a blizzard granted them the rare gift of a powder day. Another storm socked them in 14 days later, during their summit push. On several occasions near the top, Mike considered ditching his skis, but Steve's withering look, and the fraternal imperative, persuaded him to continue on. In a total whiteout, they reached what they judged (by their altimeters) to be the peak. The summit photograph, of Steve in a fog, doesn't tell you much. It could be Snowmass or Scotland. They clicked in and skied down a moderate slope, through ice and breakable crust, to advance base camp. It was the most difficult skiing they'd ever experienced. "Easy eight-thousander, my ass," Mike muttered to his brother.

The media's declaration, upon their return, that they were the first Americans to ski an 8,000-meter peak, ruffled some feathers, especially in light of the tragedy the year before. To their detractors, the Central Summit was one asterisk, as was the slim evidence of their having reached it. Later that year, Laura Bakos Ellison, a woman from Telluride, Colorado, climbed 26,906-foot Cho Oyu, the sixth-tallest mountain in the world, in her alpine ski boots and skied back down. She became, in the eyes of many, the first North American, male or female, to ski off an 8,000-meter peak. The Marolts again pointed out that they were the first to ski from above 8,000 meters. They've skied from above 8,000 once since, on Cho Oyu. They've twice skied on Everest's North Ridge, from 25,000 feet. (The summit is at 29,035 feet.) All told, they have six ski descents from above 7,000 meters, apparently more than anyone else in the world. (There is no ski-mountaineering governing body—official or otherwise.) They do it without supplemental oxygen, and they carry their own gear.

"People who haven't been up there and done this have no concept," Mike says. "It's the hardest thing you'll ever do."

Since you can't see thin air on film, the only visual hint I've had of the difficulty—and of the Marolts' unique ability to have fun regardless—is in some footage of Steve on Everest. A climber in a down suit, ascending via fixed rope and hidden behind his oxygen mask, stops and turns his head to observe Steve skiing past in a baseball cap. From the climber's bewildered body language, you get the sense that he might as well have just seen a flying turtle.

"We're not embraced by the climbing community at all," Mike told me one night. "Maybe because we've always gotten along with our parents."

"Maybe because we don't smoke dope," Steve said.

We were sitting in Mike's living room in Aspen, dining on steak and drinking Stranahan's Colorado Whiskey. Bedtime was imminent; we were looking at a pre-dawn alpine start the next morning. The plan was to hike and ski Castle Peak, a fourteener in the Elk Range—for the Marolts, a training run; for me, an occasion for a restless night.

"All those guys are jerks," Steve went on, referring to an unnamed chorus of doubters and gripers. "In mountaineering, the only way you can excel is to break other people down."

"There's no point system," Mike said, "so the only way to feel good about yourself is to bust on someone else's accomplishments."

"We don't care what they think," Steve said. "We don't need the money. We have jobs."

Mike: "Have you ever referred to yourself as a climber?"

Steve: "I can't stand the notion."

Mike: "I've never referred to myself as a climber."

"You know what makes me crazier than anything?" Steve said. "Prayer flags." Buddhism, he says, is all about letting go of ego. "And yet everyone over here puts them up to show how cool they are because they went to the Himalayas. That's all ego."

The two are identical, yet it isn't hard to tell them apart. Mike is a little wall-eyed. Steve wears glasses. Mike is earnest and effusive. Steve is more acerbic and wry. I observed, rather quickly, that, as I put it to Mike, "Steve doesn't suffer fools, does he?" Mike took great delight in the phrase. Mike suffers them quite well; he's the one who chronicles, publicizes, and raises money for their trips and who put me up, and put up with me, during my visit in May. Mike is deferential and solicitous toward Steve in their daily dealings. Steve is the expedition leader. Mike was in charge of their first Asian adventure—a 1997 climbing trip to 26,400-foot Broad Peak, the world's 12th-highest, on the Pakistan–China border—but it was a mess. Steve is slightly stronger and faster. "He's a beast above 20,000 feet," Mike says. Their mother says, "Steve is the uptight one."

"Crabby, grouchy, curmudgeonly—that's what people tell me," Steve says. "What do you expect after you've been carrying your brother on your shoulders for 45 years?" They're both very fit and very square. They go to church together on Sunday mornings.

The brothers live across the street from each other, in a development at the northern edge of town, near Woody Creek. "This is where the common folk live," Mike told me as we drove up to his place. He lives with his wife, Shelly (a painter originally from New York City), and their two young daughters (whom they adopted from China) in a red ranch house that's partly subsidized by the town. Steve is married to Charlotte, a former prenatal nurse, and has three kids. The last time the twins got in a fight with each other was 24 years ago. It began with a dispute over whose car they were going to drive into town for cash before heading back to St. Mary's College of California, where Mike played baseball. Mike's account of it has him spitting on Steve, then running and hiding in the bathroom, while Steve waited outside long enough to ambush Mike and punch him in the jaw.

Mike: "We busted up the house."

Steve: "Oh, that's nonsense."

Mike: "Haven't had a fistfight since."

Steve: "I don't think I hit you in the face."

Mike: "I guarantee you did."

Steve: "I don't remember hitting you in the face, for crying out loud."

Mike: "You did. Atrocious behavior. Unbelievable."

I met Mike a couple of years ago, when he came to the Explorers Club, in New York, to peddle a rough cut of *Skiing Everest*, a documentary he'd made, with the filmmaker Les Guthman, about the twins' adventures. The film will be released this fall, after the Marolts return from an expedition to ski 26,758-foot Manaslu, in Nepal, the eighth-highest mountain in the world. The name of the film is a little disingenuous: It implies a descent from the top. Skiing on Everest doesn't have quite the same ring, however. This is the kind of thing that irks their detractors.

A number of renowned ski mountaineers told me, without wanting their names to be used, that they resented the attention the Marolts had received for their exploits—or, more to the point, the attention the Marolts had sought out. The criticism is that the Marolts ski (and climb) unremarkable, unstylish lines ("tourist routes," as one put it), that they care less about summits than about altimeter readings, and that, above all, they make more of their feats than those feats merit. The fact that they've skied so often above 7,000 meters elicits a collective "So what?" from the sport's elites, who favor first descents and technical derring-do. One of them told me, "All it proves is that they have more time and money to waste on trying to get one boring run."

The relative youth and narrowness of the high-altitude-skiing category makes it a hard niche to define and opens it up to a host of qualifying questions. Did the skier use Sherpas or supplementary oxygen, did he ski from the summit, did he make a continuous descent, did he choose a stylish route? One day, I came across a list of first descents assembled by the Colorado ski-mountaineering pioneer Lou Dawson (the first to ski all of the state's 14,000-foot peaks) on his blog, WildSnow .com. It became an occasion, in the comments section, for a handful of the world's top ski mountaineers—including Fredrik Ericsson, Andrew McLean, and Dave

Watson (who skied on, but not from the summit of, K2)—to engage in a spirited debate about the relative merits and murky facts of various high-altitude-skiing feats. McLean wrote at one point: "For better or worse, there are no rules to this sport, which leaves it open to interpretation when somebody shouts 'I SCORED A TOUCHDOWN!' That's when the real games begin."

"There's a hell of a lot of ego in what we do. Let's be frank," says Steve.

"When you go out and do all the shameless self-promotion," Mike told me, "people think, 'Oh, Marolt's out there making money.' I haven't made a dime off of any of this, but I have been able to drag my buddies along on amazing trips around the world." He helped finance the Shishapangma expedition by selling photographs of earlier trips. "Then we got the feather on Shish, and the sponsorship came around"—mostly in the guise of free gear. Still, Mike says, the trips are 75 percent self-funded. It's the films that require the money. To complete *Skiing Everest*, he got a big loan from a family friend. Fortunately, Mike had plenty of raw footage; he's brought a camera on all their trips and has learned, through trial and error, how to deploy it. These aren't home movies.

"The glory in what we're doing, if there is any, is just the result of one thing: We decided to do it," Mike said to me one day. "Anyone can do it. It's doesn't require any special talent. It's not like hitting a major league curveball. It's not even a sport. It's high-level, high-risk recreation."

When I first met Mike, I recognized the last name. It turned out that he and Steve were nephews of Bill Marolt, a former Olympic ski racer and director of the U.S. Ski Team. Bill's older brother, Max Marolt, Mike and Steve's father, had been one of the top ski racers in the world; he competed in the 1960 Olympics.

The family has deep Aspen roots. Mike and Steve's great-grandfather, Frank Marolt, an Austrian immigrant, had walked—walked—from Ohio to Colorado during its 1880s silver rush. The early Aspen Marolts were miners and barkeeps. In the 1930s, they began raising cattle. The family sold the Marolt Ranch, which encompassed 440 acres, in the 1950s for $157,000. It's now the municipal golf course. On the one hand, Mike and Steve can regret no longer having the land in the family, as it would now be worth many tens of millions; on the other hand, as Roger Marolt, Steve and Mike's older brother, says in *Skiing Everest*, selling the land gave their parents the means to remain in Aspen as it became a glitzy, expensive resort. "Growing up, they couldn't even afford to eat the cattle they raised," Mike said of his forebears. Instead, they lived on what they could catch or kill: deer, elk, trout. This is why, later in life, the boys' father, Max, ate only beef. (Mike: "I can't eat trout." Steve: "Worms with fins.")

Max began taking the boys backcountry skiing on Independence Pass when they were 12. Once they could drive, they each bought a Willys Jeep and started heading out on their own. One year, Max, who made a living as a regional sales rep for Look bindings, Völkl skis, and Nordica boots, started an off-season ski-racing camp up in a backcountry cirque called the Montezuma Basin, at the foot of Castle Peak, where he'd often trained. Max put in three rope tows and converted an old smelting house into a bunk room. It didn't last long. The U.S. Forest Service made him shut down the rope tows because they fell within the Aspen Skiing Company's leased property, and someone burned down the bunkhouse. Still, the twins spent years exploring the nearby peaks and chutes. (Max died of a heart attack at 67, in 2003, while skiing in Las Leñas, Argentina—"with his skis on his feet," as Mike says.)

Typically, in their Colorado backcountry wanderings, the Marolt boys were accompanied by a handful of close neighborhood friends, including Jim Gile, now a computer programmer, and John Callahan, a former Olympic cross-country ski racer. This was the core group that wound up graduating from one adventure to the next, until they came to find themselves gasping for air together in Tibet. The first trip out of state, after the Marolts graduated from college, was to Mount Rainier. Next came Denali, in 1990, where they realized they had a lot to learn. (They reached, but did not ski from, the summit.) For seven years, the group made an annual pilgrimage back to Alaska, to the Wrangell–St. Elias range, where they ripened their mountaineering skills on such beastly peaks as Logan, Blackburn, St. Elias, and Bona. At that time, it was a place where not many had skied. They left their skis behind on their first trip to Asia, the 1997 trip to Broad Peak. They were accompanied by the mountaineer Ed Viesturs, who got tired of hearing them grouse about not having their skis and suggested they bring them along next time. It was Viesturs who urged them to consider Shishapangma.

After Shish, and a series of trips to South America (they go down to the Andes every year), they got to Everest in 2003. They approached it from the north: It was cheaper to do so, and they wanted no part of the notoriously dangerous Khumbu Icefall. Foul weather and extreme cold prevented them from making the summit. "It's been 60 days, and north Everest has kicked our butts," Mike said to Everest News.com at the time, via satellite phone. The Marolts wound up skiing a section of the North Ridge, from an altitude of 25,000 feet, in a storm that blinded them, helpfully, to the fact that on either side of the narrow pitch they were skiing were precipitous drops of 4,000 feet to the glaciers below. They settled for a similar result in 2007, on their return trip to Everest, when Mike, worried about his frozen feet and discouraged by thin snow cover, decided to turn back at 28,000. Earlier on the same trip, they'd climbed Cho Oyu, where Mike had an asthma attack a few hundred feet from the summit, preventing him from making the top. (Mike is also, bizarrely, allergic to aspen trees.) Steve alone skied from the summit.

Their Himalayan résumés, like those of most mountaineers, contain as many shortfalls as triumphs. Failure, if you can even call it that, is part of the deal. (Survival is success, of a kind. The only injury anyone has ever had on one of their trips was a frostbit fingertip, on Mount Logan.) For all of Mike's finely parsed categories of accomplishment, he insists they're in it for the turns, not the prize.

"I've never had regret about not making the summit of Everest," he says. "When you're climbing those peaks, you don't care if someone's been there before you."

My first day out with the Marolts was a tour in the Snowmass backcountry. It was May, and the lifts were closed, but there was still a lot of snow, all the way down to the ski area's base. Mike and Steve typically put climbing skins on their skis and hike up Snowmass and then on out to an adjoining peak called Baldy a couple of times a week, before or after work. They were inspired, in part, by Fritz Stammberger, a German climber who moved to Aspen when they were kids; Stammberger, who summited Cho Oyu in 1964 and then skied down from 23,600 feet—at the time, the high-altitude-skiing record—used to train by hiking up Aspen Mountain with duct tape covering his mouth. The Marolts skip the duct tape.

Unlike most ski mountaineers and backcountry skiers, who sneer at riding lifts, the Marolts also hit the resort a few afternoons a week, when it's open, to pound out as many runs as they can in a couple of hours before the lifts close. (Mike told me he couldn't care less about first tracks: "I've had plenty of powder in my life.") They generally ski Ajax, which is a few blocks from their offices. (They are not business partners; they get enough of each other as is.) They use giant slalom racing skis and seek out bumps and crud. The idea is that the only way to build up the muscles for skiing at high altitude is to ski hard. No matter how fast you walk up, you can't get enough turns in without the chairlift. "You can't ski those peaks without doing that," Mike said. "You need power and endurance." Still, no bump run will really prepare your legs for Everest. "It's hard to pursue an anaerobic sport in a place where you can't go anaerobic," he said.

Since I'd arrived, Mike had been needling me to come with them to Manaslu in September. And yet now, in consideration of the fact that I'd come from sea level, they'd arranged for a snowmobiler to rush us, one at a time, to the top of Snowmass. The WildSnow boys would not have approved. Mike rode up first, while Steve stayed behind with me and complained about how much he hates snowmobiles. I soon came to dislike them, too, when halfway up my pilot flipped our sled.

I bailed (helmetless) just before the machine careered, upside down, into the pines. The driver had on a helmet and was unharmed, save for his pride. The 40-minute effort to get the sled upright made me aware, for the first time, of the altitude.

The day was sunny and clear. Up high, the wind had beaten the snow into meringue; the windward aspects were bare, the lee loaded. Once Steve joined us, cursing the sled, we skinned out along the ridge toward Baldy. About 15 minutes out, Mike dropped a ski pole. It skittered to a stop on a massive pillow of snow about 60 feet down the leeward cirque, which was also baking in the sun. Steve and Mike considered it for a while and decided that it was too risky to retrieve it; the pillow had a hair-trigger look. They tried throwing rocks at the pole, to knock it loose and down to the bottom of the bowl, for later and safer retrieval, but that didn't work. They'd have to come back for it in August. For the next two hours Mike skinned with one pole. I tried to think of all the people I'd skied with over the years and concluded that the twins, who venture into more perilous terrain than most of them, might be the only two who wouldn't have persuaded themselves to go after that pole.

Our day ended with a gentle corn run down through the Big Burn, amid the eerie ghost-town appeal of a resort hill shut down for the year. The day, snow-mobile aside, had been as mellow as a backcountry outing can be, and yet after skinning for a couple of hours at 13,000 feet, I could feel the altitude getting the better of me. It was hard for me to imagine the horror of an asthma attack at twice the altitude, as Mike had experienced on Cho Oyu. Generally, asthma aside, Mike and his brother seem to be physiologically suited to high altitude: Doctors have told them that they have huge hearts and lungs and veins. On a treadmill at a MET testing site, Mike's VO2 max—the point during exercise at which the body can no longer increase the amount of oxygen it uses, despite the intensity of effort—was more than 70, double the average 45-year-old male's score.

"Our genetics allow us to have fun at altitude," Mike says.

So does the fact that they have a ready-made expedition team in the half-dozen or so old Aspen friends who've been accompanying them for 20 years.

"When everything works, it's like a line on a hockey team," Jim Gile likes to say. Gile also likes to say, at some point on every trip, that he will never go on another one. "He writes it in his journal: 'Remember this,'" Steve says.

John Callahan told me that he wouldn't bother to climb at all if not for the company—rough as that company can play. Callahan, the Marolts told me, comes in for more flak than anyone.

Steve: "Why is Callahan the brunt of every joke?"

Mike: "Because he's a know-it-all. We call him the Professor."

Steve: "Callahan failed calculus twice. In college."

Mike, for his part, gets perennial hell for an old Rainier trip, their third, in which he decided, a few feet short of the summit, that he was close enough. "It comes up constantly," Mike says. "It bugs the shit out of me, both because I was too lazy to go those extra 20 feet and because who cares? I'd already been to the top a couple of times."

~~~~~~

"THAT'S NOT his house."

"Yes, it is."

"No, it's not."

"Yes, it is."

"No, it's not."

The twins were inching along an Aspen street in the dark in Mike's pickup truck, looking for the home of their friend Mike Maple, who accompanied them on an expedition to Noijin Kangsang, a 23,642-foot peak in Tibet, last year. (It was Maple who coined the term "Tibetan corduroy," which is, as Mike described it, "a generous euphemism for corrugated boilerplate.") It was almost 5 A.M. Maple appeared, and the three of them spent most of the drive south to the Castle Creek trailhead swapping tire-rotation horror stories and gossip about acquaintances who were having extramarital affairs. "You've hung out with these guys long enough to know not to believe everything you hear," Maple told me.

First light found us walking up along a rutted jeep track over ice and rotten snow at about 10,000 feet. Sunrise came as we put on our skis and skins, revealing steep palisades of rock and snow rising up on both sides of the drainage. The Marolts pointed out prized lines. Up ahead, the valley forked where their father's ski camp had been. The Marolts decided to go for Pearl Peak, on account of the avalanche risk on nearby but higher Castle, if not also for the fact that they had along a flatlander who was already struggling to keep up. They led the way up into a vast basin of refrozen snow that rose gradually from the tree line to the foot of Pearl. We weren't even at 12,000 feet yet, and I was out of gas. The wind had a schizophrenic malevolence to it. Spring in the southern Rockies, my ass.

We boot-packed over scree and windblown snow up the face of Pearl, the two Mikes way ahead, Steve hanging back, tight on my tail, exhaling very loudly. (Mike told me later that Steve is a notorious heavy breather; the doctor's office under the Aspen gym where the brothers work out has lodged several complaints.) We reached the peak at ten and spent a few moments taking in the view of Crested Butte, as well as of Castle, which looked inhospitable from this side, too. Steve's altimeter read 13,300 feet. Now that it was time to ski, I felt fine. As Mike says in his film, "climbing without skiing is just pain and suffering with lousy food at the end of the day."

We leapfrogged our way down a chute, the snow wintry and firm. It was steep and rocky enough to suggest that any kind of fall could mean trouble but wide enough to allow for a little speed. The Marolts skied with an aggressive, heavy style; you could tell they'd raced in their youth. After the run was done, we traversed across the basin over to an adjoining mountain called Greg Mace Peak and boot-packed up its flank to access another chute, which had the shape of an hourglass. "I thought New Yorkers were always in a hurry," Maple said as the three of them waited for me to click in. The run was a dream. It started in steep chalk and ended in a giant alluvial field of corn snow that settled once and for all in my mind the utter insanity of ever walking downhill over snow.

"Once you make turns, it makes everything right," Mike said back at the truck. It was noon. We'd ascended and descended 5,000 vertical feet in a morning. Usually, they'd have done it in a couple of hours. "You could have the experience from hell, but once you make turns—even if it's bad snow—it makes everything right."

Agreed. But Manaslu? I'll pass.

(Originally published September 2010)

OPEN YOUR MOUTH AND YOU'RE DEAD

JAMES NESTOR

~~~~~~

The freediving world championships occur at the outer limits of competitive risk. During the 2011 event, held off the coast of Greece, more than 130 athletes assembled to swim hundreds of feet straight down on a single breath—without (they hoped) passing out, freaking out, or drowning. Meet the amazingly fit, unquestionably brave, and possibly crazy people who line up for the ultimate plunge.

~~~~~~

Junko Kitahama's face is pale blue, her mouth agape, her head craned back like a dead bird's. Through her swim mask, her eyes are wide and unblinking, staring at the sun. She isn't breathing.

"Blow on her face!" yells a man swimming next to her. Another man grabs her head from behind and pushes her chin out of the water. "Breathe!" he yells. Someone from the deck of a boat yells for oxygen. "Breathe!" the man repeats. But Kitahama, who just surfaced from a breath-hold dive 180 feet below the surface of the ocean, doesn't breathe. She doesn't move. Kitahama looks dead.

Moments later, she coughs, jerks, twitches her shoulders, flutters her lips. Her face softens as she comes to. "I was swimming and . . ." She laughs and continues. "Then I just started dreaming!" Two men slowly float her over to an oxygen tank sitting on a raft. While she recovers behind a surgical mask, another freediver takes her place and prepares to plunge even deeper.

Kitahama, a female competitor from Japan, is one of more than 130 freedivers from 31 countries who have gathered here—one mile off the coast of Kalamata,

Greece, in the deep, mouthwash blue waters of Messinian Bay—for the 2011 Individual Free-diving Depth World Championships, the largest competition ever held for the sport. Over the next week, in an event organized by the International Association for the Development of Apnea (AIDA), they'll test themselves and each other to see who can swim the deepest on a single lungful of air without passing out, losing muscle control, or drowning. The winners get a medal.

How deep can they go? Nobody knows. Competitive freediving is a relatively new sport, and since the first world championships were held in 1996, records have been broken every year, sometimes every few months. Fifty years ago, scientists believed that the deepest a human could freedive was about 160 feet. Recently, freedivers have routinely doubled and tripled that mark. In 2007, Herbert Nitsch, a 41-year-old Austrian, dove more than 700 feet—assisted by a watersled on the way down and an air bladder to pull him to the surface—to claim a new world record for absolute depth. Nitsch, who didn't compete in Greece, plans to dive 800 feet in June, deeper than two football fields are long.

Nobody has ever drowned at an organized free-diving event, but enough people have died outside of competition that freediving ranks as the second-most-dangerous adventure sport, right after BASE jumping. The statistics are a bit murky: some deaths go unreported, and the numbers that are kept include people who freedive as part of other activities, like spearfishing. But one estimate of worldwide free-diving-related fatalities revealed a nearly threefold increase, from 21 deaths in 2005 to 60 in 2008.

Only a few of these fatalities have been widely publicized. The famed French freediver Audrey Mestre—wife of freediving pioneer Francisco "Pipin" Ferreras—died in 2002 during a weight-aided descent to 561 feet, leading to controversy that continues still about whether Ferreras, who managed safety for the attempt, did his job properly. More recently, just three months before the 2011 world championships, Adel Abu Haliqa, a 40-year-old founding member of a free-diving club in the United Arab Emirates, drowned in Santorini, Greece, during a 230-foot attempt. His body still hasn't been found. A month later, Patrick Musimu, a former world-record holder from Belgium, drowned while training alone in a pool in Brussels.

Competitive freedivers blame such deaths on carelessness, arguing that each dead diver was going it alone or relying on machines to assist the dives—both very high-risk pursuits. "Competitive freediving is a safe sport. It's all very regulated, very controlled," says William Trubridge, a 31-year-old world-record freediver from New Zealand. "I would never do it if it wasn't." He points out that, during some 39,000 competition freedives over the past 12 years, there has never been a fatality.

Through events like the world championships, Trubridge and others hope to change freediving's shaky image and bring it closer to the mainstream. City officials in Kalamata, a freediving hub, are trying to help. To that end, they hosted an opening ceremony for the event on a Saturday night along a crowded boardwalk. There, hundreds of competitors, coaches, and crew members in matching T-shirts and tracksuits waved national flags and screamed their countries' anthems from an enormous stage—a scene that looked like a low-rent Olympics. Behind them, a 40-piece marching band played a ragged version of the *Rocky* theme as grainy video highlights from past freedives were projected onto a 30-foot screen.

"You ask me, this all looks crazy," said Xaris Vgenis, a Kalamatan who runs a water-sports shop near the beach. A video of a 300-foot dive appeared on the screen, and Vgenis shook his head. "You'll never get me to do it!"

Then the lights of the stage darkened, the video screen dimmed, and the PA system went silent. Moments later, strobe lights flashed and streams of fireworks exploded in the night sky. The participants cheered while a few hundred locals scratched their heads. The 2011 freediving world championships were on.

Two days after the opening ceremony, on a windless and hot Monday morning, I head for the Kalamata Marina, where a scruffy Quebecois expat named Yanis Georgoulis is waiting on a 27-foot boat to carry me to the first event. For all its mainstream hopes, freediving has a built-in problem: it's almost impossible to watch. The playing field is underwater, there are no video feeds beamed back to land, and it's a logistical challenge even to get near the action. Today's staging area is a sketchy-looking 20-by-20-foot flotilla of boats, platforms, and gear that looks like it was swiped from the set of *Waterworld*.

While we motor out in the shadow of toothy coastal mountains, I use the time to brush up on freediving's complicated rules. The competition officially starts the night before a dive, when divers secretly submit the proposed depths of the next day's dive attempts to a panel of judges. It's basically a bid, and there's gamesmanship involved as each diver tries to guess what the other divers will do. "It's like playing poker," Trubridge told me. "You are playing the other divers as much as you are playing yourself." The hope is that your foes will choose a shallower dive than you can do, or that they'll choose a deeper dive than they can do and end up "busting."

In freediving, you bust either by flubbing one of dozens of technical requirements during and after the dive or by blacking out before you reach the surface, grounds for immediate disqualification. While not common in competitions (I'm told), blackouts happen often enough that layers of safety precautions are put in place, including rescue divers who monitor each dive, sonar tracking from the flotilla, and a lanyard guide attached to divers' ankles that keeps them from drifting off course—a potentially fatal hazard, I'll later learn.

A few minutes before each dive, a metal plate covered in white Velcro is attached to a rope and sunk to the depth the competitor submitted the night before. An official counts down, and the diver submerges and follows the rope to the plate, grabs any of dozens of tags affixed to it, and follows the rope back to the surface. About 60 feet down or lower, the competitor is met by rescue divers who are there to assist in the event of a blackout. If he passes out so deep that the safety divers can't see him, that will be detected by the sonar. The rope will then be hoisted up and the diver's unconscious body dragged to the surface, rag-doll style.

Divers who successfully resurface are put through a battery of tests known as the surface protocol. This gauges their coherence and motor skills by requiring them, among other things, to remove their face masks, quickly flash a sign to a judge, and say "I'm OK." If you pass, you get a white card, validating the dive.

"The rules are there to make freediving safe, measurable, and comparable," says CarlaSue Hanson, the media spokesperson for AIDA. "They are set up to ensure that, through the whole dive, the diver is in full control. That's what competitive freediving is all about: control." As long as you're in control, it's all right if (as sometimes happens) blood vessels burst in your nose and you come out looking like Sissy Spacek in *Carrie*. "The judges don't care how someone looks," Hanson says. "Blood? That's nothing. As far as the rules go, blood is OK."

After an hour, Georgoulis ties up to the flotilla. In the distance, a motorboat cuts a white line from the shore to deliver the first competitors to the site. There are no fans present. Only officials, divers, coaches, and a handful of staff are allowed out here, a group numbering about 15 today.

The divers show up wearing hooded wetsuits and insectoid goggles, each moving with syrupy-slow steps as they warm up on the sailboat, staring with wide, lucid eyes lost in meditation. One, two, three—they slide like otters into the sea, then lie back, looking semi-comatose as their coaches slowly float them over to one of three lines dangling from the flotilla. A judge issues a one-minute warning, and then the competition begins.

Freediving is broken down into multiple disciplines: today's is called constant weight no fins, abbreviated as CNF. In CNF, divers go down using their lungs, bodies, and an optional weight that, if used, must be brought back to the surface. Of the six areas in competitive freediving—which include everything from depth disciplines like free immersion (the diver can use the guide rope to propel himself up and down) to pool disciplines like static apnea (simple breath holding)—CNF is considered the purest. Its reigning king is Trubridge, who broke the world record in December 2010 with a 331-foot dive. Today he's trying for 305 feet, a conservative figure for him but the deepest attempt on the schedule. Before he arrives, a dozen other divers kick things off.

An official on line one counts down from ten, announces "official top," and begins counting up: "One, two, three, four, five..." The first diver, Wendy Timmermans of the Netherlands, has until 30 to go. She inhales a few last mouthfuls of air, ducks her head beneath the water, and descends. As her body sinks into the shadows of the Mediterranean, the monitoring official announces her depth every few seconds. Two minutes later, after reaching 171 feet, Timmermans emerges and passes the surface protocol, setting a new national record. Another diver goes down on line two; another preps on three.

The diver on three takes one last breath, descends 200 feet, touches down, and, after three painfully long minutes, resurfaces. "Breathe!" his coach yells. He smiles, gulps, then breathes. His face is white. He tries to take off his mask, but his hands are cramped and shaking. Lack of oxygen has sapped his muscle control, and he just floats there, with blank eyes and an idiotic grin on his face, probably with no idea where he is.

Behind him another diver resurfaces. "Breathe! Breathe!" a safety diver yells. The man's face is blue, and he isn't breathing. "Breathe!" another yells. Finally he coughs, jiggles his head, and makes a tiny squeaking sound like a dolphin.

For the next half-hour, as divers come and go, these scenes repeat. I stand in the sailboat with my stomach tightening, wondering if this is the norm—and if it is, how the hell any of it could be allowed. All the competitors sign waivers acknowledging that heart attacks, blackouts, oxygen toxicity, and drowning may be part of the price. But I have a feeling that competitive free-diving's continued existence has more to do with the fact that the local authorities don't know what really goes on out here.

Trubridge arrives, wearing sunglasses and headphones, his lean spider limbs dangling from the oversize thorax that is his chest. I can see his gargantuan lungs heaving in and out from 30 feet away. He's so lost in a meditative haze that he looks half dead by the time he enters the water, latches his ankle to the lanyard, and gets set to go.

"Five, four, three, two, one," the official says. Trubridge dives, kicking with bare feet, descending rapidly. The official announces "twenty meters," and I watch through the clear blue water. Trubridge places his arms at his sides and floats down effortlessly until he's out of sight, drifting barefoot into the shadows of the deep.

The image is both beautiful and spooky. I try to hold my breath along with him and give up after 30 seconds.

Trubridge passes 100 feet, 150 feet, 200 feet. Almost two minutes into the dive, the sonar-monitoring official announces "touchdown"—at 305 feet—and begins monitoring Trubridge's progress on the way back up. After a total of 3 minutes and 43 seconds, I see Trubridge rematerialize from the shadows. A few more strokes and he surfaces, exhales, removes his goggles, gives the high sign, and says in his crisp New Zealand accent, "I'm OK." He looks bored, his body and brain seemingly unaffected by the fact that he just swam—without fins, without anything—30 stories down.

The next two days are rest days. By midmorning on Tuesday, the courtyard at the Messinian Bay Hotel is buzzing with the chatter of a dozen languages as teams gather around patio tables to sip bottled water, talk strategy, and e-mail worried relatives. The group here is largely male, mostly over 30, and generally skinny. Some are short, a few are pudgy, and most have shaved heads and wear sleeveless T-shirts, action-strap Teva sandals, and baggy shorts. They hardly look like extreme athletes.

"Freediving is as much a mental game as a physical one," says Trubridge, who, in his wraparound dark glasses, cropped hair, and worn-out T-shirt, fits right in. He pulls up a seat beside me at the swimming pool. "It's a sport that's open to everybody."

Well, maybe. You still have to be able to hold your breath an incredibly long time, exert yourself tremendously, and not freak out—something I find extremely challenging, even though I spend most of my spare time surfing. Recreational free-diving is one of the fastest-growing watersports—a trend that will accelerate this year when Scuba Schools International expands its free-diving courses to dozens of locations worldwide—but it's hard to imagine competitive freediving in the Olympics anytime soon. It just seems too damned dangerous. I ask Trubridge to walk me through the physics and physiology of what he endures. Before long my stomach is tightening again.

In the first 30 or so feet underwater, the lungs, full of air, buoy your body to the surface, requiring strenuous paddling and constant equalization of the middle-ear cavities to gain depth. "This is where you use up to 15 percent of your energy," Trubridge says. And you've still got 600 feet of swimming to go.

As you dive past 30 feet, you feel the pressure on your body double, compressing your lungs to about half their normal size. You suddenly feel weightless, your body suspended in a gravityless state called neutral buoyancy. Then something amazing happens: as you keep diving, the ocean no longer pushes your body toward the surface but instead pulls you relentlessly toward the seafloor below. You place your arms at your sides in a skydiver pose and effortlessly go deeper.

At 100 feet, the pressure has quadrupled, the ocean's surface is barely visible, and you close your eyes and prepare for the deep water's tightening clutch.

Further still, at 150 feet, you enter a dream state caused by the high levels of carbon dioxide and nitrogen gas in your bloodstream: for a moment, you can forget where you are and why. At 300 feet, the pressure is so extreme that your lungs shrink to the size of oranges and your heart beats at less than half its normal rate to conserve oxygen. You lose some motor control. Most of the blood in your arms and legs has flooded to your body's core as the vessels in your extremities constrict. Vessels in your lungs swell to several times their normal size so they won't be crushed by the incredible pressure.

Then comes the really hard part. You open your eyes, struggle to force your semiparalyzed hand to grab a ticket from the plate, and head back up. With the ocean's weight working against you, you tap your meager energy reserves to swim toward the surface. Ascending to 200 feet, 150 feet, 100 feet, your lungs ache with an almost unbearable desire to breathe, your vision fades, and your chest convulses from the buildup of carbon dioxide in your bloodstream. You need to hurry before you black out. Above you, the haze of blue water transforms into a sheen of sunlight on the water's surface. You're going to make it.

You resurface, the world spins, people are yelling at you to breathe. Is this just another altered-state dream? It's hard to tell. So you sit there, whacked out, trying to come to quickly enough to complete the surface protocol. You take off your goggles, flick a sign, say "I'm OK"—then you get out of the way and make room for the next diver.

~~~~~~

How do you decide this is something you want to do? That you *can* do?

"I was always drawn to the ocean," Trubridge shrugs when I ask him how he got into freediving. "My first memories were of the sea." Born near the small village of Haltwhistle, Scotland, Trubridge was 20 months old when his parents, seeking adventure, sold their house, bought a 45-foot sailboat, loaded up Trubridge and his brother, Sam, and took off. For the next nine years they lived on the boat, sailing west. For fun, William and Sam would challenge each other to breath-holding dives. "We probably made it to 25 or 30 feet," he says, then laughs. "Which, you know, in retrospect was all pretty dangerous."

By the time Trubridge was 12, the family had settled in Havelock, a tiny town near New Zealand's east coast. He studied genetic biology at the University of

Auckland, where he tested himself one day to see if he could swim 80 feet underwater on one breath. One lap soon became two. Trubridge was slowly drawn into the sport.

After a stint in London as a bellhop in his early twenties, Trubridge took off for Honduras to explore freediving. "I remember diving one day, to maybe 60 feet, and lying down in a sea garden, relaxing, meditating, watching all the life and just being part of the environment," he says. "Not having to breathe for a minute or two. It was just the most amazing and peaceful feeling you can imagine."

For the next few years, Trubridge dropped out and dedicated himself full-time to freediving, honing his body into a machine built for undersea performance. He trained for hours a day, every day, swimming, doing yoga and breathing exercises. A rower and junior chess champion, Trubridge found that the combination of mental and physical training came naturally to him. "Freediving requires body, mind, and even spirit to be aligned and directed toward a common intent," he says. "I'm the sort of person who requires a challenge." When not diving, he translated freediving manuals, taught, and studied videotapes. At the end of a two-year stint bouncing around Central America, the Bahamas, and Europe, he hit the freediving scene as one of the best in the world.

"Here's a guy who spent two years sitting on a mountain alone, just waiting," says Sebastian Näslund, a Swedish freediver. "And when he came down, he was just kind of unstoppable."

Between 2007 and 2010, Trubridge broke 14 world records (mostly his own) in the disciplines of constant weight no fins and free immersion, which allows divers to pull on the rope to gain depth and to ascend. Today he and his wife of two years, Brittany, live mostly out of suitcases, wintering in the Bahamas and summering in Europe. They teach courses between competitions to help make ends meet.

I wonder what keeps Trubridge bound to the sport. It can't be the money: at the world championships, competitors pay about $700 to dive, plus accommodations, and win nothing but a medal. He makes a pittance through sponsorships. It's not the fame, either. Few people outside free-diving know who he is.

"To me, I don't really have a choice," he says in a soft voice. "There is an immortal peace confronting the underwater world on its own terms, with your breath at your breast. The ocean is just where I am meant to be."

~~~~~~

It's Thursday, and the glassy blue waters of Messinian Bay are gray and wind-chopped from a storm that came through yesterday. It's not raining now but clouds loom overhead, and subsurface visibility has diminished to about 40 feet. By 9 A.M. the first divers are in the water.

This time they're using monofins—three-foot-wide wedges of plastic attached to neoprene boots. Compared with traditional fins (one on each foot), a monofin gives a diver more thrust with less effort. As a result, today's dives will be about 25 percent deeper than the no-fins dives on Monday. The current world record in this category (called constant weight with fins, or CWT) is 124 meters—more than 400 feet—set in 2010 by Herbert Nitsch. Until 2009, only ten freedivers in the world had reached that mark. Today, 15 competitors will be attempting 100 meters, an almost unheard-of number.

British diver David King is one of them. King surprised everyone last night by announcing that he would try a 102-meter dive (335 feet), which would be a new UK national record. According to his teammates, he hasn't gone deeper than 80 meters in the past twelve months.

The judge counts down. King wets his head, upends, and goes. I watch from the sailboat as his silhouette fades into the gray water below like a headlight disappearing in fog.

"My God, he is *flying* down," says Hanli Prinsloo, a South African freediver who has joined me on the prow of the boat. Speed isn't necessarily a good thing in free-diving, she reminds me. The faster King goes, the more energy he burns and the less oxygen he'll have for his ascent.

"Eighty meters, ninety meters," the dive official says. "Touchdown," he announces, and King starts coming back up.

"Ninety meters, eighty meters." Then the official pauses. King is coming up at about half the speed of his descent. At 60 meters, the updates come slower. At 40 meters they stop altogether.

Five seconds pass. King has been underwater for more than two minutes. "Forty meters," the official repeats. Pause. "Forty meters."

A sickening anticipation sets in. I look around the sailboat. The officials, divers, and crews all stare at the choppy water and wait. And wait.

"Thirty meters."

King appears to be moving, but too slowly. Five more seconds. He should have surfaced by now, but he's still 100 feet down. Five more seconds. "Thirty meters," the official repeats.

"Oh God," says Prinsloo, holding her hand over her mouth. Five more seconds. In the water we see nothing—no sign of King, no ripples at the surface, no movement.

"Thirty meters." Silence. "Thirty meters."

"Blackout!" a safety diver yells. King is unconscious ten stories below the surface. The divers kick down into the water.

"Safety!" the judge on line three yells. About 30 seconds later, the water around the line explodes in a cauldron of white wash. The wetsuit-covered heads of two safety divers reappear. Between them is King. His face is bright blue, and he's not moving. His neck is stiff.

The divers push his face out of the water. His cheeks, mouth, and chin are slicked with blood. "Breathe! Breathe!" the divers yell. No response. Bright drops of blood drip from King's chin into the ocean.

"CPR! CPR!" the judge yells. A diver puts his mouth over King's blood-covered mouth and blows. "CPR now!" the judge yells. King's coach, Dave Kent, is yelling into King's ear: *"Dave! Dave!"* No response. Ten seconds pass and still nothing. Someone yells for oxygen. Someone else for CPR. Georgoulis screams, "Why isn't anyone calling a medic? Get a helicopter!" Everyone is yelling.

Behind us, on line one, another diver heads down. Then another surfaces, blacked out. The safety divers move King's stick-figure form to the flotilla and punch an oxygen mask to his face. Still no response. His facial muscles are frozen into a sickly smile, his eyes wide and lost, staring out at the open sea.

The consensus on the sailboat is that King has died. But we're 40 feet away from him now, and nobody can really tell what's happening. The safety crew keep pumping his chest, tapping his face, yelling. "Dave! Dave!"

Then, miraculously, King's fingers quiver, his lips flutter, and he breathes. Color returns to his face; his eyes open, then softly close again. He is breathing deeply, tapping his coach's leg to let him know he's OK.

In the wake of all this, Trubridge attempts a 118-meter dive on line one, but he turns around early and fails his surface protocol. British free-diver Sara Campbell turns back after just 22 meters on a world-record attempt. "I couldn't do it," she says, hopping back on the sailboat. She was too shaken by King, who's now being taken by motorboat to a hospital. As it races back to shore, there's another blackout on line two. Then another on three.

"My God, this is getting messy," says Campbell. The west winds are up now, chopping the ocean, fluttering the sail above us. "It's like dominoes. Everything's falling apart. This is the worst I've ever seen."

The competition goes on for three more hours. On the last dive of the day, a Ukrainian, new to the sport, attempts a beginning descent of 40 meters. He surfaces and removes his mask to flash the OK sign, and a stream of blood gushes from his nose. Then he completes the surface protocol and is awarded a white card. The dive is accepted. Blood is OK.

That night at the hotel the divers cavort, some laugh, others casually shake their heads at all the drama. Of the day's 93 competitors, 15 attempted dives of 100 meters or more. Of those, two were disqualified, three came up short, and four blacked out—a 60 percent failure rate. King is in the hospital. Nobody knows for sure, but the rumor is that the pressure tore his larynx, which is fairly common on deep dives. A minor injury, they say.

"This kind of thing never happens," the divers repeat over and over, rolling their eyes. But I think this kind of thing happens all the time: it's just that nobody here wants to admit it. The challenge now is to see who can move beyond today's "messy" events, erase them from their minds, and dive to even greater depths on the final day of competition.

One person who seems unfazed is Guillaume Néry, a 29-year-old French free-diver and the winner of yesterday's CWT competition. The day after King's near-death episode, I meet him midmorning at a table crowded with other members of the French team.

"I was not there, so don't know exactly," he says in a thick accent. "But I think the main mistake is not for Dave King but for all freedivers. They were focused on this 100-meter number and not on their feelings, not what they really want to do." Néry, who started freediving at 14, gained international fame last year with the release of "Free Fall," a short film that follows him on a 13-story freedive in the Bahamas. The clip has been viewed on YouTube more than 10 million times.

"I learned long ago that patience is the key to success in freediving," he says. "You have to forget the target, to enjoy and relax in the water." Néry smiles and runs his fingers through his mop of sandy hair, mentioning that he hasn't blacked out in more than five years of steady freediving. "What is important now is trying to do the dive, surface, and have a smile on my face. That's what I did."

Not everybody is so philosophical. "Blacking out is like shitting yourself," Sebastian Näslund tells me. "It's an embarrassment to you and everyone else around you." Fred Buyle, who became one of the first competitive freedivers in the 1990s and is now retired, echoes Näslund. "Honestly, I think the guy is a fucking idiot," he says of King. "I thought he was dead. His coach thought he was dead. I've been freediving since 1990, and that's the worst I've ever seen."

Months later, King tells me by e-mail that he is aware of the criticism he received and offers his own perspective on what happened. "I am not a reckless diver," he writes, noting that the blackout in Greece was his only one in ten years of freediving. He argues that his work schedule doesn't allow him to train as much as other elite divers and that he had time for only three dives before the competition. "I got to 102 meters, equalizing easily," he says. "I just had problems as I reached the surface."

Saturday, the final day of competition, brings scalding sunshine, still air, and clear, calm waters—perfect conditions. The discipline today is free immersion, where divers are allowed to pull themselves down the line to reach their target depth. Free-immersion dives are a little shallower than CWT, but they can take a while, sometimes more than four minutes, making them excruciating to watch. The divers got a wrist slap last night from event director Stavros Kastrinakis, who told them, "Dive your limits." The announced dives today appear to be more conservative. Still, there are a number of world- and national-record attempts planned.

As the morning unfolds, more blackouts occur, but today they don't look so bad. Or maybe I'm just getting used to the sight of inert bodies and blue faces. Most competitors recover quickly, then swim back to the boat in silence, ashamed to have, again, pushed beyond their limits.

I keep watching as the next dozen athletes make their dives. Then the elite divers begin: Malina Mateusz of Poland breaks a national record with a dive of 106 meters. The women's world champion, Russian Natalia Molchanova, sets a world record of 88 meters. Anton Koderman dives 105 meters to set a new Slovenian mark. Néry breaks the French record with 103. Trubridge does 112, almost effortlessly. Seven national records are broken in an hour. Everyone is in control. The sport, again, is awe inspiring and beautiful.

Then, at line two, a commotion breaks out. The safety divers have lost a Czech diver named Michal Risian. Literally lost him. He's at least 200 feet underwater, but the sonar is no longer picking him up. He has somehow drifted away from the rope.

"Safety! Safety!" yells the judge. The safety divers go down but come up a minute later with nothing. "Safety! Safety! Now!" Thirty seconds pass. No sign of Risian anywhere.

On line one, Sara Campbell is preparing to dive. From below her, three and a half minutes after he went down on line two, Risian emerges—40 feet away from the line he was first attached to.

There's confusion. Campbell jerks away, frightened. Risian snaps off his goggles, saying, "Don't touch me. I'm OK." Then he swims back to the sailboat under his own steam. He plops down on a seat beside me on the hull, laughs, and says, "Wow, that was a weird dive."

Yeah, that's one way of putting it. Before Risian's dive and per the usual routine, his coach attached the lanyard on Risian's right ankle to the line. As Risian turned and plummeted, the Velcro securing the lanyard came loose and fell off. The safety divers saw it floating, unattached, and rushed down to stop Risian, but he was already gone, 100 feet deep. Risian, unaware, closed his eyes, meditated, and drifted downward. But he wasn't going straight down—he was angling 45 degrees away from the line, into open ocean.

Risian's coach, realizing that death was the likely outcome of this screwup, floated motionless at the surface, gazing at the safety divers, who were too stunned to blink. "I'll remember their looks for a long time," he said later. "Terror, awe, fear, and sadness."

Meanwhile, 250 feet below, Risian was diving farther down and farther away, oblivious to the problem. At 272 feet, he reached out to grab the metal plate, but there was no plate. "I couldn't see any tickets, any plate, any rope, nothing," he said. "I was completely lost. Even when I turned up and looked around, I saw only blue."

At 29 stories down, even in the clearest water, all directions look the same. And all directions feel the same—the water pressure makes it impossible to gauge whether you're swimming up or down, east or west.

For a moment, Risian panicked. Then he calmed himself, knowing that panic would only kill him faster. "In one direction there was a bit more light," he told me. "I figured that this is where the surface was." He figured wrong. Risian was swimming horizontally. But as he swam, trying to remain conscious and calm, he saw a white rope. "I knew if I could find the rope, I would be OK," he said.

The chances of Risian finding a line 250 feet down—especially one so far from his original line of descent—were, I would estimate, about the same as hitting a particular number on a roulette wheel. Twice. But there it was, the line Sara Campbell was about to descend, some 40 feet away from where he had first gone down. Risian grabbed it, aimed for the surface, and somehow made it up before he drowned.

~~~~~~

On the final night, the divers, coaches, and judges gather on the beach for closing ceremonies. Strobes and spotlights glare from an enormous stage, Euro pop blasts from a DJ booth, and a crowd of a few hundred dance and drink beneath a night sky sequined with stars. Behind the stage a bonfire rages, heating the bare, wet bodies of those who couldn't resist one last splash.

The winners are announced. All told, the divers broke two world and 48 national records. Competitors also suffered 19 blackouts. Trubridge won gold in both constant weight no fins and free immersion.

"Risian is the real winner here," says Trubridge, sipping a beer beside his wife, Brittany. Behind us, every 20 minutes or so, an enormous video screen shows the chilling footage of Risian's tetherless dive, which was recorded on underwater cameras. At the end of the video, the crowd cheers and Risian, who's had a few, rushes to the stage to take a bow. Dave King, the diver who suffered the horrific blackout just two days ago, walks through the crowd with the British team, smiling and seemingly in perfect health. Néry, in quintessential French style, is smoking a cigarette.

"There is such a strong community here," says Hanli Prinsloo, drinking a cocktail by the bonfire. "It's like all of us, we have no choice. We have to be in the water, we've chosen to live our lives in it, and by doing that we accept its risks." She takes a sip. "But we also reap its rewards."

I begin to understand her point. Freedivers have access to a world that the rest of us see only from the surface—from boats, surfboards, and airplanes 36,000 feet up. It's safe, where most of us are, but it's also isolating: we can never know the ocean's true wonder, power, strength, or beauty. The real mysteries of nature are revealed to those who reach farther, push harder, and go deeper.

For freedivers, access to the hidden universe that covers 70 percent of the planet is worth the price of admission—blackouts, ripped larynxes, and all. And blood? What's a little blood when you've made it to the other side?

(Originally published January 2012)

QUOOSIERS

ERIC HANSEN

~~~~~~

The Quidditch World Cup sounds dorky, and make no mistake: it is. But these sorcery-loving Harry Potter fans play pretty rough, as Eric Hansen found out when we sent him to captain a bad-news team of ex-athletes, ultimate Frisbee studs, slobs, drunks, and some people he knows from Iceland. Brooms up, and may the best Muggles win.

~~~~~~

Sunset on a Saturday in early November. The playing fields of Randall's Island, New York City. It's near the end of the first day of the surprisingly violent 2011 Quidditch World Cup, and we of the *Outside* Magazine Partially Icelandic Quidditch World Cup Team—OMPIQWCT for short—are ready to kick some Potter ass.

The 14 of us dominated our first competitors this morning and flew loop-the-loops around our second challengers this afternoon. Now, at one end of the vast spread of beautiful fields—what grass! what trees!—we're warming up for our third match, which will determine whether we progress to the quarter-finals tomorrow. Behind us looms Icahn Stadium, where the finals will be played and where a Muggle named Usain Bolt once set a world record in the 100 meters.

Some 2,000 chipper, ethnically diverse, and not wholly fit competitors, mostly high school and college students, mill around the bleachers, the Porta-Potties, the team tent area. The line for the waffle cart stretches nearly to the East River. One infield retailer does a brisk business selling championship lapel pins, while another is on its way to liquidating the Quidditch players' "broom of choice," according to the brochure, a $55 handmade model dubbed the Shadow Chaser. Everywhere there are fans—dads wearing shirts that read PROUD PARENT OF A MCGILL QUIDDITCH PLAYER, alongside teens in capes and the crimson-and-gold scarves of Hogwarts. Only five years old, this grand tournament of nonfantasy Quidditch will draw some 10,000 paying spectators. A Fox newscaster once called it "a cross between the Super Bowl and a medieval fair."

"Look here," hollers one of our offensive players, waving a hand as we trot around the field, catching and throwing inflatable balls.

At the edge of the field stand our opponents: undergrads from Rollins, a liberal-arts college in Winter Park, Florida. They have flown, or more likely ridden a bus, all the way from Florida to compete. And though they're not even warming up yet, we watched their aggressive play earlier and want to be on point. We no longer feel awkward about how we threw together our team just a few weeks ago. Nor do we grumble that some of us are old enough to be Quid Kid parents, our average age being 30. Instead, we focus on game-winning strategy.

"Let's monopolize the bludgers," says our 39-year-old co-captain Josh.

"And then just let the chasers do their thing," says our 28-year-old top scorer, Dan.

What are they talking about? I'm still not sure. In creating this real-world adaptation of the fantasy sport enjoyed by Harry and Ron and Hermione, numerous concessions to magic-quashing forces like gravity had to be made, and the result is best understood by those who score high on standardized tests. For example, the official rulebook contains illustrations of 22 different hand signals that a referee might make while blowing a whistle in any of four ways.

But here are the basics: Play happens on an egg-shaped, 50-yard-long pitch. Each team fields seven players, two of whom must be women, and all players have to wear team jerseys and colored sweatbands. Critically, *everyone* must at all times straddle a broom at least 46 inches long, to simulate flying.

The goal is to score as many points as possible in games that typically last around 45 minutes. Ten points are earned by offensive players (chasers) throwing a deflated volleyball—called the quaffle—through one of the opposing team's goals, which consist of three hula-hoops arranged vertically atop PVC-pipe stands. Thirty points are awarded, and the game ends, when a player grabs the snitch. At Hogwarts, the snitch hovers and darts of its own accord; here, it's a tennis ball in a sock hung from the waistband of an unaffiliated volunteer called the snitch runner. The snitch runner is usually an off-season cross-country star and is not limited to the field. Five minutes after he or she is "released" at the start of the game, each team gets to send one unlucky member—the seeker—in pursuit, sometimes up trees.

The quaffle is moved downfield rugby style, with running and passing. Attacks are stopped when a defenseman, called a beater, beans a player with one of three gym balls (bludgers) or when an offensive chaser uses his free arm to tackle the opposing chaser and wrestle the quaffle free. A goalie—the keeper—guards his team's hula-hoops, usually by swatting the quaffle out of the air with his hand.

Or so we thought. Ten minutes into our showdown with Rollins, we are frozen in a 10–10 tie, and their stocky, long-haired goalie isn't even near his hoops. He keeps abandoning his post and trying to blitz the length of the field to score himself.

"Wrap him up, tackle him!" a teammate yells at me when the goalie takes off a third time. I try, but he barges past with the flailing arms and unblinking eyes of a proper Potter psycho. For reasons unknown, just shy of our goal the bastard chooses to ignore the hoops and instead clobbers my wife, Hrund, who isn't even in the game.

I see the whole episode from just inches away, a dirty lock of his hair waving in my face as I sprint behind him. One moment she's relaxing on the sideline, looking away, not even holding a broom. The next, this freak lowers his non-broom-carrying shoulder and blasts her in the sternum. The impact sends her flying through the dusky air, nearly completing a full back layout before landing on her head.

Silence. The sun disappears behind skyscrapers. "I'm OK," Hrund declares, finding her feet.

But I'm not. "What the fuck's your problem?" I scream at the goalie, behaving worse than I ever have in a lifetime of competitive sports. When he doesn't respond, I shove my face inches from his, throwing my broom down like a hockey enforcer dropping his stick. "You need to fucking calm down!" I shout.

The irony only increases. After some discussion, the referee awards the goalie a yellow card, apparently based on some rule or precedent for unprovoked assault of a spectator. "We can't give him a red card," the ref explains, "because she wasn't actually playing."

Jolted to action, the OMPIQWCT goes on to score 110 mostly unanswered points, and we win 120–40. Sorry, nerds. But there's a war on out here.

~~~~~~

Quidditch was invented at Vermont's Middlebury College in 2005, when a group of buddies—fans of J. K. Rowling, of course—got tired of playing bocce and decided to improvise something more exciting that involved brooms and bath-towel capes. They drew up a loose Quidditch rulebook and encouraged other students at tony schools to play.

In 2007, a reporter from *USA Today* covered "the first intercollegiate Quidditch match." Never mind that this was just a scrimmage between the Middlebury guys and some of their high school friends at Vassar. Within months of the story's appearance, the intramural sport had magically spread from campus to campus. With an organizing committee at its helm, it attracted more teams and volunteer administrators and fresh coverage every year—"a remarkable ascension," declared *Time* magazine in 2010. The height of the mania quickly became the annual World Cup, held each fall and open to any teams registered with the Bedford Hills, New York–based International Quidditch Association.

Two months before the World Cup, this magazine's editorial director asked if I was interested in recruiting a team. Why he asked me I wasn't sure. I certainly wasn't a Potterhead, as fans call themselves. I'd never bought a pewter wand, like my nephew, or a co-branded plush toy, like my niece. I'd never visited the Wizarding World theme park in Orlando, and I certainly hadn't taken sides with Stephen King, who has maintained that the Harry Potter books will last "not just for the decade but for the ages." For that matter, I hadn't taken sides against Yale scholar Harold Bloom, who believed, conversely, that "Rowling's mind is so governed by clichés and dead metaphors that she has no other style of writing." As to the world-shaping powers of Rowling, I was happily agnostic. I hadn't read any of the books and fell asleep when the movies were screened on planes.

The more I Googled around, however, the more Quidditch piqued my interest. I imagined writing something snarky, maybe poking fun at how Quidditch started out as a decidedly preppy sport, heedless of Rowling's *Quidditch Through the Ages,* which suggests the game be played on "deserted moorland far from Muggle habitations." Or I'd lampoon its comical misfires: before settling on a tennis ball in a sock, for example, some teams had tried using a remote-controlled helicopter for the snitch.

As for the sport itself, it just seemed like a hoot. A bit of rough and tumble, not a terrible amount of running, harmless competitors. If I gathered some fit New Yorkers, we'd surely have a blast and maybe even win a few games. Injuries were the last thing on my mind.

A week after I contacted the International Quidditch Association, one of the founders—Alex Benepe, now 25 and commissioner of the IQA—e-mailed to say a spot had opened. I was bummed when he strongly suggested that we register as Division 2. Weren't we—whoever we would turn out to be—all-star material? He assured me we'd have challenges enough, playing the likes of Syracuse, Duke, and other teams that had actually been practicing for a year. Also, he wanted to know, since we would be replacing a team of New Zealanders, was there any way we could field an international squad? I told him to register us as Iceland—Hrund's homeland and one of the rare countries in the Northern Hemisphere not already represented—and we were off to the races.

Or not. We made a big recruitment push via e-mail, Twitter, and Facebook and through an announcement on *Outside*'s website, but we struggled to sign players.

"Come, win glory!" I said. No! came the replies.

"The more you tell me about this, the less interested I am," said my brother-in-law. No one showed up to the open tryouts in Central Park two weeks later, which happened to take place during a freak snowstorm, and the OMPIQWCT's only practice session, in Central Park a week before the World Cup, enticed just five strangers and acquaintances.

Our confidence grew nonetheless.

"They're history majors and competitors in the Science Cup and stuff," said Josh. "We're big and old and intimidating."

Bolstering the authority of this statement was the fact that Josh had once led an inexperienced team of New Yorkers to the finals of the World Elephant Polo Championships in Nepal, another competition of indeterminate ridiculousness. I immediately named him co-captain.

We practiced for about an hour——meaning we read and discussed how to play the complex game—and then retired for beers at an outdoor patio. "Are you guys some sort of team?" the waiter asked, noticing the brooms and Swiffer leaning against railings and chairs.

"Yeah," we said, giving him a rough overview of Quidditch.

"Oh," he replied. "I thought maybe you were a curling team."

As if! Friends and strangers signed up and dropped out right up until the midnight roster-registration deadline, but ultimately the OMPIQWCT evolved into a tight squad of 14, including two people of Viking stock: my 31-year-old wife and her badminton teammate from childhood, a 29-year-old guy named Birgir, or Biggi. We were writers and animators, a grad student, a banker and a lawyer, a hip-hop musician, a consultant, a student, and a production coordinator for a menswear company. Half our team knew next to nothing about Harry Potter, and none had played Quidditch before.

We did turn out to be athletes, though, and pretty good ones. Dan had been voted the nation's most valuable ultimate Frisbee player not long before. One of his disc teammates, 27-year-old Jack, was also a former juggler in a professional circus, and the other, 28-year-old Tim, was once captain of his high school wrestling team. Twenty-five-year-old Jen was a former cheerleading national champion. Hrund had been the women's junior national champ in snowboarding and badminton in Iceland.

Things were shaping up to be fun. But there were portents of violence, like when I spoke to a longtime player who gave me strange-sounding advice that I relayed to the team.

"'Hide your girls?'" Josh kept asking. "What does that even mean?"

Team OMPIQWCT came together for the first time less than an hour before our debut. Our collective state was, I'd say, a bit nervous. The three Frisbee boys—as we'd taken to calling Dan, Jack, and Tim—walked around to scout the competition. Twenty-four-year-old Russell, who works in animation and was our most eager player, brought a competition-level broom, while Josh fretted over the tall kitchen sweepers I'd picked up at the hardware store the night before.

"These are way too long," he groused.

"But they're lightweight," I said.

He immediately set to work shortening one, bashing the metal handle end with a rock until it was a twisted mess. How were we to know that brooms were supplied?

Our thirtysomething hip-hopper, Thaddeus, had the toughest time, and not because he was tired from an album-release party a few hours before or had dressed for game day in designer jeans and $300 sneakers. After we donned the jerseys *Outside* had supplied—red T-shirts with a big Icelandic flag on the back—people began stopping by to say how much they loved Björk or to shyly ask someone to speak the language. One girl simply prostrated herself in front of us and then moved on without a word. Thaddeus nearly drowned in the white-boy dorkiness.

"This is absolutely the least gangster thing I have ever done," he said. "The 16-year-old me would kick the shit out of the adult me for doing this."

"Anyone who goes to Outdoor Icelandic, please come to Field 9," an announcer interrupted, confusing us for a college. This was it, the moment when all our minutes of practice would be tested.

"Brooms down!" said the announcer.

Seven of us dropped a knee behind the seven wooden brooms lying on the baseline and closed our eyes, as instructed.

"The snitch is loose!" the announcer said, signaling that the man with the ball dangling from his shorts was running away from the field.

"Brooms up!" the announcer said.

Everyone opened their eyes and ran toward the center of the field, brooms wagging like dog tails, to grab the gym balls and volleyball that rested there.

For the first ten minutes, members of the OMPIQWCT ran around in pandemonium. We collided with each other, tripped and fell, and simply forgot to straddle the brooms like hobbyhorses.

"Icelander! Get on your broom," the announcer barked. "It's why we play. To *fly*."

Soon, some of us were exhausted by the ceaseless back and forth and subbed out. But not the Frisbee boys. Dan had an almost-omniscient field sense. Jack could throw a ball accurately while falling sideways. Our opponents, a short-legged group called CAMPS, swarmed toward Tim, but he covered 50 yards before they could traverse the narrow field.

Russell was also committed. He followed the snitch to the parking lot, lost him under some bleachers, and then ran back and snatched the sock near a bank of folding chairs. Some 20 minutes later, we had trounced CAMPS, 110–30.

A bloody cage fight it was not. CAMPS turned out to be made up mostly of high school kids from a youth ministry in Massachusetts—a fact I chose not to spread around.

Still, we had won our first game in a sport we hardly knew. The sun was shining and the river sparkling, and we, an endorphin-flush team of randoms, had achieved a certain esprit de corps.

"I'm really glad I came," said Thaddeus.

"I think we can take this thing," said Dan.

In our next game, against Miami University of Ohio—known for its synchronized-figure-skating program—our defense monopolized two of three bludgers while wrapping up their offense. And our forwards caught alley-oop passes, slam-dunked, and necromanced the quaffle. The announcer liked to point out that "the old-man team" often perpetrated various and sundry fouls. But when our offense picked up defensive bludgers, it was only out of confusion. We crushed: 150–90.

A fanboy ran up to one of our women. "You're the best beater I've ever seen," he said, and then ran away. Birgir led us in the Icelandic cheer he'd devised.

"*Drepa, drepa, drekka blóð!*" we shouted, thinking then that "Kill, kill, drink blood" was the height of irony.

Unlike Rowling's fictional Department of Magical Games and Sports, which is said to list 700 potential fouls in a Quidditch game, the downloadable IQA rulebook runs to a mere 55 pages and is both simple and, in places, astoundingly complex. It includes straightforward sections like "The Mounted Broom," plus many more-taxing chapters. A 15-volunteer IQA Rules Council oversees changes, and the codification evolves much faster than in, say, college football, where new rules appear only after long reviews. If a competitor chooses to study the latest edition of the rulebook, he can discern hints of the mayhem that can mar Quidditch at all levels.

"The physical contact rules contained within this book allow for rough play," an early disclaimer reads. "Players are encouraged to have first aid equipment and people trained in first aid on hand during every game."

But we didn't study the rules that closely, the organizers never asked for our liability release waivers, and I didn't catch a whiff of the terrifying stench of Quid Kid hostility until I ambled out into the parking lot at the south gate and ended up chatting with a tired ambulance driver who was having a smoke. He was one of 30 EMTs posted at the event.

"Easy duty," I said.

"This is just the quiet before another storm," he corrected. "I've had eight concussions, two people taken to the hospital, bloody noses, scrapes, twisted ankles. I stopped counting injuries after ten."

My teammates weren't as surprised by these stats as I expected. One recalled stopping a young female chaser just short of the goal, only to have the girl yell an extremely unprintable comment. Another teammate recalled watching a man in Division 1 lift a girl, spin her like the blades of a helicopter, and throw her to the dirt. The violence was not only pervasive but gender neutral. Hide your girls, indeed.

In Division 1, where teams were often hand-selected from college-wide tryouts, the savagery appeared coordinated, with flanks of rhino-like teammates blocking for Quidditch chasers who could pass as junior college running backs. Though illegal, many of their clotheslines to the neck and elbows to the face looked about as accidental as gravity.

Of course, I had almost gotten violent myself when Hrund was flattened. After my shameful display against Rollins, Frisbee Dan had tried to console me—"I would have done the same thing," he said—but I had to take a walk to cool off.

All around, there was so much happy hoopla and strangeness on display! At one point, I ran into a preposterously muscular group of guys standing under a supersize American flag.

"Who are you?" I asked one of the bodybuilders.

"America's Finest," he said, removing his American-flag T-shirt to display his shield-like abs.

"Where are you from?"

"America."

"But I mean, what unites you as a team? Do you all go to the same school?"

"We're Americans."

"How are you doing?"

"Oh and three."

I couldn't believe it. "But you're the fittest team here!"

"It's really complicated," one of their girls said. "And we have temper issues."

In the team tent area, life was more amiable. All sorts of cute circles had formed: stretching circles, jumping-jack circles, teammates-napping-heads-on-bellies circles. One of Quidditch's founders strode around in top hat and cane, an entourage trotting dutifully behind. I kept an eye out for the IQA group streaming live stats and the professional PR woman and the résumé-building undergrads—the "HR coordinator," the "executive board members," the "regional directors," the "outreach director," the editor of the Quidditch magazine *The Monthly Seer.* On the main stage, a Quidditch-themed folk duo—was it Harry and the Potters? the Whomping Willows? Snidget?—attempted the fizzy back-and-forth I had come to expect.

He: "Our Huff and Puff song is the best one."

She: "Yeah, it's the greatest!"

I couldn't believe that a crowd was actually listening to this, lapping up the allusions to Potter characters and settings and plotlines.

And that's when I got it. I *was* an old man. I'd completely missed the Potter craze, unlike so many competitors on Randall's Island, who had actually come of age in the midst of it. They, with their "knobbly knees," had hit puberty with *Half-Blood Prince.* The boys had begun to show some patchy stubble just like Harry did in *Deathly Hallows.* Maybe the girls dared to trade hoodies for their first lipstick-red dresses after seeing Hermione pull it off. Or maybe not. Whatever the case, a new book or movie had appeared roughly once a year for the past decade, and because these kids were the same age as Harry and Ron and Hermione, developments in the books had mirrored changes in their lives. Harry Potter was in their guts, in their loins. This was *their* sport. And so sometimes, sure, they had to gang-tackle or lance people in the kidneys. In the real-world Quidditch World Cup, that's just what it took to conquer evil.

The next day, at 10:20 A.M., we squared off against the team from Johns Hopkins, the not quite Ivy League school in Baltimore, in our last game of pool play. We felt super-psyched but immediately realized that we were in for a new kind of trouble: nagging.

"We've noticed them off their brooms—will you watch them?" one of their captains asked the referee.

"Yeah, we've seen 'em," their gangly co-captain said. "They're not on their brooms."

True, we were still struggling with the basics of "flying," but it also must be noted that I was wearing sunscreen on my face and worn-out tennis shoes on my feet, while the gangly co-captain had on steel-cage lacrosse goggles, a mouth guard, and cleats, and had rubbed blue war paint under her eyes.

Sure enough, the announcer shouted "Brooms up!" and the ref started handing out yellow cards—mostly to us. I got one for tackling from behind. Tim earned one for tackling with both hands. Two of our goals and one impressive snitch grab were dismissed for murky reasons. All of these were prompted by whines from the Hopkins co-captain.

"Are you refereeing this match or are they?" Birgir asked the ref at one point.

Not that Hopkins lacked muscle. They had some of the most aggressive women in all of Potterdom, and halfway through the game their snitch got aggro, too, slamming Russell to the pitch. Our biggest Quidditch fan, our tireless snitch-chasing seeker, found himself on the receiving end of a WWF-style takedown. The paramedics arrived and diagnosed a dislocated shoulder.

Unknown to us, the body slam had actually torn Russell's biceps off his shoulder. At the time, his grunts and teeth grinding simply served as a call to arms, a reminder that nothing unites a Quidditch team or a nation like a common enemy. We forced an 80–70 win in front of a packed bleachers.

Our first real fans howled. Online, friends of the International Quidditch Association posted comments like "They beat Hopkins!" and "They totally dominated" and "Icies are hardcore." Jack riled up the crowd further by throwing a standing backflip.

Two and a half hours later, at 4:45 P.M., we faced off against Hopkins again. The finals bracket seeded us third, behind Purdue and Illinois State, but in an inexcusably amateur scheduling mistake, organizers pitted us against Hopkins in the quarterfinals, our first single-elimination round.

At the beginning of the grudge match, the packed stands creaked under the weight of our newfound supporters. Many teams had lost and taken the school bus home by now; only half the fields remained in use. Goth-looking vendors were selling Deathly Hallows necklaces, but it was the hulking, shiny structure of Icahn Stadium that beckoned.

I wish I could say more, but I have little recollection of the two hours or so surrounding the game. According to my teammates, early on a slippery Hopkins chaser fumbled the quaffle near our goal, he and I lunged for it, and his broom walloped me in the back of the head. Another injury that surprised no one.

"Eric has a concussion and we walk to the paramedics," wrote Hrund, who picked up my notebook. "There is a girl with a broken wrist."

"We win the 2nd game against Hopkins by 20 points, after having grabbed the snitch four times," she continued. "The first three times were disqualified for Frisbee Tim being too aggressive/physical on the snitch. The fourth time was supposedly too aggressive as well but the snitch didn't want to be thrown to the ground anymore. He was a small, mildly injured kid with glasses and a uniform covered in dirt by the fourth grab."

Hrund escorted me from the medical tent to the north end of the fields at 7 P.M., where OMPIQWCT was battling Rochester Institute of Technology, the engineering university in upstate New York, in the semifinals. Emerging from the fog of my concussion, I saw the sport as if for the first time.

"I know we're on Randall's Island and playing Quidditch and stuff," I said, "but this is just insane."

In a cold breeze, under bright halide lights, the OMPIQWCT was shouting and running plays, steamrolling and posting up. The Frisbee boys were stiff-arming anyone who got in their way, and our beaters were throwing elbows to guard their bludgers. Two of our players substituted for each other because (1) we no longer had any other subs, thanks to the injuries and unavoidable commitments that had siphoned off six of our players; and (2) the guys' hands had been stepped on so much that they were having difficulty gripping the balls for more than a few minutes. Frisbee Jack, for example, attempted a diving tackle and missed, and an RIT girl stomped her cleated foot on his throwing hand. He yelped in pain. Seeing him roll over and clutch his throbbing paw, the girl pointed at him and yelled to the ref: "Off his broom!"

Some 30 minutes in, Frisbee Tim spied the snitch and dropped into a scary, hands-forward grappler's crouch. But an RIT player, so small as to go almost unnoticed, sneaked up and made off with the sock. RIT won, 90–70.

Hrund, Russell (in a sling), and I cheered the sweat-drenched OMPIQWCT as they dragged their exhausted selves off the pitch. Later that night, in Icahn Stadium, Purdue would go on to take home the championship vodka-bottle-spray-painted-gold-to-look-like-a-trophy trophy that went to the winner of Division 2.

I was sad to have lost in the semis but more than satisfied with third place and happy to return to my very non-magical life without any permanent injuries.

"Rugby is dangerous enough when you don't have a broom stuck between your legs," said Birgir, and we nodded in agreement.

Toasting over multiple rounds of drinks a week later, the OMPIQWCT was regaled with the story of Russell's visit to the Randall's Island hospital. Normally, the place admits drug abusers and the homeless and overflow from Harlem Hospital, he said, but during the Quidditch World Cup he and other young schoolkids were hobbling up and down the hallways with brooms. His doctor finally had to ask what the hell was going on.

"Did you tell him it was a curling competition?" someone asked.

Later, everyone e-mailed me their thoughts about the weekend, and most echoed Josh, who wrote: "I wish I could say it wasn't actually fun, and that I didn't want to win, but that would be a lie."

Russell was the exception. It took three months before orthopedic surgeons reattached his biceps to his shoulder, using five titanium pins, and he still hasn't regained full use of his right arm. "But I don't have any regrets," he wrote. "I'd go brooms up with you guys anytime." He plans to frame his cut-up jersey and hang it in his apartment, above the Shadow Chaser broom we all signed.

(Originally published May 2012)

THE BEAUTIFUL GAME

PATRICK SYMMES

~~~~~~

In Argentina, rival soccer fans don't just hate, they kill, and the violent partisans of top clubs fuel crime syndicates that influence the sport at its highest levels. Who better to investigate than our longtime contributing editor Patrick Symmes, who braved bottle rockets, howling mobs, urine bombs, and drunken grannies on a wild ride through the scariest fútbol underworld on earth.

~~~~~~

"There are two stories," a leader of the Rat Stabbers told me. We were filing through police lines toward the cylinder, the stadium of a powerful Buenos Aires soccer team called Racing. Inside, about 60,000 enemy fans waited to crucify us.

His name was Jorge Celestre—Georgie Blueskies—but he was explaining the name of his fan club, the Rat Stabbers. They were the diehard supporters of Estudiantes, a pro soccer team southeast of Buenos Aires.

The first story was about some medical students—owing to their lab work, "rat stabbers"—who founded Estudiantes more than a century ago. It was a nice story about a studious, successful Argentina, a country that started the 20th century with futuristic dreams and progressive ambitions.

"But the second story is more probable," Celestre explained as we jostled our way toward lines of police. The original fans were some unemployed men who sat around parks killing rats for fun. That squalid image evoked another Argentina, the one that ended the 20th century with riots and a currency crash, a backstabbing society where life is, as one Argentine put it to me, "a war of all against all."

I had met the Rat Stabbers by physically pushing into their red-and-white-clad column as they marched toward the Cylinder, a high-fascist coliseum built in the

1940s by dictator Juan Perón—a Racing fan—with public funds. The swooping concrete is still dominated by Perón's swan-necked tower, its omniscient eye now filled with the cameras of Copresede—a police surveillance agency called the Provincial Committee on Sports Safety—who are charged with stopping the most violent soccer fans in the world.

We squeezed through funnels of policemen watched by lines of horsemen and backstopped by rows of cop infantry in full riot gear. Specialists in nitrile gloves patted down the males in our cohort. Behind them were plainclothes Copresede agents holding mug shots of some of the 400 Rat Stabbers banned from their own team's games.

The Rat Stabbers started up their brass band, for courage, and with a hard push about 2,000 of us were swept up the stairs and jammed into the visitors' terrace. Here, penned by metal fences and more police, we were pressed shoulder-to-shoulder, immobile, for two hours, a single screaming entity heaving up and down.

Problem: we had 2,000, but the Cylinder seats 64,000. It wasn't absolutely full, but I'll stick with my guess that we were outnumbered by 60,000. They were dancing in great waves, a sea of blue and white, their noise drowning out even the Rat Stabbers' band.

The game went badly. Not for Racing, whose diehard fan club, the Imperial Guard, gathered below our terrace, taunting, calling up challenges. *Come down here and say that to my face.*

The Rat Stabbers retaliated by spitting, and they managed to heave firecrackers and a smoke bomb over two layers of fencing. Nobody would remember the game later, not even the score. But they would remember this, the battle.

Goals are nice. But fighting is forever.

I've been fascinated—or should I say terrified—by Argentina's violent brand of soccer since 1996, when I saw the Buenos Aires team Boca Juniors play in their notoriously tight little stadium, La Bombonera. Boca is famous for the quality of its play but also for its fan club—La Doce, the 12th Man—which has occupied the same north terrace for half a century, always standing, always singing, usually fighting.

That night, Boca fans began the match in style, igniting Roman candles that spewed red flames, sparks, and smoke over their heads. Enormous blue-and-gold flags unfurled from the upper levels. It was intimidating to watch from the opposite end, where I stood with a few thousand supporters of a team called Gimnasia, 50,000 people hating on me and my new friends.

The unaccountable happened: the unheralded Gimnasia handed Boca its worst defeat in half a century, a 6–0 stomper that sent waves of Boca fans crashing against the fencing that protected us. Trash and cups filled with urine rained down on us. Fleeing with Gimnasia fans, I found the streets of a great capital awash in cavalry and tear gas.

Don't cry for Argentina. Brazil may be more famous as a soccer nation, the beautiful game embodied today by the 20-year-old juggler Neymar. And Europe remains soccer's center of gravity: English clubs like Manchester United and Chelsea rule the global bandwidth, and Spanish clubs have ruled the pitch, bringing home two European championships in the past five years.

Yet, often enough the Europeans get there with an Argentine: Barcelona's striker is the shaggy-haired, fertile-footed Lionel Messi, the dominant player of this age. Sergio "Kun" Agüero and Carlos Tévez, who led Manchester City to this year's league championship, are both Argentines. So is Paris Saint-Germain's Javier Pastore. In 2009, Argentina surpassed Brazil as the world's top producer of soccer talent, farming out 1,700 players to professional leagues abroad. Soccer goes deep here—the first league was founded in 1891, the third-oldest in the world after England and the Netherlands.

But what Argentina really excels at is not so much the play of soccer as the bloodsucking financial exploitation and mob atmosphere that accompanies it. Corruption, of course, is nothing new in the sport. Italian teams are suffering their second major gambling scandal in six years, with reports of one player drugging his own team. Sepp Blatter, the four-time president of soccer's global body, FIFA—the Fédération Internationale de Football Association—has set a low standard, trailed by clouds of bribery allegations and the same marketing scandal that recently brought down Brazil's longtime soccer boss Ricardo Teixeira.

Of course, many nations produce dangerous fans. Games in Milan feature knife fights, England has long had its "firms" of hooligans, and racist "ultras" are a problem in Italy and Eastern Europe, where last year Polish fans threw Nazi salutes at Russian rivals. But the English hooligans of the 1980s fought for bragging rights, not money, and now they've been tempered by a national surveillance state. Across Europe, working-class fans have been outpriced by a move to champions or premier leagues, with their transnational schedules and sky boxes and crowd control.

Argentina's fan clubs, meanwhile, have become "not quite as violent as the Bloods and the Crips, but similar," says Andy Markovits, a University of Michigan political scientist specializing in soccer culture. In the 1980s, Markovits says, the fan experience in South America was "a cakewalk" compared with what was happening in Europe. Today it's the reverse.

With nicknames like the Drunkards of the Stands, the Garbage Men, the Blue Pirates, the Gangsters, and the Scoundrels, the fan clubs for the 40 professional teams playing at Argentina's A and B levels have been around almost as long as the teams themselves. But over the years, many of them have morphed into organized syndicates called *barras bravas*—literally "rowdy gangs"—that control most aspects of the teams. South American teams are private clubs, owned by their members. That leaves fan clubs, with their big voting blocs, able to make or break club officials and thereby control coaches and athletes. The most notorious barras—Boca's La Doce, River Plate's Drunkards of the Stands, and Quilmes's Indians around Buenos Aires, along with Rosario Central's Gangsters and the Lepers of Newell's Old Boys in the provinces—have captured their stadiums' concessions, monopolizing sales of soda, hamburgers, and jerseys. La Doce has one of the best scams, taking in somewhere around $125,000 to $150,000 a week in parking fees for home games. The barras routinely skim off players' salaries. And, like Sopranos of South America, the strongest assert a criminal influence at the global level, taking cuts of the transfer fees charged when an Argentine player leaves for the European premier leagues.

But the barras don't stop at profiteering: they have also been implicated in crime—from petty drug dealing, narcotics trafficking, and money laundering to beating not just rival fans but sometimes their teams' own players. Last October, after San Lorenzo defender Jonathan Bottinelli scored an own goal to lose a game, three barra soldiers walked onto the practice field and beat him up—in front of his teammates.

Surely Bottinelli knew the history of recent killings. In 2005, for example, there were six soccer murders, including the shooting of a Rat Stabber during a massive fight with police. Five died in 2006, including a fan killed with a rock in a train station, and four in 2007, including two in internal fan-club feuds. Six were killed in 2008, another eight died in 2009, and 2010 saw 11 deaths, including a Boca fan beaten by rivals at the World Cup in South Africa and the wine-bar assassination of the country's most powerful barra leader.

When I landed in Argentina in May, the violence was mounting faster than ever. A Nueva Chicago supporter was beaten to death with a crowbar in an internal feud; a few days later, a rival was killed as payback. A faction leader from the Drunkards was shot in the head. Three Rosario fans were gunned down by someone from Newell's, and during my visit, some Unión fans shooting at a Newell's crowd accidentally killed a bystander. By the close of the season in June, the death toll was already nine. And a new season would begin in August.

That violence has degraded the game itself. Every player who can follows Lionel Messi abroad, and when these dispersed stars do reassemble as a national team, they crumble rather than cohere. At the 2010 World Cup, Argentina covered the South African grass with talent but was humiliated: Messi was unable to score a single goal in the tournament, and the Germans packed their bags 4–0.

This sense of rising crisis, of a country and a sport destroying itself, was what lured me back to Argentina. The Argentines invented a new way to steal money, they used it to crush their enemies, and now they will ruin their own beautiful game. All while raining goals.

Sunshine kills mafias, but the sun goes down early in the autumn streets of Buenos Aires, and the evening game is still hours away as photographer Marco Di Lauro and I turn up a small street and come face-to-face with about 500 members of La Doce, Boca's notorious fan club. The hardcore of La Doce always rally before a game in a parking area three blocks from the stadium. Tetra Pak boxes of cheap wine are piled in pyramids, clouds of marijuana drift everywhere, and the testosterone flows freely. Everyone is dressed in blue and gold, including me. I've borrowed a natty blue zippered number, emblazoned in gold with an elaborate club seal: CABJ, for Club Atlético Boca Juniors.

Boca. Not just the most famous team of any sport in South America but an icon, a myth. The Boca neighborhood is a grimy working-class port, and the team represents the poor man's side in the class war that is Latin America. Boca has underdog charisma but wins like the Yankees: scores of national titles, as well as five South American championships in the past decade alone. It has its own museum, where you can buy thong underwear in team colors. Outside you can get your picture taken with a statue of Diego Maradona, the avenger who rose from the slums to dominate the global game and humiliate England with his infamous Hand of God goal at the 1986 World Cup. Twenty-five years later, the sight of Boca's blue-and-gold strikers coming up the field is enough to tighten the sphincter of any goalie.

Our guide is Sergio Caccialupi, known to everyone as Paco, a grizzled Boca fan and a member of La Doce since the 1970s. Paco has agreed to escort us for an extortionate ticketing fee ($150 apiece), typical at Boca games. He is thin-faced, jittery, and scarred—according to his autobiography, sold at the stadium store, he spent the 1980s peddling 30 kilos of cocaine a week, survived two jail terms, and once went all the way to Rio to fight supporters of another team. ("Better a thief than a policeman," his father told him.)

Despite my suit of blue armor, I'm immediately threatened with stabbing, robbery, and buggering. But that's par for the course, a sign I'm being accepted, or at least tolerated. Taunting is the core of hooligan life, and I plaster a broad smile on my face and take a nip of whatever is handed to me—red wine mixed with Coca-Cola, then red wine with orange soda, then Fernet with lime soda.

Trying to establish my bona fides, I mention that I was present here when Boca suffered its worst defeat in half a cent—

"Six to zero," Paco says.

"1996," another voice says.

"Gimnasia," a third man adds. "That was the worst day of my childhood."

I'm losing friends quickly. The men talk among themselves in *lunfardo*, the rapid Italo-Spanish dialect of Buenos Aires. "They have to pay," one man says. Another warns Paco, "Don't let them see anything." Another volunteers to his friends that he'll rob me if he gets the chance.

I call him out. "Why are you going to rob me?"

"That's what I do for a living," he replies coolly. On weekends he goes to Boca games. Monday to Friday, he robs tourists in the same neighborhood. If I go walking around, he says, "90 percent chance we will rob you."

Time for protection. We give Paco the agreed-upon fee for two entries to the La Doce terrace. Cash, no receipts. Paco assures me that numero uno himself—La Doce boss Mauro Martín—has approved our attendance, and indeed, a few minutes later Martín strolls past in a white track suit, his red eyes giving us a once-over.

We're in.

~~~~~~

Ninety minutes before the game, Paco suddenly says, "Let's go." We follow him not toward La Bombonera, its steep concrete walls painted blue and gold, but down a side street, through a quiet tennis stadium, and into some locker rooms before emerging to face a high fence of sheet steel. A knock, and a door opens. We are suddenly at the stadium gates, having skipped three lines of security. It's amusing to see a dozen Buenos Aires officers look away deliberately. We go straight to the entrance of the *tribuna popular*, the world of La Doce. It's the celebrity treatment, the Paco passage.

We do have to go through the turnstiles themselves. "Where are you from?" a policeman asks as he pats me down. America, I tell him.

"Welcome," he says. And, looking up from my ankles with a smile, "Good luck in there."

Paco hands us our "tickets," digital passes that belong to someone else—in my case, a youth named Mariano. Marco, an Italian war photographer who has spent more than 1,300 nights embedded with troops in Afghanistan, is apparently my mother, Maria.

We climb slowly up four flights of stairs—Paco, worn by hard living, has to rest on each landing—to reach the terrace, perhaps the most feared and tightly defended real estate in world soccer. "You have to sit here," Paco says, indicating a section on the left. "You can't take pictures over there," he says, turning toward the center. "Stay away from that part. It's where the boss sits. Don't even point your camera over there. You can take pictures in other directions, but don't even look over there."

The regular Boca fans pile in during the next hour. La Doce has no official membership—"Only the police keep a list," Paco says—and our terrace packs in with four or five thousand fans. But just a few minutes before game time, the dedicated core of the barra brava march in. These are our 500 friends from the parking lot, singing and waving huge flags as they follow the band to that central forbidden zone. Mauro Martín is in there somewhere, hiding from photographers behind a ring of loyalists and a drapery of banners. ("If they become famous, they get arrested," a police officer told me.)

Martín is not the only boss in the house. Diego Maradona has flown in from Dubai, where he coaches a team called Al Wasl. Various derailments—cocaine, tax evasion, a brief exile in Cuba—have only deepened the love affair between La Doce and their idol, who sits in a box at midfield.

The singing builds, the flags wave, and for a while we are inside the joyous machine of a fan club, exactly where I always dreaded, a stomping, jeering, cheering, and drunken band of warriors. The enemy—the Brazilian team Fluminense—takes the field amid a deafening chorus of 40,000 boos. When Boca comes out, La Bombonera explodes into a wall of bass drums and chanting: *Dale, dale, Bo! Dale, dale, Bo! Dale, dale, Bo! Bo-ca! Let's go, Boca!*

The Brazilians give the stadium a scare: two quick attacks on goal. La Doce only sings louder, draining the atmosphere with a version of "Volare" for 20,000 voices. Yet few of us can even see the action. There are too many banners draped over our heads, and many fans sit facing not the field but the band. Petty drug sales are one of La Doce's biggest rackets, and dark green buds are passed around openly, rolled up, and smoked in titanic quantities. Putting a buzz on top of a drunk leaves quite a few fans in the same state as Paco—so wasted, so early, that he lists to one side, nodding to the simple beat of the chants.

A string of menacing tough guys approaches, threatening us if we take pictures. One says, "This is our house. Nobody takes pictures in our house. Nobody." Paco has promised us this access, but he's too drunk to speak, and my Boca jacket has no magic here. A wiry, wide-eyed man screams at us bluntly: "You take one more picture, your cameras are going to fly through the fucking air!"

Game over. The Brazilians suffer a sudden setback, a red card to their player Carlinhos in the 34th minute. Two riot policemen escort him off the field under a hail of small objects tossed down by La Doce. The match turns into a mismatch: 11 Boca players grinding down 10 Fluminense rivals. The Boca striker Pablo Mouche eventually slides one across the mouth of the Brazilian goal.

Fluminense almost get an equalizer, but a Boca player blocks the shot with his right arm. It's one of the few plays I witness, occurring right below us. But the referee doesn't see it, and the fans don't want to. Diego "Hand of God" Maradona is in the house. Boca wins 1–0.

The first murder spawned by Argentinean soccer can be traced to 1924, when a Boca fan shot a Uruguayan rival during a tango-style showdown outside a luxury hotel in Montevideo. Sometime in the 1950s, the fan clubs organized for self-defense. La Doce took its fierce, fistfighting form in the 1970s. Then, around 1981, in the last violent days of Argentina's military dictatorship, the fan killings accelerated. Journalist Amílcar Romero, who wrote a history of soccer—this country also produces philosophers and artists specializing in the sport—divided the violence into three periods. Only 12 fans had been killed during the roughly 30 years following that first hotel murder. In the next three decades there were 102. The next 30 years saw 144 dead.

But Romero counted only game-day deaths. The antiviolence group Salvemos al Fútbol tallies 269 soccer-related deaths in its running count—with much of the killing moving off-site in recent years. In 2009, for example, the former Lepers leader Roberto "Pimpi" Camino was shot four times while leaving a wine bar late at night. Today the violence often takes place within the fan clubs themselves, in fights to control the barras' growing incomes and the benefits of their power. "They fight over money and women," one sportswriter told me. (He insisted on anonymity, saying, "No Argentine journalist could write this story," for fear of retaliation.)

One of the few to take that risk is a five-foot-three-inch platinum blond lawyer from Buenos Aires. Forty-four-year-old Fabiana Rubeo is a Boca devotee, but she grew tired of seeing soccer ruined by its fans. In 2006, she founded an antiviolence nonprofit called New Horizon for the World. Tiny and unthreatening, she charmed 160 leaders from more than 40 barras into attending a peace summit, where they agreed upon a Ten Commandments of barra etiquette.

Yet, the first thing Rubeo tells me when I show up at her office is that she has given up her campaign. She was threatened by criminals, ignored by the government, and mocked as "naive" by the Buenos Aires newspaper *Pagina 12*.

"Nobody supported us," she says. "I don't want to be Don Quixote tilting at windmills." All that's left of her effort is an agreement by gang leaders to throw back balls that land in the stands.

"Here, everything is mixed up between soccer and politics," Rubeo says. She cites the example of Bebote ("Big Baby"), the current Red Devils leader from

Independiente, whose real name is Pablo Alejandro Álvarez. Thanks to a close relationship with a trade-union leader and other politicians, Rubeo says, Big Baby got a lucrative travel concession, flying barra leaders to the 2010 World Cup at government expense. (South African authorities deported most of them immediately.) Likewise, Rafael Di Zeo, the former leader of La Doce, worked for the local legislature for years, before his love of publicity and stadium fighting combined to put him in jail.

Why doesn't anyone fight back? Politicians keep the barras on speed dial, using them as paid flash mobs in the country's *fuerza de choque*. This is the "collision of forces," an Argentinean style of politics in which rightists, leftists, unionists, and any group that wants anything must put protestors in the streets. The *fuerza de choque* is a war of perpetual demonstrations and pickets, road disruptions and blockaded buildings. Soccer-style thuggery has infected the highest levels of politics; the president's own son leads a nationalist "youth group" that stormed Congress in May, waving flags and shouting fight songs. Two years ago, an administration official who disliked a new book about inflation called on the fan club of Nueva Chicago. About 15 barra soldiers then raided the Buenos Aires International Book Fair, threw chairs, and fought security guards while chanting slogans against the startled author.

Rubeo puts me in touch with someone who knows one of these dangerous men—the head of the fan club for Lanús, a team from greater Buenos Aires. She wishes me luck but issues a warning. *"Fútbol,"* she says, "is like a Mafia family. If you are not in the family, you don't come inside."

The gangster meets me in a tobacco-stained bar on a cool autumn afternoon. He is huge, mostly muscle but wrapped in a layer of fat and covered in tattoos from his neck to his wrists.

He says that I should "gratify" him, a reference to money, not sex. A Spanish TV crew paid him $5,000, he notes. I demur.

"I've been the leader of this barra for 12 years," he says, suddenly angry. "I'm the longest-serving leader in any barra. You understand what that means? We're wanted men. We don't do this for free."

"Argentina's the best in the world at this," he boasts. If only he means soccer.

Four days later, before a Lanús home game against All Boys, three barras on motorcycles open fire on Lanús fans, killing 21-year-old Daniel Sosa and wounding five others. Police recover three guns from outside the stadium.

The game starts a few minutes later.

～～～～～～～～～～～～～～～～～～～～～～～～～～～～～～～～～～～～～～～

Murder has a way of improving things. Until 2010, the Rat Stabbers were among the worst in a nation of bad fan clubs and had driven ordinary fans away from

Estudiantes games. But late that year the Rat Stabbers went too far, killing a policeman during a brawl.

Copresede dismantled the club. Leaders were jailed, and 400 dangerous fans were banned from the games. Since then a more normal fan club has emerged. Three weeks after my first outing with the Rat Stabbers, Marco and I join them in their hometown, La Plata, a chilly city on the coast southeast of Buenos Aires. We find the fans milling around a red bus on a Saturday morning, wearing the red-and-white jerseys of their team.

Georgie Blueskies is here, leading a subgroup of the new Rat Stabbers. Stout and deep-voiced, he embodies the reformed, middle-aged new fan—his ponytail going silver, his demeanor reflective. Women and even children are back at the games, a glimpse of what *fútbol* could be in this most productive of *fútbol* nations.

"These are normal people," Celestre emphasizes as he drives us across town in his (red) muscle car, following the (red) bus to pick up more (red-clad) fans. "We'll see how long that lasts." Without constant police pressure, he says, the old violence will return, because the opportunities for corruption are always present in soccer.

"Here at the local level, it's normally just ticket sales, parking, a portion of travel costs," he says. "In other clubs there's more money: the sale of shirts, even a percentage of a player's salary. The leaders are always allied with politicians, with whichever party is in power." The barras are becoming "executive gangs," he says; some leaders are lawyers and professionals who mix with politicians in the expensive seats.

Celestre isn't impressed with Copresede, whose list of 400 banned fans turned out to include a lot of dead people and children. "They are useless," he says. "They never protect us from anybody." He complains that some Rat Stabbers were recently attacked with stones and bottles by my old friends from Gimnasia, their rivals across town.

We end up at a traffic circle outside La Plata, massing for the drive to a game with archrivals Banfield, southwest of Buenos Aires. Their last game was canceled after Rat Stabbers threw firecrackers at the Banfield goalkeeper.

There are thousands of other fans, in 13 buses and a fleet of private cars. We're surrounded by 100 or so cops, including a police bus, a dozen squad cars, and motorcycle officers riding tiger-striped bikes and wearing shotguns slung across their backs. The cops frisk anyone suspicious, meaning all the dark-skinned or rough-looking young men.

I briefly meet the Rat Stabbers' leader, the extremely tall Ruben Moreno, who is very mellow, befitting the Spicoli-grade stoning he appears to have going. ("Welcome, welcome, no problems here.") He is one of the Rat Stabbers banned from the games, so he won't be traveling with us. But he has to stand around in the mud handing out the fundamental currency of his patronage network: free tickets.

The cops toss the buses, throwing (empty) wine cartons out the windows, and after some negotiation—we're warned off one bus set aside for extra-heavy pot smokers—we board the musicians' bus, a relatively calm one with some grannies on it.

Our convoy moves at a crawl, stretching the 75-mile drive into a three-hour parade. We roll like contractors in Fallujah, preceded by a flying squad of motorcycle policemen, the 13 buses interspaced with squad cars, more motorbike cops patrolling the flanks. As soon as we are moving, the beer comes out (it was hidden by the driver, under his legs) and then the weed (it was stashed inside a drum). The clouds of dope are kept to the back of the bus, somewhat, but I think the grannies are affected, because the whole way they are singing at the top of their lungs: *We're the Rat Stabbers / We smoke marijuana / And run from the police!* Or this one, specially composed, perhaps: *Everyone from Banfield is a whore! / Everyone from Banfield is a whore!*

Finally, we shudder to a halt near the pitch. "Women first!" every-one shouts, which leaves a thousand men free to urinate on every fence in the neighborhood. Hundreds of grilled chorizos are bought and wolfed down in seconds, and we jog toward the stadium like a red tsunami. Inside, the younger fans unfurl their flags and the Rat Stabbers begin to sing and jump in place, overwhelmed by the joyful, forging power of being outnumbered during a raid on hostile territory. Even better, Estudiantes scores early, and then scores again, creating an ecstasy not seen since the Oracle at Delphi.

The Banfield fan club—called the Band of the South—isn't amused, but the reactions of a mob are notoriously hard to predict. Every Argentinean game is rated in advance as low, medium, or high risk for violence; today is high risk. But the police have learned a lot over the past decade of murder and mayhem, and enormous riot fences separate us from Banfield's seething barra brava.

It turns out that the cops welcome journalists for the same reason the barras don't: publicity hurts criminals. I climb a surveillance tower looming six stories over the stadium and join a Copresede security team in a small control room. The officers are using cameras to zoom in on a young Rat Stabber trying to tear down the fencing. Walkie-talkies let them coordinate with a uniformed cop reporting a fight in the Banfield section. As the fighting builds, a pudgy, curly-haired officer in a dark blue sweater, Guillermo Suarez, cries out, "We're going to have a *quilombo*," slang for a huge mess. "Get an infantry cordon over there!" But some fans intervene, and medics soon pull the victim away.

Bored, Suarez shows me how to aim a camera at any part of the stadium, even the hallways. The passivity of watching everything all the time brings out the psychoanalyst lurking in every Argentine. "There's no line between barra and not-barra," he observes. "Look at those stands over there. Those are good seats. You'd think they were rational people. Professors. Good people. But it's incredible. They go crazy."

From up here, I watch the Band of the South, which has unfurled banners demanding the release of their jailed leaders. Banfield is going down—the final score is 3–0 Estudiantes—but the Banda is up, roaring, cacophonous, undoing some of the misery of their defeat.

After the game, the hardcore barras from Banfield wait outside their stadium. A hundred men in green track suits are chanting their loyalty in the cold, muddy street. It's a frankly fascist scene: the agitated young fans displaying power, their heads shaved or cut close, their chants, their groupthink, their insistence on the superiority of their own side. Juan Perón loved soccer crowds.

While Marco and I are gawking, police cordons push the Rat Stabbers back onto their buses, and they drive back to La Plata. Stuck on foot in nowheresville, we dodge the angry Banfield mob and grab a public bus heading back to Buenos Aires. But the Rat Stabbers' day isn't over. During a roadside stop, some local men throw rocks at their caravan; everyone defends themselves, the younger Rat Stabbers pouring off the buses to retaliate. Police fire tear gas and rubber bullets, and the bus with the grannies has its windows smashed by rocks.

This smackdown doesn't make the news. Not even the soccer news, where a "temperature report" in the national newspaper *Clarín* records the week's *fútbol* outrages. (Fans of a team called Italia threw syringes at their own coach; the president of Independiente got another death threat; after a loss, 44 members of a Cordoba fan club ambushed their own players' bus, threatening "a bullet for everyone" if the team didn't advance a division.)

A riot. Some rocks. Gas guns. It's just background noise.

In the end I find a *clásico*, a match between historic rivals. This turns out to be Boca at Racing, the same stadium where it began for me three weeks earlier with the Rat Stabbers. Now it was La Doce's turn to force their way into the Cylinder.

La Bombonera is only a few miles away, so La Doce always marches there, across the dirty Río Riachuela on the Old Bridge. It's more an invasion than a parade, and Marco and I narrowly avert a beating from a fan leader who recognizes us from the previous game. He draws a finger across his neck and tells me, "If you take a picture, we're going to throw you in the fucking river."

His threat is backed by a surging crowd of several hundred hardmen pushing toward us across the bridge. Chanting and waving flags, La Doce pours toward the Cylinder, with Marco and I running just ahead of them. We find refuge in a taxi, duck down, and are scooped up at the stadium entrance by friendly Guillermo Suarez from Copresede. "You just saved our lives," Marco says.

Racing's Imperial Guard puts on a huge display of sound and fury; there is confetti, a blazing red marine flare, and firecrackers thrown across the moat at the Boca goalie (they miss). The Guard have a nearly 60,000-man advantage over La Doce, but the Boca fans unfurl some old Racing banners they stole during previous street fights, a dangerous taunt. Copresede phones a Boca leader, and the war prizes disappear within minutes.

Finally, here is a real game, worthy of the title *clásico*. Our pals in the police let us onto the field itself, where we sit at the midfield line, smelling sweat and the acrid tang of smoke bombs. We're so close that Boca's hawk-faced coach, Julio César Falcioni, nearly runs me over while disputing a call.

For a moment, I can live in the beautiful game. Some of the world's top athletes are tearing up the grass, and the play is fast, passionate, and clean—men shaking hands after knockdowns, a display of sportsmanship so missing in the stands. Protected by perhaps 1,000 cops, I finally feel safe in an Argentinean stadium.

A bit later, up inside the swan-necked tower, I join Suarez and five of his colleagues in the cramped Copresede surveillance center. Fifteen screens show feeds from 14 fixed cameras and 13 mobile units. The very top of the tower holds a swiveling camera with a super-powerful telephoto lens that Suarez controls with a joystick. We watch a man lighting a joint, then another pissing in a corner and a third getting beaten up by members of his own fan club. ("Copy," Suarez says to an officer out in the terraces. "It's to the right of the Rolling Stones banner.")

Someone is shining a green laser in the eyes of the referee. Abusing the ref is normal—at Maracanã stadium in Rio, I saw fans shoot flare guns at one official— but Suarez and two colleagues rewind the footage and quickly track the laser to one corner of the Imperial Guard terrace. Suarez swivels his joystick and the camera locks onto an acned, monobrowed individual in a striped Racing jersey, holding his left hand to his ear. "Got him," Suarez says. A beefy technical assistant hits the print button, and four copies of the kid's photo are dispatched to police at the four exits used by the Imperial Guard.

The game is playing on a small television in the corner, ignored. I go back down to the smoke-filled arena, to my privileged spot beside the grassy action. In the first half Racing presses hard, dominating the ball, running triangles and through passes, to the delight of the Imperial Guard. But in the second half, the Boca striker

Lucas Viatri receives a lofted pass to the middle. Facing away from the goal, he splits his momentum—a back-footed tap to the right, a quick turn to the left.

It takes only a second to relieve an hour of tension. Stepping around a flat-footed defender, Viatri reunites with the ball on the first hop, drilling a roundhouse. Time stops, physics takes over. The back of the net billows out. It is improbable, beautiful. Not just a *gol* but a *golazo,* according to the next day's *Clarín.*

In Argentina, tomorrow is always better than today.

(Originally published October 2012)

ALL THE JITTERY HORSES

WILL GRANT

~~~~~~

Will Grant was once an intern at Outside. *The first thing I noticed about him was that he speaks like a cowboy. Turns out that's because he is one. And when he told us about the Mongol Derby—the longest, hardest horse race in the world—we couldn't resist his enthusiasm. So we sent him halfway around the world to try to win it.*

~~~~~~

The toilet paper startled the horse. I was relieving myself, and a gust of wind had unfurled the tissue in my left hand. The red and white spotted pony lifted his head when he saw the flutter, and the rope to his bridle slipped through my fingers. He looked at me with eyes full of white and his front feet spread wide, ready to bolt. We both froze. He knew he was loose. I lunged forward in a full Pete Rose slide, bloodying both my knees and scraping my exposed parts on the rocks and the short prickly grass. Just as I grabbed the rope, he jerked it out of my hand and wheeled away, kicking a hind leg at me as he sprang off.

I collected myself and concluded my business while he quietly grazed about 20 yards from me. I spent the next half-hour trying to walk him down, cursing his name, or rather, because he didn't have a name, his number, which was painted on his shoulder. Finally, he quit me and, with almost all my gear aboard, trotted off over the pale green horizon.

It was 6:30 P.M., and I was now on foot on the broad and treeless steppe of Outer Mongolia's Tamir River Valley. Below me, about a mile away, I could see the white yurts of a herder camp. Within a quarter-mile of that, I could see a man watching me. Guard dogs milled around the camp, a stark reminder that, in spite of my meticulous preparation, I had failed to renew my rabies vaccination.

I decided to stop and wave. It was easy to see that I was a horseman without a horse, and the man watching me hopped on his and galloped off in the direction mine had gone.

Twenty minutes later, he rode up with my pony beside him. I thanked him as best I could, with smiles and hand gestures, and he in turn made it clear that I now owed him something. I offered him my hat—a baseball cap from my hometown of Alma, Colorado—and cash, some Mongolian tugriks worth about $20. He shook his head no and pointed at my wrist.

Getting my horse back—my third mount of the day—cost me an hour and my alarm clock, a fancy Timex Ironman watch. Considering the day I'd had, it was a bargain. That morning I had crashed with the first horse I'd been issued; he had stepped into a marmot burrow at full gallop, and we did a synchronized somersault that would have been impressive to observe but hurt like hell. A few hours later, I sank my second horse to his chest in quicksand and then swam him across a furious river.

Now this nag was too tired to make the next checkpoint, which, according to my GPS, lay eight miles ahead. It was mid-August, the sun would set in about an hour, and temperatures would start dropping into the forties. I needed to find a place to camp and to somehow make a fire in this treeless landscape. I was about halfway through the Mongol Derby, and it was shaping up to be a long day.

When I told Jack Brainard, a legendary master horseman and my mentor as a cowboy and professional horse trainer, that I was riding the Derby, he said, "Why in hell would someone want to ride them little horses for 1,000 kilometers?" Brainard, now 91, had spent most of his life in the saddle. "I'll bet you get halfway through the race and throw down your pencil and your notepad and say, Me and my big mouth. What have I got myself into now?"

Except for the two South African adventure racers and a chain-smoker from Holland who had done the race the year before, none of us—an eclectic bunch of 35 international riders—really knew what we were getting ourselves into. The Mongol Derby is a loose re-creation of Genghis Khan's 13th-century communication system—a fast-horse mail relay, a precursor to our Pony Express of 600 years later. Unlike the Khan's riders, we had no time-sensitive communiqués. But, like them, we did get issued a new horse every 25 miles, riding from *urtuu* (horse station) to *urtuu*. We would start approximately 60 miles south of Ulan Bator, ride in a clockwise arc to the west and north and, 24 *urtuus*, three mountain passes, countless rivers and creeks, and one surreal dune field later, finish at the foot of a dormant volcano about 250 miles northwest of where we began. The route would entail some 650 miles of riding; organizers figured the first rider would finish in about eight days.

Staged by the London-based company the Adventurists, whose slogan is Fighting to Make the World Less Boring, the race is a logistical behemoth, employing more than 1,000 horses and a support staff of over 300 mostly Mongolian interpreters, drivers, wranglers, cooks, and veterinarians. In a conference room at the Ramada Inn in Ulan Bator, race staff barraged us with an eight-hour briefing. They handed out satellite images of the route, loaded our GPS units with more than 2,000 waypoints, and showed us how to use the Spot personal tracking devices we were issued.

Then came the rules. We were allowed to carry only 11 pounds of gear, not including water, loaded into a backpack or saddlebag—sleeping bag, camera, GPS unit, headlamp, spare batteries. There were penalties for everything from straying outside the 12-mile-wide corridor between horse stations to riding longer than the proscribed 14-hour period each day to falsely issuing an SOS with our Spot trackers. Each rider needed to complete at least three 25-mile legs a day, to keep pace with the support staff, but otherwise you could do as you pleased: sleep alongside race organizers and fellow riders at each station or bed down on the steppe wherever you happened to be when the day's riding time had expired. The goal was simply to cross the finish line first. To ensure that the horses weren't being driven too hard, each rider was required to carry his mount's vet card, which recorded condition and heart rate, the time of arrival at a horse station, and the time of departure. If the animal's heart rate didn't come down to 64 beats per minute within a half-hour of arriving, the rider served a two-hour penalty.

After the briefing, we had two days to make final preparations and get to know the steeds. Native Mongol horses haven't changed much over the past 800 years and remain as scrappy as they are small, about six inches to a foot shorter than a typical Western horse. "They're not much to look at," Harry McKerchar, one of the vets, told me, "but they're powerful little beasts." They're also extremely sensitive and will spook at any number of things, from a belly laugh to a discarded vodka bottle. Sometimes they just buck wildly and run hell-bent for the horizon for no apparent reason. Saddling one can require three Mongolians to muscle the horse into submission.

Four of my fellow racers, plus myself, had been professional horsemen; along with a few others, including the veteran South African adventurers and a pair of good-natured Irish jockeys, we wanted to win. But a good number of the other riders entered the race with the idea of having a leisurely Mongolian holiday. And a few, like a soft-spoken Emirati woman whose family thought she was in Turkey on vacation, and a female journalist from Dubai who smoked a lot of very thin cigarettes and showed up with comically inadequate gear, were clearly in over their heads.

I've been riding horses since I was old enough to know which end the hay goes in and was arrogant from the start. Figured I'd show these people how we do it out west. I had done my homework, repeatedly sizing up my fellow competitors via their online bios. I had the organizers send me the required race-issue saddle so I could break it in. I ran around the foothills and peaks outside Alma, did a couple hundred sit-ups and push-ups every day, and was riding harder than I had since I quit cowboying professionally four years ago.

The night before the race, drinking a warm beer by the fire, the event's videographer told me I was his pick to win. An hour before the start, the head medic told me the same thing. "My money's on you," he said. At the finish line, the two Irish jockeys said they had expected me to be on the podium with them. But things don't always work out as planned.

It didn't help matters that I showed up at the starting line with a blinding hangover. I had stayed up late drinking vodka around the campfire with Mongolian cowboys and, on the way to my bedroll, fell in a marmot hole the size of a small child. I woke up that morning with a bad limp, a throbbing headache, a cut below my right eye, and blood on my shirt.

When the gun went off, the horses about jumped out of their skins and a surge of adrenaline sobered me up. The mayhem began almost immediately. Less than ten miles from the start, Paul de Rivaz, a 64-year-old former British special-forces soldier who entered the race with his son, fell and broke his collarbone. When de Rivaz's riderless horse galloped past Linda Sandvik, a Web designer from Norway, her horse spooked, jettisoning Sandvik, who hit the ground so hard that she fractured her pelvis and collapsed a lung. Two hours later, Erin Shanson, a lawyer from London, wrenched her knee while trying to dismount her skittery pony. Before the first 25-mile leg was completed, three people had suffered race-ending injuries.

The strict head-protection rule now made sense. Leading up to the event, the thought of racing in a helmet—or, more specifically, of incriminating photos of me racing in a helmet—was depressing. So much so that I told race organizer Katy Willings that I had never worn a helmet before (a lie) and that I was worried one might throw off my balance (another lie), thus endangering my safety.

"Endanger your vanity is more like it," she replied. "If I see one picture of you without a helmet on, you're disqualified."

Because the mark of a cowboy is his spurs, I was also determined to wear my favorite pair. Willings nixed that idea, too. But she and her cohorts couldn't do anything about my Wrangler jeans, pearl-snap shirt, silk bandanna, or worn-out leather boots. It was the Wranglers they especially objected to; they were convinced the denim would rub abscesses into my legs. Nearly all the other riders were decked out like adventure racers, in tights and technical fabrics. Exasperated, I finally told them they'd obviously never ridden with an actual cowboy and that I'd take a photo of my shiny white legs for them at the finish.

By the start of day two, I had fallen in with two other riders, Paul de Rivaz's son, Ben, 29, a British investment manager, and Campbell "Cozy" Costello, a 25-year-old veterinarian from Australia. Ben, an Ironman and former member of the British army's polo team, was just as tough as his dad. He was also the only guy I saw shave during the race—maintaining standards, he called it. Cozy grew up mustering cattle in the outback and was as indefatigable as the country he grew up in.

The three of us rode well together. We got along and laughed and quickly figured out the best way to urinate from the saddle (pull the horse's head to the left, pee off the right). It could be messy—so much for standards—but it was faster, and safer, than stopping.

Our depth perception slowly changed as we crossed the steppe and learned how to interpret the scale and scope of the land. We learned that the rust-colored seedpods of an aquatic grass looked like an orange haze from three miles away. A light tan hillside meant pieces of sandstone coming through the grass—hard on the horses' hooves. A brown-tinted fluvial plain was the worst. Our horses would trip and stumble over the spongy, uneven terrain. Half a mile of that could take close to an hour, and it sapped a horse's energy as though you were galloping uphill.

Nothing was so frustrating as a horse that ran out of energy. Most of the time, Cozy was soft-spoken, polite, and gracious. But when a horse began to fade on him, he'd turn the air blue. *Orangutan* was about the only inoffensive term he used for horses.

"You have a way with words, Cozy," I said, "none of it printable."

"That's alright, mate," he said. "Just show a picture of a #$!% and that'll do."

It was about 3 P.M. on my second day riding with Ben—Cozy had gone ahead—when Ben's horse ran out of energy for anything but a walk. The sun was high, and the heat had taken its toll on the horses, his in particular. We decided to get off and walk to let them air up. Galloping, which we were doing more often than we weren't, is obviously hard on a horse. But riding a horse at top speed is a full-body workout for the rider, too, and we were hot and muscle sore. While the horizon seemed a long way off from the back of the horse, it seemed a lot farther on foot.

Ben pulled out a flask of single-malt whisky. In addition to being the fittest guy in the race, he also had the best booze. Most riders carried prescription painkillers and muscle relaxers—two riders from Sweden were hopped up on morphine for much of the race—but no one seemed to carry as much or as many kinds of liquor as Eton-educated, clean-cut Ben. He unscrewed the cap of the pewter flask and handed it to me.

"It's Bowmore Tempest, 112 proof," he said. "Space was an issue, so I figured I'd go for the most alcohol for the volume."

A couple of swigs changed everything. We figured it might take us a while, like five or six hours, to get to the next camp. But one way or another we'd get there, and there was no sense worrying about it. After an hour or so we got back on and rode.

As we plodded along on tired horses, a Mongolian man on a motorcycle waved us down. He made motions of drinking tea and pointed to a white yurt a mile away. We could push the horses, make the next station, and maybe cover another leg of the race before nightfall. Instead, Ben and I looked at each other and agreed: damned horses are played out, might as well have a look.

Our host was a good-looking man, about 35, with wind-burned cheeks, strong hands, and broad, square shoulders, and when we first glimpsed his home, we knew we were cut from similar cloth. Drying meat hung from the rafters inside. Guns were leaned in the corner, and he proudly showed us the medals he'd won for horse racing, wrestling, power lifting, basketball, and martial arts.

He served us milk tea, a bowl of hard, home-made dumplings, and some sort of broth. Mongolians love to eat fat, and several large chunks floated in our bowls. I heard Ben gag twice and make a sound like water coming up a hose, but he choked down whatever was troubling him and, in classically polite British style, managed to cap his performance with a hard swallow and a smile.

After the meal, the man challenged us to arm-wrestle him. Ben went first and lost quickly. I went second and lost even faster. I could see where this was going: soon we would be drinking heavily and wrestling, and as much as we'd have loved to stay, we had a race to get back to. We exchanged gifts, he made sure our saddle girths were tight, and we rode off into the sunset.

~~~~~~

The river was as wide as the Colorado and ran the color of chocolate milk. Parts of trees rolled in the current. It was late afternoon on the fifth day of the race, and I'd been riding with a Kiwi named Sam Wyborn for most of the day. Sam and I had ridden together on and off throughout the race, and I still didn't quite understand what he did for a living back home. He definitely spent a lot of time hanging out in Fiji, at a house owned by his father, who was rumored (falsely) to be the second wealthiest man in New Zealand. What was certain: we had four more hours of legal riding time ahead of us, and we wanted to cover one more leg before we were through. The next station lay a quarter-mile away, within sight, on the other side of the Tamir River.

We had been told at the prerace briefing to take the highway bridge, which we blew by about eight miles ago, to get across the river. But the vet at the previous station, even while looking at the maps and discussing the best route with us, had failed to mention it. The briefing had faded so far into memory, and was such a blur at the time, that I was surprised the race organizer, who rode the Derby in 2009, thought we wouldn't need additional reminders. I'd had some grievances about how the race was being run—like the fact that we were issued Google Earth images rather than topographical maps—but now I was straight-up mad as hell. The river, at this level, could kill man, beast, or both.

"I think we just try it," Sam said.

I wasn't so sure. The horses were tired, and I thought we should look for a shallower place to cross. We spread out and rode up and down the bank. When I turned around, I saw Sam and his horse emerging on the opposite side, 200 yards downstream. That settles that, I thought, and I walked my light gray horse up the bank, whipped him over the hindquarters, and jumped into the current.

Hitting the water was like grabbing hold of a passing freight train. Immediately, I could feel that the horse had nothing under him. I kicked out of my stirrups to swim beside him, grabbed a handful of mane with one hand, and held my camera over my head with the other. Only the horse's head was above water, and he was sucking all the air he could hold. The bank flew by as we bobbed downstream. If he goes under, I thought, I'll drop the bridle reins and turn him loose.

Mongolian ponies don't give up easy, and some 15 seconds later we reached the opposite bank. Sam's horse was larger than mine and fared better. My poor pony just stood there trembling and wouldn't move.

Turns out we weren't the only ones who had missed the bridge, and I was still so pissed off that when we finally hobbled into the station, and the interpreter asked me to choose my next horse, I told her I couldn't give a damn. That cost me. She gave me a heavy-strided pony that felt like he had cinder blocks for feet. Sam's horse was faster, and after an hour I told him to ride ahead without me. A few hours later, the toilet paper incident delayed me further. But the thought of an open bivy on the steppe kept me moving, and in the failing light I rode into a camp unconnected with the race.

I had been riding for nearly 14 hours, and I was still cold and wet. Walking inside the heated yurt was euphoric. The men were apparently gone for the night, and there was just a young woman, her infant daughter, and her grandmother.

Oogii, the young woman, spoke a bit of English, and they offered me milk curds but no water. After some attempts at small talk, we rolled out two pads on the floor. I took a prescription-strength muscle relaxer, and in accordance with Mongolian custom, we laid down with our heads to the north, away from the door. I didn't undress, for fear of offending the women, and crawled into my sleeping bag in my still-damp jeans.

~~~~~~

I rode by myself for most of the next day. Sam was now at least a station or two ahead of me, and I hadn't seen Ben or Cozy since I left them on day three. In the early evening, I came into station 17 cold and wet from heavy afternoon storms and with a difficult decision to make. I'd been riding hard all day and making good time. It was 6:30, and the back of the lead pack was now just 25 miles ahead of me, over a mountain pass that was currently hidden in purple storm clouds. With a fast horse, I figured, I might be able to make the next station in two and a half hours and be within striking distance. I looked at my GPS, then the sky. The vet in camp, a young, attractive woman from Belgium, watched as I deliberated. Eventually, she smiled over her clipboard and said, "Just so you know, I am going into town to get some beers. You're welcome to come."

"Where do I put my saddle?" I replied.

Later that night, Ben and Cozy, who had been trying to catch me for two days, rode into camp in the dark. Drinking cold beer with them in the warm yurt, I knew I'd made the right decision. We rode hard together the rest of the race, often pushing the horses to their limit, but always stopped for tea with strangers, admired the shrines, and never turned down a drink. On the afternoon of the ninth day, we finished the race in a three-way tie for 14th place.

I didn't take a photo of my shiny white legs, but I could have. I was so invigorated by the whole experience, I would gladly have turned around and ridden the damn thing in reverse. Most of my fellow racers didn't fare as well. Only 18 of the 35 riders completed the race, many of them limping across the finish line. There were broken ribs, avulsion fractures, torn ligaments, and a full-blown physical collapse. (It seemed like one of the Swedes had a hard time coming off the morphine.) The Hollander who'd done the race the year before had one of the scariest injuries; he broke two vertebrae in his neck when he was thrown from his horse on day five. He lay on the steppe for an hour, unable to feel his arms, before the medics could get their Land Cruiser to him. Then he waited for another three hours while race headquarters tried to coordinate a helicopter to evacuate him. When it became clear that there would be no bird for an airlift, they strapped him to a stretcher with his stirrup leathers, loaded him into the back of the SUV, and bounced over the foothills.

Remarkably, he recounted all this at the post-race party, with his doctor beside him and a brace around his neck. "I think I will try again next year," he said.

After dinner we got to talking about American cowboys and using a lariat rope. I figured if I could rope a calf, I could rope a Mongolian goat, and I was eventually persuaded to demonstrate. It took a few tries and a lot of running, but I got one roped. I'd like to think old Jack Brainard would have been proud.

(Originally published April 2013)

THE BULLFIGHTER CHECKS HER MAKEUP

SUSAN ORLEAN

This is one of my all-time favorite Outside *headlines, and, fittingly, it was later used as the title of Susan Orlean's first story collection. The juxtaposition of one of the most historically masculine sporting events with the female pronoun is intentionally jarring. It immediately tells you everything you need to know.*

I went to Spain not long ago to watch Cristina Sánchez fight bulls, but she had gotten tossed by one during a performance in the village of Ejea de los Caballeros and was convalescing when I arrived. Getting tossed sounds sort of merry, but I saw a matador tossed once, and he looked like a saggy bale of hay flung by a pitchfork, and when he landed on his back he looked busted and terrified. Cristina got tossed by accidentally hooking a horn with her elbow during a pass with the cape, and the joint was wrenched so hard that her doctor said it would need at least three or four days to heal. It probably hurt like hell, and the timing was terrible. She had fights scheduled each of the nights she was supposed to rest and every night until October—every night, with no breaks in between. It had been like this for her since May, when she was elevated from the status of a novice to a full matador de toros. The title is conferred in a formal ceremony called "taking the alternativa," and it implies that you are experienced and talented and that other matadors have recognized you as a top-drawer bullfighter. You will now fight the biggest, toughest bulls and will probably be hired to fight often and in the most prestigious arenas. Bullfighting becomes your whole life, your everyday life—so routine that "sometimes after you've fought and killed the bull you feel as if you hadn't done a thing all day," as Cristina once told me.

When Cristina Sánchez took her alternativa, it caused a sensation. Other women before her have fought bulls in Spain. Many have only fought little bulls, but some did advance to big animals and become accomplished and famous, and a few of the best have been declared full matadors de toros. Juanita Cruz became a matador in 1940, and Morenita de Quindio did in 1968, and Raquel Martinez and Maribel Atienzar did in the eighties, but they all took their alternativas in Mexico, where the standards are a little less exacting. Cristina is the first woman to have taken her alternativa in Europe and made her debut as a matador in Spain.

There was a fight program of three matadors—a corrida—scheduled for the Madrid bullring the day after I got to Spain, and I decided to go so I could see some other toreros while Cristina was laid up with her bad arm. One of the three scheduled to perform was the bastard son of El Cordobes. El Cordobes had been a matador superstar in the sixties and a breeder of several illegitimate children and a prideful man who was so possessive of his nickname that he had once sued this kid—the one I was going to see—because the kid wanted to fight bulls under the name El Cordobes, too. In the end, the judge let each and every El Cordobes continue to be known professionally as El Cordobes.

The kid El Cordobes is a scrubbed, cute blond with a crinkly smile. Outside the rings where he is fighting, vendors sell fan photos of him alongside postcards and little bags of sunflower seeds and stuffed-bull souvenirs. In the photos, El Cordobes is dressed in a plaid camp shirt and acid-washed blue jeans and is hugging a good-looking white horse. In the ring, he does some flashy moves on his knees in front of the bull, including a frog-hop that he times to make it look like he's going to get skewered. These tricks, plus the renown of his name, have gotten him a lot of attention, but El Cordobes is just one of many cute young male matadors working these days. If his knees give out, he might have nothing.

On the other hand, there is just one Cristina, and everyone in Spain knows her and is following her rise. She has gotten attention far outside of Spain and on television and in newspapers and even in fashion magazines; other matadors, even very good ones, fuse in the collective mind as man-against-bull, but every time Cristina kills a bull she forms part of a singular and unforgettable tableau—that of an attractive, self-possessed young woman elegantly slaying a large animal in a somber and ancient masculine ritual—and regardless of gender she is a really good matador, and she is being painstakingly managed and promoted, so there is no saying where her celebrity will stop. This is only her first season as a full matador, but it has been a big event. Lately El Cordobes or his publicist or his accountant has been igniting and fanning the rumor that he and Cristina Sánchez are madly in love, with the hope that her fame will rub off on him. She will probably be more and more acclaimed in the four or so years she plans to fight, and she will probably be credited with many more putative love affairs before her career is through.

Before the fight in Madrid, I walked around to the back of the bullring and through the patio de caballos, the dirt-floored courtyard and stable where the picadors' horses and the donkeys that drag away the dead bull after the fight relax in their stalls and get their hair combed and get fed and get saddled. I was on my way to the bullfighting museum—the Museo Taurino—which is in a gallery next to the stalls. It was a brilliant day with just a whiff of wind. In the courtyard, muscle men were tossing equipment back and forth and unloading a horse trailer. Another 20 or so men were idling in the courtyard in the few pockets of shade or near the locked door of the matadors' chapel, which is opened before the fight so the matadors can stop in and pray. The idlers were older men with bellies that began at their chins and trousers hiked up to their nipples, and they were hanging around just so they could take a look at the bulls for tonight's fight and see how they were going to be divvied up among the three matadors. Really, there isn't a crumb of any piece of bullfighting that goes unexamined by aficionados like these men. I lingered for a minute and then went into the museum. I wandered past the oil portraits of Manolete and Joselito and of dozens of other revered bullfighters, and past six stuffed and mounted heads of bulls whose names were Paisano, Landejo, Mediaonza, Jocinero, Hermano, and Perdigón—they were chosen for the museum because they had been particularly mean or unusual-looking or because they had killed someone famous. Then I stopped at a glass display case that had in it a picture of the matador Juanita Cruz. The picture was an eight-by-ten and looked like it had been shot in a studio. Juanita Cruz's pearly face and her wedge of a chin and her pitch-black hair with its tiny standing waves were blurred along the edges, movie-star style. She looked solemn, and her eyes were focused on middle space. In the case next to the picture were her pink matador knee socks and her mouse-eared matador hat and one of her bullfighter suits. These are called *traje de luces*, "suit of lights," and all toreros wear them and like to change them often; Cristina has half a dozen, and Juanita Cruz probably owned 20 or so in the course of her bullfighting career. This one was blush-pink with beautiful gold piping and sparkly black sequins. It had the classic short, stiff, big-shouldered, box-shaped matador jacket but not the capri-like trousers that all matadors wear, because Juanita Cruz fought in a skirt. There is no such thing as a matador skirt anymore—Cristina, of course, wears trousers. I looked at the skirt for a while and decided that even though it looked unwieldy it might actually have been an advantage—in a skirt, you can bend and stretch and lunge with a sword unconstrained. On the other hand, a skirt would have exposed so much fabric to the bull that in a fight it would have gotten awfully splashed and smeared with blood. Every matador has an assistant who is assigned to clean his suit with soap and a toothbrush after every fight. Juanita Cruz was popular and well accepted even though she was an anomaly, but late at night, as her assistant was scrubbing her big bloody skirt, I bet he cursed the fact that she had been wearing so much fabric while sticking swords into bulls.

I went to visit Cristina at home the morning before she was going to be fighting in a corrida in a town called Móstoles. It was now a week since her injury, and her elbow apparently had healed. Two days earlier, she had tested it in a fight in Cordobes and another the following day in Jáen, and a friend of mine who reads Madrid's bullfight newspaper told me Cristina had gotten very good reviews. It turns out that I was lucky to catch her at home, because she is hardly there during the bullfighting season—usually she keeps a rock star schedule, leaving whatever town she's in with her crew right after she fights, driving all night to the next place on her schedule, checking into a hotel, sleeping until noon, eating lunch, watching some television, suiting up, fighting, and then leaving again. She was going to be at home this particular morning because Móstoles is only a few miles from Parla, the town where she and her parents and sisters live. She had come home the night before, after the fight in Jáen, and was planning to spend the day in Parla doing errands. The corrida in Móstoles would start at six. The assistant who helps her dress—he is called the sword boy, because he also takes care of all her cutlery— was going to come to the apartment at five so she could get prepared and then just drive over to the bullring already dressed and ready to go in her suit of lights. Parla is an unglamorous place about 40 minutes south of Madrid; it is a kernel of an old village that had been alone on the wide open plains but is now picketed by incredibly ugly high-rise apartment buildings put up in the midsixties for workers overflowing the available housing in Madrid. The Sánchez apartment is in a slightly less ugly and somewhat shorter brick building on a busy street, on a block with a driving school, a bra shop, and a bank. There is no name on the doorbell, but Cristina's father's initials are barely scratched into a metal plate beside it. These days it is next to impossible to find Cristina. The nearly unmarked doorbell is the least of it. Cristina has a magician press agent who can make himself disappear and a very powerful and self-confident manager—a former French bullfighter named Simon Casas—who is credited with having gotten her into the biggest bullrings and the best corridas in the country but is also impossible to find and even if he were findable he would tell you that his answer to your request to speak to Cristina is no. He is especially watchful of her international exposure. Simon Casas didn't know I was coming to see Cristina in Parla and he might have disapproved simply to be disapproving, and after I saw him later that afternoon in Móstoles, prowling the perimeter of the bullring like an irritable wild animal, I was that much gladder I'd stayed out of his way.

Anyway, Cristina wasn't even home when I got there. I had driven to Parla with my translator, Muriel, and her bullfighter husband, Pedro, who both know Cristina and Cristina's father, Antonio, who himself used to be a bullfighter—if it sounds like just about everyone I encountered in Spain was or is a bullfighter, it's true. No one answered the doorbell at the apartment. Cristina's car wasn't around, so it looked like she really was gone. A car seems to be the first thing matadors buy themselves when they start making big money—that is, when they start getting sometimes as much as tens of thousands of dollars for a major fight. The bullfighter car of choice is a Mercedes, but Cristina bought herself a bright red Ford Probe, which is much sportier. She also bought her mother a small business, a gift store. We decided to wait a bit longer. Pedro killed time by making some bullfight business calls on his cellular phone. Just as we were debating whether to go looking for Cristina at her mother's store, Mrs. Sánchez came around the corner, carrying a load of groceries; she said Cristina was at the bank and that in the meantime we could come upstairs. We climbed a few flights. The apartment was tidy and fresh-looking and furnished with modern things in pastel tones, and in the living room there were a life-size oil painting of Cristina looking beautiful in her suit of lights, two huge photographs of Cristina in bullfights, one of her as a civilian, a large photograph of the older Sánchez daughter getting married, and a big-screen TV. On almost every horizontal surface there was a bronze or brass or pewter statuette of a bull, usually bucking, its withers bristling with three or four barbed harpoons called banderillas, which are stuck in to aggravate him before he is killed. These were all trophies from different corridas and from Cristina's stint as a star pupil at the Madrid bullfighting school. Lots of Cristina's stuff was lying around the room. On the dining table were stacks of fresh laundry, mostly white dress shirts and white T-shirts and pink socks. On the floor were a four-foot-long leather sword case, three hatboxes, and a piece of luggage that looked like a giant bowling-ball bag, which is a specially designed case for a matador's $20,000 suit jacket. Also, there was a small black Kipling backpack of Cristina's, which cracked me up because it was the exact same backpack that I was carrying.

Mrs. Sánchez was clattering around in the kitchen, making Cristina's lunch. A few minutes later, I heard the front door scrape open, and then Cristina stepped into the room, out of breath and flustered about being late. She is 25 years old and has chemically assisted blond hair, long eyelashes, high cheekbones, and a tiny nose. She looks really pretty when she smiles and almost regal when she doesn't, but she's not so beautiful that she's scary. This day, she was wearing blue jeans, a denim shirt with some flower embroidery, and white slip-on shoes with chunky heels, and her hair was held in a ponytail by a sunflower barrette. She is not unusually big or small. Her shoulders are square and her legs are sturdy, and she's solid and athletic-looking, like a forward on a field hockey team. Her strength is a matter of public debate in Spain. The weakest part of her performance is the very end of the fight, when she's supposed to kill the bull with one perfect jam of her sword, but she often doesn't go deep enough or in the right place. It is said in certain quarters that she simply isn't strong enough, but the fact is that many matadors mess up with the sword. When I brought it up, she shook her head and said, "People who don't understand the bullfighting world think you have to be extremely strong, but that's not the case. What is important is technique and experience. You have to be in good shape, but you don't have to match a man's strength. Besides, your real opponent is the bull, and you can never match it in strength."

Her mother came in and out of the room a few times. When she was out, Cristina said in a low voice, "I'm very happy with my family, but the time comes when you have to be independent." The tabloids have reported that she has just bought a castle on millions of enchanted acres. "I bought a small piece of property right near here," she said, rolling her eyes. "I'm having a house built. I think when I come back from my winter tour in South America I'll be able to move in."

What I really wanted to know was why in the world she decided to become a bullfighter. I knew she'd grown up watching her father fight, so it had always been a profession that seemed normal to her, even though at the ring she didn't see many girls. Plus she doesn't like to sit still. Before she started training to be a matador, she had worked in a beauty parlor and then as a typist at a fire-extinguisher factory, and both jobs drove her crazy. She is a very girly girl—she wears makeup, she wants children, she has boyfriends—but she says she was only interested in jobs that would keep her on her feet, and coincidentally those were jobs that were mostly filled by men. If she hadn't become a matador, she thinks she would have become a trainer at a gym, or a police officer, or perhaps a firefighter, which used to be her father's backup job when he was a bullfighter, in the years before he started advising her and became a full-time part of her six-person crew. She didn't become a woman matador to be shocking or make a feminist point, although along the way she has been shunned by some of her male colleagues and there are still a few who refuse to appear in a corrida with her. Once, in protest, she went to Toledo and instead of having a corrida in which three matadors each killed two bulls, she took on all six bulls herself, one by one. She said she wants to be known as a great matador and not an oddity or anecdote in the history of bullfighting. She simply loves the art and craft of fighting bulls. Later that day, when I saw her in the ring, I also realized that besides loving the bullfight itself, she is that sort of person who is illuminated by the attention of a crowd. I asked her what she'll do after she retires from the ring in three or four years. "I want to have earned a lot of money and invested it wisely," she said. "And then I want to do something in the movies or on TV."

She mentioned that she was eating early today because she had a stomachache. With a fight almost every night for months, I suppose there would be nights when she felt crummy or wasn't in the mood. Cristina laughed and said, "Yeah, sometimes you do feel like, oh God, I don't have the slightest desire to face a bull this afternoon!" Personally, I'm not a huge coward, but the phrase "desire to face a bull" will never be part of my life, any afternoon, ever. I figured that nothing must scare her. She shook her head and said, "Failure. My greatest fear is failure. I'm a woman who is a fighter and I always think about trying to surpass myself, so what I most fear is to fail."

Just then, Mrs. Sánchez came into the room and said the sandwiches were ready, so Cristina started to get up. She paused for a moment and said, "You know, people think that because I kill bulls I have to be really brave, but I'm not. I'm a sensitive person, and I can get super-terrified. I'm afraid of staying home by myself, and I get hysterical if I see a spider." I asked if bulls ever haunted her dreams, and she said, "I don't dream much at all, but a few times I've dreamed that a bull was pursuing me in the ring, up into the stands. And the night before my debut in Madrid, I did dream of bulls with huge, twisted horns."

I had seen the first bullfight of my life a few days earlier, on that night in Madrid, and it was a profound education. I learned that I should not eat for several hours beforehand and to start looking away the minute the picadors ride in on their stoic-looking blindfolded horses, because their arrival signaled that the blood and torment would begin. At first, in Madrid, I had been excited because the Plaza de Toros is so dramatic and beautiful, and also the pageantry that began the corrida was very nice, and when the first bull galloped in, I liked watching it bolt around the ring and chase the matador and his assistants until they retreated behind the small fences around the ring that are there for their protection. The small fences had targets—bull's-eyes, actually—painted on them. The bull would ram into them with its horns and the fence would rock. The more furious bulls would ram again and again, until the matador teased them away with a flourish of his cape. The bulls were homely, with little heads and huge briskets and tapered hips, and they cornered like schoolbuses and sometimes skidded to their knees, but they had fantastic energy and single-mindedness and thick muscles that flickered under their skin and faces that didn't look vicious at all and were interesting to watch. Some of the fight was wonderful: The matador's flourishes with the shocking pink and bright yellow big cape and his elegance with the small triangular red one; the sound of thousands of people gasping when the bull got very close to the cape; the plain thrilling danger of it and the fascination of watching a bull be slowly hypnotized; the bravery of the picadors' horses, which stood stock-still as the bull pounded them broadside, the flags along the rim of the ring flashing in the late-afternoon light; the resplendence of the matador's suit in that angling light, especially when the matador inched one foot forward and squared his hips and arched his back so that he was a bright new moon against a sky of sand with the black cloud of a bull racing by. I loved the ancientness and majesty and excitement of it, the way bullfighting could be at once precious and refined yet absolutely primal and raw. But beyond that I was lost and nauseous and knew I didn't understand how so many people, a whole nation of people, weren't shaken by the gore and the idea of watching a ballet that always, absolutely, unfailingly ends with a gradual and deliberate death. I didn't understand it then, and I doubt I ever will.

In the little brick bullring in móstoles, Cristina killed two bulls well but not exceptionally—for the first kill the judge awarded her one of the bull's ears, but for the second she got no award at all. A once-in-a-lifetime sort of performance would have earned two ears, a tail, and a hoof. After that second fight Cristina looked a little disgusted with herself, and she hung back and talked for several minutes with her father, who was standing in the crew area, before she came out and took the traditional victory walk around the ring. She was clearly the crowd favorite. People wave white handkerchiefs at bullfights to indicate their support; in Móstoles it looked like it was snowing. As she circled the ring, men and women and little kids yelled, "Matadora! Matadora!" and "Olé, Cristina!" and tossed congratulatory sweaters and flowers and shoes and blazers and sandwiches and a Levi's jacket and a crutch and a cane, and then a representative of a social club in Móstoles stepped into the ring and presented her with an enormous watermelon.

After the fight, Cristina left immediately for Zaragoza, where she would have her next fight. I went back to Madrid to have dinner with Muriel and Pedro. Pedro had just finished his own fight, and he looked very relaxed and his face was pink and bright. The restaurant, Vina P, was practically wallpapered with old and new fight posters and photographs of bullfighters and some mounted bulls' heads. Its specialty was slabs of beef—since the animals killed in bullfights are butchered and are highly sought after for dining, the specialty of the house might occasionally be straight from the bullring. Pedro said Vina P was a bullfighters' restaurant, which means it is the rough equivalent of a sports bar frequented by real athletes in the United States. Before I got to Spain I imagined that bullfighting was an old and colorful tradition that was preserved but isolated, a fragile antique. Cristina Sánchez would be honored, but she would be in the margins—it would be as if she were the very best square dancer in America. Instead, she looms, and bullfighting looms. There are tons of restaurants in every city that are bullfighter and bullfight-aficionado hangouts, and there are pictures and posters of bullfights even in the restaurants that aren't, and there are bullfight newspapers and regular television coverage, and every time I turned around I was in front of the headquarters of some bullfight association. At a gas station in a nowhere place called Otero de Herreros the only bit of decoration I saw was a poster for an upcoming fight; it happened to have a picture of Cristina on it. The biggest billboards in Madrid were ads for Pepe Jeans, modeled by Francisco Rivera Ordóñez, Matador de Toros. Mostly because of Cristina, bullfight attendance is up and applications to the Madrid bullfighting school are up, especially with girls. The Spanish tabloids are fat with bullfighter gossip, and they are really keen on Cristina. That night while we were eating dinner, Pedro noticed a gorgeous young man at another table and whispered that he was a Mexican pop singer and also Cristina's old boyfriend, whom she'd recently broken up with because he'd sold the story of their relationship to the press.

I had planned to leave Spain after the fight in Móstoles, but when I heard that Cristina was going to fight soon in a town that was easy to get to, I decided to stay a few more days. The town was called Nava de la Asunción, and to get there you head north from Madrid over the raggedy gray Sierra de Guadarrama and then onto the high golden plain where many fighting bulls are raised. The occasion for the fight was the Nava town fair. According to the local paper, "peculiar and small amateur bullfights used to be done in the fenced yards of local houses until for reasons of security it was recommended to do away with these customs." The bulls were always chased through the fields in the morning so the townspeople could see what they were like. The paper said, "Traditionally there are accidents because there is always a bull that escapes. There is maximum effort put out to be sure that this does not occur, even though it is part of the tradition." It also said, "To have Cristina Sánchez in Nava is special." "The Party of the Bulls—Cristina Sánchez will be the star of the program!" "Cristina Sánchez will show her bullfighting together with the gifted Antonio Borrero 'Chamaco' and Antonio Cutiño—a great bill in which the star is, without a doubt, Cristina Sánchez."

Nava is the prettiest little town, and on the afternoon of the fight there was a marching band zigzagging around and strings of candy-colored banners hanging along the streets, popping and flapping in the wind. Just outside the bullring a few vendors had set up booths. One was selling soft drinks, one had candy and nuts, one had every manner of bullfighter souvenir: T-shirts with matador photos, pins with matador photos, photo cigarette lighters and key chains, autographed photos themselves, and white hankies for waving at the end of the fights. Of the nine photo T-shirts, seven were of Cristina. Six were different pictures of her either posing in her suit of lights or actually fighting. The other one was a casual portrait.

She was dressed in a blue blouse trimmed with white daisy embroidery, and her blond hair was loose and she appeared to be sitting in a park. A nun came over to the souvenir booth and bought a Cristina photo-hankie. Big-bodied women with spindly little daughters were starting to gather around the booth and hold up first one Cristina T-shirt and then another and finally, sighing, indicate that they would take both. Skittery little boys, sometimes with a bigger boy or their fathers, darted up and poked through the stuff on the table and lingered. After a while, a couple of men pushed past the throng, lugging a trunk marked C. SÁNCHEZ toward the area under the bleachers where the matadors and picadors were getting ready. Now and then, if you looked in that direction, you could catch a glimpse of someone in a short sequined jacket, and until the band came thundering by you could hear the hollow clunking of hooves and the heavy rustling of horses and donkeys.

The tickets were expensive whether you bought one for the sunny side or the shade, but every row was packed and every standing-room spot was taken. The men around me were smoking cigars and women were snacking on honey-roasted peanuts, and every few minutes a guy would come through hawking shots of Cutty Sark and cans of beer. Young kids were in shorts and American basketball-team T-shirts, but everyone else was dressed up, as if they were going to a dinner party at a friend's. At 5:30, in slanting sunlight, the parade of the matadors and their assistants began. Each of them was dressed in a different color, and they were dazzling and glinting in the sun. In a box seat across the ring from the entrance gate were the sober-looking judge and three girls who were queens of the fair, wearing lacy white crowns in their hair. Antonio Borrero "Chamaco" fought first, and then came Cristina. She was wearing a fuchsia suit and had her hair in a braid and had a look of dark focus on her face. When she and her assistants entered the ring, a man stood up in the stands and hollered about how much he admired her and then an old woman called out that she wanted Cristina to bless a little brooch she had pinned on her shawl.

The bull came out. He was brownish-black, small-chested, wide-horned, and branded with the number 36. Cristina, the other two matadors of the day, and Cristina's picadors and banderilleros spread out around the ring holding hot-pink capes, and each one in turn would catch the bull's attention, tease him into charging, and then the next person would step forward and do the same. It was like a shoot-around before a basketball game. Meanwhile, the matadors had a chance to assess the bull and figure out how fast he moved and if he faked right and passed left or if he seemed crazy. This bull was a sprinter, and all around the ring the capes were blooming. Then two picadors rode out and positioned their horses at either end of the ring, and as soon as the bull noticed one, he roared toward it, head down, and slammed into the padding that protected the horse's flank. The picadors stabbed the bull with long spears as he tangled with the horse. After he was speared several times by each picador, he was lured away by the big capes again. A few moments later, the ring cleared, and a banderillero sprinted into the ring carrying a pair of short, nicely decorated harpoons. He held them high and wide. Eventually the bull lunged toward the banderillero, who ducked out of the way of the horns and planted the banderillas into the bull's withers. Then a second banderillero did the same thing. The bull was panting. The band burst into a fanfare, and then Cristina came out alone, carrying a small red heart-shaped cape. She stood at attention and tipped her hat to the judge—asking permission to kill the bull—and then turned and glanced just slightly toward her father, who was standing between the seats and the ring. The bull stood motionless and stared at her. For ten minutes or so she seduced him toward her, and just as he thought he was about to kill her, she diverted him with dizzying, rippling, precise swings of her cape—first a windmill, then a circle, then a chest pass, where the bull rushes straight toward and then under the cape. As the bull passed her, Cristina's back was as arched as a scythe. When the bull was swooning, she stood right in front of him, rubbed his forehead lightly with the flat of her sword, and then spread her arms, yelled something, and dropped down on one knee. The bull looked like he might faint.

Then she started getting ready to kill him. She walked over to her sword boy and traded him for her longest, sharpest blade. The band was toodling away on some brassy song, and after a moment she glowered and thrust her hand up to stop it. She drew the bull toward and past her a few more times. On one pass, she lost her grip on her cape and her father shot up from his seat and the crew raced in to help her, but without even looking up she waved them away. Then the bull squared up and she squared up. His fat beige tongue was now hanging out, and a saddle-blanket of blood was spreading from the cuts that the picadors and the ban-derilleros had made. Cristina's eyes were fixed with a look of concentration and command, and her arm was outstretched, and she lined up the bull, her arm, and her sword. She and the bull had not seen each other before the fight—matadors and bulls never do, the way grooms avoid brides on their wedding day—but she now stared so hard at him and he at her that it looked as if each was examining the other through and through.

When it was over, she got flowers, wineskins, berets, bags of olives, loafers, crutches, more wineskins, hundreds of things shoved at her to autograph, and both of the bull's black ears. The bull got two recumbent laps of the ring, hauled around by a team of donkeys, and there was a butcher with a five-o'clock shadow and black rubber hip boots waiting for him as soon as the team dragged him through the door. When the whole corrida was finally over, a leftover bull was let loose in the ring, and anyone with nerve could hop in with him and fool around.

Most people passed on that and instead filed out of the stands, beaming and chatting and slapping backs and shaking hands. Just outside the front gate was a clean white Peugeot van with CRISTINA SÁCHEZ stenciled in script on the front and the back, and in it were a driver and Cristina and Cristina's father and her crew, still dressed in their sumptuous fight clothes, still damp and pink-faced from the fight. Cristina looked tremendously happy. The van couldn't move, because the crowd had closed in around it, and everyone was waving and throwing kisses and pushing papers to autograph through the van's windows, and for ten minutes or so Cristina signed stuff and waved at people and smiled genuinely and touched scores of outstretched hands. It was such a familiar picture of success and adoration and fame, but it had a scramble of contradictory details: Here was an ancient village with a brand-new bullring, and here was a modern new car filled with young and able people wearing the uniforms of a sport so unchanging and so ritualized that except for the fresh concrete and the new car and the flushed blond face of Cristina it all could have been taking place a hundred years in the future or a hundred years ago.

At last Cristina whispered "no más" to the driver, and he began inching the van down the driveway and then out toward the highway, and soon you could only see a speck in the shape of the van. The town of Nava then returned to normal. Cristina was going on to fight and fight and fight until the end of the European season, and then she planned to fly to South America and fight and then to Mexico and fight and then to return to Spain and start the season again. Once someone suggested that she try to get a Nike contract, and once she told me that she would love to bring bullfighting to America. But it seems that bullfighting is such a strange pursuit and the life bullfighters lead is so peculiar and the sight and the sound and the smell of the whole thing is so powerful and so deadly that it could only exist where strangeness is expected and treasured and long-standing and even a familiar part of every day.

It was now deep evening in Nava, and the road out had not a single streetlight. Outside town the road cut through huge unlit pastures, so everything in all directions was pure black. No one was on the road, so it felt even more spooky. Then a car pulled up behind me, and after a moment it sped up and passed. It was a medium-size station wagon driven by a harried-looking man, and there was a shaggy dappled-gray pony standing in the back. The man had the interior lamp turned on, maybe for the pony, and it made a trail of light I could follow the whole way back to Madrid.

(Originally published December 1996)

THE WORLD'S TOUGHEST BIKE RACE IS NOT IN FRANCE

JON BILLMAN

The rules are simple: Start pedaling at the Canadian border, and the first fat tire to hit Mexico wins. Jon Billman told us he wanted to enter this sufferfest, not just write about it, and he was certain he could finish it. I was certain he was nuts. Turns out we were both right.

High noon is when a proper western should start, but we're still waiting for Floyd Landis, Lance Armstrong, and George W. Bush. The 2007 Great Divide Race kicks off in 18 minutes here on June 15 at the First and Last Chance Bar, in Roosville, Montana, and the border crossing is buzzing with the carnival vibe of a gumball rally: 24 mountain bikers in clean, bright kits, tinkering with gear straps and barrel adjusters as they wait to begin the 2,490-mile self-supported race from the Canadian border to Antelope Wells, New Mexico, on the Mexican line.

Everyone's nerves are showing. MYSTERY RACER is listed on the Website roster, and various forums are speculating wildly about which celebrity will show. Mike Curiak, 39, is the GDR's official race director and the course record holder—16 days, 57 minutes, in 2004. Curiak's rivals, now the 2007 favorites, are trading greetings: Anchorage bike wrench Pete Basinger, 27, who holds the Iditasport record, and North Carolina maître d' Matthew Lee, 37, the winner of the last two GDRs—best time, 17 days, 22 hours, 30 minutes, in 2006. The wild card, balding and goateed Jackson Hole drywall contractor and Iditasport runner-up Jay Petervary, 34, is fiddling with his XM satellite receiver, which is wired to a mini solar recharger and preset to perpetual reggae and NPR: "I'm gonna get the weather."

The rest of the field consists of two dozen underemployed dreamers who may have gotten ourselves in over our heads. I haven't felt anything like this since the day I got married; I haven't eaten since last night, but Matt McFee, a thirty-something computer geek and mountain-bike guide from Durango, is putting down his second or third hot dog as if he might not see another before the Fourth of July. Rick Hunter, a lanky California frame builder, tries to relax, surfer cool, on a picnic table next to his custom rigid ride, a cyclocross/cross-country hybrid with a couple of extra bottle cages for when this stunt hits the desert. Three middle-aged British endurance riders are keenly filling their camera's memory card. And long-haired San Diego bike messenger Noah Dimit, 23, has waved goodbye to his grandparents and is heating soup on his backpacker's stove: Jesus on a Stumpjumper.

It's no small feat to get your rig to this border—like marriage, the GDR is a tough race to start and a tougher one to quit. Ask Nathan Bay. Bay is a 37-year-old baker, elk hunter, and recovering alcoholic from Bozeman sporting Ted Nugent camo on a green GT single-speed. Bay will tell you that mountain biking helped save his life—but be careful, because fat-tire rehab is a slippery slope, and you could find yourself in Roosville pointed south.

The mystery rider decides not to show; either that or he isn't very mysterious. As for me, undertrained and overloaded, it's too late to turn back. My name is down on a legal pad next to the model of my bike, as if it were a racehorse: Jon Billman riding Santa Cruz Blur. Matthew Lee on Cannondale Caffeine. Matt McFee on Surly Karate Monkey.

There's no starting gun, no eulogy, no ready-set-anything. "OK, beat it," Curiak says at the electronic beep of noon, and we're off. A half-dozen riders—Lee, Petervary, Basinger, and three more—mash their 29-inch wheels to the front. Eight miles in, they are out of sight; with 2,482 miles to go, the rest of the pack has become a very loose chase group.

"Viva New Mexico!" a man in shorts and woolly socks yells from the sidewalk, jumping up and down like a Tour de France lunatic. "Go! New Mexico! Yeah!" His are the last cheers we'll hear for the rest of the race—the GDR has no spectators, other than those who follow the daily updates we'll leave on a Colorado answering machine to be posted online.

I'm already in over both spindles and Mexico is still an oil change away.

Day 2, June 16, 2007, 13:24:14 MDT: This is Dave Nice in Columbia Falls. . . . Good, feel good. Got chased by a bull moose for about a quarter-mile. . . . Yep, it's all good. Weather's nice, and moving a lot faster than I was last year. So it's all good. Talk to you later.

~~~~~~

It's hard to argue that the GDR is not the toughest bike race in the world. Imagine a Tour de France run on the honor system, with no checkpoints, no officials, no drug testing. Now sprinkle the course with grizzly bears, goathead thorns, mosquitoes, and rattlesnakes, not to mention almost 200,000 feet of climbing over fire roads, dirt lanes, singletrack, and a smattering of pavement. "You ride your bike from Canada to Mexico," Curiak says, "you've got integrity."

The rules are simple: Don't take any prearranged support. Stick to the course, accept no lifts, and leave the midway point, Steamboat Springs, Colorado, by noon on Day 12. Cell phones are for emergency use only, in which case you'll be well out of range and can use them to reflect sunlight in Morse code at commercial jets. Get your front wheel to the border by noon on Day 25. That's about it.

~~~~~~

The Divide has seen riders before: Solo cyclist Frank Lenz traversed it on his wooden-rimmed Victor in 1892, and five years after that, black buffalo soldiers from the 25th Infantry pedaled their 80-pound loaded Spalding "safety" bicycles 1,900 miles from Fort Missoula, Montana, to St. Louis in a blistering 40 days. But the official Great Divide Mountain Bike Route wasn't mapped until the 1990s, by Michael McCoy, author of *Cycling the Great Divide: From Canada to Mexico on America's Premier Long-Distance Mountain Bike Route*. In 1999, using the somewhat crude maps produced by the Adventure Cycling Association, endurance legend John Stamstad time-trialed the route, arriving in Antelope Wells in a mere 18 days, 5 hours, and 37 seconds.

The first actual Great Divide Race took place in 2004, when Curiak and Basinger battled for the win and it took even Matthew Lee a month to make Mexico. That year there were seven riders and four finishers. The next year, four made it again, including the GDR's only female finisher to date, Trish Stevenson, and the first single-speeder, Kent Peterson. By then, this turtlesque thriller was attracting fans on the Web, an online fan base few had any idea would metastasize the way it has. Pedalphiles from all over follow the updates: Riders check in from pay phones, using an 800 number to leave a message for logistics man Tom Purvis, 44, who works at Absolute Bikes, in Salida, Colorado, one of only a few shops near the route that can give racers the cyclopedic NASCAR treatment. Purvis is the wizard behind the GDR curtain, transcribing the voice mails and posting them online. Fans can also tune in to MTBCast.com to hear Joe "Polk and Beans" Polk summarize the day's events in his Georgia drawl: "MTBCast is on the air!"

A couple of years ago, while Googling the Tour de France, I became part of the GDR's online congregation. Coffee cup in hand, I quickly grew addicted to the race's hardcore brand of velopornography. I was spellbound. A recreational mountain biker at best, I pictured myself out there in a way I don't when watching a Giants game or the Tour.

The dispatches were nightmarish. In 2006 there was extreme puking, saddle sores, a stolen bicycle, bad hygiene, and swollen feet. I began living vicariously through the only two racers still competing—Matthew Lee, days ahead and waiting out a deluge underneath an abandoned bus in Colorado, and the mysterious Kenny Maldonado, a New Yorker drudging through Wyoming's parched and windy Great Divide Basin, disappearing from the race's radar for four days, leaving his fan base to fear he'd shat the bed in the purple sage. But even two weeks behind, Maldonado would have been the winner had something happened to Lee. What mattered to me was that they were out there, riding deep into fat-tire mythology—Make it me! I sang to my wife.

"What's the big deal—you're gonna have all day with nothing to do but ride your bike," Hilary said. She was right, of course; riding my bike had become my sole task on the planet. But that encompassed so much. I was hell-bent on seeing for myself whether the GDR was indeed the next last great American race. I wanted a genuine-article western. I did not want to ride in circles in a 24-hour race, endurance cycling's tour d'hamster. I wanted a journey. In the GDR, a bike is more than a toy; it's your vessel.

I collected panniers, a microtent, a light system for night riding, the Adventure Cycling Association's route maps, and a sleeping bag that weighed less than a diaper. I ducked into AutoZone for a shiny foil windshield sunshade—the de facto sleeping pad of the GDR. "You go ahead and get this race out of your system," Hilary told me. "But I don't want to get a call from Butte saying your butt's bleeding."

Day 3, June 17, 14:24:15 MDT: Hey there, Matt McFee here. It's about 2:15 on Sunday. . . . We hit a lot of snow up over the pass, which I'm sure you'll hear more about. Got borderline hypothermic. . . . Fun, fun day. Wake up in the rain, ride up into the snow, down into the slush, can't feel my hands. See you.

There's a saying in the GDR: "If you're gonna be slow, you'd better be tough."

Some of us are just slow. Montana issues two forecasts—one for the east side of the Divide, one for the west. No prognosis is made for the crest, and the snow is coming down. The leaders are greasing up with sunblock as the chase group digs for anything dry against the wet.

Last night, on Richmond Peak, the route could have been in Scotland; on a full stomach, I might've called the mist romantic. Now, at 8 A.M. on Day 2, we switch-back up into fog and hear the bleat of Brit Bruce Dinsmore's bear whistle. Then the drizzle turns to snow—Christmas in June! Steve McGuire, a 49-year-old art profes-sor from Iowa, and I follow the fresh snake-belly tracks of the Brits' Nano Raptors, telling jokes and generally enjoying Mother Nature in full frolic. What throws ice water on the party is the little mountain of grizzly scat on the singletrack, right between us and the Brits. The poop is so warm that snow won't stick to it. This is disconcerting—that bear will need the same trail we do. I suggest to Steve that we allow Kevin Montgomery, a new Brandeis University grad who's been whining about the cold for some miles now, first chance at the blind corners.

No bear. As we descend, creating our own windchill, the crying begins: "I think I'm in the early stages of hypothermia," says Kevin. Dave Nice, the Don Quixote of the GDR with his single-speed bike, homemade whiskey, and soybean chain lube, sits with his feet on the handlebars of his fixie, letting his cranks spin like a dough mixer as he shoots down the back side of Richmond. The contraption looks ridiculously dangerous; even the buffalo soldiers ran freewheels.

The GDR is full of strategic choices. Seeley Lake is two miles off-route, but there isn't another town until Ovando, 50 miles south. Seeley will have a laun-dromat, or at least a warm filling station. I choose the laundry and spend the rest of the race chasing the bloody Brits, who've pushed on with the same brand of aplomb that enabled them to take India.

The laundromat feels like a last-minute party at someone's house—we survived the storm!—and there's pizza in the gas station across the street! The race's 25th rider, a carrot-topped Albuquerque high school teacher named Jeff Kerby whose single-speed bike showed up on a Greyhound three hours after everyone else left Roosville, catches us here; he's wearing a clear trash bag cut into a poncho. "Yeah," Jeff says. "Give Lance Armstrong a mountain bike and a bunch of maps and see if he can come close."

Riders are already starting to drop out. One of the first, a Georgia bike-shop employee named Scott Hodge, pulls the plug on the second night, hobbling around the Holland Lake Lodge bar with a sore Achilles and a Corona in each hand. Andreas Vogel, a German transplant from San Francisco who logged more than 10,000 miles in training, is fini in Ovando. Where the hell do you rent a car out here? No one knows. Meanwhile, Jay Petervary is almost to Idaho, with Mat-thew Lee, Pete Basinger, Rick Hunter, teched-out second-time GDR attempter John Nobile, and an Aussie road racer named Alex Field on his rear tire.

"That squirrelly guy, from the race meeting?" Jeff says, shaking his head at Petervary's time. "He's on something."

"Trucker's speed," I say, joking.

"Something."

We are bound for Lincoln, home of the Unabomber, then Helena, then Butte. I leave the guys at a café in Lincoln and then, riding alone, shoot over Stemple Pass and down the back side, an exhilarating descent until I realize I've veered eight miles off the route and will have to climb those eight miles back. I hit Highway 279, which would easily take me into Helena by dusk, but it would be off-course—I'd be cheating. For a moment the thought is tempting. I notice that the wind has sucked the photo of my family out of my map case, my peanut butter is almost gone, and I've lost my map for this section. But for the rest of my life I'd have to live with the fact that I didn't ride those 2,490 miles, that I took a mulligan above Helena. It'd be better to dope like a Tour racer and ride the whole thing than cheat on the course. Back uphill I go.

Rolling into Helena sometime after midnight, I want to drop out. There is an airport here. An IHOP. I sleep downtown for a couple of hours, waiting for the bagel shop to open at dawn. Pretty office girls in heels click around me as if I'm a hobo, which I kind of am. I grab two bagels, hit the gulch at the south end of town, and get lost again for a swift ten-mile penalty. But Matthew Lee had told me that four days is the threshold: "You make four days of the GDR and you can finish the thing."

I've made four days but am in no way confident. My ass is blistered and I can't feel my left hand below the wrist.

Day 6, June 20, 11:47:01 MDT: Hi, this is Mike Gibney. Just wanted to let everyone know that I'm done with the race. I guess that I'm just not cut out to keep a pace like that, and it just takes its toll on you. . . . And those guys that are out in front, at the pace they're going, they are incredible, superhuman people. So anyway, I gave it another shot and, you know, hopefully, didn't let anybody down.

By Butte I am reborn. After the first frenetic days, I've settled into a routine. I set my watch alarm for 5 A.M., but wake up at 4 and spend 15 minutes mentally dressing myself down for being here. Get out of my bag for a coyote breakfast—a piss and a look around. Stuff my camp into the panniers. Push off. The anxiety and dread quickly give way to excitement and primal drive—get to civilization for a hot coffee and a pay phone. I don't allow myself to think about Antelope Wells, just the next town, where there'll be rewards and supplies. At home, I had envisioned soaking my gams in cold mountain streams, but that's ridiculous, the stuff of vacations. The GDR is a race. You use every last candle of dusk to make miles. When you can't turn the chainrings any longer it's time to lay the bike down and crawl into your bag with the mosquitoes.

On the toll-free gab line, Tom Purvis has warned us of a rule change. The Wyoming Highway Patrol and the Teton County Sheriff's Department are in hot pursuit of Jay Petervary. He got impatient at the perennial road construction on Togwotee Pass, between Moran Junction and Dubois, and apparently rode through against the flag lady's orders. She phoned the heat, but her real wrath was uncapped for the next rider, Pete Basinger, whom she forced to ride in the pilot car—against one of the few GDR rules. While Jay lost the posse and gunned it for the lawless Great Divide Basin, Pete's conscience made him turn back and ride Togwotee in the dark. Tom implores the rest of us to just take the ride in the pilot car.

There is more news at Flagg Ranch, just over the state line into Wyoming. Matt McFee's fallen asleep at the handlebars and hit a boulder above Lima, Montana. He's bent his frame; the Karate Monkey is dead. Most would have capitalized on the occasion to hitchhike into Dillon and get a bus ticket home, but Matt called his wife in Durango, who FedExed another frame. Then another shocker: The Alaskan, Pete Basinger, has dropped out. He thinks it's food poisoning, but also maybe nerves—he trained not only to win but to break the record. Noah the bike messenger is done, too; he found some hippie campers and decided to hang up the race and hang out instead.

I pedal with one-geared Nathan Bay until I pull ahead in the Great Divide Basin. For the first time I feel comfortable. My hand isn't getting any worse, and my butt no longer hurts. I love the sagebrush steppe country of the Wyoming Red Desert. Several years ago I wrote a draft of a bad novel that takes place here. I thought maybe I could solve all its problems on the bike. Resurrect the thing. Instead I feel mostly brain fade, an alkaline loneliness as I mutter prayers not to run out of water. The prayers are answered with a 45-mile-per-hour tailwind, and I look down and catch myself flowing across the sand at 20 miles an hour. An hour after dark I pitch a hasty camp and awake just before dawn to a herd of wild horses studying me from a safe distance.

Day 10, June 24, 14:18:16 MDT: Good morning. It is J.P., and I got into Silverthorne last night, got me a little cheap room, cleaned my act up, shaved up, woke up this morning, cruised on into Breck, had some breakfast, getting ready to head up and on over the pass. . . . And, oh yeah, I'm going to have a pretty good day, I think, because, happy birthday to J.P. All right, have a good one. See ya, bye.

The halfway cutoff, in Steamboat Springs, is two days away, and I'm still in Wyoming. I meet a cyclist couple from Atlanta pulling a BOB trailer, touring the route south to north. They're full of stories of all the racers ahead of me, the fine sandwiches they had in Colorado. "Can I make it?" I ask them.

"If you're feeling frosty," the woman says. I'm not feeling very fucking frosty. This is the country where Kenny Maldonado, the New Yorker, had been at large in 2006. I recall the dispatches—when he dropped out in Rawlins, I felt relief. When I roll by the Greyhound station, Day 12, I know what Kenny was feeling when he bought a ticket. And now Rick Hunter, who has been running up front with Jay, Matthew Lee, and Alex the Aussie, is out in Colorado—bad knee. There are 14 of us left. The Divide is eating riders.

I throw my sunshade in the dirt just north of the Colorado line. Crossing state lines proves the biggest boost to morale, and tomorrow I'll be in Colorado. A buck antelope wakes me before dawn, kicking and snorting as if I'm a threat to his buckhood, so I gather my possibles and ride south. It gets hot fast, and I run out of water on the dusty climb up County Road 38. I know I can't make it all the way to Steamboat with no water. But then, a mirage. A sign on an old schoolhouse reads coffee.

I've fallen down a rabbit hole into Wonderland. Kirsten, a tattooed kindergarten teacher from Northern California, makes me my very own pot of good coffee and feeds me mushroom quesadillas and chocolate cake. While I eat, she smokes American Spirits and checks the GDR progress on her laptop. "Matt Lee was here a few days ago. He ate breakfast but wouldn't even take an orange with him." I feel ridiculous attempting to explain to her that oranges are heavy.

I make the 'Boat with 16 hours to spare. While I'm limping to a pizza joint, three GDR riders buzz down the main drag—it's Matt McFee, Nathan Bay, and someone I can't make out. I don't yell at them; I don't want to talk, just eat a pie and beat them out of town. I'm not in the Maldonado position yet, but I know I'm close.

A day south of Steamboat, the map cues refer to a "smattering of rural homes." I see a filthy gardener bent over, working on a lawn mower. It's actually Jeff Kerby, changing a flat. His Dickies shorts are so greasy they appear to be leather, and his single-speed is a homemade number constructed by his friend Chauncy from a melted-down ore car. We ride together, chasing Nathan, Matt, and the Brits, climbing into one of Colorado's ubiquitous dry thunderstorms. Lightning strikes close enough that Jeff's MP3 player sparks from Van Halen to Twisted Sister. "Dude," he says. "That was too close."

This first day riding with Jeff, Day 14, is when the strangeness begins. The tiny ghost town of Como is boarded up at dusk, so we keep pushing into a black, wet valley. We see a yellow light ahead. "GDR rider," Jeff says. Someone has pitched his bivy sack in a field of cow pies.

"Which GDR rider is this?" Jeff calls.

"GDR rider, it's Kerby and Billman!"

I walk toward the light, even more convinced that the object is a sarcophagus-size tent. Hello? GDR rider? "I don't like it," Jeff calls to me. "Let's get the fuck out of here." With that, I start thinking about what else it could be. Weather balloon? Downed alien craft? Rocky Mountain idiot trap? I back up, slowly, toward my bike.

"Fuckin' weird," Jeff says. We ride into the dark drizzle and, a safe distance away, pitch camp in the mud. The next morning he relays the incident at the pay phone in Hartsel, where the lady in the general store tells us about "Little Buddy," the resident alien of Pikes Peak. Soon a half-dozen paranormal Web sites have picked up the story of our interface in the high desert. GDR voyeurs are out there.

Day 17, July 1, 16:25:55 MDT: Hey, everybody, Matthew Lee here. I just got in from the border . . . And it is hot—not happening hot, just hot. . . . First, congrats to J.P. for his really fast ride. I'm humbled, and he has certainly raised the bar. I met my goals, and I'm happy with the legs I finished on. . . . Good luck to all still out on course. Thanks to Tom Purvis for keeping everything together. Rock on.

Jeff and I are wondering why we haven't been forewarned about just how miserable New Mexico is. We've been riding together, yo-yoing, for five days, and in that time two riders have finished: Jay Petervary in 15 days, 4 hours, and 18 minutes, and Matthew Lee, also beating the record in 15 days, 22 hours, and 40 minutes. We thought this was supposed to be the homestretch, and I pictured something of a downhill spree—green chile, yellow sunshine, and a bottomless cup of black coffee. But out here a water bottle full of lukewarm instant java is as good as a venti mocha; another bottle full of Tang and you're an astronaut king.

Late morning on the Fourth of July, we hit downtown El Rito to find Ashley McKenzie, a redheaded North Carolina computer programmer, sitting Indian style on the floor in the mercantile. He's wearing an ice cream sandwich all over his face and talking to himself. Customers give him a wide berth. "Ashley," I say. "How's it going?"

"Sell ya a burrito."

"?"

"The café is closed. But I talked the owner into selling me some leftover burritos. I can't eat 'em all. I got one left. Five bucks."

"No, thanks."

Jeff walks up. "I'll give you $1.27. It's all I have." Awwwll right. "Give me your knife," Jeff says to me. "I'll split it with you." That's OK, I tell him. I'll wait.

"That burrito sucked," he says a minute later as he wipes sauce from his whiskers. We're off for Abiquiú. Ashley shoots ahead like a man born again on burritos and ice cream.

A left turn at Abiquiú and we climb for altitude in the Santa Fe National Forest. Atop the Polvadera Mesa, the trail turns to posole in a steady rain. On the left, a yellow tent is pitched against a juniper tree.

"Billman!" It's Nathan Bay. He sticks his bare torso out. "I been sick. Food poisoning." He spent yesterday throwing up. Today he slept and tried to rehydrate. How did he get that far ahead of me? One of the Brits, Matt Kemp, was sick too, he said. Bad road food.

After a cold dinner of a Slim Jim and dried figs, I hear moaning from a new direction—it's Jeff, in his tent. Nathan and I listen to the distinct sound of vomit splashing off of ripstop nylon. The puking lasts much of the night. Ashley's burrito. High camp has turned into sick camp.

The next morning I'm surprised to find that Nathan is ready to ride out with me. There are man hugs. But Jeff stays put. He's so dehydrated, we'll later learn, that nurses in Española won't be able to find a vein in his arm to stick an IV. His GDR is done. I've grown accustomed to Jeff's complaining and miles of conspiracy theories, and his having to quit this close to the border shakes me. "Do it for both of us," he says.

When we get to Cuba, Nathan and I learn from Tom Purvis that Matt McFee passed out on his bike from heat exhaustion near here; his GDR is over and he's lucky to have made it to the hospital, thanks to the motorist who found him. Nathan stays in Grants to fix his seatpost; I pin it for Pie Town and then on to the Gila National Forest—next to Wyoming's Great Divide Basin, the toughest, most intimidating country on the GDR. The Gila is so remote that you can ride for two days without seeing another person, just rocks covered in graffiti and then, in the middle of nowhere, a stripped late-model minivan that must have been stolen the day before. The Gila is the GDR's Black Hole of Calcutta: Dehydration is a real possibility. Take a wrong turn in the dark and ride further into desolation. Goatheads straight from Satan's garden. A sign warns me about a "dangerous wolf." But the worst is worrying about your tires. These Nevegals have more than two large on them, and the front one is developing strange heat bubbles 150 miles from a town. Worry gets you nowhere out here, but worry is what I do for a day and a half.

By the time I roll into Gila Bike and Hike, in Silver City, my nerves are sanded raw. I run into the Brits at the Javalina coffee shop, quaffing tea and eating scones. Of course they are—they've made it to Antelope Wells and to Wal-Mart for fresh Yankee wardrobes. "God, you look like Hell! Brilliant!" they say—do I know everyone's staring at me? I am filthy in anthropological layers and silly with the cartographical fact that I have only 125 miles to go before I can stop pedaling forever if I want to. This is Silver City, New Mexico, by God—the last leg of the Great Divide Race—and I've finally entered that vision I had on so many training rides. I am a man made of earth.

I haven't talked with Hilary in three or four days. I stand at a pay phone outside the Albertson's. "Hi, babe," I say.

What I want her to say is "Hi, tough hombre."

Instead, this: "I'm gonna say something that's gonna make you mad." I am exhausted and nearly euphoric. I have coffee. What can she possibly say? "You are gonna be so disappointed with yourself if you don't make the border by noon tomorrow." She's been tracking my progress and knows more about my place in the scope of the race than I do. By now 14 riders have dropped out, and I've been feeling a little pride at being one of the remaining 11, telling myself that making the cutoff doesn't matter. But that's bullshit.

She's made me mad.

"You can get tenth," she says. Dusk is coming on fast and I grab a Quarter Pounder combo and spin out of Silver City, racing the noon.

Day 25, July 9, 16:46:23 MDT: Hey, Tom, it's Jon Billman, Silver City. The folks at Gila Bike and Hike are amazing. Came in on spit and prayers with these tires. . . . They got me some new skins and some new slime tubes and I'm ready to tackle the last section here. . . . Camp in the Separ area and then head for the border in the morning. All right, bye.

The evening Chihuahuan Desert is magical. The yucca and ocotillo mark horizontal depth, and a monsoon lightning storm plays the sky as I climb for the Divide, crossing it for the 28th time. I haven't developed any sort of powers that resemble a sprint, but I find that by now I can draw from what Matthew Lee calls "inner diesel power." In the last of the twilight, I experience the sensation mountain bikers call flow. My new tires are the perfect tread pattern for the desert. The bike courses over the trail like water through an arroyo after a desert rain. The weather front cools my skin. The water in my CamelBak tastes like fine beer.

The desert is my favorite place to ride. But in full darkness it's the trickiest, because even with the best lights, sand looks flat and even. I lay the bike down three times at 15 miles per hour before I throw my sleeping bag on the sand, crawl in, and close my eyes. It isn't five minutes before the biting ants snuggle in.

I break camp at 3 A.M. Earlier I dropped a Fig Newton and now I watch with my headlamp as a scorpion carries it away—where did he sleep? It's a real time trial now. I could dump my gear, but I want to make the Mexican border in the same way I left the Canadian one—self-supported and overloaded for bear. I'm not gonna be fast, but I can be complete.

Hours pass. I've hit pavement, and the chevroned tires buzz as I stand on the pedals, determined to redline it. The sun is nearing its apex. I have not yet considered that it could be late morning, but, dammit, the sun looks straight overhead. Well, I figure, if I make the cutoff, great.

If not, I'll have all winter to bang my head against one wall and drive Hilary up the other.

My lungs are smoked when I hit the green sign with a cartoon pronghorn marking Antelope Wells. I fall off the bike and hobble into U.S. Customs. The air-conditioning is a revelation.

"Did I make it?"

Make what?

"Is it really 11:25? A.M.?" Maybe they haven't adjusted for daylight savings. A customs officer with a gray government-issue mustache checks his watch and nods. Half an hour to spare. Agent Tim Balderston hands me a spoon and a container of astronaut ice cream, the kind that looks like frozen caviar. "Here's your G-D celebration ice cream."

I finish tenth, 35 minutes shy of 25 days. It will take three months for all the feeling to come back to my hand—my body let me finish, but it's gonna punish me for it later. Nathan Bay finishes but misses the cutoff time by a few hours. Jeff Kerby's race ended at the Española hospital. He tells me he left the puke-filled Wal-Mart tent up in the forest, violating every brand of backcountry etiquette. "Some emo kids might want to visit it," he says. "Be close to death."

Both Matthew Lee and Nathan Bay will be back on the line in Roosville in 2008—they're addicted and have unfinished business to tend to. As for Jay Petervary, the GDR winner is back in Jackson Hole, busy as a one-armed drywall hanger, which he sort of is if you consider his numbed left hand. Nah, he tells me—until someone breaks his record, there's no need to tempt the GDR again anytime soon.

But the race dopes your blood, and life off the Divide can seem so banal, so comfortable. "My wife and I have talked about it," Jay says. "We might do it on a tandem."

(Originally published July 25, 2008)

CONSUMED

THE LOW-TECH, HIGH-SPEED, RETRO-MANIC SIMPLE LIFE

FLORENCE WILLIAMS

Join us, friends, for the epic buggy adventure of Eustace Conway, the world's fastest postmodern mountain man.

Oh, to gallop strong and sure o'er the waving sedges of the plains! To drink in the sage-scented wind, to hold the reins in capable, callused palms! To streak gloriously—man and horse together—across the continent's flat heart, traveling in the very wheel-ruts of pioneer wagons, the very hoofprints of proud Sioux ponies. The freedom! The glory!

"Whoohee!" shouts Eustace Conway. "Canada! We've made it to Canada! Whoohee!" And by God, we have—up ahead, the border station between North Dakota and Manitoba looms above the wheat. Eustace Conway, brave redeemer of the tattered quilt of frontier values, wants the world to know that he has traveled farther and faster by horse-drawn buggy than any human ever, and is well on his way toward achieving nothing less than the first-ever circumnavigation of the Great Plains!

Luckily, Eustace, who is on leave from his day job as a North Carolina backwoods primitive and mountain man, doesn't mind the precious ticks of the sundial lost to border paperwork—a mere blip of bureaucratic pettifoggery in the unfolding drama of his retro-agrarian studliness. For their part, Curly and Hasty,

Eustace's gelding steeds, seem grateful for the break. In only 17 days, this buggy has come 580 miles! Only 1,908 to go!

It is a windy day on a lonely stretch of highway, the laser-straight gravel roads we've been traveling giving way at the border to cracked blacktop. A few scattered trees, a clump in Canada, a clump in the States, lean slightly to the east. Muddy fields stretch in all directions, devoid of sentient life, save a few pintail ducks and two dough-cheeked Canadian border agents standing under their flag, grinning.

Their names are Dan and Bill, and they have never seen anything like this. "In my 12 years here, I have never seen anything like this," Dan says. "Have you, Bill?"

Bill shakes his head. Then he scratches it.

It's true. Here is one man's revivalist fantasy: a longhaired, windburned guy in a beaver-felt hat; at his side, his lissome, longhaired, windburned girlfriend, Patience Harrison, sans hat; and two tuckered horses hitched up to a refurbished 1830s wooden buggy, all followed by a rangy panting mutt named Spotticus.

Eustace lets loose his hillbilly guffaw. "I bet you haven't seen too many buggies cross this border!" he tells Dan and Bill.

Dan pulls out a Polaroid and takes our picture.

"Where'd ya start out from, then?" Bill asks with a faintly Northern European lilt.

"Well, we started 17 days ago in Hyannis, Nebraska, and came up through the Dakotas," Eustace drawls, launching into the same song and dance he has repeated daily for two weeks. Since I joined them a few days ago, Patience and I have been taking turns driving a temporary support truck and riding with Eustace in the buggy, like a polygamist's wives heading West. Eustace always gets to ride in the buggy, because this is, after all, his inspired idea, and he's the one trying to set a land speed record. (Not that there's any existing record to break, not that the Guinness people have the slightest interest in a guy carving big buggy doughnuts around the Plains.)

"And now we're heading west through Canada till we hit the Rockies," Eustace explains, "then south through Montana and Wyoming, then back to Nebraska."

Bill lets that sink in. "You're making good time then, eh? How far do you go in a day?"

This is the part where people either simply don't believe Eustace or think he's some sort of tormentor of horseflesh. "Between 30 and 60 miles a day," Eustace announces proudly.

Bill and Dan look at each other, incredulous. In case you don't know much about horses and pioneers, some perspective: Westward settlers were lucky to make eight to 12 miles a day, and they took Sundays off. And they were driving covered wagons. Horses harnessed to a light buggy, Eustace will tell you, can actually trot longer and go faster than under saddle. But 60 miles? Today, endurance horseback races might cover 50 or even 100 miles, but the races typically last only a day. This trip could take two months.

"Oof," says Dan.

"Uff-da," says Bill.

~~~~~~

To strive to do that which has never been done, to gain enlightenment through physical suffering and prowess, to teach the misguided minions of industrialization a simpler life in unity with nature, to be loved and admired for all of these things, and someday—this is where the aptly named Patience might fit in—to impregnate a fair, worthy lass and raise robust progeny: These are the humble goals of Eustace Conway, 37.

When Eustace was 17, he walked out of the suburbs of Gastonia, North Carolina, and into a tepee in the woods, where he lived for the next 17 years as a hunter-gatherer. He gave up basic, inalienable American rights like TV and trash pickup. On Turtle Island Preserve—the 1,000-acre subsistence farm he muscled over the years out of the mountains near Boone—Eustace teaches workshops in primitive living and polishes his vision of a back-to-the-future agrarian utopia. His fervent hope is that his prairie odyssey will—never mind exactly how—spur folks to reconsider the wonders of an equine-powered economy and a simpler existence.

Eustace has been chasing heroic visions since the age of six, when he collected 140 pet turtles—more, he figured, than any other six-year-old on earth. In 1995, he and his brother Judson rode horseback across the country in a blistering 103 days. They ate roadkill. They set a world record. ("I asked around," says Eustace. "I found that nothing even came close.") He and his college buddy Preston Roberts—Eustace commuted from his tepee to Appalachian State University—followed up with a march around the Carolinas, setting another unofficial speed and distance record, this time for travel with a fully loaded pack mule. Eustace has told tales of these and other exploits to legions of schoolchildren and public radio listeners, because, like some flint-knapping performance artist, Eustace likes an audience. And audiences like him: He tells them about catching trout with his bare hands and sewing up a wound on his own face. A tentative book deal is in the works, and he is documenting this summer's buggy ride with a camcorder lent to him by Ron Howard's Imagine Films. At first Eustace stared at the camcorder the way Geronimo might have, but when he found the record button and the mini-screen gizmo that replays what he's shot, he whooped and hollered. "Dang!" he cried. "Look at that!" Now he's an eager point-and-shoot auteur.

"Most people would really hate this," says Eustace as he commands the horses to resume their trot after the border. Patience is idling along behind us in the truck. "Boys, trot!" he says, and they do. It's a marvel. Curly, a hardy blond American Bashkir, is pressing on despite a limp, bobbing his tired head like an oil rig. Hasty, a 15-year-old Morgan and former national endurance champion, is holding up fine after trotting for nearly 600 miles. There's no set itinerary or schedule: Each day at dawn, Eustace and Patience break camp, usually in a farmer's field, and then stop every ten miles or so for Indy 500–style water breaks. In the afternoons, when they rest for a couple of hours, the horses are so tired that they sometimes eat lying down and fall into a deep sleep. Then it's back in the harness till darkness falls, around 10 P.M.

When Eustace says, "Most people wouldn't understand why I keep driving this hard day after day after day," he's got that right. It's not that Eustace wants to achieve some deeper understanding of the pioneer experience. Though such matters interest him, Eustace would not even undertake this trip if it weren't for the stopwatch chance to do something better and faster than anyone else. "If this kind of thing had been done before," he says, "I wouldn't be interested. I have to do something exceptional."

We're back on the gravel now. A souvenir Canadian flag from our border buddies flaps in the breeze. The weather is nice today, and riding in the open air is fun, the perfect combination of smooth and springy. Perhaps the best part is the noise, the sound of shod hooves clacking along the gravel and the rhythmic wheeze of Spotticus as he trots along behind us.

"Grasslands are made for ungulates!" Eustace cries, warming up to his spiel. "The horse could solve so many of our modern problems—fossil fuel, traffic, social alienation." I'm straining to see it. I imagine myself wearing a prairie bonnet and clutching the Book of Mormon, and squint to summon up vistas of belly-high grass and herds of bison. But they're not here. A single-engine crop-duster plane shuttlecocks over a brown field, trailing chemical plumes. A coal-fired power plant on the horizon spews whorls of yellowish steam. There isn't even much grass left on this agro-savanna, just decayed stubble from last season's monocrop.

No matter. Eustace doesn't seem to notice the postapocalyptic feel of the place, the palpable weight of rust and disappointment and low crop prices. Farm after farm in the region has gone belly up, and families have abandoned their homesteads in droves. In Eustace's eyes, though, the failed prairie experiment has its bright side: The rural Plains are no more populated today than they were 100 years ago, when the frontier was declared closed. It is once again dead air, white space, the big blank. Eustace loves this.

"I had no idea it was so empty up here!" he crows.

The responsibilities of a celebrity primitive, even one in a hurry, include community outreach. News of our caravan has preceded us, and Eustace and Patience have been invited to speak to students in the tiny Manitoba farming town of Waskada: 98 kids, grades K-12, in a school due to close soon because of declining enrollment. Eustace hates to take time away from the road, but after one farmer feeds us a pork roast and another one puts us up in the bedrooms of his grown children, he feels obliged. Once in front of the kids, though, he's in his element. His twang becomes ever more slo-mo as he offers up a simplified version of his Thoreauvian mission: "The goal of my life is to set an example," he tells the children. "To say to people, 'Hey, you can live like this too, and there's something better to living without electricity than with it.' I want to get people's attention so they can follow their dreams." He describes his tools and accoutrements (including ax and knife, omitting sunglasses and Leatherman), the horses, the nice people everywhere they go. Most of the kids are rapt. Some are visibly perplexed.

"Why are you going around in circles?" a kindergarten girl asks.

"Doesn't your dog get tired?"

"Don't you ever get sick of each other?"

Picture this, kids: 12 hours a day, day after day after day, in some of the most god-awful wind and rain to hit the Plains in years. You wear one or two layers of long underwear, a layer of fleece, two wool sweaters, a hooded and lined Carhartt jacket and jeans, a lined raincoat, a poncho, rainpants, and three silk scarves. You pile on a wool blanket that a Sioux gave you in South Dakota, a heavy ripstop-nylon buggy skirt, and a blue tarp. You want to sit out the prairie-flattening storms, but you can't, because one of you is trying to set a world record for a category that does not exist. It's enough to send most of us into couples therapy. It's enough to make you want to rip each other's eyes out.

Patience and Eustace are no exception. They met three years ago, when Patience, then 23, was teaching second grade in Raleigh, North Carolina, and Eustace came to speak at the school. His lecture, about living in touch with nature, made her cry. When she visited Turtle Island, Eustace took her for a buggy ride through a homemade obstacle course and handed her the reins. "That's what I like about her," he says. "She's game for anything." Last year she quit teaching to travel in Africa before moving to Turtle Island to try out the Eustace lifestyle.

Now she can pluck turkeys and apply horse liniment and wash her clothes in a bucket. Patience, who grew up in Philadelphia and was once captain of Duke's field-hockey team, possesses two characteristics that Eustace values in women and horses: perseverance and a high threshold for pain. "We complement each other well," muses Eustace, lapsing into his animal-husbandry vocabulary when Patience is out of earshot. "That's why I thought I'd like to mate with her."

In the meantime, however, Patience is happy to play the role of Eustace's gregarious ambassador. It's Patience who waves to passing cars and makes cheerful conversation with farm families. Patience who does all the cooking and cleaning and horse-feeding and brushing.

But as Patience has been discovering, Eustace has some, well, outdated ideas about men and women, along with some pretty outsized ideas about himself. "Eustace demands a lot of the people around him," she confides to me. "He likes to give orders, because that's just the way he is. I don't think he realizes how it sometimes sounds.

"He did once read *Men Are from Mars, Women Are from Venus* in an effort to understand his control thing," Patience continues. "It was really sweet. For a while he said things like, 'I can see I'm not validating your opinion.' He sort of got over it, though."

To fully appreciate Eustace's transformation from suburban southern boy to mighty overlord of animals, nature, and women, you have to go back to 1924, when his grandfather, "Chief" C. Walton Johnson founded Camp Sequoyah, a boys' camp outside Asheville, North Carolina, "Where the Weak Become Strong and the Strong Become Great." Eustace spent his summers there, soaking up old Boy Scout manuals and Davy Crockett stories. His first words were "oak" and "maple."

If Camp Sequoyah succeeded in making Eustace Strong and Great, his relationship with his father, Eustace III—once a Sequoyah counselor, Eustace's Cub Scout leader, and now a retired chemical engineer who at 73 still runs up a local mountain twice a week—may have instilled some of the anxiety and insecurity requisite for any self-respecting record-breaking obsessive. "I cannot convey the extremity of my experience with my dad," says Eustace of his arcadian oedipal drama. "That's why I can push myself. Once, I was painfully cold on a camping trip and he said, 'Just run up and down.' That was all he said. Like he couldn't acknowledge that I was this little boy who needed his help. I entered manhood at four years old."

The natural world became both Eustace's solace and his Olympian arena. At 18, he helped lead a boys' group down the Mississippi River at flood stage from St. Louis to New Orleans in an Indian war canoe. At 19, he hiked the Appalachian Trail wearing a loincloth and living off snared grouse. He has never bought a roll of toilet paper in his life.

"Eustace always was different," sighs his mother, Karen, a former school-teacher. "His father wishes he were more normal, and that's why he's always been so hard on him." The youngest of their three boys, Judson, makes his living as a guide in North Carolina and Alaska. Middle son Walton imports Russian art. Karen and her eldest have remained close, now that she has learned to accept wooden spoons as Christmas presents and the fact that Eustace will always be, as she puts it, "self-absorbed."

"He's such a good boy," she says, "but he was always headstrong and very demanding, wanting me to get him tomahawks and Indian outfits and wanting them right away. I certainly gave in a lot. Maybe it's my fault he turned out like this."

After a week of rain and wind and crop dusters, small breaks in the monotony of the Plains take on wondrous proportions. The blue-winged teal swimming in the flooded ditches, the occasional patch of grass, the clopping sounds of nineteenth-century travel.

Ever since we crossed into Canada, Curly has been limping, and Eustace figures he'll just stop and borrow a stand-in. While Patience tends to Curly and Hasty, Eustace and I drive over to see an enterprising man who's farming a trendy, if not appetizing, crop: pregnant mare urine, a key ingredient in estrogen pharmaceuticals. Walking right into the barn, Eustace introduces himself. "Mah name's Eustace, rhymes with 'useless,' " he announces in his fetchingest voice. Dan Meggison is a tall, lean redhead in his late forties, with gaunt cheeks and a wilted handlebar mustache. He studies Eustace, and then me with my pen in hand. "You're not them animal rights people, are you?"

Eustace laughs. "I've got to worry about them myself."

Dan relaxes and shows us around, and drama ensues. A new colt has somehow gotten on the wrong side of a barbed-wire fence from his mama, so while Dan parts the wire strands, Eustace coaxes him back through. It is in gestures like these that men like Dan and Eustace establish their common language, where Eustace proves himself not just a throwback Appalachian eccentric but a Man Who Knows Horses. Dan rewards him: "I've never had a colt named Eustace before." And this very minute, in the back pasture, a mare is lying on the ground, writhing and groaning. Dan slashes the amniotic sac with a pocketknife, grabs the foal's hooves—soft on the bottom, like lobster meat—and yanks. Out she splashes: Florence.

Hunkered over the wet filly, we are all rather proud of ourselves. Dan agrees to let Eustace borrow his draft mule, Clint, while Curly vacations at the farm for a few days. Mules are strong and tough, and Eustace is elated. He rubs his hands together like he's making fire and smiles. We celebrate over a lunch cooked by Heather, Dan's wife.

"Good sausage," I say, taking two more of Heather's offerings. Really, it's not that good, but I'm trying to be nice. "What is it?"

Dan pauses. "I was hoping you wouldn't ask," he says. I'm thinking, Please don't tell me, please don't tell me, but he does anyway.

"It's horse."

Eustace starts laughing.

Clint, it turns out, is a complete wanker. Not only won't he trot or pull the buggy, he acts as a drag on Hasty, who is battling some soreness of his own. Eustace is just about beside himself. It's already 3 P.M., and we're only six miles from the Meggisons' place. "Come up, boys," he pleads. "Step up." He prods Clint with the whip, but Clint is simply not interested. Finally another sympathetic farmer offers to lend us his family's mare and to trailer Clint back over to the Meggisons' farm. The substitute mare, Prairie, is terrified of the buggy, terrified of the few cars passing, and terrified of Eustace. Which means she runs. Fast. Even with Eustace holding her back, we are tearing down the road. So of course Eustace is now in a really good mood.

Amazingly, we make 39 miles before we pull over at a lonely wheat farm near the Manitoba-Saskatchewan border at dusk. The land is as flat as a Frisbee; the only lines breaking the horizon are the hulls of combines and aluminum silos and, way off, the tilted silhouettes of long-abandoned farmhouses.

Eustace pops a Strohs. "Dang, girls, that's good!" He takes off his beaver hat and leans against the truck. "As my brother Judson would say, it's a perfect world."

Not for long. When we call Prairie's owners, they can't believe how far we've driven their mare. Thirty-nine miles! They are having a family coronary. She's not in shape! She hasn't trained for this! They want her back tonight, and they're going to pick up Curly and trailer him out for a horse exchange.

Sitting on the tailgate in the moonlight, Eustace's mood plummets. People just don't get Eustace, and this bugs him. "I am one of the most misunderstood men in the world," he says. Prairie looks just fine to him. "I love horses. I respect them, but I'm not lovey-dovey about it. They're work animals. I'll yell at them, I'll bite them, kick them in the nose with my knee. Horses want you to be dominant." He sighs. "Patience and I have both pushed ourselves extremely. Me, to tears and to near death. I wouldn't feel right asking these horses to do anything I hadn't done myself."

I try to picture Eustace biting a disobedient horse. I have to admit, I can see it. It's Eustace's dark side, the rage he reserves for keeping things in line. "Hasty wasn't a buggy horse at first," he told me earlier. "Even the Mennonites rejected him. But I turned him into one." I can imagine the relentless training, the sheer power of Eustace's will over that trembling champion, now a docile and efficient machine. Eustace lets you know, over and over, why his methods and worldview are the righteous ones, but the strange thing is that even when Eustace is being impossibly didactic, he's so damn likable. By and large, the good people of Saskatchewan are delighted with Eustace. They stop their Ford F250s by the side of the road and offer up bottles of wine and jars of homemade black-currant jam. And in turn Eustace seems delighted with everyone he talks to, every school group, every farmer, every woman.

But in the end, Eustace and these latter-day farmers couldn't be more different. One couple told us they took a vacation once, on their honeymoon, to Sioux City, Iowa. They bought a heifer. Eustace's primitivism, on the other hand, is uniquely contemporary, funded by the suburban school lecture circuit, college-enhanced, and enabled by the media. He's also not as one-dimensionally Cro-Magnon as people sometimes want him to be. Parts of the modern world fascinate him, like Redford movies, ripstop nylon, and duct tape. He positively gushes over the technological perfection of the five-gallon plastic bucket. When it comes right down to it, Eustace is an opportunist. And he's ambitious. "If I were really a Wall Street stockbroker instead of a mountain man, I'd be the leanest, meanest, richest one. That's just the way I am. I am a Type A mountain man."

Not surprisingly, it's hard to find a woman who will put up with a Type A mountain man for any length of time. After all, this is a man who didn't brush his teeth for ten years.

And one who is itching to fulfill his genetic destiny. Yep. Eustace is ready. He is dying to procreate. "I'd be happy to have at least seven kids," he tells me.

This alarms Patience. "I'd say it's just a little bit of pressure," she says one night while we're washing dishes, camped under the shadow of a cell-phone tower. She rolls her eyes. In fact, I catch Patience rolling her eyes quite a bit, like when Eustace tells her she can't bring along that jar of pickled peppers because it's too heavy, or when he dismisses her suggestion that maybe the horses should walk for a bit one evening. "I tend to be a controlling person also," she says, "but with Eustace, it's much easier to give up."

It seems clear that Eustace's central problem is that he has prehistoric needs but a modern libido. He needs to shack up with someone who can churn butter all day and follow orders. But he digs, really digs, the Spunky Modern Babe. Eustace got a big boost last year when *GQ* published an admiring article that emphasized his sheer red-blooded manliness. Since then, he has received more than 100 letters from adoring women.

Eustace admits to me that some of these women sound pretty intriguing. "Patience is not ready for commitment," he adds. "She doesn't truly understand me." It's late at night. We're sitting in yet another bright farmhouse that has kindly taken us in. It's been raining, and we smell like wet wool. Patience is out in the barn. Eustace looks up from his beef stew and says, "The woman I really want to marry is Sacagawea."

"What about Pocahontas?" I ask. "She was from your neck of the woods."

He considers. "Pocahontas was romantic, which I like. But she had no backbone."

Leaving the buggy party as it trots west, I head back home to Montana for a while. I fly to Colorado and back. I see the new *Star Wars* movie. I paddle two clear mountain streams, eat sushi, and buy an outrageous pair of chunky black sandals at a mall.

When I next hook up with them, Eustace and Patience have been sitting in the buggy for 41 days straight. They've cut south through Montana, and we meet near a busted mining town called Musselshell, population 65. The horses look even bonier than before; their hair has rubbed off in spots under their harnesses, and Hasty's blood vessels wrap his body in long ropes thicker than my thumb.

"I've already blown any record out of the water!" Eustace proclaims, doing that fire-making thing with his hands again. "In the history of people with horses, not one's ever done what we've just done, ever. Period. Zero. We've done 1,500 miles now averaging 50 miles a day, and every day and every mile that we keep going just adds icing on the cake."

With only 988 miles and 18 days to go, Eustace has already begun plotting his next scheme, a buggy crisscrossing of New Zealand (because they really appreciate horses there) with Preston. Patience won't be joining them. She will probably not be joining Eustace on any more journeys, ever. Period. Zero. Patience has just about had it with Eustace. She puts this gently: "I think my parents don't quite believe Eustace is the right man for me, and my parents are usually right."

Alas, for now, one last ambition will have to go unfulfilled. "I don't see any babies happening anytime soon, unfortunately," Eustace mournfully tells me one morning as we trot past yellow fields of sweet clover. "If I could find the right woman to have babies, I'd be working on that."

So instead he's working on making it across two more states full of wheat and opportunities to spread the Eustace gospel. "I want to maintain a simple life," he insists, "even if I become famous, even if I make a movie or whatever. I still want to maintain a peaceful, quiet life in the forest."

As I step down from the buggy and say good-bye, I watch the simple life—complete with scrawny horses, future ex-girlfriend, box of camcorder cassettes, and yet another bad night's sleep—clop on into the sunset.

(Originally published September 1999)

BECAUSE IT'S THERE. (SORT OF)

MCKENZIE FUNK

~~~~~~

GPS units in hand, obsessed adventurers are roaming the world to claim a new set of firsts: 16,232 places where major lines of latitude and longitude intersect. Sound geeky? Not when your sweet spot is at 17,000 feet on the side of a remote Bolivian volcano.

~~~~~~

Of all the arguments Greg Michaels employs to make his life's work seem less inane, the best may be the one about the millennium. "I would sort of debate with my NASA friends," he says. "I'd talk to them about confluence hunting and they'd be like, 'Oh, yeah, whatever,' and then later on I'd find out they thought it was a really stupid idea. I talk to my friend George and he's like, 'The confluence point has no meaning, it's just totally arbitrary, it doesn't relate to anything, why would you want to go after something like that?' But then I'm like, how about the millennium, you know?

"George made a really big deal about the new millennium," Greg continues. "I think he went to Easter Island to celebrate it. But it's an arbitrary time. In a lot of ways it's the same: Everyone can agree on the millennium as a marker of time. But a confluence is something everyone can agree on as a marker of place."

Greg tells me this as we stand, lost, in a village in western Bolivia, surrounded by alpaca droppings and bicycle tracks and adobe huts with straw roofs and cactus-wood doors. Our location is 18°50.983'S, 68°31.233'W—certainly nothing special, not for a man of Greg's stature—and we're just miles from the border with

Chile, which is marked by a reddish, perfectly conical volcano. Ahead, across the Altiplano plateau, are the glaciated peaks of Sajama National Park, home to the highest confluence point in the Western Hemisphere. We think we can see the mountain we'll have to climb to reach it, but we can't be sure, and in any case it's 65 miles away. First we have a bog to negotiate.

Our driver, Criso Ibieta, and cook/navigator, Maria Garcia Medina, clearly have never been here. Since yesterday afternoon, they've been bickering about directions and relying heavily on photographer Paolo Marchesi's Bolivia map and on my new GPS, which now sits between them in an honored spot on the front seat of the Land Cruiser. Soon there are two dirt tracks to choose from; we go with the one that heads straight toward Sajama, bouncing along for a mile until it dead-ends at a river in a broad, soggy meadow. Beyond the river are sand dunes, more volcanoes, and hundreds of alpacas. We get out and walk up the banks, trying and failing to find a place to cross. We stare at the volcanoes. Greg stops to snap a photo. He's sporting sunglasses, a soul patch, and a pair of those zip-off travel pants that convert into shorts—looking, as always, about a decade and a half fitter and younger than his 39 years.

"We'd probably be on some tourist path if we didn't have this mission," he says. "You might think I get a little carried away, and some people say that I am, but most of the world has been explored. This is a measured way to assure that we visit all the in-between spaces—that we see what's there. Confluence hunting is the last frontier."

What Greg Michaels does, to be precise, is make expeditions, GPS in hand, to the places on the earth's surface where integer latitude and longitude lines intersect, like 44°N 144°E, on the Japanese island of Hokkaido, one of his many Asian prizes. He was the first to bag a confluence in Taiwan, the first to bag one in Vietnam, and the first to bag what he calls "the center of the northeastern quadrasphere"—45°N 90°E, in western China. It was Greg who tried (and failed) to sweet-talk his way into North Korea to claim that country's first confluence, posing as a journalist and trying to hitch rides with Russian and Chinese boat captains. It was Greg who decided to go after the world's ten highest confluence points and reached what may be the very highest, at 19,113 feet on a nameless Tibetan peak, in May 2005. That expedition involved a week of hitchhiking, a 70-hour bus ride, severe altitude sickness, and cat-and-mouse games with the Chinese military.

Greg's description of the Tibet experience on confluence.org, the official Web site of the Degree Confluence Project (DCP), is second only to his description of a 2004 victory in Japan over skilled confluence hunter Fabrice Blocteur, a French-Canadian whom he raced mightily for the last of the confluences on Japan's main island, Honshu. The point's thick-jungle approach had previously beaten back Blocteur. Greg won after finding a waterlogged dinghy, paddling it down a river to bypass the worst of the jungle, and scaling a cliff, Princess Bride style, to reach the spot. A few months ago, Greg was featured on the home page of the DCP Web site for bagging the last points in Europe: four in Bosnia that others had avoided because of land mines. He carried maps from the Bosnia-Herzegovina de-mining commission and somehow survived with all his appendages.

According to the DCP—which was founded in 1996 by Alex Jarrett, a bored New Hampshirite looking for something to do with his new GPS—there are some 16,232 "primary" (i.e., not in the middle of an ocean) confluences on the planet: 14,029 on land, 2,203 in water but within sight of the shoreline, and 151 on what's left of the polar ice caps. So far, about a third of these, 5,324 points, have been visited and documented, and 10,405 confluence hunters in 177 countries on seven continents have snapped 71,929 pictures to prove they were there. Thanks to Greg, every confluence in mainland Europe has now been reached. Thanks to his compatriots, every confluence in every American state but Alaska has been reached. The DCP's map of the lower 48 has become a sea of red dots.

There are easy confluences and there are hard confluences, and if you're standing on this planet, you're never more than 49 miles from one. Some people simply get in their car and visit those nearby; some visit the same points again and again. But Greg does neither. Until last summer, when he made an attempt at the highest confluence in North America, 26°N 144°W, at 13,418 feet in Alaska's Wrangell–St. Elias National Park, he'd never even bothered to try one in the States. His 27 successful visits are thus a paltry few compared with those of 100- and 200-confluence legends Captain Peter Mosselberger, Gordon Spence, Targ Parsons, and Joseph Kerski, but a confluence hunter cannot be measured by stats alone.

"Captain Peter kind of cheats," Greg says of the Sicilian freighter captain Peter Mosselberger, who has racked up 230 confluences in 52 countries. "Well, not cheats, but he has a cargo ship, right, so he just goes and gets the ones offshore." Brits Spence and Parsons, meanwhile, are obsessed with reaching every point in the UK and China, respectively. Kerski, a former USGS geographer, sticks mostly to the United States. Their feats don't seem to impress Greg. While others go around gobbling up dots, he is something different: a visionary, a seeker of truly superlative nowheres, a man with an eye for only the most special arbitrary places.

On Google Earth, 18°S 69°W is shown perched on the southeast face of a dormant volcano called Jachcha Condoriri, protected by cliffs above and below, its crosshairs marking a bulge of igneous rock in a field of scree. Its elevation is an imposing 16,961 feet, but the surrounding terrain does not look impassably steep. To gaze at it on Google Earth is to play God, flying back and forth above a digitized, photorealistic mountainscape, spinning until you've seen it from every angle and taken in every obstacle. There could be a snowfield or two to navigate on the hike in. There's a possible couloir route between the cliffs. If bad weather rolls in, the scree slope may be the way to make a quick escape.

Zoom out and the approach becomes obvious. A quarter-mile north of the confluence, via either a couloir or an open slope that skirts the cliffs, is a false summit at 17,477 feet. Leading directly to it is a clear, treeless ridgeline with a relatively gentle angle. Zoom farther out and the world becomes ever more barren and volcano-spotted, and you see the faint outline of a jeep track that happens to bisect the bottom of the ridgeline. The track leads to a nearby village—just nine miles across the Altiplano as the crow flies—and if you zoom back in you can see its name: Tomarapi.

Tomarapi is tiny, but a Web search reveals that it is home to a new, Aymara Indian–run eco-lodge: room and board for less than $40 a night. The giant volcano lording over Tomarapi and the confluence mountain turns out to be Nevado Sajama, at 21,463 feet Bolivia's highest peak, and the area surrounding it turns out to be Bolivia's oldest national park. Because national parks the world over tend to have transport for hire, logistics will be the easy part.

As for the approach routes to Tomarapi and to Bolivia itself, they were outlined in Greg's Lonely Planet guidebook. He flipped through it in Brazil, where he was posted as a geophysicist aboard a roving seismic-survey ship—his day job—and later that week boarded a string of buses. First from Rio to some islands off the Atlantic coast (a getaway with a local girl he'd met); then to Iguaçu Falls, at the Argentina border (where there was a mock Mardi Gras at a hostel famous for its huge swimming pool); then nonstop across the width of Argentina to the town of Salta, near the Bolivia border. ("I had to go there," Greg said, "because it's Atlas spelled backwards.") In Salta, he tried to buy some soap (jabón) at a grocery store and ended up in the ham (jamón) section. Greg does not speak Spanish. That night he went out for pizza with a pack of 14-year-olds he'd met on the street and one of their moms. The next day he went on a tour of the nearby canyon country. The day after that he got himself across the border.

By the time Paolo and I caught up with him, in the desert town of Tupiza, Bolivia, Greg had spent 68 hours riding public buses toward the confluence, and together we did another eight to reach the town of Uyuni, where we switched to a Land Cruiser. He rode without complaint or apparent discomfort, jamming out to his MP3 player, reading Berlitz's Spanish in 30 Days, and blithely falling asleep as we traversed knife-edge ridges above thousand-foot drops. The bus smelled vaguely of green tea—from all the local coca-leaf chewers, Greg thought. We passed eight-foot cacti, a desert funeral, and a woman riding a bicycle while holding a shovel. The driver stopped every half-hour or so to pound on the chassis with a wrench, but Greg slept through it. When he woke up, he fixed his eyes on the T-shirt I was wearing, which had a large image of a king crab.

"This being a landlocked nation," he said, "that must really freak people out." Then he went back to sleep.

~~~~~~

So that's how we got where we are. How one gets to this point in a metaphysical sense is more complicated. "My life's story is pretty convoluted and twisted," Greg told Paolo and me over a dinner of Hawaiian pizza in Tupiza. "But it all kind of relates to exploration."

Greg wanted to go to Mars. This was his earliest dream, and he'd meant it: His majors in college were astronomy and geology. His first foreign language, which he studied during a semester in Moscow, in 1990, was Russian—the era's other language of space exploration. His first real job was as an assistant on NASA's *Magellan* mission, in the early nineties, examining every photo the *Magellan* space-craft sent back from Venus, becoming the first human to "see" large swaths of the planet. His master's was in planetary geology. And his moment of disillusionment came not when he applied to be an astronaut and was rejected—only a handful of the 5,000 applicants made the cut, and he could apply again—but when he realized that modern astronauts were going only as far as the International Space Station.

"My dream was to go on land somewhere," he told us. "I decided I just wanted to explore Earth more." In the grad-school library at Arizona State, he flipped through career books until he found the geophysical firm that worked in the most countries across the globe. That it turned out to be a petroleum-surveying company bothers the environmentalist in him, but Greg's story illustrates how hard a guy has to work these days to find something to explore. He's had to make some sacrifices.

For Greg, the end of the Cold War was a window of real, if fleeting, opportunity. One of his favorite stories is about when the walls were coming down, and he happened to be in Vienna, and he happened to have a raft, and he happened to notice that the Danube River flowed straight into Czechoslovakia. He climbed in and floated to Bratislava. "There was no passport control, and nobody said anything," he recalled. "I just noticed that all the buildings looked different." When he reached the city, he was surrounded by patrol boats with machine guns. When the police realized he was an American—one of the few they had seen—they gave him a hero's welcome, stamping his passport on the spot.

Greg's first geophysical assignment was in the Caspian Sea, which allowed him, during a drunken port call with the mostly Azerbaijani crew, to sneak visa-free into Turkmenistan—a place few Westerners have seen to this day. When the Caspian job was done, in 1999, he and a friend bought a Niva—an old Soviet jeep—and spent months driving it around Georgia and Russia. Siberia was close to China, and China was opening up, so he drifted east, traveling overland until he'd crossed the entire continent. He went to Taiwan, where he became obsessed with learning Mandarin, which he studied until the oil money ran out. "I had to start teaching English," he says.

Globalization kept creeping on, and Greg kept teaching—first in Taiwan, then in Japan. During summers he began leading tours in China for the growing horde of outsiders coming to see it. Asia was becoming less exotic, though Greg himself wasn't. One time he went alone to a Chinese zoo and noticed that everyone was staring at him instead of the monkeys. Trying to lighten up an awkward moment, he hunched over, scratching himself and making ape noises, while the crowd, still expressionless, stared harder.

You might say the confluence project gave Greg newfound purpose. But his brand of modern, confluence-driven exploration poses problems of its own. Our trip to Bolivia, for instance, was originally meant to be a trip to Peru. After I first contacted him, I invited myself along on his next expedition, and we planned it for months—a trek to 12°S 76°W, in the Andes, supposedly the highest confluence in the Western Hemisphere. Then I got a late-night e-mail from him slugged "interesting development." On the DCP Web site, he told me, the Peru confluence had suddenly been demoted to number two, and an obscure point in Bolivia had been elevated to highest in the Americas. The reasons were unclear, and were only slightly less so after Greg's techy explanation:

It looks to me like the project is now using elevations from Google Earth. They originally used elevations from the GT30 1km footprint elevation data. Then, in 2005, I got a hold of the SRTM (Space Shuttle Radar Topography) data (the best data to date), and convinced them to change the data for the top 50 highest confluence points. Now it has changed again, and I've already contacted the project to find out their source. I want to make sure it is worthy.

Greg went into overdrive to find the source of the updated elevation data, spending weeks e-mailing back and forth with a shadowy Google Earth authority code-named Penguin Opus, a German- and French-speaking Scottish topography expert with an Italian name, and various DCP coordinators in Canada, Russia, and the Middle East. I received messages from him with titles like "Russian plot," "a plot of points," and, eventually, "Bolivia." It was finally confirmed: We were going to 18°S 69°W, a confluence that was—according to all the best data sets—at least 300 feet higher than the one in Peru.

A truism of confluence hunting is that you never really know what the obstacles will be. In a string of last-minute e-mails from Brazil, Greg advised Paolo and me to be ready for anything. What looked "so inviting" on Google Earth could be treacherous in real life. We should bring crampons and ice axes. We should bring a tent and a stove. We should factor in extra time for things to go wrong.

"It could be a walk in the park," he wrote, "but, as in a lot of confluence hunting, you just need to be prepared for the unforeseen."

We arranged to rent a Land Cruiser in a dimly lit office in Uyuni, arriving at 6 P.M. and hoping they could have it ready by six the next morning. Time was running out for Criso and Maria, who we were told would pilot the jeep, to buy fuel and supplies, but Greg was meticulous, almost rudely so, reading a checklist out loud and asking repeatedly about water, food, spare tires, hotels along the way, what the food was, what the hotels were like, how many spares there were, how well Criso knew his vehicle, etc.

"I've had problems with Land Cruisers in Tibet," he explained. He was agitated, as if the closer he got to the confluence, the more it weighed on him, the more he wanted to control the variables. In the morning, he got up at 5 A.M., an hour early, waking himself just to organize his backpack and ensure all his gadgets were in order. He was so thorough that he was still the last one ready.

Between Uyuni and the confluence is the world's largest salt flat, some 65 miles by 65 miles. The Salar de Uyuni sits at 12,000 feet, is shaped like an amoeba, and is filled, unsurprisingly, with salt: man-made salt mounds, a salt hotel, a salt highway, saltwater springs, and blinding salt-pan views from cactus-dotted "islands." We rolled onto it at dawn, and Greg was serene again, happy about Criso and Maria's (short-lived) familiarity with our surroundings. We stopped briefly at a salt-mining operation. We ate breakfast at the salt hotel, at a table made of salt. Undisturbed, the Salar's perfectly white surface had dried to form a mosaic of interlocking hexagons that stretches miles across the emptiness, and in the distance we sometimes saw mirages or speeding trucks whose hum sounded like a jet taking off. Greg bent over to lick one of the ridges "just to make sure" it was salt. It was.

Our route took us less than a mile from 20°S 68°W, low-hanging fruit that had been bagged twice before. Perhaps for the benefit of Paolo and me, Greg decided we should go for it anyway, so after lunch he and I pulled out our GPS units and watched the numbers tick down. On Greg's wrist was an altimeter/compass watch. He had the Google Earth screen shots on his music player as well as printouts of the same, plus photocopies of some military topos. He had a backup GPS, a backup camera, and a backup compass in his bag. Combined with the arsenals Paolo and I have, this brought us to a total of three compasses, four GPS units, six cameras, and perhaps three dozen maps. We were ready for action, and I could not deny the excitement of the moment when it came.

"Tell him to slow down and go to the left," Greg told me, and I relayed his message in Spanish. Criso veered off the track, and the hum of our wheels quieted. My GPS showed the distance dropping rapidly: 1.35 kilometers, 900 meters, 250 meters, 45 meters. "Now, now, now . . . Stop!" Greg yelled. We threw open the doors. It was windy out and very cold, and the salt crunched underfoot as I waved my GPS back and forth, trying to follow it in.

"Now I usually get out my compass and try to figure out where I need to go to make the zero," Greg said. "The GPS read .007, which meant we were a little south." We strode north, then slightly east, and my newer GPS locked it in: 20°00.000'S, 68°00.000'W, accuracy plus or minus three meters. "Photograph it as quickly as possible," Greg advised. "It'll change." He lurched back and forth, trying to get his own GPS to zero out—the "confluence dance." Soon he hit it, too, and grabbed for his camera. We snapped photos in the four cardinal directions—of salt, salt, salt, and salt, respectively. Greg pulled out a pad and scribbled some notes. He smiled. We were done. As we left, he took a one-boliviano coin from his pocket and placed it on the confluence—a gift for any brave explorers who followed.

Thus baptized, we drove out of the Salar and into the unknown, following a web of dirt roads toward Sajama, stopping for directions in almost every windswept village, relying more and more on the GPS and map. In one village, Llica, Criso asked the guys at an auto shop which direction we should go. Straight, they said. We passed a family of quinoa farmers working a barren patch of dust, Maria hopped out, and we all watched as they pointed back the way we'd come.

We found our way across a smaller salt flat, then rumbled through the Altiplano, passing deserted villages, sand dunes, and Stonehenge-like clusters of rock tombs, called chullpas, which Maria said are filled with the bones of an ancient race of midgets who were killed by the sun. We picked up—and got directions from—a hitchhiking grandmother and her four grandchildren, backtracked out of the bog, talked down some soldiers who wanted a bribe, got lost and found our way a half-dozen times, and overnighted in a truckers' hostel in a run-down border town. Now, on the afternoon of the second day, we've finally reached Sajama National Park, where we see a herd of alpacas grazing on the flanks of the namesake volcano.

Opposite the volcano is the confluence peak—we recognize it on sight—and Greg has a final request for Criso and Maria: that we use the remaining daylight to detour toward the peak and scout our line. They bristle. "Our job was to take you to Tomarapi," Criso says.

"No, no, no—we need to get as close as we can," Greg says, his voice tense. "It's so ridiculous. Of all the out-of-the-way stuff we did today, we can't do this? This is the most important thing."

They go silent and make long faces, hoping he'll relent. He doesn't. Just before Tomarapi, we turn off and drive most of the way up the jeep track and stare at our destiny. It looks more or less like it did on Google Earth. Even so, we use Paolo's long lens to shoot close-up photos of the confluence, the volcanic bulge it sits upon, and the cliffs guarding the approach. That night, after a quinoa-and-soup dinner at the eco-lodge, we pull out my laptop, upload Paolo's photos, and compare them with maps and printouts until we're certain our ridge route is best. Paolo and I go to bed early, but Greg stays up late, shuffling and organizing, readying his pack, his cameras, and his multiple GPS units.

~~~~~~

At 5:30 A.M., with the world still dark, Greg sits upright in bed and flicks on his headlamp. For 15 minutes he stays wrapped in his blankets and barely moves, the beam of his headlamp conveniently pointed across the room at my face as I try to keep sleeping. Various alarms—on watches, cell phones, etc.—begin going off, but he doesn't move to disarm them, instead grumbling about the cold and loudly blowing his nose. He gets up and puts on deodorant, then begins walking back and forth across the room, pulling things out of bags, putting them in other bags, scattering his gear about the floor. Paolo and I get dressed. When Greg finishes his shuffling, he remembers his contact lenses and walks to the bathroom to put them in. He takes a moment to slick back his hair in the mirror. We're ready to go.

A park employee picks us up, and after 20 minutes we're at 14,700 feet, throwing on our packs in a boulder field near the foot of the ridge. The temperature hovers around freezing. A herd of wild vicuñas stands a few hundred yards uphill, and the clouds hugging the surrounding volcanoes are already burning off. Before we start walking, Greg pulls out a bag of coca leaves Maria gave him. He kneels and sticks a few down an animal hole near a big rock—his way of currying favor with the native goddess of the earth: "Uh, OK, Pachamama, here you go." He also sticks a few leaves in his mouth, hoping they'll make his altitude headache go away.

We walk up the scrub slope, passing juniper-like queñua trees—the highest-altitude trees in the world. The false summit is dead ahead, bathed in early sunlight; glacier-covered Sajama is directly at our backs.

"I think this is going to be easy—a piece of cake," says Paolo.

"I think it's going to be harder than we think," says Greg.

"Tomorrow we should go on a jeep tour," says Paolo.

"Let's think about tomorrow tomorrow," says Greg. "Right now let's think about the confluence."

After an hour and a half, we gain the ridge, which greets us with a blast of cold wind that nearly knocks Greg and Paolo down. The confluence is before us, somewhere on an escarpment in the middle of a vast bowl of scree—our first good view. Greg waves his arms and yells through the wind: "I've got to take a bearing!" When he's done, we back away from the edge until we're out of the wind. He fiddles with his altimeter watch and peers up the hill. "You know," he says, "people thought it was stupid when Edmund Hillary tried to climb Everest, too."

The altitude sinks in. My head starts to pound. Greg starts taking break after break, hunching over with his right hand on his knee, almost hyperventilating. Only Paolo seems unaffected: He's bounding ahead, waiting for us at every rise and flat spot. We reach the final pitch just after 2 P.M., and Greg stuffs his mouth with the rest of the coca leaves. He surges forward—the first to reach the false summit, the first to take in its vertiginous views of Sajama, the twin volcanoes to our west, and the twin lakes at their base. Paolo and I follow, and in that instant, confluence hunting makes perfect sense: It's an excuse to see places like this. For 20 minutes, we take photos in every direction. Greg gets antsy. "All right, all right, let's go get it," he says. "Let's go." We snap a few last shots. When we look up again, he's gone, running with newfound energy downhill toward the confluence.

Paolo and I follow Greg's footsteps down a scree slope, skirting the couloirs and the first band of cliffs, then sliding on our tails down a ten-foot patch of steep, icy snow. Greg waits just long enough at the saddle for me to catch up. "We're 134 meters away," he says, breathless. We run up a small knoll, weave through vertical fins of reddish rock, and start dropping again. "One hundred meters!" he yells. Up ahead, the escarpment appears to fall off into nothing. "What the hell is on the other side of this?" he asks—this isn't how Google Earth said it would be.

We proceed slowly. The rock underfoot is loose. The wind picks up. At 40 meters out, we begin downclimbing a steep slope that rolls over into a true cliff; at 17 meters, Greg ditches his pack and descends alone into a scree-filled chute. Below him, one slip away, is a yawning drop tens or hundreds of feet high—we can't see the bottom. The wind sends pebbles avalanching over the edge. "I'm going to try to get all zeroes," Greg yells. He inches downward, his left hand on the rock wall, his right hand holding the GPS. He swings the receiver right, then left—17°59.994'S, 69°00.008'W . . . 17°59.993'S, 69°00.006'W. He's still a dozen meters away. Shaking, with gloved hands, he documents the imperfect visit—photos of the north, east, south, and west—and then gets a slightly better reading, 17°59.994'S, 69°00.000'W, that appears as he and I scramble out. And he's not done.

Back on the rim we find a shivering, suddenly delirious Paolo, who's being blasted by the wind as he shoots photos of Greg's conquest. His Camelbak has frozen; his head hurts; he's dehydrated. Greg jogs past him. "Wait, wait, where are you going?" Paolo asks. Greg tells him we're going the long way around—a route back that could take us closer to the base of the cliff, closer to the confluence. "It's getting really windy," Paolo growls. "It's getting late. If anything happens now, it's a big deal. If anyone gets hurt, it's a big deal."

Greg is unmoved, and I, admittedly, back him up—I want to see him bag it. We climb to the saddle and race down a scree field, surfing on sliding rocks and kicking up clouds of sulfurous yellow dust. Our shadows grow long. Once parallel to the base of the cliff, Greg begins to traverse a steep slope of loose rock—an inch or two of gravel over frozen earth, too slippery to stand on. He pulls out his ice ax for extra purchase. He crawls eastward like a crab, confluence-bound, and for a moment I believe nothing will stop him. But then he slips and falls, and he slips and falls again, and he sits down and stares wistfully at his prize, 200 yards away. Reality sets in. He starts to descend.

The slope funnels us to the bottom of a broad valley, and we're alone in the Andes, our footprints the only ones as we tromp through the sand. Sajama is a beacon, the last thing illuminated by the fleeting daylight, and the wind is gone, the air calm. We walk toward the volcano and slow our pace. Greg gives Paolo some of his water. He looks up at the cliff. "Well, we got the confluence," he says. "We didn't get to check out that bottom part, but we got it. We got the highest confluence in the Americas." He pauses. "I might have to come here someday with ropes," he says. He pauses again. "We can still go back tomorrow and get the bottom," he says. "I mean, if you guys want to."

(Originally published June 2008)

THE BROTHERHOOD OF THE VERY EXPENSIVE PANTS

STEVEN RINELLA

Brit Eaton is the best of a curious breed of fortune hunters combing old mine shafts and barns across the West for vintage denim. He's discovered $50,000 worth of clothes in a single day, and his clients include Ralph Lauren and Levi's. We dispatched Steven Rinella to join him on a search for the blues.

When I say that Brit Eaton was in the doghouse, I don't mean that he was in trouble with his wife. I mean he was literally inside a dog's house, with just his boots sticking out the door.

I shone my flashlight over Brit's back to watch as he picked through the layers of old rags and clothes making up the bed of the occupant, a heeler with a baseball-size cyst on her belly. The dog's owner, a sixtyish rancher named Mike, from Modena, Utah, was too distracted to pay much attention to his visitor's behavior. Just that morning, Mike had learned that a mountain lion had somehow infiltrated the eight-foot-tall fence surrounding the headquarters of the Meathook Ranch, which his grandfather had established in 1903. He was cautiously watching a juniper thicket above a corral of calves. "I'm a son of a bitch on following tracks," he was saying, "so you better believe when I say it was a big cat." Mike turned back toward the doghouse and was surprised to see Brit's backside. He pointed a thumb at Brit. "People make money all sorts of ways, don't they?"

Brit, 38, is of medium height and solid build. He has a stern, square face that would be suitable on an evening newscaster if it weren't for a tangled scar above his lip that resembles a strand of barbed wire. He makes his living scouring the old ranches, ghost towns, abandoned homesteads, and forgotten antique shops of the American West in search of vintage clothes. When most people hear the word vintage, they think of bell-bottoms from the seventies, but Brit's definition of that word goes many decades deeper into American fashion. He has a particular interest in denim workwear from the late 19th and early 20th centuries. His company's name is Carpe Denim, and he sells his products, or "pieces," to a disparate array of clients, including Hollywood wardrobe departments, private collectors, and companies like Levi's, Ralph Lauren, the Gap, and Dickies.

He is unabashed about his prowess; he freely admits to being "the best person in the country at finding old clothes, maybe the best in the world." In a career spanning more than ten years, he has found hundreds of thousands of sellable vintage-clothing items. He once sold a pair of chinos with links to a soldier from the Spanish-American War to a Japanese collector for $12,000, his personal record for a single piece, and he's discovered as much as $50,000 worth of clothes in a single day. Brit is deathly afraid of competition—there are a handful of other vintage-denim hunters—so he's skittish talking about money. It's clear, though, that he earns an annual income pushing well into six figures.

Despite these numbers, Brit has yet to find a piece that approaches the pinnacle of the vintage market. In the summer of 2008, an eBay seller going by "Burgman" auctioned a pair of circa-1890s, candle-wax-encrusted Levi's that he claimed were found in a mine in California's Mojave Desert. On July 30, the bidding closed at $36,099. In 2001, an anonymous person sold a pair of 100-plus-year-old jeans, discovered in a Nevada mining town, on eBay through Butterfields, a San Francisco–based auction house. The jeans were purchased by their original manufacturer, Levi Strauss & Co., for $46,532. With stakes this high, Brit isn't eager to reveal his hunting grounds, but I'd arranged to spend a week with him on what he calls a "denim safari" and had met up with him at his warehouse, in Durango, Colorado. He was in good spirits; the day before, a couple of designers from Dickies had visited and made a substantial purchase. The warehouse is a garage-like structure with overhead doors, chaotically stacked wall to wall and floor to ceiling with plastic crates of vintage clothes bearing cryptic labels that Brit himself can hardly understand. "I hide stuff from myself so I can't sell it right away," he said. "It's a retirement plan."

From the warehouse, we'd driven to Brit's home, on the outskirts of town along the Animas River. In the morning, he said goodbye to his wife of four years, Kelly, and their three-year-old son, Zealand. Brit loaded a barebones collection of camping gear into the back of his Toyota Tundra and we headed west toward the Great Basin, between the Rocky Mountains and the Sierra Nevada. "There's a chance we won't find anything out there," he warned, "but it's the best place to be if you want to find something that's going to shake up the world."

Late the following morning, we'd rolled into Modena, Utah, a once-thriving railroad community reduced by time to little more than a ghost town. The bank, hotel, and bars were all closed and permanently shuttered. The only sign of life was a middle-aged woman in a sedan who was sorting mail she'd pulled from a P.O. box. Brit's intuition suggested, correctly, that this woman lived on an old ranch, and he stepped out of his truck to make the somewhat preposterous suggestion that she let him dig through her closets and attics. Earlier, Brit had complained that the rain was a detriment to this particular approach. "People associate storms with strangers and trouble," he said.

If the storm didn't scare her off, I was thinking, Brit's clothing might. He was wearing an olive-green 1940s canvas hunting vest, oversize 1950s fatigue pants, beat-to-hell leather boots of indeterminate age, and a white henley-style shirt from the 1920s. He explained to the woman that he pays good money for the sorts of things he was wearing and that it's not uncommon for him to fork over a thousand dollars for a piece that most people wouldn't even give to the Salvation Army.

"You know how kids nowadays buy jeans that are faded and full of holes?" he asked her. "Well, clients rely on guys like me to find things for design inspiration." The woman looked at Brit as if he were asking her to strip right then and there, and she said that we better talk to her husband, Mike, about eight miles up the canyon. "But wait an hour," she said. "He's dealing with a lion right now."

Brit Eaton's path into the vintage-denim business was as circuitous as the occupation itself. The son of an investment banker and a mother with an interest in archaeology, he was born in Princeton, New Jersey, in 1970 and raised in a home dating back to the 18th century. His mother, Landis, believes that Brit inherited "the looking-for-things genes" from her. During spring-cleaning season, she would strap him into a car seat and drive around to see what their neighbors had put out on the curb. "He never liked to wear anything but old stuff, and he was always an entrepreneur," she says. As a kid, he sold pumpkins and lemonade at a roadside stand, and when he got a little older he tried expanding his product line to include lead toy soldiers that he produced with a Bunsen burner and a hand-casting mold. He remembers taking some of his product to a local Kmart in an unsuccessful bid to broker a wholesale contract.

In 1988, Brit enrolled at Rollins College, in Winter Park, Florida. He spent his junior year in a semester-at-sea program that took him around the world, and the journey left him with a deep wanderlust. After graduating, in 1992, he shipped an old Harley-Davidson to Rotterdam, Holland, thinking he'd tour Europe on two wheels. He rode the bike up to Norway, where he sold it for twice what he'd paid. Brit knew a solid business opportunity when he saw one, so he returned to the U.S. and escorted three more Harleys to Europe in 1993. He might have stayed in the motorcycle-import-export business if he hadn't gone to a party one night in Princeton, fallen into a window well, and broken a few ribs. "That made it pretty much impossible to kick-start old bikes," he says.

Over the next few years, he racked up an impressive roamer's résumé: He was thrown in jail in Greece; drove a cab in Madison, Wisconsin; created and sold T-shirts at Grateful Dead concerts; sold ice cream on nudist beaches in Holland; got caught up in a multilevel marketing scheme in Florida; and worked for a company that organized trekking expeditions for Americans traveling in Europe. In early 1997, he took a job working on a swordfish long-liner out of Puerto Rico. He was confined to his quarters for insubordination, but the trip had a positive outcome. A fishing captain from another boat mentioned to Brit that his mother worked for an import-export agent who had a 1,000-pound, compression-packed bale of used Levi's in a Florida warehouse. It reminded Brit of something he'd heard a few years before, when a Norwegian Harley-Davidson customer suggested he import vintage Levi's along with bikes.

Brit returned to Florida in April 1997 and bought the bale for $750, then took it to a home where he was staying in Fort Lauderdale. When he cut the bale's straps, it exploded into a room-size pile of denim that his friends called Mount Levi. "Those jeans were in horrible shape," Brit recalls. "Full of holes, ripped up." Rather than ship them overseas, he spent his nights patching the jeans and his days trying to sell them at flea markets, three pairs for $10. Profits were skimpy. "It was absolutely the lowest point of my life," he says.

But Brit noticed something unusual at the flea markets. Some vintage dealers would inspect his stacks of jeans and excitedly pluck out individual pairs for purchase regardless of condition. That's when Brit began to learn about big E's and little e's. Before 1971, Levi's jeans had an uppercase E printed on the tab sewn into the rear right pocket. After 1971, the company switched it to lowercase. In a general sense, a pair of Levi's is considered vintage when it has a big E, and these are much more valuable in the eyes of connoisseurs. (Vintage big E's are unrelated to Levi's premium Capital E line.) Brit learned about dozens of such categories for different brands, including classifications exclusive to the earliest types of jeans. He educated himself in the nuances of rivets, stitching, denim types, labels, and suspender buttons. "Jeans have their own language," he said. "It takes a while to figure it out."

Levi's is easily the most deep-pocketed consumer of vintage jeans. The company's historian, Lynn Downey, a self-described "obsessed vintage lunatic," explained that Levi Strauss effectively invented "jeans" when he began putting rivets into the seams of denim pants in 1873. In 1906, the company's four-story warehouse burned down after the great San Francisco earthquake, destroying their inventory. Currently, the oldest piece in their collection is from 1879. "Levi's has produced items that I've never seen," she said. This is a problem because vintage clothes represent the history of fashion and also mark the future. "Levi's designers are the primary users of our archives," she said. In 1996, the company launched its Levi's Vintage Clothing line, featuring replicas of recovered pieces. Brit has conducted a few deals with Downey, and he refers to her type of high-dollar denim as "big game."

Because Levi's didn't start selling jeans in the eastern U.S. until after World War II, there was an inherent limit to what could be found there. So in August 1997, Brit loaded his Jeep and migrated to Durango, Colorado. He began traveling up and down the Rocky Mountains until he knew the location and hours of just about every small-town thrift shop where someone might unknowingly drop off an item of surprising rarity and value. He would buy pickup loads of clothing at Goodwill prices and then sort out the more valuable items for shipment to his growing clientele of domestic and international vintage-clothing dealers. Jeans remained his passion, but he also developed an eye for other items that would get snapped up by savvy shoppers and Wild West enthusiasts: canvas work clothes, concho belts, biker jackets, hand-tooled cowboy boots, decorative saddle blankets, antique fur coats, riding chaps, cowboy hats, army surplus, and even homemade apparel.

Perhaps the most important thing Brit learned while hunting vintage clothes in thrift shops is that thrift shops are not the best places for guys like him to hunt vintage clothes. He didn't want the things that a person had recently quit wearing and donated; rather, he wanted the things that a person's great-grandfather had quit wearing and tossed into a dusty corner on a homestead, where it was forgotten about for a few generations. "I used to walk into a good thrift shop and my palms would get sweaty," Brit told me. "And then one day I couldn't get excited by thrift shops. It's like I used to enjoy firecrackers, but now it takes dynamite to get me high."

Finding a $40,000 pair of jeans requires luck and daring, but, most important, it requires leads. Brit collects leads while talking to people in bars, cafés, hotels, gas stations, and antique shops. Good leads include the phone numbers of multigenerational ranch families, addresses of small-town historical societies, favorite saloons of modern-day miners, and even descriptions of landmarks leading to the properties of crazy old hermits who live up in the hills with collections of junk and arsenals of weapons.

As he follows these tips, Brit sometimes stumbles into a series of unusual events that cascade along for days. Before we even made it to the Meathook Ranch, where the lion had been trapped inside a fence, we had stopped in western Utah to visit the home of a retiree named Theo who spends his days tinkering with a vast collection of antique steam-engine tractors and compressors. Brit suspected that there might just be some old denim mixed in with all that old iron.

Theo was skeptical. "If it had been around that long, I would have sopped up some grease with it by now," he said. His comment reminded me of something Brit had told me earlier: "My number-one rule in this business is to never believe anything I hear. The more someone tells me they don't have anything, the more I know they do." Sure enough, Brit reached beneath a leaky outdoor spigot and picked up a small-game item that I would become very jealous of. It was a black T-shirt with MACBETH printed on the front in an ominous font, and it resembled the faux-faded, distressed T-shirts that college freshmen buy at Urban Outfitters. Except this shirt's fading had happened thanks to endless doses of sun and occasional spurts of water, so it was infinitely cooler. Clutching the ten bucks that Brit gave him, Theo was beginning to agree. "It was all just rags to me," he said. "Not no more!"

We spent much of the next day at the Meathook Ranch, where Mike the rancher segued seamlessly between searching for the lion and telling stretchers. "My grandfather didn't buy this ranch," he bragged. "He just paid the outlaws and murderers who were living here to move along." As we walked around, Mike pointed to various places where he'd allegedly killed 250 lions over the years. Brit scurried behind us like an unleashed dog, prying and poking into every trash pile, junked car, corral, smokehouse, and outhouse. After an hour of searching, he realized that the good stuff was long gone, having met its usual fate over the years in burning barrels and county dumps. "I was dying to get in here," he whispered in my ear. "Now I'm dying to get outta here."

When we finally shook free of the Meathook, we stumbled into a coyote trapper outside Modena whose trailer home fronted a collection of ramshackle log cabins. Right away, I saw the waistband of a pair of jeans stuffed between two cabin logs as chinking—a common frontier use for old rags. The jeans had a buckle and straps riveted into the waistband in the back. Known as "bucklebacks," such work pants were prevalent from the earliest days of jeans until about 1940.

We were on the right track. We crawled down into a root cellar and found banks of shelves still stocked with the fractured remains of canning jars. An ancient shirt was wedged into a doorjamb, but it turned to powder when Brit tried to carefully pull it free. When I creaked open the door of a neighboring cellar, I was greeted by the unmistakable snicker of a rattlesnake. I eased the door shut and remembered a story Brit had told me about the time he crawled into a mine and heard the hissing sound of a snake coming from the vicinity of his crotch. He retreated from the serpent with a mad dash while an excruciating burning sensation spread across his groin. Once outside, he realized that he'd actually been "bitten" by a canister of pepper spray he'd pocketed in order to defend himself against cave-dwelling beasts.

After Modena, Brit swore me to secrecy about the places we'd be visiting in "the vintage happy-hunting grounds." We were on our way to visit a man I'll call Cowboy, who lived on the outskirts of a small mining town whose claim to fame is that, during its infancy, 75 citizens died in gunfights before a single person died of natural causes. Brit wanted to question Cowboy about a rumor he'd heard from the man's ex-wife that involved a mysterious building full of 1920s clothing.

"Cowboy is six-four and weighs 270 pounds," said Brit. "He's a Korean War vet and a mountain man and, well, basically a hobo junk collector." We found Cowboy at the center of the vast, moatlike collection of junked cars he uses as a security barrier around a small refuge of trashed camping trailers. His specific location inside an aluminum motor home was betrayed by a rising column of smoke out front where a pot of coffee was resting on a Weber grill packed full of smoldering sagebrush. Cowboy was passed out, his head propped on a stack of rags near an open window. Brit yelled inside to wake him, which startled the hell out of the man. He was drunk, or seemed to be, and he ranted and raved for a few minutes while expressing an intense lack of interest in talking about old clothes.

Brit and I drove into town and parked in front of the diner where Cowboy gets his mail. We went inside and took a seat next to Uncle Teddy, a man in his seventies with a severe comb-over hairstyle. Brit introduced Uncle Teddy as someone who'd once sold him a buffalo-hide jacket. As they talked, Brit made the mistake of dropping the name of his associate, Cowboy. "He wouldn't make a pimple on a cowboy's ass," said Uncle Teddy. Then he told us that Cowboy had recently been prosecuted for stealing another man's outhouse.

"What was so special about the outhouse?" I asked.

"What was special is that it didn't belong to Cowboy," said Uncle Teddy.

We had just enough daylight for one more lead, and we headed to a mining camp occupied by an old man who was sacked out in another trailer. It was getting dark. There was no immediate reply when Brit honked his truck's horn and rapped on the door, but a frantically barking dog suggested that someone was around.

After about 15 minutes, the man revealed himself by kicking open the trailer door from the inside. He had a long white beard and screamed "What's going on out here?!" in a voice that would have made John Wayne soil his pants. He was toting a shotgun, and he detained us at gunpoint while shouting indecipherable commands. It took a few moments for us to realize that he was stone deaf. Brit started yelling, "We'll never come back!" while we walked backwards with our hands in the air and then eased into the truck and sped off.

We settled into a bar that I'll call the Peephole and had a couple of shots to toast that the man hadn't pulled the trigger. When I lifted my third vodka, an hour later, my hand was still shaking. Brit was at the end of the bar talking to a drunken man who was covered in coal ash and wearing a denim chore coat. "This guy's got great leads," he said.

~~~~~~

The leads from the Peephole kept us busy for a couple more days, though they didn't produce any exciting finds beyond a human leg bone that I plucked from a hole in the ground after being directed to the location by a local landowner. The waistband from the buckleback jeans outside Modena was the closest we'd come to a big-game find, though the back of the truck continued to pile up with small-game items that might fetch $10 or $50 or $200. In addition to Theo's MACBETH T-shirt, we had a stack of saddle blankets, assorted western-style button-up shirts, a pair of 1970s corduroy pants, a beat-up piece of Filson luggage, a Victorian-era women's coat made of velvet, a homemade coat rack of welded horseshoes and fencing staples, a leather rifle scabbard, old riding chaps, assorted trucker's hats, and a pair of cowboy boots that were so stiff with age, they felt bronzed. (Brit soaks leather goods back to life in neat's-foot oil, which he buys by the drum.)

It was better stuff than you're going to see in 90 percent of college-town secondhand stores, but Brit was hardly impressed; in fact, he was growing increasingly annoyed over our inability to make a major score. He likes to describe his occupation as equal parts Antiques Roadshow and The Crocodile Hunter, but I was beginning to see traces of the Tasmanian Devil creeping into the mix. I'd been marking my notebook every time we went into a building (I registered more than 40 marks the first day), but now Brit was flying through structures with such rapidity that I hardly had time to pull it out. Rather than walking around the perimeter of a 30-foot-deep chasm in the center of an abandoned mill, Brit went over it by trotting along a partially rotten six-inch beam, his arms flailing out to his sides for balance. Several times I watched him pull himself up through holes in rotten ceilings only to bust through in a shower of pigeon shit and dust. One time, blasting down a dirt road, I looked at his truck's speedometer and saw he was driving three times the posted speed limit while packing his mouth with carrots and bread washed down with a Starbucks Frappuccino.

The numbing speed of our travel was punctuated by a few short moments of crystalline excitement. On our last full day in the field, we ran into a farm kid and his pack of hunting dogs in a wide irrigated valley bordered by rugged, chalk-white mountains. He said it'd be OK to poke around for old clothes in a chain of abandoned farm buildings scattered along the river to the north. Brit pored over most of the buildings, leaving his truck running outside and wielding his flashlight in a way that reminded me of an FBI agent conducting a drug raid. Instead of yelling "Police!" he constantly shouted "Snakes!" in an effort to scare off rattlers.

But there was one old house where Brit slowed his pace and came to a complete stop. When I stepped inside the kitchen door, I could see why. It seemed as though someone had wandered off decades ago, leaving behind evidence of a very simple life. Mice-gnawed food crates were scattered about. A cupboard contained the sopping-wet pages of a novel published in 1918. A woodstove and chimney stood against the wall. In a corner by the door was an old pile of clothing that had rotted into a dirt-like mound. I walked into the main room and was startled when a large raptor dropped down from a rafter and, with a pump of its wings, pushed itself out a window.

"Take a look in that second chimney," Brit said. I noticed a single section of stovepipe poking through the living-room ceiling and attached to nothing but air. I peered upward into the pipe and was surprised I couldn't see sunlight. When my eyes adjusted to the dark, I let out a whoop. What I was seeing was unmistakable: Some bygone resident had grown weary of the cold drafts from the chimney and had plugged it with fabric. I climbed up to fetch it, but the roof was so decrepit that the chimney rolled off and landed outside in the tumbleweed. I raced outside and removed from the pipe a cylindrical wad of denim. The top of the ball was bleached white from the daily doses of sun that managed to peek inside. The underside was still blue, like the color on the knees of a pair of 501's when they're finally ready to give out. The denim crackled as it unfurled, and the bleached spot spread in a tie-dye pattern. I checked the label: J.C. PENNEY.

Brit said the pants might be from the 1940s or even earlier, a great find if it weren't for the size. I held them up to my waist, and the hems barely came down to my knees. They were made for a little boy. I was still holding the jeans as we walked back toward the truck, and I couldn't help but wonder about the slow line of circumstances that might have played out inside that house. A couple of times I looked over my shoulder, irrationally expecting to see some poor little kid off in the sagebrush wearing nothing but his underwear. I found myself thinking that this family might've liked that their old clothes were actually worth something in this day and age. I recalled something from just a few days before, when Brit was negotiating with a rancher's wife over a cowboy hat that Brit had found in a ten-antless house on her property. He made an offer for the hat, and after accepting the price, the rancher's wife noted that it had belonged to her husband's dead father.

"I shouldn't take the hat then," Brit said. "He might be upset."

The woman silently compared the price of her husband's anger with the price of the hat. Apparently, the hat was worth more.

"Don't worry," she said. "You'll be long gone by the time he gets home."

(Originally published January 2009)

WATERSHIP DOWN DOWN DOWN DOWN DOWN AND (ALAS) DOWN AGAIN

CHRISTOPHER SOLOMON

~~~~~~

Are you the persistent type? Not compared with Dallas Trombley, who's spent countless hours (and about $200,000) on six failed attempts to build and float a raft down the Hudson River from Albany to Manhattan. Even he's not sure why this obsession keeps bringing him back for more dunkings and disappointments— so we sent Christopher Solomon on a quest to figure out what, exactly, floats Trombley's boat.

~~~~~~

Dallas Trombley can't stop himself. He can't stop building rafts and boats, and he can't stop trying to take them down the great river. Six times over the past four summers, he and a shifting array of friends have launched homemade watercraft onto the mighty Hudson and attempted to ride from Albany, New York, to Manhattan—147 scenic miles in all.

Six times they've failed, often spectacularly. Only a few miles into his first voyage, in June 2006, Dallas hit a river buoy and sank. The second time out, he was washed overboard. Once while he was docking, a trolling-motor propeller came loose and plopped into the Hudson's chocolate-milk waters. Dallas, who isn't much for swimming, had to splash for shore with a mooring rope gripped in his teeth.

In pursuit of his Huck Finn dream, he's been shipwrecked, fly-bitten, sunburned, starved, reduced to penury, nearly drowned, and ticketed by the marine police.

Still, he can't stop. During his quest, he's built rafts with a junkyard's worth of materials—rotten fence posts, discarded pallets, fugitive chunks of dock, plastic barrels from a tomato-sauce factory, a motorcycle exhaust pipe, rare-earth magnets, a Katchakid pool safety net, a rowing machine, cement blocks (used as anchors), three citronella candles (for running lights), and deep-cycle batteries, among much else.

Here's the really odd thing, though: Dallas doesn't like building rafts all that much. He just wants to float to New York on one. But even that's not exactly right: He has to do it. The incompleteness is like a sickness Dallas can't get over. He wishes this need didn't consume him so totally. He dreams of a time without rafts—a day, perhaps soon, when he can pack up the tools and the life preservers and do other things. Find a girl. Write a novel. Backpack through Europe.

But for now, he can't think about much else. So he keeps trying. Because this year ... this year will definitely be the year he makes it.

"If there are a thousand steps to this, then we're on step three," Dallas is saying, "and I'm hoping to accomplish steps four through 27 this weekend."

It's a Friday in early April, quitting time, and Dallas is sitting on an Albany barstool, thinking about the weekend construction schedule for his latest raft, Assembly Required, the seventh he'll put in the water. Cool weather is in the forecast. He's worried that the epoxy he's planning to slather on the boat's twin hulls won't dry fast enough.

"Everyone keeps telling me I'm wrong about this," he says, swigging from a Coors Light. "But why can't we just set a number of small fires around the outside of the raft while the epoxy hardens? I mean, it's flammable, but it's not like ... well, it's extremely flammable. But if we do it right, I think we should be OK."

Dallas is a slim, handsome 26-year-old with sleepy eyes, a hairline deep in retreat, and a tattoo on his right biceps that reads live free or die. He works for the state government, as a legislative analyst for the Labor Committee of the New York State Assembly. The job, he says, is "like a mixture of reading Milton and VCR instructions." Still, he enjoys it and he's good at it. He has a love of language and a philosophical bent. Sometimes he'll quote John Locke or George S. Patton out of the blue. Today, he came into the bar with a fedora set far back on his head—like a gambler at the racetrack—and a copy of *Washington: The Indispensable Man*.

Between more gulps of Coors, a confession: This year's raft is a little behind schedule, and he's worried that he won't make his hoped-for launch date of July 29.

As Dallas sketches the boat on a bar napkin for me, it's obvious why he's running behind. This craft is no simple log platform lashed together with rope. Over time, Dallas's designs have become increasingly lavish in their complexity and aesthetic. This year, he's drawn up plans for a sleek, catamaran-like boat, with two enclosed fiberglass hulls joined by a center cockpit. Building it, he estimates, will take 500 hours and cost around $8,000.

"The idea in my head was a '69 GTO," he says. "I don't want there to be any square angles on it. I want it to be all curves." Propulsive power will come from humans (rowing) and from a pair of four-foot wind turbines, spinning on poles, that will supply juice to a trolling motor. As far as Dallas is concerned, this raft— the ne plus ultra of all previous hard lessons learned—is missing only one thing. "If we didn't think we'd get in trouble," he says, "we'd build a PVC-pipe cannon filled with confetti to fire when we got to New York City."

Why this obsession? It began with an offhand comment. In the fall of 2005, at the start of Dallas's senior year in college at SUNY Albany, he and a few friends were sitting on the shores of the Wallkill River in New Paltz, shooting the breeze. Somebody said, "Wouldn't it be awesome to take a boat all the way down to New York? Get some good friends, some beer, and just float with the rhythms of the big river—no gas engines allowed!"

Everybody laughed. But in Dallas something clicked. "All you'd need is some wood and a bunch of, like, you know, floaty shit," he said. "We'll say we're protesting America's reliance on fossil fuels." Everybody laughed again.

"You guys are full of shit," Dallas's girlfriend at the time said, "but I hope you do it."

"Oh, we will," he and a friend said at the same time.

Five years later, at the home of Dallas's parents in the town of New Baltimore— where the raft's shell awaits—Dallas and Rob Babcock-Ellis, his friend since the fifth grade and a frequent first mate, are eating Saturday-morning breakfast before getting down to work. A framed sign in the den reads, welcome to the nut house.

Over bacon and eggs, the rafters discuss their epoxy-drying problem. Dallas asks his mom, Sandra, if he can use her hair dryer.

"If you burn it out, you'll buy me another," she says.

"We've gone through more tools from these boat-building expeditions," barks Dallas's dad, Kirk. "My father had a whole garageful of tools we can't find anymore."

"We can find 'em," says Dallas, standing to get to work. "We just need sonar."

Outside, the guys apply strips of fiberglass fabric to the hull they've started, brushing on epoxy that they've warmed in an empty paint can that sits on a hot plate (also belonging to Mom). The epoxy smokes, overheats, turns rock-hard in the can. The guys have to start over, and it occurs to the uninitiated observer that there are unforeseen problems here that might have been foreseen.

Rob, who's 26, is the duo's laconic half, a sales-tax auditor for the state. Unlike Dallas, who finds raft construction onerous—like having to build your own car before racing in the Indy 500—Rob looks forward to the puzzle of it. "I do thoroughly enjoy the building process, and being on the river is a lot of fun, too," he says. "I guess I just really like the whole spectacle of it." What Rob doesn't say is that he's the pragmatic one. Sometimes it seems that his role in the raft-building process has been to make sure Dallas doesn't build his own coffin.

Meanwhile, they plod on, nobly—or perhaps mulishly. Strands of fiberglass drift in the perfumed April air like dandelion fluff, sticking to shirts, to faces.

"Wow, I wonder if we should use safety goggles," says Dallas. Then, like the breeze that carries the strands, the thought passes, and he bends again to his work.

From its source at Lake Tear of the Clouds, in the Adirondacks, all the way down to Battery Park, where Vietnamese immigrants cast for stripers, the Hudson is only 315 miles long, but the imprint it's made on American history and culture is so large that it's hard to put your arms around it. An enormous finger of the Atlantic, the tidal river rolls past Revolutionary War battlefields, vistas painted by Thomas Cole, and the Sleepy Hollow countryside where the Headless Horseman galloped. It rolls past other things, too: past a Superfund site where for years General Electric pumped PCBs straight into the river, and past a sewage plant where an alarm sounds just before scrubbed wastewater boils up beneath you. A drift down the Hudson would treat anyone to a panopticon view of the whole messy beauty and tragedy that is America.

Dallas knew little of the river growing up. Though he was raised just a mile from its banks, the closest he came to nautical experience was eating soft-serve down at the Muddy Rudder. Still, the June after his college graduation, in 2006, Dallas and three friends finished building their first raft. It was square, fashioned from rotting plywood, pallets, and fenceposts, and buoyed by plastic barrels. The finished product flexed like a piece of Velveeta. They dubbed it USS *Crablegs* and provisioned it with five cans of beef stew, a jar of peanut butter, mixed nuts, and a 30-pack of Keystone Light. On launch day, Dallas wore a wide-brimmed leather hat and a canvas jacket with epaulets. Before weighing anchor, he had his comrades load a broken wooden filing cabinet onto the deck.

"Why the fuck are we bringing this cabinet?" Rob complained.

"For effect," Dallas said. "You know, it's like a strongbox."

"The door doesn't shut, the lock doesn't work, and we have nothing of value to put inside it."

"That's why I said 'for effect' and 'it's like a strongbox.'"

At the dock in Coeymans, a few miles south of Albany, Dallas's mother swung a bottle of champagne against the hull. It didn't break. She swung again. It still didn't break. The wood was too soft.

That first trip went … poorly. The raft hit a navigation buoy. The crew was nearly killed by a tanker coming upriver and, soon after that, by a barge. By noon the next day, the raft had begun to tilt and sink. The crew beached against another navigation marker in the middle of the river and, within sight of the Rip Van Winkle Bridge, called the police for a rescue. They'd floated only 15 miles.

Dallas wanted to try again. His crew didn't. At a party in Vermont that summer, he met two strangers who were hiking south on the Appalachian Trail and recruited them to man the second raft. *Crablegs 2.0* would be unsinkable: an old piece of dock yanked out of the weeds behind the Boat House restaurant, in New Baltimore, with a homemade, bicycle-powered paddle wheel in the stern.

If the first raft trip was a farce, the second one was a debacle. The paddle wheel broke. Dallas fell overboard and lost his cell phone and binoculars. Storm waves washed away the tide chart and map. The crew ran out of food. The horseflies were biblical; to elude them, the crewmen held on to the sides and floated in the river. And then there was the wind. Come summer, the prevailing winds on the Hudson blow north, upriver. (This was news to Dallas.) They blew so relentlessly that the raft moved backwards.

"And, God, we ran out of beer," recalls Dallas. "That was really a disaster." After ten days—starving, welted, sunburned, and thirsty—they gave up. Dallas called his parents from a pay phone to get a ride. The next day he dropped the hikers off at the AT.

Dallas thought he was through with his riverman phase. But within several months the urge came back again—with force. In the interim, he'd lost his car, his computer had broken, his girlfriend had dumped him. He had the post-college blues, and it seemed to him that, somehow, rafting to Manhattan would give him purpose. It would be a middle finger to adulthood and its pissant responsibilities; to the ex-girlfriend who was already dating someone else; to the naysayers who couldn't imagine the possibility of success.

It would also be the sort of thing that made a few friends and relatives wonder: Has Dallas lost his mind? No. The way he saw it, he'd found the perfect way to put it to use.

Dallas has a memory from when he was a child. "There'd be a coaster on a table, and it wasn't aligned with the grain of the table," he says. "I'd be watching TV by myself, and I'd just be annoyed by it, and keep lining it up, and having to keep touching it." Later, there were rituals he had to perform before bedtime, and noises he had to make, or a shirtsleeve in the laundry pile he had to fold until it was just so. By 19, the tics had gotten so disruptive that he went to see a doctor. The doc's conclusion: Dallas had obsessive-compulsive disorder.

With OCD, researchers believe, the part of the brain that handles emotional processing is overactive. Sufferers are tortured with anxiety—anxiety about the rumple of a shirt, or germs, or sin. People with OCD try to control their anxiety with rituals, but the rituals themselves become compulsive as they try to keep chaos at bay, like the boy who scrubs his hands raw because he's obsessed about dirt. Sufferers become trapped by the very remedies that are supposed to help. Time vanishes beneath the obsessions and compulsions.

Medications helped Dallas, but he hated the way he felt—nearly too sluggish to move. "Fuck doctors and side effects," he told himself. "I can do it myself." He went off the meds and relabeled his condition "obsessive-compulsive advantage," a signal that he was in control. The self-therapy has worked—mostly. Though Dallas still has OCD, he likes what his mind can do. "I can focus in on something and obsess on it, and work on it all day without doing anything else. So why don't I accept that and try to use it as much as I can?"

Dallas acknowledges that his OCD probably channels into a rather outsize perseverance in the face of poor odds. (He once lost 66 games of darts in a row to Rob but kept playing until he won.) "I really have a hard time letting some things drop," he says. "I want to do something else, but I just can't. It's like an annoying feeling when I haven't mastered something"—he pauses here—"like the Hudson." He laughs. Then his voice lowers. "You fucking river," he says, no longer laughing.

That kind of determination led, in June 2007, to raft three. *The Manhattan Project* consisted of two old dock remnants donated by New Baltimore's Shady Harbor Marina, with a homemade cabin nailed on top. It was the most ambitious raft yet—20 feet long, with a 15-foot mast sporting a tarp sail and a big American flag, and a solar-powered trolling motor at the stern. It looked like a patriotic garage.

It lasted less than a day. The night of castoff, Dallas and three crew members went ashore for provisions. Vandals discovered the raft, snapped the oars, ripped the sail, tossed the motor and batteries overboard, and cut the mooring lines. The marine patrol found it floating, abandoned, and towed it back to the scene of the crime. A quick repair was impossible. Worse, the cops said the guys couldn't leave the raft where it was. Dallas & Co. had spent five months building The Manhattan

Project; now they had to disassemble it plank by plank and burn it in a bonfire. "So much for helping out the environment with our raft trips," Rob said as black smoke lifted into the sky.

Nature's indifference was one thing; human cruelty was another. Dallas was defeated. Then a story ran in the local paper about the vandalized boat. Soon after that, a letter arrived from an old couple urging him onward. Then came a letter from a father with a leukemia-stricken son, who had said, "He can't quit now, Dad, he's got to try again." The letters nagged at Dallas. So did the obsession chewing inside.

The fourth raft was a two-man, stitch-and-glue-construction trimaran that cost nearly $4,500 and took six months to build. When finished, it looked like a handsome little toy boat, riding high in the water, with a comically oversize captain's wheel for steering. Dallas christened it *Excelsior*, the motto of the state of New York.

With each raft, Dallas was learning—about carpentry, marine navigation, knots. If he was failing, he was failing better, as Samuel Beckett said. But still he failed. Floridly. The July 2008 voyage of *Excelsior* redefined "fiasco." The crew forgot sunscreen; fair-skinned Rob blistered horribly. At one point the raft grounded, which bent the keel, making it hard to steer.

Mostly, though, the high-riding raft couldn't beat the southerly winds. Finally, on day seven, dry-heaving and exhausted, Rob said he needed to leave. Dallas put him ashore. A few hours later, Dallas was also fed up. He came ashore and started the six-mile walk along the railroad tracks back to civilization, weighed down with everything he could salvage. Little by little, as he staggered along the tracks, he jettisoned items into the woods until, finally, he hoisted the captain's wheel. Howling and shaking with frustration, he threw it into the bushes.

That did it, Dallas thought. He recognized defeat when he saw it. Then, one night that fall, he dreamed about a new raft. It was big. It had two paddle wheels. "And the waves were going with us, and we were moving, like, ten miles an hour and there was this feeling: 'Yes! We're going to make it!'" Dallas says. "And then I woke up that morning and I just started researching all this stuff on electricity."

All through autumn, in secret, Dallas studied and drew up plans. On New Year's Day he presented them to Rob. They would call it, appropriately, *Assiduity*—the motto of the city of Albany.

The previous rafts had been relatively cramped affairs. Not *Assiduity*. This would be the Queen Mary of homemade rafts: 24 feet long, 12 feet abeam, with a flying bridge rigged for steering, a biodiesel-powered paddle wheel attached to flea-market bike rims, and a screened cabin with a little hunter's stove that the construction crew anointed by frying up a batch of cheese dogs. The raft bobbed atop 50-gallon barrels.

The crew of three spent nearly every weekend for seven months making it. By the time it was completed, in July 2009, it weighed 3,500 pounds, had cost nearly $10,000, and had to be licensed by the state as a marine vehicle.

But the raft's grandiosity would be its undoing. Even before setting sail, the rudder broke. The paddle wheel's $50, special-order belts melted. Dallas switched the propulsion to a propeller turned by a biodiesel engine. In mid-July he took it for a shakedown dash across the river. The setup shook so horribly that all the bolts worked loose. The exhaust pipe fell into the river. The cabin filled with black smoke. Then the prop and shaft dropped off. *Assiduity* was a golden turd.

Dallas decided that he'd lost his simple dream with this pattern of building ever-bigger boats. But there was still some summer remaining to salvage a win. In just three days, he and Rob cobbled together a new raft, a trimaran, from two aluminum canoes and a battered Sunfish sailboat bought from a riverman. He dubbed the new craft *The Mother of Inventions*. Last August, he and Rob made it the farthest yet, 91 miles, before the unrelenting southerly winds finally forced them to give up a mile shy of West Point.

It was the best trip yet, says Dallas. Finally, they'd found the romance of being out on a big river: drifting under the steel webwork of the Hudson's bridges as they growled with car traffic, lying back under the sugar-spill of stars at night as waves licked at the sides of the canoes. "Out on the river at night," says Dallas, "you can't tell where the fireflies end and the stars begin."

It was all too good. They knew they had to try one more time.

The Hudson at New Baltimore is calm and not so wide, and it twinkles in the April sunshine. Trees and pocket parks line its shores. Far downstream, a barge appears from around a bend and thrums slowly upriver. Sitting on the deck of the Shady Harbor Marina, drinking a beer with the raft builders, you can understand the urge to climb aboard something "floaty" on that twinkling river and see what lies beyond the bend.

Sometime during the first week of August—if all goes according to plan—Dallas and Rob will drift south into New York Harbor, take a left at the Statue of Liberty after dodging a few fast-moving ferries, and finally nose up to a park at the base of the Brooklyn Bridge to find expectant friends and family waiting with beer and hugs.

And then what? "The plan is to just enjoy the success there, then turn around and head back," says Dallas, drinking his beer in the sunshine. "I would love to have enough time to get back to Albany." Then he'll be free. Free to write that novel. Free to go to Europe. Free to find that new girlfriend. Just … free. At least until the next obsession comes along.

Later, back at home, his mother whispers, "I hope it works this time."

"We're pushing for Tarrytown this year," says his father.

But the rafters, beers in hand, feel good about their chances. "I don't see anything that could possibly go wrong," says Dallas.

(Originally published September 2010)

REVERSAL OF FORTUNE (LUCKY CHANCE)

ELIZABETH WEIL

Maybe you've never heard of Lucky Chance—born Toby Benham—but the Australian climber, circus act, and all-around stunt monkey was testing the limits of BASE jumping in 2011 when he survived a horrible mountainside crash in France. What happens when a highflier falls to earth? He starts over—no matter how daunting the prospect.

Last January, three months after Lucky Chance woke up from a coma in France and a week after he arrived back home in the suburbs west of Sydney, he put on his oversize monkey costume and hobbled across the street to a playground. There, his mother held a camera and helped Lucky, now 28, make a video.

Lucky had been creating short films since he became Lucky Chance, a name he legally adopted after he dropped out of high school at 15, lived as a rock-climbing bum, and joined Australia's Lennon Brothers circus. The videos are beautiful and terrifying, halfway magical, two-thirds nuts, exploring what it looks like when a young man in his prime pushes his body hard up against the edge of risk. In them, Lucky does handstands on the lips of cliffs. He hurls himself off rock walls holding only a rope. He BASE-jumps from unfamiliar exit points on days when clouds obscure the landing zone. He sets up a diving board on a sheer rock face, inches backward toward the end, and leans back.

"It's physical image creation—art through physicality," explains Lucky, who was born Toby Benham. We're sitting in front of his mom's computer at her house in Emu Plains, where he's come to convalesce and figure out what to do next.

Carol Hahnfeld, a preschool teacher, is one of only a few people who still calls him Toby. Her office is small and stuffy, cluttered with filing cabinets, an ironing board, and old family photos, homey enough to make anyone with a strong taste for adventure want to cannonball from a ledge.

Much of the world met Lucky in July 2011, when a video surfaced of him doing just that. Or, to be more precise, when the world saw Lucky, wearing a pirate costume, do a triple backflip with a double layout from the end of a 100-foot-long climbing rope bolted to a cliff in the Blue Mountains, about two hours from Sydney. Lucky called the apparatus the Death Swing, and in July 2010, a camera crew working on a climbing movie called *Smitten* was there to film him as he flew off and landed with a parachute. But as he rotated, his legs splayed. The chute tangled around one leg, and Lucky fell 560 feet before it finally deployed, 30 feet from the ground. He hit the earth standing and walked away. Lucky's sister, Melanie, a 30-year-old account manager for a financial-analysis firm in Melbourne, told me that the event made her brother feel "a little bit invincible." A video clip of the fall went viral—more than 400,000 hits.

The man sitting next to me in his mother's house looks quite different from the man in that video. His handsome face is lined with scars. The light in his eyes flickers like a wonky fluorescent bulb. His legs get stiff. On August 16, a little over a year after his miracle on the Death Swing, Lucky's name and the cloak of protection it implied betrayed him. In what he estimates was his 500th BASE jump, he hiked down from the village of Les Carroz to a thousand-foot cliff in Magland, near Chamonix in the French Alps. The place is known as a good, accessible spot—the first cliff many BASE jumpers approach upon arriving in France. Lucky chose to jump from Dérivator, a side exit point less steep than the main one, which requires a running start. He planned to leap off and practice his trademark somersaults and flips in flight.

Lucky remembers, or says he remembers, no details of that day. All he knows or will acknowledge is that he was jumping with his best friend, fellow Australian Alex Duncan (who did not respond to interview requests), and that he did the two things he always did before a BASE jump: he checked the wind direction and speed and pushed negative thoughts from his mind. "It is commonly the case that you overestimate the difficulty of a particular jump. This may have been my undoing, but I would never have had it any other way," Lucky told me in his grand archaic style. Much of the short, fantastic life of Lucky Chance feels like a fable: dramatic, timeless, containing a moral—and a little vague. On principle he refused to surrender to risk.

That day in Magland, Lucky's persona or worldview or whatever you want to call it caught up with him. With his wide harlequin's smile and BASE-jumping backpack, he launched himself off the cliff, threw a complicated set of aerials, and hit a rock ledge almost 450 feet below the exit point. According to reports from other jumpers, the day was very windy, and Lucky freestyled (did airborne gymnastics) where he needed to track (put his body in the best position to gain distance from the wall). When he bounced off the granite his chute partially opened, and he wound up suspended, unconscious, from his canopy, which was caught in a tree 300 feet above the grassy landing zone. He suffered a fractured jaw, a broken pelvis, open fractures in his left femur and heel—and a traumatic brain injury. Three French jumpers later retrieved his canopy, which was full of cuts and holes. As one of them, Jean-Michel Peuzin, said, "A canopy in a cliff is no good for karma."

In the first video Lucky made after returning to Australia, he is not Lucky at all. Instead he is a character he calls Stunt Monkey. Before showing me the video, Lucky stood up and walked with his stiff, wide gait across the hall to his childhood bedroom. There, stacked in the corner, next to the twin bed with the floral coverlet, sat a pile of three football-mascot-type costumes: a monkey, a dog, and a bunny. "You have to meet Stunt Monkey," he said. "He's my alter ego. Monkeys like to do all the same things I like to do: climb and swing." Before the accident, Lucky had given Stunt Monkey cameos in several videos. Stunt Monkey—who has a head filled with foam, a brown body, black eyes, and a tan face and belly—front-flipped off the Death Swing cliff wearing a rope and harness. He walked down the sidewalk in Sydney, glanced up at a building, and scaled it unroped. Near the top, Stunt Monkey sat to rest on a windowsill. Then he climbed back down.

That first post-accident video is unbearably sad. Stunt Monkey, his balance off and his confidence tattered, wobbles on crutches around a tiny playground. The sky is gray, the music melancholy. The adventures du jour do not involve handstands on cliffs, skateboarding prostrate downhill at 45 miles per hour, or double back layouts through the sky. Instead, Stunt Monkey flails his arms through the bars of a jungle gym built for a toddler. He crawls on hands and feet up a flight of three stairs. He pauses timidly at the top of a tiny slide. Then he inches down.

Following the accident, Lucky was evacuated by helicopter to the village of Sallanches, but his injuries were so severe that doctors there sent him on to the University Hospital of Grenoble. The Grenoble doctors searched for Lucky, who was still unconscious, on YouTube to learn more about who he was. He started waking up six weeks later. When he was finally coherent, eight weeks after the accident, and the doctors told him what had happened, Lucky said, "That sounds exactly like something I would do."

According to Carol, Lucky has been seeking high-altitude trouble all his life. When he was a child, if she wanted to find him, she needed to look up. Lucky—then still Toby—spent a lot of time on the roof of the house and of his school and on top of the bus-stop sign. His younger cousin Ben Ko, 23, describes him as that awesome, terrifying older cousin you always wanted to be around even though he'd feed you 30 packets of sugar just to see you freak out. Toby, a smart but disinterested student, didn't have much of a superego. "There was very little difference for him between thinking and actualizing," Ben said. "Toby would say, 'You know what I'd really like to do? I'd like to climb naked.'" Then he would.

Toby's parents divorced when he was 12. Shortly after, he signed up for a rappelling class in Glenbrook, in the Blue Mountains. Carol encouraged this—she'd just made her son move to a small house in a new suburb, and she wanted to give him something positive. Toby's love for the mountains was fierce and magnetic. He already possessed that sparkling ambition and love of heights that characterizes the *puer aeternus.* French pilot and writer Antoine de Saint-Exupéry is the classic of the type: charming, impractical, talented, short-lived. Toby started climbing. Then he started jumping off a nearby highway bridge, 60 feet down into the Nepean River. School felt deadly: too boring and too many rules. The day his mother flew to Germany for a honeymoon with her new husband, a postman named Knuth Hahnefeld, Toby dropped out of high school and moved about an hour away to a climbing campground. He was 15.

The hand-to-mouth dirtbag life suited Toby, as did free soloing—climbing without a rope. Toby was never a sponsored climber, never well-known outside Australia, but he was a talented athlete with a magic about him. (This magic seems to have been less charming up close; by Lucky's own admission, those who loved him found him colossally self-centered.) He also had a bottomless appetite for daring, free-soloing routes close to the edge of his ability—climbing walls he'd never climbed before, without safety gear.

Over breakfast one morning near the city of Parramatta, Lucky told me about his formative on-sight solo route, Ferrets and Berts, rated 5.11c. The line is overhung at the crux, near the top, so, already exhausted, he threw a hand—a "dyno"—toward the final hold. "That was a massive, massive experience for me," Lucky said while wolfing down a plate of French toast and bacon with his fingers. "My friends were not keen to do it themselves. But the rope was unnecessary! It was unreasonable! If I knew I wasn't going to fall, what was the point?"

On an extended trip to Mount Arapiles, in southern Australia, Toby picked fruit for farmers in exchange for food and did his first backflip off a rope swing into a reservoir. He loved the feeling of tumbling midair, and he started flipping compulsively off ever higher objects: fences, stairs, buildings. Six months later, when he returned to the Blue Mountains, climbing in any traditional way no longer interested him. As he puts it now, "I wanted to keep making mental gains along with physical ones, and that was only achieved through danger."

In 2002, Toby, then 19, traveled around the world, hitting the climber-vagabond highlights and sharpening his skills. He ate candy and watched TV while sitting in lawn chairs at the Kmart in Bishop, California. He got tendinitis in his forearms and, while he was grounded, learned to cartwheel on a slackline. He shoplifted food in Salt Lake City and spent four days in jail. In Europe, Toby fell in love with a French girl. In Germany, he found ticks, he says, embedded in "both my Johnson and my butt."

Then he encountered England's famous gritstone scene—a dangerous, technical head game, as the rock is nearly featureless and the local ethos prevents climbers from placing bolts. With his tendinitis in check, he hurled himself at the walls, meeting a British climber named James Pearson at a crag in northern England's Peak District and crashing on Pearson's parents' floor.

Pearson, 26, is now sponsored by North Face, La Sportiva, Adidas Eyewear, and others. As he recalls, Toby returned to England the following year, 2003, and the two embarked on a "gritstone rampage."

"We were psyched out of our tiny little minds," Pearson told me. "We climbed pretty much every day, in all weather." According to Pearson, at that time only one or two other guys in the world could match their skill on the hard grit. "We would try routes in really bad conditions so that when we went for the lead on a cold, crisp day, it would feel relatively easy. We were playing a dangerous game, and we both came close to losing."

In late 2003, Toby soloed Knockin' on Heaven's Door, graded E9 6c (the rough equivalent of 5.14), with no mats and no ropes, after a night of dancing on ecstasy. On Christmas Day, which he spent with Pearson's family, he climbed Harder, Faster—rated E9 7a. The route was the pinnacle of his climbing career. His tendinitis was returning so regularly and ferociously that he could no longer climb enough days in a row to progress. Soon, Toby got what Pearson calls "itchy feet" and flew to Spain to learn to BASE jump.

"If I'm honest, nothing Toby did surprised me," Pearson said recently. "And if I am really honest, I expected one day to hear that he had gone too far. From our time climbing together, I would say that while Toby had a huge desire to enjoy life to its absolute maximum, he actually had a fairly low appreciation of the gift he had. Last year, when I saw news of his accident, I remember thinking, Well, shit, here it is—he finally pushed things too much."

Lucky says his reaction to BASE jumping was like a junkie's to heroin. "From my first jump I wanted more. It was like a drug—just a taster was never enough."

BASE jumping is far more dangerous than anything else we consider a sport. It has what statisticians call a crude death rate of 43 per 100,000 people. (By comparison, skydiving's rate is 1 per 100,000 and rock climbing's is 0.31 per 100,000.) Regardless of the statistics, Lucky soon began trying new jumps no one else would dare try. He gravitated toward the fringe sport of freeBASEing—climbing with only a BASE-jumping parachute for protection, which on Australia's low cliffs pretty much means climbing with no protection at all. But Lucky never achieved much notoriety outside of Australia. (Neither Dean Potter nor Jeb Corliss, two of the most cutting-edge jumpers in the world, had heard of him before his accident.) *Smitten* played in five Australian states, and clips aired on TV and in festivals in Europe. Director Ed Thornhill described Lucky as an "athlete who could often make vastly complicated stunts appear effortless." Still, his approach worried many who knew him, including Gary Cunningham, president of the Australian BASE Association. "His raw talent and background in other extreme sports allowed him to quickly excel to a level well beyond that of the average BASE jumper," Cunningham said. "He would do advanced jumps that most people would not even consider. Many took the view that it was only a matter of time before he got injured or killed."

Toby Benham's short life came to an end in August 2008, when he walked into the Registry of Births Deaths and Marriages in the town of Wollongong, an hour south of Sydney, and legally changed his name to Lucky Chance. He was 24 and working as a circus performer, traveling across Australia doing what he describes as a high-wire spider-man routine. After Europe, he'd enrolled in a two-year program at the CircoArts school in New Zealand to perfect his balance, body control, and tumbling skills for flight. Before choosing the name Lucky Chance, he considered Phoenix in Flames. He loved the ancient myth, the bird that dies in a fire of its own making and then rises from its ashes. When he turned 18, he had a phoenix tattooed on his back.

His first six months as Lucky did not go as planned. He tore a muscle. His slackline snapped. The LEDs in his costume short-circuited. He lost his phone. A girl stood him up. He worried that his new name might be undermining his karma and tempting fate. But then his luck seemed to turn. He landed a great job riding jet skis and diving off 50-foot masts in the Pirates Unleashed show at Sea World, on Australia's Gold Coast. By the summer of 2011, he considered his luck restored, perhaps even augmented. That's when, in his red-and-white-striped pirate shirt, he fell 590 feet from the Death Swing and walked away.

"Oh my god, you don't know who he is?"

The women working the desk at the Edge, a climbing gym in a suburban strip mall, are Googling Lucky and watching his YouTube videos. Behind them on the floor, Lucky, in his Edge work shirt, is putting up sport routes for high school groups. He's grateful to have the job; he needs the money and the distraction. But as anyone with a Web browser can see, Lucky is a broken-down version of his former self, a former emperor of the air who now looks exhausted and walks like a golden retriever with hip dysplasia.

Lucky grips the railing as he descends the stairs to find more footholds for gossiping high school kids. The other guys who work at the Edge bounce along on their toes, all smooth skin and popping veins. "It's hard to lose so much physical ability," Lucky admits in an unguarded moment. When his shift ends, he leaves immediately. His mother is driving him to another doctor's appointment.

Lucky has lived in limbo since the crash. He doesn't remember the first couple of months—those were for Carol to endure. She'd been half-waiting for the call for years. He takes calculated risks, she'd tell herself. He takes calculated risks. Three days after the fall, his mother and his sister, Melanie, flew to France. Lucky's then girlfriend, 20-year-old acrobat and stuntwoman Nandalie Campbell Killick, met them there. When they finally saw their boy, comatose in the ICU, he was swollen almost beyond recognition. Carol later learned that Lucky's doctors didn't think he was going to live. "He had loads of tubes everywhere going in and out of his body," she said. "A machine was breathing for him. It was very surreal. We could only touch his arms. I just kept holding his fat, puffed-up hand and thinking, He's so big."

The day after they arrived, a doctor cataloged Lucky's injuries: the broken jaw, the fractured pelvis, the open fractures to the left foot and femur, the blunt contusion to the left side of his brain, the twisted neck, the air between his lung and thoracic spine, and the lacerations down the left side of the face. The pressure inside his skull was 30 mmHg, two to four times normal—a dangerous situation, as high intracranial pressure can lead to crushed brain tissue, brain herniation, and damaged oxygen supply. He lay with his upper body elevated 45 degrees. Given his condition, doctors couldn't yet operate on Lucky's broken bones, but no one considered this a major problem. Either his brain was going to survive the trauma or it wasn't.

Early on, James Pearson visited as well. Lucky's family spent the night telling funny stories about Lucky, but as Pearson recalls, "Things seemed bleak, to say the least. I left feeling that in a few days, weeks, or months, I would learn of Toby's death—something that touched me more than I would have imagined." Lucky or Toby or whoever he was then finally woke up one day when Carol stayed back in the apartment she and the girls had rented in Grenoble. Carol had a cold. Lucky assumed he'd get right back to being Lucky. Only slowly, he told me, did "the reality of how much I fucked myself up dawn on me."

That is not to say the fall broke his spirit. In the hospital's purgatorial-sounding post-reanimation ward, with a steel rod bolted to what remained of his left femur and infections raging in his foot and lung, Lucky tried to wiggle off the mattress and slide to the floor. In mid-October, once he could sit in a wheelchair, he appeared to break free. Nurses found his bed empty and called security. Friends on Facebook rejoiced: Lucky had made a runner! A grand gesture! The trickster had survived! Lucky, however, deflates that interpretation. "My aim was to get to the cafeteria to buy a *pain au chocolat.* They had these donuts with no holes and Nutella inside. They were mighty good."

When Lucky returned home to Australia last November, three months after his fall, he set about rebuilding his body and his life. He still quickly fatigued, both mentally and physically, but his work ethic served him well. He set up a gym on his mother's back porch. He relearned to walk on an old elliptical machine and gained strength with a chin-up bar and an ancient universal weight machine. But repairing his finances hasn't been so easy. Lucky was not insured for the accident; not even the traveler's insurance on his credit card covered him for "airborne activities." Climbers, friends, and family donated a total of $30,000 to offset the cost of his medical-transport flight back to Australia. But Lucky owes an estimated $280,000 to the hospital in Grenoble, and he worries that his wages will be garnisheed for the rest of his life.

Lucky's world has contracted since his fall. Some of his close friends stuck by him, but the Australian BASE community has distanced itself, party because Lucky was always a little too interested in risk. They claim to revere safety, though promoting this message has required some political jujitsu over the years. Dwain Weston, one of Australia's best jumpers and a childhood inspiration to Lucky, literally cut himself in half when he BASE-jumped from an airplane and hit Colorado's Royal Gorge Bridge in 2003.

On the shelf of Lucky's bedroom is his collection of Rubik's Cubes: three-by-threes, four-by-fours, five-by-fives. One of his signature tricks, before his crash, was solving a Rubik's Cube while standing on a slackline. (This is even harder than it sounds, because it means you can't use your eyes for balance.) His cognitive function seems quite good, considering. Lucky declined to put me in touch with his doctors, but according to Alan Weintraub, medical director of the Brain Injury Program at Craig Hospital in Denver, even patients who've been in comas as long as Lucky was can improve dramatically. "Unexpected functional recoveries are entirely possible," he told me. "Usually, this is the result of relentless effort and motivation by those patients, families, and loved ones." Already, Lucky's conversation and writing are lucid. But according to his mother, he still has some short-term-memory problems and what she describes as trouble "planning." He can no longer solve Rubik's Cubes at all.

Lucky is adamant that his crash not be viewed as a tragedy. "I'm excited about this second chance at life, and I will live it completely differently," he told me. "Instead of living for myself, as I've done in the past, I will live for other people. Maybe volunteer overseas, teach English, work in conservation—try to be of use."

The question of who to be kept nagging Lucky during my last day in Australia, when we drove to the Blue Mountains, the place Toby started climbing, where Lucky launched off the Death Swing. For the entire hour-long ride in the rain, Lucky hummed the Simple Minds song "Don't You (Forget About Me)." When I asked why he seemed so melancholy, he told me what I'd suspected since I first met him, looking hollow in the Sydney airport: Lucky Chance died in Chamonix. He was trying to think of a new name.

"I consider this a new life," he said when we stopped for breakfast before heading out to get soaked on the crags. "Lucky's been great. He's given me lots of amazing moments. But I've changed exponentially. I can't feel bad about it or wish it didn't happen, but I need a new name for these next years." He was considering Avant Garde, though he didn't think Avant was a great first name. He was also thinking about Stunt Monkey, but he didn't particularly want to be called Stunt, either.

After breakfast we parked near a trail leading to the Three Sisters rock formation. A half-mile into our hike, a fence barred the track, announcing that it was closed. Still we walked on. Almost all BASE jumps are illegal. Lucky long ago made a habit of ignoring signs. He tottered wide-legged through puddles and over branches like an old man or a gremlin, experienced but wracked. He still has a steel rod in his leg; lingering damage to his left hip and both ACLs means his body can't withstand the impact of landing BASE jumps anymore. But he's got a few plans. He'd like to walk a gondola cable in the Jamison Valley, just below where we are now. He'd also like to walk municipal power lines. At an overlook, Lucky hoisted himself onto the railing along the cliff's edge. You could tell he yearned for the freedom of falling, the freedom of not knowing what risks cost. "I'm glad to be out here instead of sitting at home," he said, looking down toward the waterfalls and sandstone towers, none of which we could see through the clouds. "And we're not dead! That's fantastic! If you're dead, you feel nothing."

On the way back to the car, we played one of Lucky's favorite games: What's the most useless superpower? His initial vote was the power to see two seconds into the future—too short to alter it. Then he changed his mind. The most useless superpower would be the ability to see the future but to be mute, unable to warn anybody.

A few weeks later, I received an e-mail from Lucky. "The time has come to change my name again. It's as good as done," he wrote. "I really feel like a different person yet again." The ones Lucky was considering required only a new first name. He'd call himself Second, or maybe Next Chance.

(Originally published July 2012)

HEART OF DARK CHOCOLATE

ROWAN JACOBSEN

You know this one: German guy heads into tribal jungle deep upriver, sends the company crazy reports full of radical ideas . . . and then goes totally rogue. Only this time it's not ivory he's after. It's a secret lost for centuries: the finest cacao on earth.

They called it Cru Sauvage.

The impeccable Swiss packaging alluded to its aboriginal provenance, and inside were two bars wrapped in golden foil, 68 percent cacao. I'd paid $13 (plus shipping!) for these skinny little planks of chocolate, just 100 grams' worth of "Wild Vintage." That's $60 a pound. After savaging its wrapper, I placed a square of the dusky stuff on my tongue and closed my eyes.

Chocolate is one of the most complex foods we know. It contains more than 600 flavor compounds. (Red wine has only 200.) Chocolate can be bitter, sweet, fruity, nutty, and savory all at once. It takes the vast library of taste and blends it into one revelatory package. The tropical cacao tree has secret things to tell us about flavor and desire, and for more than a decade I've made a hobby of tracking down those secrets.

This incredibly rare and expensive chocolate was produced by the venerable firm of Felchlin, which claimed that it was unique in the world, made from an ancient strain of cacao native to the Bolivian Amazon—i.e., wild cacao, au naturel, unmolested by millennia of botanical tinkering. It hit me with an intense nuttiness, but without the slightest hint of bitterness, a combination I'd never experienced. Aromatics burst in my sinuses. Citrus and vanilla. The flavor dove into a deep, rich place, and then, just as I thought I had a handle on it, the bottom fell out and it dove some more. That might sound ridiculous, but I've spent an inordinate amount of time "researching" the best chocolate in the world, geeking out on it like the most obnoxious sommelier, and this was something entirely new.

When the feeling finally began to subside, I opened my eyes and started looking for the man responsible.

His name was Volker Lehmann, and he was the only reason Cru Sauvage existed. Before I'd even tasted the chocolate, I'd gleaned the basic elements of the story from the folks at Felchlin: Agronomist enters Bolivian rainforest and makes startling discovery. Volker was the visionary connoisseur on the ground, in the shit. Felchlin was just smart enough to recognize what he'd found. The company invested in specialized equipment, began production, and brought the first fruits of Volker's labor to the European gourmet market, in small quantities, in 2005. It was three years before I heard of it.

After my own chocolate enlightenment, I had to know more. It wasn't easy making contact with Volker, but once I did, he told me he was just scratching the surface. Demand greatly exceeded supply, and there was much, much more out there. He was planning a trip to Bolivia's Río Grande, a remote tributary of the Amazon that, it was said, held vast chocolatales, as the forests of wild cacao are called. There he would visit the Amazonian tribespeople who lived along the banks, offer them employment as cacao gatherers, and eventually, he hoped, set up jungle processing stations in their villages. Did I want to tag along?

Yeah, I was in.

Six frustrating months later, on the other side of a series of false starts, logistical snafus, tropical deluges, and cruel vaccinations, I finally met the bald, athletic 53-year-old in the jungle city of Santa Cruz, Bolivia. From there, we hopped on a 16-seater to Trinidad, a swampy town with frogs trilling in the crumbling gutters. It was early March, the tail end of the rainy season; the rivers had risen 30 feet and spilled across the forests. Trees stood in six feet of water. Piranhas had abandoned the river channels for better hunting in the woods.

To get within a reasonable distance of the indigenous settlement of Combate, a purported cacao hot spot on the Río Grande, we opted for a one-hour, $400 bush-plane ride instead of a four-day boat trip. Every landing strip along the river was underwater except one near an abandoned hunting lodge. As we approached, our pilot, a squat, mustachioed Bolivian of few words, pointed and shook his head in sad disgust. It was unsettlingly overgrown. Down on the river, two men in a dugout canoe waited. We swooped down for an inspection and—good God, he was landing in that stuff! Death smirked at me: All for a goddamned chocolate bar. But we punched into the brush and came to an amazingly soft stop.

I gave our (sad, disgusted) pilot two happy thumbs-up, hopped out, and landed on the home of some warlike ant tribe, which opened up a can of whup-ass on my sandaled foot. As he stood watching me do the first of many ant dances, Volker smiled thinly and said in Teutonic tones, "Welcome to the Amazon. If you stay, we eat you."

~~~~~~

Wild cacao? A myth, disappeared ages ago, extinct—that's what my industry sources had said, anyway. Chocolate is made by fermenting, drying, roasting, and grinding the almond-size fruit seeds of Theobroma cacao, which has been farmed—and therefore much changed by humans—for thousands of years. The ancestors of the Maya perfected the process in Mesoamerica, and it was later passed on to the Aztecs. In the 16th century, conquistador chronicles tell us, the Maya were cultivating vast cacao orchards throughout the Yucatán and Chiapas. It was thoroughly domesticated. Until recent genetic testing proved that the tree is actually native to Amazonia, many scholars believed it hailed from the Maya homelands.

Cacao was used as both drink and currency by the Maya: Ten beans got you a rabbit or a prostitute. When Hernán Cortés entered the Aztec capital of Tenochtitlán, in 1519, he found nearly a million cacao beans in Montezuma's coffers. Liquid chocolate played the role of blood in some Aztec rituals involving human sacrifice. The cacao pod seems to have reminded the priests of the heart.

The Spanish didn't quite get chocolate until they learned to mix it with sugar, and by the 17th century, Europe was cuckoo for cacao. The groves of Central America and southern Mexico couldn't keep up. Enter Brazil, where an inferior variety was being farmed. Though this cacao was higher-yielding and more disease resistant, it was also bitter as hell, so they cut it with lots of sugar. Europeans never knew the difference. Neither do you. The finer-flavored domesticated cacao of the Maya was long ago abandoned, so crappy Brazilian cacao—farmed primarily in Africa these days—is all most of us have ever known.

Ninety-five percent of chocolate is made with "bulk beans," meaning they taste like shit. If you think dark chocolate is bitter and nasty, blame the bulk beans. The tiny supply of good domesticated stuff—from makers like Valrhona, Scharffen Berger, and Amano—comes from old cultivars, grown mostly in remote corners of the Americas on farms that were never able to afford the switch to modern, high-yield varieties.

All of this I knew from researching gourmet chocolate for my book *American Terroir*. Then I stumbled upon the Cru Sauvage. Its wild cacao had always been harvested like any other fruit by the indigenous tribes, but it had never been shipped out of the country before, just hauled to Trinidad by middlemen, in poor condition, and sold on the domestic market. While working in the Bolivian Amazon as a consultant in 1991, Volker filed a report on the great potential he saw in the wild cacao. It was roundly ignored. He would later leave the idiots to their bureaucracy and pursue his vision alone.

Uh-huh, I thought, I've heard this story before, courtesy of Joseph Conrad: German guy hops on a boat, heads deep into the jungle, and then sends some freaky communiques before going rogue. Well, if Volker was Kurtz, I figured I was Marlow, fated to tell his story.

Dante was our guide—a very inauspicious name, it seemed. Volker and I climbed into his dugout, and he yanked its outboard to life, steering us between curtains of endless rainforest. Combate lay three hours downstream. It was classic Amazon: flocks of green parrots and blue-and-yellow macaws flying across two by two; pink river dolphins surfacing; the drumroll of cicadas running up and down the river. I began to feel really, really good. It could have been the jaw-dropping wildlife and the sweet, clean tropical air, but it was probably the big fat wad of coca leaves in my cheek.

The sacred plant of Bolivia, coca is chewed by most of the indigenous population, and Dante seemed to have an eternal quid of it in his maw, so I'd asked for a little. I stuffed the dried leaves inside my cheek, added a smear of baking soda to start the chemical reaction, and let the alkaloids slowly ooze into my bloodstream. First, my tongue and cheek went numb, then things began to occur to me. One was that there is no better way to float down the Amazon than on the wings of a mild coca high. Another was that it's a crying shame that cocaine, a superconcentration of the alkaloids, has screwed things up, because natural coca is one of the world's best drugs. It simply makes whatever you happen to be doing the most deeply satisfying thing in the world. Three hours on a hard wooden seat? Twenty-four hours without food? No problemo, señor.

Curled up in the bow of our boat with his rifle, scanning the banks for tasty monkeys, was Aurelio Rivero. Aurelio, who grew up on a remote homestead in the area, made his living as a cacao trader, plying the river system in his dugout, buying sacks of cacao from the indigenous families that lived along the river, piling them precariously in his canoe, and selling them down in Trinidad, where Volker met him in 2008.

By then, Volker was already buying wild cacao from several traders and trying to generate interest outside of Bolivia. But in recent years, word of the chocolatales' existence had leaked out, and they'd become something of a cause célèbre with conservation organizations, both international and local. "This cacao was lying in front of their eyes all of the time!" Volker told me. No one had ever thought it was worth much. "And then I put my own money behind it and did it. And then people started saying, 'He's taking our resources! Getting filthy rich!' "

In reality, his goal is the same as the conservationists': to preserve the chocolatales, which he thinks should be UNESCO World Heritage sites, and move ever closer to "long-term sustainability in every economic, social, and environmental aspect." But he believes in the market-driven approach: "These forests have no value except for cacao. If they have no value, they'll be cut down [i.e., landowners will sell the timber instead]. The more interest you have in cacao, the more you save the forest. The most sustainable thing we can do is to raise the interest." But a decade of groundwork in Bolivia had taught him to respect the bizarre intricacies of the Amazonian economy. "Many, many people have lost their fortunes in Latin America. There's no Bolivia for Dummies! You have to figure it out yourself."

And that, he thinks, is where the nonprofits have failed. "They make a deal with an indigenous group, get some nice photos, then run to the grant funds, overpaying for almost any type of cacao, no quality whatsoever," and then selling it domestically. Rather than conservationism's old "Buy the land, create a beautiful park" approach, this is the new school's "Help people and places function together healthily and indefinitely" tack.

"They kicked the ball out of my hand," said Volker. "Many people here look for a certain threshold of money, and then they stop harvesting. Once the beer is secure, there's no reason anymore. Westerners think that by giving more and more money incentive, people will do more. Actually, they do less. Leisure is very highly valued in this culture. They have no bills. They're not hooked into the system."

Alex Whitmore, co-founder of Taza Chocolate—a company that also does business in Bolivia and is considered the paragon of direct, supportive relationships with Third World cacao farmers—agrees: "If they get free money, they don't want to work. Nonprofits pumping money into a community stymies the growth of sustainable agriculture. There's a balance that needs to be struck between nonprofit aid and for-profit industry. It's pretty messed up because of the coca."

As in cocaine. A strange cacao–coca codependency exists in Bolivia. "You get all this assistance and money to develop other opportunities for locals if, and only if, you have lots of coca production," said Whitmore. "They plant coca so they can get money to stop planting coca. That's USAID, U.S. government aid." It's a beautiful sell: Help transition the poor Bolivian farmers from coca to cacao, from the evil alkaloid to the acceptable one. "These aid programs basically exist to support the salaries of those who work for them, not necessarily to provide the communities with sustainable growth."

While Volker battles the nonprofits on one flank, he must contend with domestic chocolate makers on the other. One competitor even filed a complaint with the Ministry of Agriculture, claiming that Volker was robbing Bolivia of its natural wealth (as was done with rubber trees a century ago).

"They're just protecting their business," Whitmore opined. "They're trying to grow very aggressively, and they don't want anyone else doing cacao in Bolivia. He's not just buying and exporting; he's actually trying to organize the farmers. They would see that as a direct, competitive threat."

So Volker was going where no sane capitalist had gone before. He had to reach the cacao first. He also hoped to improve the quality. Only 20 to 40 percent of the cacao in Trinidad is good enough to be used in Cru Sauvage. The rest is rotten, moldy, or poorly fermented. Volker painstakingly picks the good beans from the bad and leaves the rest for the domestic Bolivian market, which is not picky. The problem is that the tribes, who don't eat chocolate themselves, have neither the knowledge nor the equipment to ferment and dry premium beans. Volker hoped to change that by setting up buying stations along the rivers and raising the level of coordination. "My role is to bring order to the jungle," he said.

If anywhere needed his services, it was the Río Grande. Thousands of acres of chocolatales lining the river. Some of the last known wild cacao on earth, much of it going unharvested or rotting before it got to market. Or so Aurelio claimed. "Show me," said Volker.

It didn't take long. At a bend in the river, Aurelio gestured. I peered into the gloom. The understory was filled with yellow pods the size and shape of Nerf footballs hanging directly from tree trunks. A sheet of river was bleeding into the forest. Volker broke off a pod and stared at it intensely.

"Very impressive," he muttered to himself. "I've already learned something new: Cacao can be very productive in understory riverbanks." Earlier, I'd told Volker that people I knew considered wild cacao a myth, and now he turned to me. "No wild cacao? Bring them here! Show them this!" He laughed, smacked the side of the pod against the edge of the canoe, and twisted it open. Inside were dozens of maggoty-looking things. He held it out for me. I stuck a handful of the white seeds in my mouth and sucked. A sweet, lemony, delicious pulp came off. This, of course, was what had attracted people and monkeys to cacao for thousands of years before some hungry and desperate soul decided to see what would happen if you roasted the dried seeds.

I sucked seeds all the way to Combate, one of a scant few settlements on the Río Grande. With a population of perhaps 80 people, Combate represented the largest cluster of potential labor on the river. It was key to Volker's vision. For two years he'd been laying the groundwork through people like Aurelio. And now it was time to make his pitch.

A dozen thatch-roofed palapas came into view. The entire settlement was underwater, the palapas on posts. Toddlers waded through the current. Chickens perched on carts, stumps, or any other dry thing they could find. The settlement was full of mango, guava, banana, and cacao trees and weird pets: wild piglets, macaws, coatis.

We pulled up on the flooded bank next to a larger wooden boat festooned with children, who were soon clustered around us. The large boat belonged to Francisco Brito, a spokesperson for the Yuracare tribe, who lived farther upriver. Francisco also traded in cacao. He was here to meet Volker and set up a deal for the upper Río Grande. Francisco had brought 20 cases of Colônia, a cheap Brazilian brew smuggled across the border. Bolivia and Brazil meet along some 2,000 miles of navigable rivers and uninhabited mush, and across that border flows all manner of goods. Cocaine goes east; pirated CDs, stolen Chinese motorbikes, and beer come west.

Beer is the Dom Pérignon of the Amazon. At about 80 cents a can, it's a sign of conspicuous consumption. In the lowlands, the surest way to get everyone's attention is to show up with an obscene amount. We had everyone's attention.

At least, we would have if we'd turned up a few hours earlier. Francisco had already spread the wealth, and the men of Combate were now drooping from his boat like tree sloths. A small, handsome man in his thirties with bloodshot eyes, spade-shaped earlobes, and a sailor's gait roused, stumbled over, and identified himself as Guillermo Figueroa, spokesman for Combate. "You're too late," he said, weaving. "Today we're drinking. Tomorrow we'll meet." Then he grabbed a fresh case and splashed off with his buddies.

There was nothing to be done but crack a few ourselves. Somebody handed me a beer and a bowl of fried piranha, and a crew of locals grabbed our hammocks and packs to set us up for the night in a simple pavilion in the middle of the settlement, their church. When I tried to hang my own hammock, it seemed to upset everybody.

"People here relate differently," Volker explained. "It's still the old patron system. They respect hierarchy. They want me to order them." Ultimately, that was why we were here. "They want to see the boss, to see if it's real. Who calls the shots? Who has the cash? That very minute, things really start. But if you become the boss, you have responsibility. They come to you and say, 'Look, I need this, and

I need that.' Or something happens. Somebody gets hurt and has to be flown out. Then I hire a plane and get that guy out and take him to a hospital. There's no discussion. I can't say, 'Oh, no, that costs too much. I can't do it.' Then I've lost. It's tricky, but it's quite a straightforward system if you know it."

If Volker could sometimes sound alarmingly German, this no-bullshit approach was refreshing, and you had to respect his experience. Anachronistic, decidedly "insensitive" order in place? Roll with it. This is business.

Beer cans and cacao pods floated past, and Volker lit a cigarette. As the darkness and mosquitoes began to ooze in, the sky turned all mango and papaya.

"Kitsch," he said.

Looking surprisingly chipper, Guillermo turned up in the morning and began whanging on an old piece of outboard with a length of pipe. If this was the church, then that, we supposed, was the bell. There was instant coffee, fried plantain, and more piranha. Guillermo popped open a Colônia and waited.

An hour later, the only people assembled were Volker and me. Guillermo pounded on the metal again in frustration. Grudgingly, the rest of Combate joined us. Guillermo and Volker made small talk in Spanish as the others gathered. Why was the village called Combate? No one could remember, Guillermo said. Some trouble with another tribe.

I was the first person Guillermo had met from the States. He was stunned to learn that coca was illegal there. Volker asked Guillermo if any of the children were his.

"Actually, I have 21 children," he replied.

"Wow, the Church must have told you to go forth and multiply," Volker said.

"No, they tell us we should have only two or three."

"Then what happened?"

"I have no television," said Guillermo with a sly smile. The crowd laughed, and Guillermo basked in the attention. He was wearing a green soccer shirt and jean shorts and his fly was open.

Volker turned to me and said, in English, "There's always one like him. He has no actual power. He doesn't make decisions. There are some quiet ones observing, possibly women, who really decide. We have to get closer to the women. Because they care for the children, they tend to be more sensible."

Then Volker made his case. The cacao that the people of Combate collect, he told them, is some of the finest in the world. But it's worth lots of money to the rest of the world only if it's perfectly fermented and dried. And right now, it isn't. Just look around.

The village was littered with comical attempts to dry beans in an inundated rainforest. Cacao was heaped anywhere that promised to stay clear of the rising waters—canoes, huts, bags hanging from mango trees. None of it was getting terribly dry, and some of it was starting to germinate.

"If you work with me," Volker proposed, "I'll build a station where you can bring the cacao. I'll have people—local people like Aurelio—to take care of it. I'll pay you immediately. I'll even bring you gasoline in advance, so you can use your outboards to get to the cacao. I'll have a nice boat to carry the cacao downriver." He smiled at Guillermo. "Maybe I'll even build you a brewery."

The crowd laughed again. Guillermo put his hand to his mouth in a shoveling motion. "What about food? I need to feed my people. Why don't you pay us now for next year's cacao crop, so we can get the things we need?"

Volker shook his head. He would pay a premium for good cacao, but he would not pay in advance, and he would not overpay. (Cash in advance disappeared in a spree of beer and Speed Racer T-shirts. "If you increase the price for no reason," he had explained to me earlier, "then the quality actually goes down, because they think you're stupid.")

The people of Combate didn't think Volker was stupid. They said, Sure, set up your buying station, upgrade our boats, take the drying off of our hands. The meeting adjourned and Volker broke out some paper and crayons and held a cacao-drawing contest for the kids, who looked as though they'd never seen a crayon.

A woman watching the kids approached us. "Next time you come," she said, "please don't bring any beer."

~~~~~~

Volker grew up outside of Berlin, near the coal mines where his father put in double shifts six days a week. After getting a degree in tropical agriculture (on his dad's day off, they gardened together), he began working for the German Volunteer Service in the Dominican Republic. This was the 1980s. Volker planted cacao and other tree farms and was later put in charge of a rabbit-breeding program, which didn't go so well. Locals refused to eat the varmints: "They're too close to rats. Same long teeth." The program ended with Volker throwing a party for his friends and grilling 80 rabbits.

The GVS moved him to Bolivia in 1991, where he entered the jungle with a Chimane Indian guide and first discovered the wild cacao. He then returned to Germany to work in Frankfurt for a number of years. When he came back to Bolivia in 2000, he was amazed to find that no organization had yet begun developing the cacao. In the Amazon, he consulted for a number of Fair Trade groups, evaluating the sustainable-harvest potential of everything from rubber trees and Brazil nuts to palm oil and a red tree latex known as dragon's blood. But the wild cacao captivated him. As he tasted more of the beans, he became the first person to identify a staggering disconnect: Bolivia had a vast supply of some of the best cacao on earth, and no one knew it.

Convincing the gourmet chocolate industry, however, was another story. ("Nobody even knows that Bolivia has cacao," he told me. "They think we grow llamas.") Part of the problem was that the wild beans were only half the size of cultivated beans and couldn't be processed with standard equipment.

"I was running around with these small beans for two years. Nobody wanted them. I sent them to Scharffen Berger. I sent them to Japan. No good, no good, no good. Everyone. It was a very uncertain situation. I started investing more effort, time, money, everything, with no promise that it would work out. I was just convinced that the cacao was wonderful."

He learned of some land for sale that included hundreds of acres of cacao forest. He borrowed money from his father-in-law and paid $13,000 for the 1,500-acre property in 2003. With the success of Fair Trade coffee spilling over into cacao, and with makers of ultra-high-end chocolate suddenly warring over access to the finest beans, he figured it was only a matter of time.

Eventually, hundred-year-old chocolatier Felchlin took notice and—as only a small-scale, high-end maker would—adapted some antique equipment to Volker's unusual beans. Then they summoned him to Switzerland. "They brought me into a conference room," said Volker. "All these serious faces sitting around a table. Very Swiss. There were five chocolate samples on the table. They said, 'Pick out the one made with your cacao.' I tasted all five. I said, 'That one.' They said, 'You're right, and we love it.'"

~~~~~~

We bought all the cacao worth buying in Combate. It would travel by boat with us down to Trinidad, then by truck, over the carnage known in Bolivia as the road system, more than 900 miles to Volker's warehouse in La Paz. At an altitude of 13,000 feet, La Paz is the highest major city in the world. Visitors regularly conk out, their brains sputtering in the low oxygen. The cool Andean air makes it the perfect place to store cacao year-round without air conditioning. Volker uses a defunct racquetball facility, 100-pound sacks of dried cacao piled high on lovely wooden floors.

From La Paz, the cacao is trucked over a 15,700-foot pass and then hurtles down the Pacific slopes to the Chilean port of Arica, where a feeder ship carries it to Panama. There, it gets loaded onto a large container ship for the trip through the canal and across the Atlantic to Rotterdam, where it gets transferred to another feeder ship and brought up the Rhine to Felchlin's warehouse in Basel, Switzerland. "I think the price of Cru Sauvage is very cheap for what we all do," said Volker.

We left Combate at dawn, carving chunks out of a local sausage and washing it down with beer. "German breakfast," Volker said approvingly. I nibbled on some raw cacao beans. There was a hint of greatness in them, but they were a long, long way from being chocolate. We had switched to a larger wooden boat, which included a trellis roof with a blue tarp to block the punishing sun. The tarp didn't reach the back of the boat, so Dante had thrown a salted pig carcass—our meat for the next two days—over the top for shade. We had no radio or backup, and the outboard had no casing and a number of jury-rigged parts. I was impressed with everyone's confidence in its ability to deliver us through three days of wilderness.

Between the bags of cacao, the backpacks, the hammocks, the piranha carcasses no one had cleaned up, the beer cooler, and the bottles of water and gasoline, the only place to sit was on the narrow gunwales—torture no amount of coca could disguise. Our goal was to visit several cacao-gathering homesteads, as well as the settlements of Palermo and Jerusalem, Aurelio's childhood home. "First Palermo, then Jerusalem," Volker muttered. "Sounds like a crusade."

Cacao was everywhere. We found an old, shirtless man with a skin disease devouring the right side of his body. He sat in a hut surrounded by well-manicured cacao trees. His name was Pedro, the last of a community of Trinitario Indians, and he'd lived there for 45 years. Pedro said there were 2,500 acres of chocolatales in the area, but there was no one left to harvest them. I couldn't believe it. In other parts of the world, chocolate companies fight like hell over the paltry supply of high-grade cacao varieties. People have even been shot in Venezuela. Here, it rotted in the forest.

"What if I helped you get pickers here during the season?" Volker asked. "And I provided food, training, and boats? And you ran the show? And we paid you a premium for everything you harvest?"

"Why not?" said Pedro. They shook on it.

Palermo, we soon discovered, had been abandoned to the floods. After 12 more back-breaking hours, we reached Jerusalem, still a foot or so above the floodwaters. Aurelio and his brothers had inherited a shack surrounded by 7,500 acres of swampy rainforest rich in cacao. The family had been hard at work: Every square inch of ground we could see was covered in a thick carpet of empty, composting cacao pods. I was thrilled to be off the boat, but as we walked toward the shack over the crunching pods I suddenly noticed that they seemed to be rippling. The entire grounds, even the floors of the shack, were alive. The ants had moved in.

By this time, I had a relationship with the jungle like that of a beaten dog to its master: I loved it, but it just kept hurting me. I'd worried about all the wrong critters. It wasn't the jaguars; never saw one. It wasn't the caiman; those we ate ceviche style, raw tail meat sliced thin and marinated in fresh lemon juice. Ditto for the piranhas and snakes. (You don't even want to know about the countless tiny vertebrae.) I even got along famously with the tarantulas, which have a personality not unlike the Dude of The Big Lebowski.

But the fucking ants. Mosquitoes, ticks, chiggers, and gnats? Awful. But the ants, streaming through the forest in black rivulets of sadism, are the real lords of the jungle. There is far more ant biomass than human in Amazonia. They attacked from the ground, came boiling out of old canoes, fell from trees. Staying in Jerusalem was suicide. Dante, who'd absorbed enough coca alkaloids to keep the city of Medellín partying for a week, voted for motoring blindly through the night. Overruled. "I know a place," said Aurelio.

We puttered down an old, dead-end arm of the river as it turned purple, mirroring the sky. Carpets of green dragonflies seeped over the water as river dolphins surfaced and fireflies winked in the trees to the rhythm of the frogs. At the end of a lagoon, a single hut rose out of the water on stilts. As we approached, a gnarled old couple tottered out. If they were startled by the sudden turn their evening was taking, they didn't show it.

I had high hopes of making it back to Trinidad the next day—Volker had promised me the best steak of my life when we arrived, and even a skanky hotel room with cold running water was starting to sound like purest hedonism—but the outboard gave up the ghost midmorning. Dante and Aurelio proceeded to do the desperate and hopeless things with screwdrivers that men always do in such situations.

With the engine dead, the sounds of the jungle rushed in. One has this idea of the rainforest ringing with dulcet birdcalls, but for whatever reason, most birds in the Amazon sound as if they have hairballs. The parrots screech. The macaws hack. The hoatzin, an evolutionary throwback, looks and sounds like Billy Idol. Walking the rainforest is like making the rounds in a tuberculosis ward.

They worked on the engine for hours. Black cumulonimbus anvils approached from the west. I watched lightning flick between them as howler monkeys tried to outroar each other. I wondered how long we could all live on the bags of raw cacao beans in the boat. I wondered how it was possible that I'd been on the world's greatest cacao river for days without tasting a single piece of local chocolate.

Our aluminum cooking pot was sacrificed. It took two hours to hacksaw a piece of metal out of it and bend it into the needed shape. It was an impressive display of Latin MacGyverism, and for a moment after Dante fired up the motor, my heart flushed with hope. Then the aluminum disintegrated like taffy.

This time Dante just yanked up the outboard, threw it on deck, and stared as we drifted. Then he reached for his coca pouch. Rain came sizzling up the river and lashed my face. Thunder rumbled in the distance, and the roaring on the banks closed in, as if the jungle itself were screaming in anticipation.

The river led to Aurelio's brother Angel's store, in the village of Camiaco, less than two miles from where we'd broken down. We managed to limp downriver and arrive at cocktail hour. I considered asking why, if they knew Angel's place was just downstream, they'd felt it necessary to spend five hours, by God, engaged in ad-lib engineering, but the Marlow part of my brain whispered, "Don't—that line of questioning leads to madness."

Instead, we talked cacao with Angel. He bought from all the collectors in the area. "I can get you ten tons a year," he told Volker. I timidly asked if he might have a little stash of homemade chocolate around. Angel disappeared into his store and soon emerged with a two-pound lump of fruity, fragrant magic. Its otherworldly aroma hit me from 20 feet away. After all the miles, the bugs, the rancid pork, I grabbed it and held it close to my face, whimpering like Gollum with his ring.

"The volume of cacao from this river—" said Volker, looking giddy, "it's much better than I thought. If I can take out 60 percent, I'm good."

The next day, after some radio calls and Escher-esque logistics, we found ourselves back in Trinidad, where Volker made good on the steak. Trinidad is surrounded by millions of acres of marshy grasslands filled with white zebu cattle. At restaurants on the main square, seven dollars gets you a free-range, grass-fed slab that would make Fred Flintstone weep. Volker and I were carving into two, watching the people of Trinidad sweep by on Haojin 150s, sometimes two, three, even four people to a bike, when his assistant walked up. There was good news. Indians from an entirely different river system (I promised not to reveal which one) had turned up in town, desperate to sell their cacao. They had hundreds of miles of chocolatales, they said, and there were no buyers. Might Mistah Volker be interested?

Volker grinned, finished his steak, and lit a cigarette. Business was good. Felchlin was fielding inquiries about new partnerships and recipes. The local market was completely sated on subpar beans. The nonprofits were off chasing funding. A virgin river in Amazonia was ripe with yet more cacao, and the only person in the whole wide world in a position to pluck it was Volker Lehmann. "Find another boat," he said. "Go upriver. Buy cacao, buy cacao, buy cacao."

"You must eat a ton of chocolate," I said wistfully.

"I don't have a taste for it," said Volker, dry as a stone. "I like Gummi Bears."

(Originally published September 2010)

RAGE AGAINST YOUR MACHINE

TOM VANDERBILT

I first learned of Tom Vanderbilt after hearing him on NPR's Fresh Air *with Terry Gross discussing his book* Traffic. *I was struck by the way he'd turned a seemingly dull topic into a fascinating investigation of human behavior. An avid bike rider to boot, he was the perfect writer to examine our question about road rage at the center of this story: What is it about cyclists that can turn sane, law-abiding drivers into shrieking maniacs?*

The U.S. Census Bureau defines an "extreme commuter" as someone who spends more than three hours getting to and from work.

This is usually understood to be by car. It's not clear, then, how the Census would categorize Joe Simonetti, a 57-year-old psychotherapist who lives with his wife in Pound Ridge, New York. His commute takes him from the northern reaches of exurban Westchester County to his office just south of Central Park.

It's about three and a half hours each way.

By bike.

When I heard about Simonetti's commute—some 50-odd road miles as Google Maps flies—I was vaguely stupefied. It may or may not be the longest bike commute in America, but it's certainly the most improbable. In my mind's eye, there was the dense clamor of New York City, then a netherland of train yards and traffic-clogged overpasses, then an outer belt of big-box retail, and then you were suddenly in the land of golf courses and five-acre zoning—where middle managers crowd the bar car on Metro-North and hedge-fund analysts cruise in 7 Series BMWs down I-95.

The idea that this landscape could be traversed on a bike struck me as fantastic. This is America, where 65 percent of trips under one mile are made by car. But at 7 A.M. on a mid-November Thursday—among the last of the year on which Simonetti was going to ride—I packed my bike into the back of a hired minivan and headed for Pound Ridge, noting with subtle alarm the ticking off of miles as we pushed north.

Simonetti obviously isn't the typical bike commuter. For one thing, he does it only twice a week, weather permitting. For another, he doesn't ride home the same day; he has a crash pad in the city where he can shower and sleep. But in following this supercommuter, I wanted to open a window into what it means to be a cyclist in a country where the bicycle struggles for the barest acceptance as a means of transportation.

Over the years and the miles, Simonetti has experienced just about everything a cyclist can on the roads today: honked horns, cramped bike lanes, close calls with cars, and even a few crashes—the last one landing him in the hospital. I was curious to ride with him for the sheer novelty of it, and also to get a handle on what seemed to be an increasingly prevalent culture war between cyclists and drivers, one that was claiming actual lives. At least for one beautiful morning, I wanted to move beyond the alarming headlines and toxic chat rooms and into the real world, to get a sense of how, why—and if—things had gotten so bad.

My interest isn't because I'm a cyclist, though I am, in the loose recreational sense. Rather, the issue was forced upon me by the publication of my 2008 book *Traffic*, which looked at the oft-peculiar psychology of drivers. Cyclists were among the book's most devoted readers, although I'm still not sure if it's because they found my dissection of drivers' foibles educational or cathartic. After all, the little things that drivers think are excusable—forgetting a turn signal, weaving a bit as they fumble for their Big Gulps—can range from frustrating to life-threatening for a cyclist.

Simonetti's house, a cozy ranch that he jokes is the smallest in Pound Ridge, sits on a twisting country lane. The walkability-measuring Web site Walkscore .org gives his address a rating of zero, meaning, basically, that you can't get around without a car. Tall and trim, with a professorial salt-and-pepper beard, Simonetti is waiting with his LeMond Buenos Aires, a 50th-birthday gift that, he jokes, makes him look "like a real cyclist." Clad in a helmet, gloves, and a blue cycling jacket, he fills our bikes' bottles with a mixture of juice and water, checks that his back pouch has spare tubes (I've forgotten mine), and clicks his shoes into his pedals.

On a still-brisk morning—it's 8:30, and Simonetti's first appointment is at noon—we push off onto a route that Simonetti has refined over the years. It was, in fact, a bike ride that brought him here from the city. After a ride across America for charity in 1998, he returned to New York feeling "a bit midlifey." His daughter was already a teenager, and he craved nature. He and his wife, Carol Goldman, a social worker, were searching for a house that "felt country" but was still within cycling reach of Manhattan. "I never want to commute five days a week by train," he says. He is surely the only person in the history of Westchester County to arrive for a house showing by bike from Manhattan. "They thought I was pretty weird," he says of the realtors. He stresses that he is purely a "functional" cyclist: he rides when he needs to get somewhere, be it the hardware store or Midtown.

Our route snakes through preternaturally quiet daytime suburbs whose streets seem plied primarily by women in SUVs and tradesmen in pickups. A Latino landscaping crew smiles at us as we ride through the leaf storm they've blown up in Greenwich, Connecticut. We don't see any other cyclists until New Rochelle, and even then it's two young girls riding on the sidewalk. In the town of Rye Brook, a little after 10 A.M., we pause at a deli for Simonetti's traditional pit-stop fare: an egg-white omelet with Swiss on a whole-wheat bagel. They all know him here, and a clipping from a local paper detailing his commute is stuck on the wall, behind a picture of the clerk's daughter.

Here, Simonetti is not some "Lycra lout," some "Lance wannabe," or any of the other epithets often hurled at cyclists. He's simply Joe. He's the guy who rides his bike to work. And, thanks to me and my questions and my questionable pace, he's late.

Somewhere south of Pelham, Simonetti tells me of a crash last summer, in the Bronx, that left him with a broken collarbone. It was a "right hook," one of the most common crash types for cyclists: a driver, traveling in Simonetti's lane ahead of him, suddenly turned right—without signaling—directly into Simonetti's path. An ambulance responded quickly, but the police did not. The paramedics told Simonetti the police would deal with the driver when they arrived, he says. "But the guy left. I don't blame him." When the police, investigating what was now a hit-and-run, came to the hospital, they asked him if he'd gotten the license-plate number. "I was laid out on the ground," he laughs. The driver was never found.

Judging by recent headlines, it's not hard to believe that riding a bike has become a little like entering a war zone. No story blew up more than that of Steven Milo, a prominent New York anesthesiologist who was struck near Vail, Colorado, last July 3 by Martin Erzinger, a Denver money manager who specializes in "ultra-high-net-worth individuals." After veering off the road and hitting Milo from behind, throwing him off his bike, Erzinger drove to a Pizza Hut parking lot and called Mercedes roadside assistance. Milo, meanwhile, sustained spinal injuries, lacerations, and, according to court documents quoted by the *Vail Daily*, "bleeding from the brain." When the district attorney, citing "job implications" for Erzinger should he be convicted of a felony, downgraded the hit-and-run charges to a misdemeanor, the cycling blogosphere went off like a supernova. Erzinger had told police that he'd never seen Milo; among the more outlandish of his lawyer's later defenses was that "new-car smell" had impaired his client. Ultimately, the judge accepted the prosecutor's misdemeanor plea deal and sentenced Erzinger to probation, a suspended jail term, and community service.

Last September, in Maryland, Natasha Pettigrew, a Green Party candidate for U.S. Senate, was training at dawn for a triathlon when she was fatally struck by a Cadillac Escalade. No charges have yet been filed against the driver, who said that she thought she'd hit an animal until she got home and found Pettigrew's bike lodged under her car. In Florida, the country's deadliest state for cyclists—119 deaths in 2007, ten more than California despite having half the population—two riders participating in last year's annual Memorial Day ride were stabbed by a driver after words were exchanged on the road.

In 2009, the last year for which records are available, 630 cyclists were killed by cars in the U.S. (compared with 4,092 pedestrians). That's arguably a big improvement over the 1,003 cyclist fatalities that occurred in 1975, when, as Census data hint, far fewer people were commuting by bike and still fewer wore helmets. And yet, even if things have gotten safer, at least in terms of absolute deaths (which are easier to measure than where or how much people are actually cycling), a sense of hostility—and sometimes outright violence—seems to be on the rise.

When accidents do happen, they can generate as much vitriol as concern, as drivers circle their station wagons and trot out now familiar arguments: that the roads are meant for cars, or that cyclists don't pay for the roads—a particularly unwarranted charge, given that local streets are paid for primarily by sales and property taxes. There's a feeling among many drivers that cyclists, either by their ignorance of the law or by their blatant disregard for it, are asking for trouble. "If the door opens into a bicycle rider," opined Rush Limbaugh on his radio show in 2009, "I won't care."

In one sense, the so-called bikelash has little to do with transportation modes. In the late 1960s, a pair of British psychologists set out to understand the ways in which we humans tend to split ourselves into opposing factions. They divided a group of teenage schoolboys, who all knew each other, into two groups and asked them to perform a number of "trivial tasks." The boys were then asked to give money to fellow subjects, who were anonymous save for their group affiliation. As it turned out, the schoolboys consistently gave more money to members of their own group, even though these groups had just formed and were essentially meaningless.

"The mere division into groups," wrote the psychologists, Henri Tajfel and Michael Billig, of the University of Bristol, "might have been sufficient to have produced discriminatory behavior." Though not exactly Lord of the Flies, the experiment was a demonstration of the power of what's called "social categorization"— and the penalties inflicted on the "out-group."

This dynamic appears on the road in all kinds of ways. "We know that merely perceiving someone as an outsider is enough to provoke a whole range of things," says Ian Walker, a researcher at the University of Bath who specializes in traffic psychology. "All the time, you hear drivers saying things like 'Cyclists, they're all running red lights, they're all riding on sidewalks,' while completely overlooking the fact that the group they identify with regularly engages in a whole host of negative behaviors as well." This social categorization is subtle but dominant, he points out. When people are given a piece of paper and asked to describe themselves, "men never write, 'I'm a man.' Whereas women will write 'woman' because being male is the 'default' status in society."

And so it is with cyclists. In a country like the Netherlands, which has more bikes than people and where virtually the entire population cycles at one time or another, the word cyclist isn't meaningful. But in the U.S., the term often implies something more, in both a good and a bad sense.

On the one hand, cyclists have a strong group affiliation, with clubs, group rides, and a flourishing network of bike blogs. And yet the oft-invoked idea of "bike culture" itself betrays cycling's marginal status in America, observes Eben Weiss, creator of the blog Bike Snob NYC, in his book *Bike Snob: Systematically and Mercilessly Realigning the World of Cycling*. "The truth is," he writes, "real cultures rarely call themselves cultures, just like famous things rarely call themselves famous."

The dark side of the "cyclist" label is that it becomes a shortcut to social categorization. Suddenly, that messenger who cut in front of you becomes the face of an entire population. And the next time you have an unpleasant encounter with a cyclist, it isn't just a matter of his (or your) carelessness: it seems intentional. Simonetti sees this type of reaction all the time, on the road and in his practice.

"As a couples therapist, I tell people that we take things so personally," he says as we near the Whitestone Bridge, on the first dedicated bike path we've seen in more than two hours. It's easy, when a car edges too close or cuts him off, to "go to that paranoid place where they're just trying to fuck with me. We're so worried that someone else can steal our sense of self that we fight for it at every turn." But it could have been just that the driver didn't see him. Under the spell of what's called "inattentional blindness," people have been known to miss obvious things simply because they're not looking for them. Either that or what seems inconsequential in a car—passing by within a foot or two—can be terrifying to someone on a bike.

One way to find out what drivers are thinking, of course, is to actually stop and ask them, which is precisely what one Wisconsin cyclist has been doing, with interesting results, for the past few years.

The first thing Jeff Frings wants you to know is that he's not out to get drivers. (He is one, after all.) The second thing is that he doesn't have a persecution complex.

"The majority of drivers go out of their way to give me room, and are decent and good drivers around cyclists," says Frings, a news cameraman and avid rider who lives in the suburbs of Milwaukee. "The problem is, it only takes one mistake to end your life or put you in a wheelchair."

A few years ago, Frings found out what happens when you encounter someone who isn't a good and decent driver. Out on a weekday ride, he was nearly sideswiped. Heated words followed. The driver accelerated away, then screeched on his brakes right in front of him. "I said, 'This is out of control,'" says Frings. "I called 911." This wasn't the only time. A similar incident ended not with a reprimand of the driver but with a threat by the responding officer to book Frings for disorderly conduct. Rattled by these experiences and dismayed by the lack of evidence, Frings mounted two small video cameras: one on his helmet, one rear-facing on the handlebars.

Frings started filming every one of the 100 to 250 miles he rides in a week, to provide proof against the claims of drivers, who are typically the only ones left standing after a serious bike-car crash. He posts the worst encounters on his Web site, bikesafer.blogspot.com, which could provide grist for a reality show: America's Douchiest Drivers. The incidents tend to follow a pattern: (1) Driver cuts him off or nearly runs him off the road. (2) Frings catches up to driver at red light. (3) Frings points out error of driver's ways. (4) Driver says something like "Get on the sidewalk where you belong, jag-off!" (5) Thus ensues what Frings calls "the Conversation," in which he notes (sometimes to police officers) that it's in fact illegal for him to ride on the sidewalk, and that while the law dictates that he be "as far to the right as practicable," that doesn't mean the shoulder, and so forth.

Typically, this goes about as well you'd expect. "I'm trying to be less confrontational," says Frings. He's embracing politeness. "Can I just ask you one favor?" he will say. "Can you give me a little more room next time?" He takes his victories in handshakes, promises to do better, and the occasional ticket police give a driver after seeing Frings's evidence. And while he's not optimistic about converting the "haters"—those who believe bikes have no place on the road—he hopes that if he can just get one driver to be more empathetic toward cyclists, it's worth it. "Because the next time," he says, "could be my time."

The confusion over the laws pertaining to cyclists unfortunately echoes throughout the entire legal system, argues Bob Mionske, a two-time Olympic cyclist and Portland, Oregon–based lawyer specializing in cases involving bikers. "Enforcement is really where it all starts," he says. "If the police don't respect your mode of transportation, don't expect the rest of society to."

Laws are often unenforced. In researching a case in Tennessee where a driver hit a cyclist (who was "lit up like a Christmas tree," says Mionske) while passing, he found that the driver hadn't been given a ticket for violating the state's three-foot passing law—in fact, he couldn't find a case where a ticket had ever been given. Even worse, laws are sometimes used against cyclists. In 2008, a cyclist in Madison, Wisconsin, who'd been hospitalized after being "doored" was actually ticketed for riding less than three feet away from parked cars—even though, as most state traffic codes note, it's the driver's responsibility not to obstruct traffic of any kind when he opens his door. But the biker had only bad choices: ride too far into traffic and risk getting hit, or ride to the right and risk getting doored. Wisconsin has since changed the law.

In Mionske's view, justice for cyclists is often invisible, handled with civil settlements that rarely draw public attention. And criminal justice often hangs on a knife-edge. When a 14-year-old teenager in Connecticut was fatally struck by a speeding driver, Mionske notes that it was the driver's prior convictions—including multiple DWIs—that helped land him in jail. For anything but the most egregious cases, Mionske says, a driver who strikes a cyclist—even fatally—is rarely even brought to trial. In the case of the Vail hit-and-run last July, what changed things was that the victim was a successful doctor. "He wasn't going to sit down on this," Mionske says. "Can you imagine if the guy had been collecting aluminum cans?"

Like many cyclists, Mionske would like to see some version of the liability system used in the Netherlands and other European countries, in which the burden of proof in a car-cyclist crash is on the driver—the idea being to encourage the user of the far deadlier vehicle to act more cautiously around the more "vulnerable road users," as cyclists are called in road-safety parlance.

Of course, if calling cyclists "vulnerable" makes it seem like they're never to blame, that's not true, either. It's not just those hipsters on fixies sealed off from the world by earbuds who give bikers an image problem. Plenty of well-meaning bike commuters aren't aware of the laws, or fail to use bright flashing lights at night, or turn without giving hand signals. Statistically, some studies show cyclists running more red lights than drivers—for a number of complicated reasons, whether to conserve momentum, to get ahead of traffic and be more visible, or, more profoundly, perhaps because their out-group status leads them to act that way.

But the red lights may be a red herring. The way cyclists get hurt seems to have less to do with their own culpability and more to do with getting hit by cars— either from behind or when a car turns right, the way Simonetti was struck. Echoing research in the UK, a recent three-year study by Australia's Monash University found that in 54 recorded crashes among a sampling of cyclists, drivers were at fault nearly nine out of ten times.

Regardless of fault, there's another twist here. As various studies have found, the more cyclists and cycling infrastructure a town has, the safer it becomes statistically, not just for cyclists but for drivers and pedestrians alike. When New York City put a protected bike lane on Ninth Avenue, some protested it as unsafe for people on foot. But since the lane's opening, pedestrian injuries on Ninth have dropped by 29 percent. Last year, as miles of bike lanes were added, New York had its best pedestrian-safety record ever.

While Mionske is generally positive about recent initiatives like Oregon's Vulnerable Road User law, which stiffens penalties for striking a pedestrian or cyclist, and the bicyclist bills of rights passed in a number of other states, he believes that laws are not enough. "Until the public attitude changes, you're not going to change the experience everyone has out there in the world," he says, "whether it's other kinds of discrimination or modism—discriminating against people because of their mode of transportation."

~~~~~~

There are times, however, when the gulf seems too wide to span. On one of his rides, Frings was hailed by a man standing in his front yard. The man announced he had passed him earlier in his car. He told Frings he had almost hit him, because he was riding too far into the road. "I tried to explain to him the concept of 'taking the lane'—that the lane's too narrow for us to be side by side, and drivers would think they could pass me even when there's oncoming traffic," Frings says. "That concept, before I talked to him about it, was completely foreign to him. He couldn't understand how it would be safer for me to ride farther out."

Hence one of the major fault lines of driver-cyclist relations. While virtually every cyclist in America is also a driver, relatively few drivers are also cyclists. "People either don't know how to handle you," says Andy Clarke, president of the League of American Bicyclists, "or they don't want to handle you." There's an empathy gap that, as you know if you've spent much time on cycling blogs, can cut both ways.

In one study in which drivers were asked how they feel about cyclists, one of the recurring labels was "unpredictable." When asked to elaborate, drivers often blamed the "attitudes and limited competence" of the cyclists themselves, rather than the "difficulty of the situations that cyclists are often forced to face on the road." When asked to describe their own actions or those of other drivers, however, they blamed only the situation. Psychologists call this the "fundamental attribution error."

So drivers, perhaps already stressed out from being late for work or stuck in traffic, then have to negotiate their way around a vehicle they essentially don't understand, causing even more stress, which they tend to attribute to something about cyclists. It's a vicious cycle—most vicious, in terms of actual harm, for cyclists.

Cyclists, too, can be as susceptible as anyone to "modal bias," thinking that one's mode of travel is the "normal," even superior, one. After researching my book, there may be no more conscientious—or paranoid—driver on the American road than me. But I am still occasionally flummoxed by some wrong-way night rider wearing black. I want to tell them, "Don't ruin it for everyone!" Then again, I wouldn't tell a rude fellow driver not to ruin the image of drivers.

Yes, cultural politics are getting weird, which may also explain some of the tension, as Brian Ladd, author of the 2008 book *Autophobia*, argues. "Most Americans," he wrote in a December post on the urban-planning Web site Planetizen .com, "know one thing about the bicyclists they see on the roads: they are losers, and you thank God you're not one of them." But wait, he says, noting the fashion-ability of cycling: Who's doing the sneering here? "It's harder to dismiss cyclists as beneath contempt," he says, "when you suspect that they might just be contemptuous of you."

In thinking about how to improve driver-cyclist relations in America, the easiest thing is to simply get more people on bikes. Growing up in the small Wisconsin town of Twin Lakes, Mionske notes, he "didn't see more than two road bikes in my entire childhood." Now, he jokes, "you've got packs of 40 guys riding around pissing people off." But with each new cyclist, he says, it's no longer "the Other; it's us."

Few American cities have done a better job of getting people on bikes than Portland, Oregon, where around 7 percent of the population bikes to work and children cycle to school in huge "bike trains." And yet, last year, like many recent years, no cyclist was killed. (By comparison, Tampa, Florida, a city where fewer than 1 percent of the population commutes by bike, had nine cyclist fatalities in four months in 2009.) Greg Raisman, a traffic-safety specialist with Portland's

Bureau of Transportation, says one key to getting people biking is providing infrastructure—actual or symbolic. The city features "bicycle boulevards" and bike-only traffic signals, and it's planning new six-foot-wide bike lanes. It recently put some 2,100 "sharrows" bike symbols on 50 miles of residential streets. He says the symbols send messages to motorists and are, as many Portlanders have told him, changing "people's mental maps of the city."

"We need to get people to change the way they think about transportation," Raisman says. While all road users need to step up in terms of behavior, he believes, calling for cyclists to be licensed, as some critics have lately done, isn't the right place to start. "I recently got my driver's license renewed," he says. "They just asked me if my address was the same." Among the things he was not asked was whether he was aware of traffic-code changes like the 2007 Vulnerable Road User law or a new Oregon rule that makes it legal for cyclists to pass on the right so they can filter to the front past queues of cars stopped at traffic lights.

The greenways of Portland seem very far away as Joe Simonetti and I pedal down a street in the Bronx that looks like the nightmare underbelly of America's car culture. In front of myriad body shops sit subcompacts with mashed-in crumple zones and SUVs with spidery shattered windows. A billboard urges auto-accident victims to dial 1-800-I-AM-HURT. Cars honk and weave, delivery trucks wait parked in the bicycle lane. "The Bronx is lawless," says Simonetti. "It's the Wild West, dog eat dog—or car eat car."

We cross the Madison Avenue Bridge into Manhattan and a few minutes later reach the Central Park loop, one of the few car-free spaces of the day. Our ride has gone off without conflict, not that it's always so. "It's hard to ride ten years without some incident," Simonetti says. There's a crash—not always major—every season or so, not to mention logistical concerns like bathroom breaks. He says he enjoys two-thirds of the ride but admits to having to "push myself" through the final third.

But the benefits are clear. For one, Simonetti, despite being nearly two decades my senior, seems ready to keep riding, whereas I'm struggling from an old knee injury that's come wriggling up like worms after rain. For another, knee notwithstanding, I feel fantastic. In a study by the University of Surrey, car commuters reported having the "most stressful" commutes, while cyclists saw their journeys as "interesting and exciting." Indeed, where driving into New York City always leaves me feeling edgy and irritable, I now feel curiously alive.

To cycle in America today is to engage in an almost political act, but what's often obscured is the simple idea of pleasure. Andy Clarke notes that bike-component maker Shimano, in some research it conducted with the design firm IDEO, found that when you talk to adults and ask them about their earliest childhood memory, "it invariably involves a bike—exploring their neighborhood, careening down a hill, ditching the training wheels." We need to rediscover that, he says. "They don't want to feel like they have to be Lance. People want to be normal, and they want cycling to be a part of normal life."

Returning from a visit to Cape Cod last summer, I was staggered to see a traffic jam stretching for dozens of miles, heading to the beaches. Almost every car had several bikes lashed to it. You could almost feel the collective urge to escape traffic and get on a bike. I thought: This is the country that hates cyclists, that sees them as a road menace?

Simonetti and I draw to a stop outside his office building, two people on bikes amid Midtown gridlock. I ask him why he does it. "I have a tremendous feeling of accomplishment," he says. "No matter what else happens in the day, I can feel good about the ride. There aren't many other things that make me feel that way."

How many people can say that about their commute? After saying goodbye to Simonetti, I head home myself, riding over to the Hudson River Greenway, that jewel of New York's expanding—and controversial—bicycle network, where none of the larger thoughts about cycling in America intrude. I'm just enjoying the breeze off the river and thinking about that final climb over the Brooklyn Bridge.

(Originally published February 2011)

THE ONE THAT GOT AWAY

IAN FRAZIER

~~~~~~

In 2012 we sent Ian Frazier to profile a celebrated Deschutes River fly-fishing guide called Stealhead Joe, an angling master with a long list of devoted clients. A few weeks after Frazier filed his draft, Joe took his own life. Frazier went back out to Oregon to re-report the story. His new draft on the tragedy was a heartbreaking meditation on the complications of life, resulting in one of the best pieces we've ever published.

~~~~~~

The police report listed the name of the deceased as Joseph Adam Randolph and his age as 48. It did not mention the name he had given himself, Stealhead Joe. The address on his driver's license led police to his former residence in Sisters, Oregon, where the landlord said that Randolph had moved out over a year ago and had worked as a fishing guide. In fact, Randolph was one of the most skilled guides on the nearby Deschutes River, and certainly the most colorful—even unforgettable— in the minds of anglers who had fished with him.

He had specialized in catching sea-run fish called steelhead and was so devoted to the sport that he had a large steelhead fly with two drops of blood at the hook point tattooed on the inside of his right forearm. The misspelling of his self-bestowed moniker was intentional. If he didn't actually steal fish, he came close, and he wanted people to hear echoes of the trickster and the outlaw in his name.

~~~~~~

I spent six days fishing with Stealhead Joe in early September of 2012, two months before he died. I planned to write a profile of him for this magazine and had been trying for a year to set up a trip. Most guides' reputations stay within their local area, but Joe's had extended even to where I live, in New Jersey.

Somehow, though, I could never get him on the phone. Once, finding myself in Portland with a couple of days free, I drove down to Sisters in the hope of booking a last-minute trip, but when I asked for him at the Fly Fisher's Place, the shop where he worked, I was told, in essence, "Take a number!" Staffers laughed and showed me his completely filled-out guiding schedule on a calendar on an office door, Joe himself being unreachable "on the river" for the next x days.

The timing sorted itself out eventually. Joe and I spoke, we made arrangements to fish together, and I met him in Maupin, a small town on the Deschutes about 90 miles from Sisters. Joe had moved to Maupin for personal and professional reasons by then. On the day we met, a Sunday, I called Joe at nine in the morning to say I was in town. He said he was in the middle of folding his laundry but would stop by my motel when he was done. I sat on a divider in the motel parking lot and waited. His vehicle could be identified from far off. It was a red 1995 Chevy Tahoe with a type of fly rod called a spey rod extending from a holder on the hood to another holder on the roof like a long, swept-back antenna.

I have seen a few beat-up fishing vehicles and even owned one or two of them myself. This SUV was a beaut, and I chuckled in appreciation as Joe got out, introduced himself, and showed me its details. The Tahoe's color was a dusty western red, like a red shirt that gets brighter as you slap dust off of it. (To maintain that look, he deliberately did not wash his vehicle, a girlfriend of Joe's would later tell me.) The grille had been broken multiple times by deer Joe had hit while speeding down country roads in predawn darkness in order to be on the water before everybody else, or returning in the night after other anglers had gone home. He had glued it back together with epoxy, and there was still deer hair in the mends.

Hanging from the inside rearview mirror was a large red-and-white plastic fishing bobber on a loop of monofilament line, and on the dash and in the cup holders were coiled-up tungsten-core leaders, steelhead flies, needle-nose pliers—"numerous items consistent with camping and fishing," as the police report would later put it. While Joe and I were admiring his truck, I didn't guess I was looking at the means he would use to take his life. He died in the driver's seat, which he pushed back into its full reclining position for the occasion. The report gave the cause of death as asphyxiation from carbon-monoxide poisoning.

Something momentous always seems about to happen in canyon towns like Maupin, where the ready supply of gravity suggests velocity and disaster. Above the town, to the east and west, the high desert of central Oregon spreads its dusty brown wheat fields toward several horizons. Below the town, in a canyon that is wide in some places and narrow in others, 4,500 cubic feet per second of jade-colored river go rushing by.

Four-hundred-some people live in Maupin in the winter; several thousand might occupy it on any weekend from June through Labor Day. People come to whitewater raft, mainly, and to fish. Guys plank on bars in the wee hours, tequila shots are drunk from women's navels, etc. Sometimes daredevils pencil-dive from Maupin's one highway bridge; the distance between the Gothic-style concrete railing and the river is 98 feet. They spread their arms and legs in the instant after impact so as not to hit the bottom too hard.

Maupin, an ordinary, small western town to most appearances, actually deals in the extraordinary. What it offers is transcendence; people can experience huge, rare thrills around here. Fishing for steelhead is one of them.

Steelhead are rainbow trout that begin life in fresh-water rivers, swim down them to the ocean, stay there for years, and come back up their native rivers to spawn, sometimes more than once. They grow much bigger than rainbows that never leave freshwater, and they fight harder, and they shine a brighter silver—hence their name.

To get to the Deschutes from the ocean, the steelhead must first swim up the Columbia River and through the fish ladders at the Bonneville Dam and The Dalles Dam, massive power-generating stations that (I believe) add a zap of voltage to whatever the fish do thereafter. Some are hatchery fish, some aren't, but all have the size, ferocity, and wildness associated with the ocean. "Fishing for steelhead is hunting big game," says John Hazel, the senior of all the Deschutes River guides and co-owner of the Deschutes Angler, a fly shop in Maupin.

Steelhead are elusive, selective, sometimes not numerous, and largely seasonal. They seem to prefer the hardest-to-reach parts of this fast, rock-cluttered, slippery, rapid-filled, generally unhelpful river. On the banks, you must watch for rattlesnakes. Fishing from a boat is not allowed. You wade deeper than you want, and then you cast, over and over. You catch mostly nothing.

Casting for steelhead is like calling God on the telephone, and it rings and rings and rings, hundreds of rings, a thousand rings, and you listen to each ring as if an answer might come at any moment, but no answer comes, and no answer comes, and then on the 1,001st ring, or the 1,047th ring, God loses his patience and picks up the phone and yells, "WHAT THE HELL ARE YOU CALLING ME FOR?" in a voice the size of the canyon. You would fall to your knees if you weren't chest-deep in water and afraid that the rocketing, leaping creature you have somehow tied into will get away.

Joe's other nicknames (neither of which he gave himself) were Melanoma Joe and Nymphing Joe. The second referred to his skill at fishing for steelhead with imitations of aquatic insects called nymphs. This method uses a bobber or other floating strike indicator and a nymph at a fixed distance below it in the water. Purists don't approve of fishing this way; they say it's too easy and not much different from dangling a worm in front of the fish's nose.

For himself, Joe believed in the old-time method of casting downstream and letting the fly swing across the current in classical, purist style. But he also taught himself to nymph, and taught others, and a lot of Joe's clients caught a lot of fish by this method. In one of Joe's obituaries, Mark Few—Joe's prized and most illustrious client, the coach of the highly ranked men's basketball team at Gonzaga University, whom Joe called, simply, "Coach," who liked to catch a lot of fish, and who therefore fished with nymphs—praised Joe's "open-mindedness" as a guide.

The nickname Melanoma Joe came from Joe's habit of fishing in board shorts and wading boots and nothing else. Most guides long-sleeve themselves, and lotion and hat and maybe glove themselves, and some even wrap a scarf around their heads and necks and faces like mujahedeen. Joe let the desert sun burn him reddish brown. Board shorts, T-shirt, sunglasses, baseball cap, flip-flops—that was his attire when we met. He grew up mostly in California and still looked Californian.

He smoked three packs of Marlboros a day.

For a guy as lost as Joe must have been, he gave off a powerful fatherly vibe. Even I was affected by it, though he was 13 years my junior. An hour after we met, we waded out into the middle of the Deschutes in a long, straight stretch above town. The wading freaked me out, and I was frankly holding on to Joe. He was six-five, broad shouldered, with a slim, long-waisted swimmer's body. I wore chest waders, and Joe had put on his waders, too, in deference to the colder water. I held tightly to his wader belt. Close up, I smelled the Marlboro smell. When I was a boy, many adults, and almost all adult places and pastimes, smelled of cigarettes. Joe had the same tobacco-smoke aroma I remembered from dads of fifty years ago. I relaxed slightly; I might have been ten years old. Joe held my hand.

That day we were in the river not primarily to catch fish but to teach me how to cast the spey rod. I had been dreading the instruction. Lessons on how to do any athletic activity fail totally with me. Golf-coach reprimands like "You're not opening up your hips on the follow-through" fall on my ears as purest gibberish, talking in tongues, like the lost language of a tribe of Israel that has been found again at Pebble Beach—

—Where Joe was once a golf pro, by the way, as he told me in passing. The only athletic enterprises he had never tried, he said, were boxing and wrestling. Now he demonstrated to me the proper spey-casting method. Flourishing the rod through positions one, two, three, and four, he sent the line flying like a perfect tee shot down fairway one. From where we were standing, above our waists in water, it went 90 feet, dead straight. You could catch any fish in the river with that cast.

Regular fly-casting uses the weight of the line and the resistance of the air to bend the rod—or "load" it—so that a flick of the wrist and arm can release the tension and shoot the line forward. Spey casting, an antique Scottish technique from the heyday of waterpower, uses a longer rod, two hands, and the line's resistance on the surface of the river to provide the energy. You lay the line on the water beside you, bring the rod up, sweep it back over the line against the surface tension, and punch it forward with an in-out motion of your top and bottom hands. The spey cast is actually a kind of water-powered spring. It throws line farther and better than regular fly-casting does, and because it involves no backcast it is advantageous in closed-in places like the canyons of the Deschutes.

~~~~~~

If Joe showed any signs of depression in the first days we fished together I did not notice them. Walking along the railroad tracks beside the river on our way to a good place to fish, he seemed happy, even blithe. As we passed the carcass of a runover deer with the white of buzzard droppings splattered all around, he said, "I've been fly-fishing since I was eight years old. Bird hunting, too. My grandfather sent me a fly rod and a 12-gauge shotgun for my eighth birthday, because he fished and hunted and wanted me to be like him. He was a Cajun from south Louisiana. His last name was Cherami. That was my mom's family, and my dad's family was also from the South, but they were more, like, aristocrats. My last name, Randolph, is an old Virginia name, and I'm actually a direct descendant of Thomas Jefferson. My dad's father is buried at Monticello."

We went down the riprap beside the tracks and held back the pricker bushes for each other. They were heavy with black raspberries; the smell in the cooler air by the water was like someone making jam. He stopped to look at the Deschutes before wading in. "This is the greatest river in America," he said. "It's the only one I know of that's both a great steelhead river and a blue-ribbon trout stream. The way I came to it was, I was married to Florence Belmondo. Do you know who Jean-Paul Belmondo is? Famous French movie actor? You do? Cool! A lot of people never heard of him. Anyway, Florence is his daughter. She's an amazing person, very sort of withdrawn in a group, but warm and up for anything—like, she has no fear—and knockout beautiful on top of that. We met on a blind date in Carmel, California, and were together from then on. Flo and I got married in 2003, and we did stuff like stay at Belmondo's house in Paris and his compound in Antigua."

I looked at Joe, both to make sure he was being serious and to reexamine his face. I observed that he looked a bit like Belmondo himself—the same close-set, soulful eyes, big ears, and wry, down-turned mouth.

Florence skis, Joe was a snowboarder. They began to visit central Oregon for the snow at Mount Bachelor, Joe discovered the Deschutes, Florence got him a guided trip on the river as a present, he fell in love with the river, they moved to Sisters, and she bought them a big house in town in 2005. "After I learned the river and started my own guiding, I think that was what created problems between Florence and me," Joe said. "Being a kept man sounds great, but it's really not. To be honest, there were other problems, too. So finally we divorced. That was in '08. We tried to get back together once or twice, but it didn't work out. Well, anyway—man, it was awesome being married to her. I'll always be grateful to her, because she's the reason I came here and found this river. And I have no desire to fish anywhere else but on the Deschutes for the rest of my life."

The railroad tracks we were walking on belong to the Burlington Northern and Santa Fe Railway. During the day, the trains sound their horns and rattle Maupin's stop signs and bounce echoes around the canyon. At night they are quieter; if trains can be said to tiptoe, these do. The rhythmic sound of their wheels rises, fills your ears, and fades; the silence after it's gone refills with the sound of the river. We were out in the night in Maupin a lot because first light and last light are good times to catch steelhead. It seems to me now that I spent as much time with Joe in the dark as I did in the light.

On my second night, he and I went to a fish hatchery downstream from town. We parked, zigzagged down a slope, passed dark buildings, crossed a lawn, and wrong-footed our way along the tracks, on whose curving rails the moon had laid a dull shine. After about a mile, we plunged through some alders and into the river and stood in the water for a long time waiting for dawn to start. This all felt a bit spooky and furtive to me.

My instinct, I later learned, was right. I had a fishing license, and Joe had licenses both to fish and to guide. He did not, however, possess a valid permit to be a fishing guide on the Deschutes. Two months earlier, he had left the Fly Fisher's Place in Sisters (actually, he had been fired), and thus he had lost the guiding permit that the shop provided him. His attempt to jury-rig a permit from a rafting guide's permit loaned to him by an outfitter in Maupin was not enough, because it allowed him to guide rafters but not anglers. Joe was breaking the law, in other words, and the consequences could be a fine of up to $2,500, a possible prison term, and the forfeit of his guiding license—no small risk to run.

On some evenings, after fishing, Joe and I went to Maupin's bars. They were packed with a young crowd that included many rafting guides, and everybody seemed to know Joe. He sat drinking beers and watching two or more baseball games on the bar TVs while young guys came up to him, often asking for advice— "She's kissed me twice, Joe, and I mean, *she* kissed *me*. But I haven't even brought up anything about sex." Joe: "Hell, tee her up, man, and ask questions later!" At the end of the night a barmaid announced last call, and Joe told her, "I'll have another beer, and a cot."

When Tiger Woods fished the Deschutes some years ago (with John Hazel, not with Joe), he did not pick up the spey cast right away, so I guess it's no surprise that I didn't, either. I simply couldn't get the message, and I told Joe I wanted to go back to the fly rod. Not possible, he said. He had no fly rod; and, at his insistence, I had not brought mine. He was a patient and remorseless coach, smoking and commenting on each attempt as I tried over and over. "You fucked up, Bud. Your rod tip was almost in the water on that last one. Keep the tip high." A failed spey cast is a shambles, like the collapse of a circus tent, with pole and line in chaos, and disgrace everywhere.

But he wouldn't give up. I worried that it might be painful for him to watch something he did so beautifully being done so wrong, but now I think his depression gave him a sort of immunity. The tedium of watching me may have been nothing compared with what he was feeling inside. And when occasionally I did get it, his enthusiasm was gigantic: "That's it! *Money!*" he would holler as the line sailed out.

So I'm in my motel cabin the night before our three-day float trip, and I can't sleep. I keep practicing the motions of the cast—one, two, three, four—like the present-arms drill in a commercial for the Marine Corps on TV. I practice the cast when I'm pacing around the motel-cabin floor and when I'm lying on my back in the bed. Joe has told me that the first pool we will fish is the best pool on the entire lower river.

If I don't catch a fish there, I figure, my chances for success will go way down. He has shown me how to cast from the right side of the river and from the left;

you turn the motion around, like batting from opposite sides of the plate. He has said we will fish this first pool from the right side, so I practice that cast only. I keep remembering that I have never caught a steelhead. I do not sleep a wink.

He has told me to come to his house at 3:45 a.m. The early start is essential, he has assured me, because another guide is likely to be in the pool before us if we're late. At 3:15 I put on my gear and drive to his house. All his windows are dark. The moon is up, and I wait in the shadow of Joe's trailered driftboat. No sign of activity in the house. At the tick of 3:45, I step noisily onto the front porch in my studded wading shoes and rap on the door. Through the window I can see only darkness, and the corner of a white laundry basket in a patch of moonlight. I call Joe's name. A pause. Then, from somewhere inside: "Th'damn alarm didn't go off!"

He comes out, rumpled and sleepy, and puts on his waders, which were hanging on the porch rail. We get in the Tahoe and take off, stopping on the way to pick up some coffee and pastry from the free breakfast spread at a motel considerably more expensive than my own. Joe assures me this is OK; no one is around to disagree.

We rattle for half an hour down a county road beside the river, leaving dust behind, and then pull into a location he asks me not to disclose. He backs the driftboat down to the river and launches it and we get in. At the second or third scrape of the oars against the boat's aluminum sides, headlamps light up at a place not far from the boat launch. Guys are camped there so as to get to this pool at first light, and we have beaten them to it, Joe says with satisfaction. We go a short distance downstream and stop under the branches of trees on the right-hand bank.

The moon is not high enough to reach into the canyon, so the water is completely dark. We wait, not talking. I unwrap and eat the Heartland Bakery cinnamon Danish from the more expensive motel's breakfast spread and crumple the wrapper and put it in the top of my waders and rinse my fingers in the river. The sky lightens and the water becomes a pewter color. Faintly, its ripples and current patterns can now be seen. Joe puts out his cigarette and applies ChapStick to his lips. We slide from the boat into the river.

My fear of wading has receded, thanks partly to my new wading staff. We go halfway across the pool. Joe tells me where to put the fly—a pattern called the Green Butt Skunk—and I begin to cast. Suddenly, I'm casting well and throwing line far across the river. Joe exclaims in astonishment and yells, "Money! Goddamn! You're throwing line as good as Abe Streep!" (He is referring to an editor of this magazine, a fine athlete who fished with Joe the year before.) I am elated and try not to think about how I am managing to cast this well. I fish the fly across and downstream as the line swings in the current. I strip in the line, take a step downstream, and cast again.

Cast, step, cast again; I work my way down the pool, Joe next to me. We pause as a train goes by, hauling a collection of graffiti on the sides of its white boxcars. I notice a purple, bulbous scrawl that reminds me of something. Joe tells me to cast toward a pile of white driftwood on the bank. I send 50 or 60 feet of line straight at it, lay the fly beside it, swing the fly across. The light is now high enough that the ripples and the lanes of current are distinct. At the end of the swing, a swift, curved disturbance appears in the pewter surface of the river, and the line pulls powerfully tight.

~~~~~~

Joe's father, William Randolph, was a navy pilot who flew many missions in Vietnam and could be gone for months at a time. Brenda, Joe's mother, stayed home with Joe (called Joey), his older sister, Kay, and his younger sister, Fran. The family spent much of the kids' childhood at Naval Air Station Lemoore, south of Fresno, California, where Joe often rode his bicycle down to the Kings River to fish.

Sometimes he hunted for ducks with family friends. Later he even had a scabbard on his bicycle in which he could carry his shotgun. His friends had shotguns, too, and sometimes they would stand about a hundred yards apart in a field and shoot at each other with the lighter sizes of birdshot. The pellets did not penetrate but "stung like crazy" when they hit. Once, when Joe was speeding along on his bicycle without a helmet, he came out from behind a dumpster and a passing garbage truck ran into him and knocked him unconscious. There was not much male supervision on the base with the dads away at war.

Joe's mother had problems with depression, which the kids did not understand until they were in their twenties. Once or twice they went to stay with relatives while she was hospitalized. When Joe was in grade school, she and his father divorced. Joe's main emotional problem, as Kay remembers, was getting angry, often at himself for personal frustrations. As a boy, he played tennis and traveled to tournaments and earned a national junior-level ranking. Being tall, he had a big serve, but his inability to avoid blowups on the court ruled out tennis for him. Other sports he excelled in were basketball, baseball, track, and volleyball.

He went to high school in Fresno but did not graduate, although he did get his GED. To acquire a useful trade, in the late 1980s, he attended a school in the Midwest where he learned to be a baker; then he decided that was not for him and returned to California. He was kicked off the basketball team at Monterey Peninsula College for skipping practice to fish. Various injuries—elbow, knee, a severe fracture of the left ankle—interfered with his promising college baseball career. He once watched a doctor chip a bone spur off his knee with a chisel and did not pass out.

In his thirties, in Monterey, he tried to qualify for the semipro beach-volleyball circuit and took steroids to improve his game. The drugs caused him to feel invincible and aggressive and righteously angry, and added a foot to his vertical leap, but he did not make the roster. While playing volleyball he met a woman named Tricia, and they married. The couple had two children—Hank, born in 1995, and Maddi, born in 1997. He and Tricia separated in about 2000 and later divorced.

Now the sun had risen over the canyon, and Joe was navigating us through rapids whose splashes wet my notebook as I recorded the details of my first steelhead—a six-pound hatchery fish from far upstream, according to the identification made by Joe on the basis of the fish's clipped maxillary fin (a tiny fin by the mouth).

"The tug is the drug," steelheaders say, describing that first strike and the fight that follows. This was true, as I could now affirm. The afterglow was great, too. I looked up at the canyon walls rising like hallelujah arms, their brown grasses crossed by eagle shadows, and at the green patches where small springs came up, and the herd of bighorn sheep starting mini rockslides behind their back hooves, and the hatch of tiny crane flies like dust motes in the sunlight.

Happiness! The pressure was off, I had caught the fish, defeated the possible jinx, the article would now work out. In this mood, I could have fallen out of the boat and drowned and not minded, or not minded much. The morning had become hot, and Joe asked if I wanted some water. He opened the cooler. Inside I saw a few bottles of spring water and a 30-pack of Keystone beer in cans. Joe's assistant for the trip, a young man named J. T. Barnes, went by in a yellow raft loaded with gear, and Joe waved. He said J.T. would set up our evening camp downstream.

Every fishing trip reconstructs a cosmogony, a world of angling defeats and victories, heroes and fools. Joe told me about a guy he fished with once who hooked a bat, and the guy laughed as the bat flew here and there at the end of his line, and then it flew directly at the guy's head and wrapped the line around the guy's neck and was in his face flapping and hissing and the guy fell on the ground screaming for Joe to get the bat off him and Joe couldn't do a thing, he was laughing so hard.

"Do your clients ever hook you?" I asked.

"Oh, hell yes, all the time. Once I was standing on the bank and this guy was in the river fly-casting, and he wrapped his backcast around my neck, and I yelled at him, and what does the guy do but yank harder! Almost strangled me. I'll never forget that fucking guy. We laughed about it later in camp."

The next pool we fished happened to be on the left side. I had not practiced the left-side cast during my insomniac night. Now when I tried it I could not do it at all. The pool after that was on the right, but my flailing on the left had caused me to forget how to cast from the right. Again the circus-tent collapse, again chaos and disgrace. My euphoria wore off, to be replaced by symptoms of withdrawal.

I liked that Joe always called me "Bud." It must have been his standard form of address for guys he was guiding. The word carried overtones of affection, familiarity, respect. He got a chance to use it a lot while trying to help me regain my cast, because I soon fell into a dire slump, flop sweat bursting on my forehead, all physical coordination gone.

"Bud, you want to turn your entire upper body toward the opposite bank as you sweep that line.... You're trying to do it all with your arms, Bud.... Watch that line, Bud, you're coming forward with it just a half-second too late." I was ready to flip out, lose my temper, hurl the rod into the trees. Joe was all calmness, gesturing with the cigarette between two fingers of his right hand. "Try it again, Bud, you almost had it that time."

By midafternoon Joe started in on the 30-pack of Keystone, but he took his time with it and showed no effects. Our camp that night was at a wide, flat place that had been an airfield. J.T. served shrimp appetizers and steak. Joe and I sat in camp chairs while he drank Keystone and told more stories—about his Cajun grandfather who used to drink and pass out on fishing excursions, and Joe had to rouse him so he wouldn't trail his leg in the gator-infested waters; about a stripper he had a wild affair with, and how they happened to break up; about playing basketball at night on inner-city courts in Fresno where you put quarters in a meter to keep the playground lights on. At full dark, I went into my tent and looked through the mesh at the satellites going by. Joe stayed up and drank Keystone and watched sports on his iPhone.

I was back in the river and mangling my cast again the next morning while Joe and J.T. loaded the raft. Out of my hearing (as I learned afterward from J.T.), their conversation turned to J.T.'s father, who died when J.T. was 15. Joe asked J.T. a lot of questions about how the death had affected him.

J.T. misunderstood Joe's instructions and set up our next camp at the wrong place, a narrow ledge at the foot of a sagebrush-covered slope. Joe was angry but didn't yell at him. During dinner that evening, J.T. told us the story of his recent skateboarding injury, when he dislocated his right elbow and snapped all the tendons so the bones of his forearm and hand were hanging only by the skin. Joe watched a football game and talked about Robert Griffin III, who was destined to be one of the greatest quarterbacks of all time, in Joe's opinion. As I went to bed I could still hear his iPhone's signifying noises.

At a very late hour, I awoke to total quiet and the sound of the river. The moon was pressing black shadows against the side of my tent. I got out of my sleeping bag and unzipped the tent flap and walked a distance away, for the usual middle-of-the-night purpose. When I turned to go back, I saw a figure standing in the moonlight by the camp. It was just standing there in the sagebrush and looking at me.

At first I could not distinguish the face, but as I got closer I saw that it was Joe. At least it ought to be, because he was the most likely possibility; but the figure just stood in silence, half-shadowed by sagebrush bushes up to the waist. I blinked to get the sleep out of my eyes. As I got closer, I saw it had to be Joe, unquestionably. Still no sound, no sign of recognition. I came closer still. Then Joe smiled and said, "You, too, Bud?" in a companionable tone. I felt a certain relief, even gratitude, at his ability to be wry about this odd moonlight encounter between two older guys getting up in the night. Now, looking back, I believe that more was going on. I believe that what I saw was a ghost—an actual person who also happened to be a ghost, or who was contemplating being one.

~~~~~~

The poor guy. Here I was locked in petty torment over my cast, struggling inwardly with every coach I'd ever disappointed, and Joe was... who knows where? No place good. In fact, I knew very little about him. I didn't know that he had started guiding for the Fly Fisher's Place in 2009, that he'd done splendidly that year (the best in modern history for steelhead in the Deschutes), that he had suffered a depression in the fall after the season ended, that he'd been broke, that friends had found him work and loaned him money.

I didn't know that after his next guiding season, in 2010, he had gone into an even worse depression; that on December 26, 2010, he had written a suicide note and swallowed pills and taped a plastic bag over his head in the back offices of the Fly Fisher's Place; that he'd been interrupted in this attempt and rushed to a hospital in Bend; that afterward he had spent time in the psychiatric ward of the hospital; that his friends in Sisters and his boss, Jeff Perin, owner of the fly shop, had met with him regularly in the months following to help him recover.

I didn't know that after the next season, in late 2011, he had disappeared; that Perin, fearing a repetition, had called the state police; and that they had searched for him along the Deschutes Valley with a small plane and a boat and eventually found him unharmed and returning home. Joe later told Perin he had indeed thought about killing himself during this episode but had decided not to.

I didn't know that Perin had refrained from firing Joe on several occasions—for example, when Joe was guiding an older angler who happened to be a psychiatrist with the apt name of Dr. George Mecouch, along with one of Dr. Mecouch's friends, and a repo man showed up with police officers and a flatbed, and they repossessed Joe's truck (a previous one), leaving Joe and his elderly clients stranded by the side of the road in the middle of nowhere at eleven o'clock at night. Dr. Mecouch, evidently an equable and humorous fellow, had laughed about the experience, thereby perhaps saving Joe's job. I did not know that Perin had permanently ended his professional relationship with Joe when Joe refused to guide on a busy Saturday in July of 2012 because he had received no tip from his clients of the day before.

The spot where Joe killed himself is out in the woods about six miles from Sisters. You drive on a rutted Forest Service road for the last mile or two until you get to a clearing with a large gravel pit and a smaller one beside it. Local people come here for target practice. Splintery, shot-up pieces of plywood lie on the ground, and at the nearer end the spent shotgun-shell casings resemble strewn confetti. Their colors are light blue, dark blue, pink, yellow, forest green, red, black, and purple. Small pools of muddy water occupy the centers of the gravel pits, and the gray, rutted earth holds a litter of broken clay-pigeon targets, some in high-visibility orange. At the clearing's border, dark pine trees rise all around.

Probably to forestall the chance that he would be interrupted this time, Joe had told some friends that he was going to Spokane to look for work, others that he would be visiting his children in California. On November 4, 2012, he spent the afternoon at Bronco Billy's, a restaurant-bar in Sisters, watching a football game and drinking Maker's Mark with beer chasers. At about six in the evening he left, walking out on a bar tab of about $18. The bartender thought he had gone outside to take a phone call. At some time after that, he drove to the gravel pit, parked at its northwest edge, and ran a garden hose from the exhaust pipe to the right rear passenger-side window, sealing the gaps around the pipe and in the window with towels and clothes. A man who went to the gravel pit to shoot discovered the body on November 14. In two weeks, Joe would have been 49 years old.

He left no suicide note, but he did provide a couple of visual commentaries at the scene for those who could decode them. The garden hose he used came from the Fly Fisher's Place. Joe stole it for this purpose, one can surmise, as a cry for help or gesture of anger directed at his former boss, Jeff Perin.

Over the summer, Joe's weeks of illegal guiding had caught up with him when the state police presented him with a ticket for the violation. He would be required to go to court, and in all likelihood his local guiding career would be through, at least for a good while. Joe thought Perin had turned him in to the authorities; and, in fact, Perin and other guides had done exactly that. Joe was often aggressive and contentious on the river, he competed for clients, and his illegal status made people even more irate. But, in the end, to say that Joe's legal difficulties were what undid him would be a stretch, given his history.

Joe's friend Diane Daviscourt, when she visited the scene, found an empty Marlboro pack stuck in a brittlebrush bush next to where Joe had parked. The pack rested upright among the branches, where it could only have been put deliberately. She took it as a sign of his having given up on everything, and as his way of saying, "Don't forget me."

<hr />

John Hazel, the Deschutes River's senior guide, said Joe was a charismatic fellow who took fishing too seriously. "I used to tell him, 'It's only fishing, Joe.' He got really down on himself when he didn't catch fish. Most guides are arrogant—Joe possessed the opposite of that. Whoever he was guiding, he looked at the person and tried to figure out what that person wanted." Daviscourt, who had briefly been Joe's girlfriend, said he was her best friend, and made a much better friend than a boyfriend. "He fooled us all," she said. "I haven't picked up a fly-fishing rod since he died."

She made a wooden cross for him and put it up next to where she found the Marlboro pack. The cross says JOE R. on it in black marker, and attached to it with pushpins is a laminated photo of Joe, completely happy, standing in the river with a steelhead in his hands and a spey rod by his feet. On the pine needles beside the cross is a bottle of Trumer Pils, the brand Joe drank when she was buying.

Just before Joe died, J. T. Barnes was calling him a lot, partly to say hi, and partly because Joe had never paid him for helping on the trip with me. (He did split the tip, however.) For someone now out $600, J.T. had only kind words for Joe. "He was like the ideal older brother. And he could be so up, so crazy enthusiastic, about ordinary stuff. One day we were packing his driftboat before a trip, drinking beer, and I told him that I play the banjo. Joe got this astonished, happy look on his face, and he said, 'You play the banjo? No way! That is so great—I sing!' That made me laugh, but he was totally being serious. I play the banjo, Joe sings!"

Joe had six dollars in his wallet when he died. Kay, his sister, who lives in Napa, thought Joe's chronic lack of money was why he lost touch with his family. "Joe was always making bad decisions financially. Maybe, because he had a lot of pride, that made him never want to see us. But he was doing what he loved, supporting himself as a famous fishing guide. He had no idea how proud his family was of him."

Alex Gonsiewski, a highly regarded young guide on the river, who works for John Hazel, said that Joe taught him most of what he knows. When Gonsiewski took his first try at running rapids that have drowned people, Joe was in the bow of the driftboat helping him through. "It's tough to be the kind of person who lives for extreme things, like Joe was," Gonsiewski said. "His eyes always looked sad. He loved this river more than anywhere. And better than anybody, he could dial you in on how to fish it. He showed me the river, and now every place on the river makes me think of him. He was an ordinary, everyday guy who was also amazing. I miss him every day."

~~~~~~

The paths along the river that have been made by anglers' feet are well worn and wide. Many who come to fish the Deschutes are driven by a deep, almost desperate need. So much of the world is bullshit. This river is not. Among the many natural glories of the Northwest that have been lost, this valley—still mostly undeveloped, except for the train tracks—and its beautiful, tough fish have survived.

Joe was the nakedest angler I've ever known. He came to the river from a world of bullshit, interior and otherwise, and found here a place and a sport to which his own particular sensors were perfectly attuned. Everything was OK when he was on the river... except that then everything had to stay that way continuously, or else horrible feelings of withdrawal would creep in. For me the starkest sadness about Joe's death was that the river and the steelhead weren't enough.

At the end of my float trip with Joe, just before we reached the river's mouth, he stopped at a nondescript, wide, shallow stretch with a turquoise-flowing groove. He said he called this spot Mariano, after Mariano Rivera, the Yankees' great relief pitcher, because of all the trips it had saved. I stood and cast to the groove just as told to, and a sudden river quake bent the spey rod double. The ten-pound steelhead I landed after a long fight writhed like a constrictor when I tried to hold it for a photograph.

The next evening, not long before I left for the airport, Joe and I floated the river above Maupin a last time. Now he wasn't my guide; he had me go first and fish a hundred yards or so ahead of him. Dusk deepened, and suddenly I was casting well again. I looked back at Joe, and he raised his fist in the air approvingly. At the end of his silhouetted arm, the glow of a cigarette could be seen. I rolled out one cast after the next. It's hard to teach a longtime angler anything, but Joe had taught me. He knocked the rust off my fishing life and gave me a skill that brought back the delight of learning, like the day I first learned to ride a bicycle. I remembered that morning when we were floating downstream among the crane flies in the sunlight. Just to know it's possible to be that happy is worth something, even if the feeling doesn't last. Hanging out with Joe uncovered long-overgrown paths back to childhood. Peace to his soul.

(Originally published August 2013)

THE BIGHORN SHEEP WHO WAS YOUTUBE FAMOUS

MICHAEL KRUSE

It's not easy to get inside an animal's head. Nor is trying to do so a particularly safe approach to your first-ever assignment for Outside. *Michael Kruse tried it anyway, succeeding brilliantly with a story about a bighorn sheep who was too charismatic for his own good.*

A sheep was dead.

A bighorn sheep.

Earlier in the day, in Wyoming's Sinks Canyon, the workers at the state park had organized a fun run and bake sale to raise money to stuff and mount the sheep, so he could come home, either in a standing pose or a walking pose, life-size and lifelike, once and for all and forever. At the visitor center, a sign hung from the rail around the deck. BRING BAM BAM BACK! Down in the town of Lander, his disembodied horns and coarse, tanned hide remained ensconced in a taxidermy shop, waiting to be mounted.

Now, in the cooling dusk of a 2013 summer evening, surrounded by the vast, impossible beauty that can start to feel almost commonplace in this part of the country—to the left, the conifer-covered north-facing slope; to the right, wildflowers and clusters of boulders and great granite walls—a couple dozen mourners and spectators sat in small, cheap chairs made of metal. They watched a lengthy slide show set to melancholy music. They looked at a portrait of the sheep, his regal gaze fixed in a frame trimmed with a black canvas shroud. They listened to sheep experts say what they felt needed to be said at such an unusual event, this tutorial meets memorial.

"The animal actually perished, ceased to have a heartbeat, last winter," said Stan Harter, a biologist with Wyoming Game and Fish. "But in my opinion, he died in 2009, when we had to move him out of the park."

"It's disturbing, what has occurred…," said Joe Hutto, a local naturalist and author. "I just never thought I'd see the day where the sheep weren't here."

Under the darkening sky, Suzan Moulton, the executive director of the National Bighorn Sheep Interpretive Center, in Dubois, reminded the gathering how many sheep there once were, and how few there are now. She posed a blunt, compelling question.

"What is wilderness," she asked, "without something like this?"

~~~~~~

The sheep that people would come to call Bam Bam was the last of his herd. The last in Sinks Canyon. In 2013, an obituary ran in the state's largest newspaper, in Casper. It called him an international star.

Based on the number of rings on his heavy curled horns, he was believed to be around seven years old. That means he was likely born in the spring of 2005, probably in the canyon, certainly high in the cliffs, somewhere hidden and hard to get to. His mother nuzzled him and nursed him, and he stretched his neck to drink her milk. She hurried to lick him dry, to lessen the scent of birth so attractive to opportunistic attackers.

Within his first hour on earth, his hooves hardened, the bottoms of his still knobby-kneed legs becoming something like tough, durable suction cups, appropriate for his treacherous, high-altitude habitat. For the first week or so, he stayed close to his mother, and then they joined a larger group of sheep known as a nursery band, a handful of ewes and their lambs.

Bighorns' best defense from predators is their vision. They have binoculars for eyes and practically peripheral sweep—and the more eyes the better, letting them watch together for coyotes, mountain lions and bears, and hungry eagles circling in the sky, searching for chances to swoop down and grab lambs from the edges of cliffs.

The ancestors of this lamb and his mother evolved in the ice ages at the shifting bases of glaciers, spreading successfully around mountains from North America to Europe, from Africa to Asia, adapting and advancing, living in extreme heat or extreme cold, the species in this way lasting from the Pleistocene to what many scientists now are calling the Anthropocene—a wholly new epoch, in which we, humans, are the preeminent influencers of the planet and its changing ecosystems.

"A particularly durable ice age creature," Valerius Geist called bighorns in his book *Mountain Sheep: A Study in Behavior and Evolution*. They are, and have been, he said, "survival artists."

As spring turned to summer, the lamb and his mother and the rest of the ewes and their offspring followed the snow line up the mountain, even higher, where the brief seasonal melt leaves the land rich, spongy, and lush, an alpine pasture verdant with nourishing grasses and forbs. He added this vegetation to the diet of his mother's milk by the time he was a few weeks old.

His kind, at least when healthy and fit, is playful and gregarious. It starts almost immediately. The lambs of bighorn sheep run and jump and twist. They push against each other. They butt heads. They stand atop rocks and play king of the hill. It isn't just for fun. The game hones dexterity. And it begins to establish where each lamb stands within the herd. The identity of a bighorn sheep, especially a bighorn ram, depends on where it ranks in relation to those around it. They never stop playing king of the hill.

By the beginning of the winter, the first of his life, the sheep who would be Bam Bam had grown to roughly 80 pounds and was almost as tall as his mother. Furious subzero weather chased the nursery band back down to valleys and lower sides of slopes, where the lambs learned how to use their hooves to paw through the windswept snow to get at what was left to eat.

For people, part of the appeal of the wilderness of the American West is the perspective it elicits: trip and fall in some snow, in 20 below, and you could be dead in half an hour. Animals don't need this reminder. Certainly not sheep. The specter of starvation always looms in winters. Existence is extraordinary happenstance, and survival is a desperate effort, a mixture of undeniable vigor and remarkable luck. It's a fight that never ends, until it does.

Starting in 2000, some 70 miles from Sinks Canyon, a handful of smart, serious men had studied the sheep in a part of the Wind River Range called Middle Mountain. They collected fecal samples, tracked radio-collared ewes, monitored the chemical makeup of the precipitation and therefore the plants and the soil. And they watched the sheep. They saw undersized lambs with patchy coats and swollen, watery eyes. They saw some so sick they crawled on their knees to their mothers. They heard chronic coughs.

Over in Sinks Canyon, the workers at the state park heard the hacking, too. It cut through the air and echoed off the rocks.

Joe Hutto, from the memorial, was one of the men on Middle Mountain. He wrote about his experience. "An obscure wave of sickness is quietly passing across the high and remote mountains of the Rocky Mountain West," he noted in his book *The Light in High Places*.

A journalist from the *Los Angeles Times* arrived in Wyoming to report on the scientists' findings, saying "profound environmental changes are beginning to ripple through the food chain and into the bodies of lambs."

For these wild sheep, maybe more than ever, the odds against a first breath were phenomenal. The odds against the next were the same.

~~~~~~~~~~~~~~~~~~~~~~~~~~~~~~~~~~~~~~~

The so-called Sheep Eaters band of the Shoshone tribe used bighorns for everything—the meat for sustenance, the hides to make warm clothes, the horns for bows to shoot their arrows. They left behind rock art, ancient etchings, the depictions of the sheep featuring horns of exaggerated length. In bighorns they saw majesty and power, and in North America as it existed then—before white men, before gold, before Manifest Destiny, before unchecked hunting, before ranches and cattle and domestic sheep—the number of bighorns, some have estimated, approached two million. Maybe the population wasn't quite that high. Probably. By the late 1950s, though, it was as low as 25,000. In Wyoming it was 2,000. These days, those numbers are up, to 80,000 and 6,700, respectively. That's mainly because of successful human intervention—restoration efforts based in part on taking sheep from larger, healthier herds and transferring them to other areas, hoping they will flourish and reproduce. But these efforts also have been frustrating and puzzling. In some spots, the sheep do reasonably well. In others they don't. They disappear.

In Sinks Canyon, in the 1980s, the transplanted herd hovered around 150. In the 1990s: more like 50. In the 2000s: the sheep that would be Bam Bam was one of only a handful of lambs.

In a few years, his baby teeth gone, he was the dominant male among the few sheep left in Sinks Canyon—a couple of rams, two or three ewes, and two or three lambs. His horns, their solid bands reflecting his increasing strength and age, had grown to the three-quarter curl that hunters covet.

His look was the look that has made his species iconic. Snapshots of bighorns have backdrops that—at no more than a glance—are identifiable as the West's impenetrable wilds. The big sky. The snow on the sharp tips of peaks.

That sentiment persists. Suzan Moulton, the director of the national sheep center, called bighorns the real "rugged individualists" in a region filled with people who aspire to be exactly that. Joe Hutto described them to me as "this symbol of an absolute, inaccessible wilderness." They live where humans don't. Where humans wouldn't. They do their best where we are not. But the unfortunate flip side of this inaccessibility is their surprising vulnerability. Bighorn sheep, some have said, are just a pair of lungs looking for a place to die. These muscular mammals, weighing up to 300 pounds, are unusually susceptible to the viruses that cause pneumonia—viruses that are latent in domestic sheep but almost always lethal to wild bighorns. And because bighorns are so social, if one of them catches it, pretty much all of them do.

If what's getting bighorns at the base of the mountains are infected domestic sheep, what's getting them at the top, of late, is what's falling from the sky—rain made more acidic by fossil-fuel pollution. The measurements taken by the men on Middle Mountain showed dangerously low levels of selenium, a critical component of the bighorn diet, which strengthens their muscles and bolsters their ability to grapple with disease. "The chemical changes occurring in alpine soils today are radical and mind-numbing in their complexity and implications," according to Hutto. He says the rain that high is so acidic it burns his eyes.

The acute sensitivity of the sheep makes them a species worth paying attention to, according to Kevin Hurley of the Wild Sheep Foundation, in Cody. If a bighorn herd can thrive in an area, it indicates that a lot of other species, like deer and elk, can thrive there, too. And the indication is that something is wrong. It's hard to say precisely what, because there's not just one thing. Domestic sheep, invasive animals, invasive plants, rule-breaking ATVs, wildfire suppression, interstate highways, acid rain, and massive water diversion—in aggregate, two letters, one word. Us.

So in 2008, in Sinks Canyon, state-park superintendent Darrel Trembly saw one lamb. Then he didn't. And at some point, the canyon had just two sheep left. Two rams. They started coming down the slopes and moving closer to the road, to the parking lot, to the visitor center. It was hard not to notice them. One in particular. He had a habit of using his horns to butt car bumpers. They heard him.

Bam.

Bam bam.

The name stuck.

They named the other one, too, the moniker reflecting their respective ranks. The first sheep was Bam Bam. The second was Bam Bam's Buddy. Bam Bam pushed Buddy around, not vice versa. Buddy ceded ground to Bam Bam, not the other way around. Bam Bam led, Buddy followed. They were seldom ever not together.

In 2009, though, after winter broke, once the snow melted, Buddy wasn't around anymore. Maybe he wandered off. Probably he was dead. Bam Bam, though, was not, so Bam Bam lingered by the side of the road that sliced through the canyon, watching people ride past on their bikes, loitering by parked cars and trucks. He seemed interested in their shiny bumpers and doors. He butted at them halfheartedly. He clambered up the steps onto the deck of the visitor center and stood in front of the windows. He stared at his reflection.

Then in May, one late afternoon, a local man named Mark James drove his black Toyota 4Runner up the road in the canyon. He saw Bam Bam standing on the shoulder. The ram stood so still that for a second James thought he was a mounted, stuffed sheep. Then Bam Bam moved his head. James made a U-turn and drove back down to get a better look. Bam Bam watched him from the other side of the road. Bam Bam crossed the road and walked toward the 4Runner. James turned on his video camera. His girlfriend, sitting shotgun, talked to Bam Bam.

"Hi," she said.

Bam Bam reared up from a standstill a few feet into the air. He reared up on his hind legs and came back down, his front hooves touching the asphalt. He bowed his head, showing the 4Runner the top of his three-quarter-curl horns. He lifted his head and turned it, showing the 4Runner one side of his horns, and then turned his head again, showing the 4Runner the other. He walked toward the vehicle, extending his horns toward the shiny bumper, touching it, tapping it. James backed up, revving the engine. Bam Bam closed the distance, touching, tapping. James backed up, revved the engine, and Bam Bam reared up and lowered his head and horns, this time giving the 4Runner's left front bumper more than a tap.

Bam.

The vehicle jolted.

The camera rolled.

It got dark and James went home. He posted a two-and-a-half-minute clip of the encounter on YouTube. He titled it "Bam Bam, the Bighorn Sheep Attacks Toyota 4Runner." People clicked. People watched. They kept clicking and they kept watching—100 views, 1,000 views—and soon enough some in Sinks Canyon started to say Bam Bam was famous.

Famous.

What's that mean?

What's it mean to be famous?

For a person, it means people know you, or think they do, even though they don't. It means they saw you on a screen, and so now they want to see you for real.

And for a bighorn sheep?

Throughout the summer of 2009, May to June, July to August, Trembly and park worker Randy Wise watched Bam Bam. They watched him lounge in the handicapped spot. They watched him walk into the visitor center, look around, turn around, and walk back out.

One day they looked out the window of the visitor center, and in the parking lot a man, a father, had set his child, an infant, on Bam Bam's back, and a woman, the mother, was taking pictures. They were laughing. Bam Bam didn't seem to mind. Trembly hurried outside, approaching the man as calmly as he could.

"Sir," he said. "This is a wild animal. You need to take your baby off the back of the bighorn. You need to give him some space."

At other times, and often, they watched people feed him. Peanuts and candy bars. Potato chips and Doritos. Wise confronted these people, telling them, in tones as nice as he could muster, that feeding Bam Bam wasn't helping him. A fed bear is a dead bear, or so goes the saying in these parts, and this was no different. "You're killing him," Wise told the people. "You're killing this animal by giving him this food."

Trembly and Wise and staffers from Wyoming Game and Fish tried to chase him off. They snapped plastic bags at him, hoping they would startle him up the hill, to the rocks of the south-facing slope, back to where he belonged. They even used firecrackers. Bam Bam scurried up. Waited for a bit. Ambled back down. Stan Harter from Game and Fish made a sign and posted it at the edge of the visitor center parking lot. BIGHORN SHEEP ARE WILD ANIMALS. DO NOT APPROACH. ATTACKS ARE POSSIBLE.

Meanwhile, on YouTube, people kept clicking, kept watching. Thousands became tens of thousands. Tens of thousands became hundreds of thousands. Viewers thought it was funny. The fact that this bighorn sheep was doing something they had never seen a bighorn sheep do should have been a signal that something wasn't right. An indicator. But they didn't know what they were watching. They didn't know that Bam Bam was behaving the way he had to behave. That he was obligated by his evolutionary code to vie for dominance. The way he did when he was a week-old lamb, drinking his mother's milk, watching for shadows of circling eagles, butting his brothers with the nascent nubs on the top of his head. Only now he was alone. There were no other rams. There were no other sheep. So he pushed on Mark James's Toyota 4Runner. He butted at it. He had it on the run. He proudly showed his horns.

Trembly and Wise worried. Bam Bam, with his ice-age body and his hard, 30-pound horns, packed three times the strength of an NFL linebacker. He could crush a person's chest or skull. Kill a child. Kill somebody elderly. Kill anybody.

A local nature photographer named Bill Briggs got to where he could sit close to Bam Bam, 25 feet away, and take pictures. He talked to him.

"What are you doing, big guy?"

One day, Bam Bam sat on his favorite flat-topped rock, not too far from the road, and Briggs watched a hyperactive college kid stop his car and get out. The kid bounded up the hill toward Bam Bam and then spotted Briggs.

"What is that thing?" the kid asked.

"Bighorn sheep," Briggs said.

The kid walked closer.

"You might not want to do that."

Bam Bam stood up. He lowered his head. He showed the kid his horns.

"You better move."

Bam Bam reared up. Came down. The kid turned and raced back down the hill, all the way to his car.

"Way to go, Bam Bam," Briggs said.

A different day, down the canyon at the home of a retired biology professor named Jack States, Bam Bam was eating the roses by the path to his front door. States called to him. Bam Bam looked up for a second and kept eating the flowers. He walked to the door and lowered his head. He put his nose on the screen. States worried the same way Trembly and Wise did. What could Bam Bam do? What would he do?

A few weeks later, a woman stood by the rail of a deck overlooking a fishpond. Bam Bam walked toward her, *clickety-clack,* hooves on planks of wood. The woman turned around. Bam Bam had her cornered. He walked closer. She held still. He lowered his head, showed the woman the top of his horns, and approached her. He touched his horns to her stomach, holding them there. Trembly saw what was happening and walked slowly over to Bam Bam and the woman, telling her he probably just wanted her to scratch his head. So she did. And Bam Bam backed off.

He couldn't stay. He had to be taken from the canyon. That August, Game and Fish came to pick him up. They took him to a different part of the range some 20 miles away. "It was only a matter of time before someone got hurt," Trembly told a newspaper reporter.

But Bam Bam found his way back. It took two weeks. He brought with him a ewe and a young ram. Those two left after a short while, though, and he was alone again.

Bam.

Bam bam.

Harter and others from Game and Fish returned to take him away for good. He was up a bit on the south-facing slope when they arrived. They tried to lure him with alfalfa pellets. Didn't work. One of the Game and Fish guys crinkled a silver wrapper from a candy bar. Seeing that, Bam Bam trotted over to their horse trailer and into it. They drove him east, past sagebrush and billboards, past cattle and the wires and slats meant to hem them in, past the derricks extracting liquid cash from the ground, past the ridges lined with rotating dervishes harvesting wind, past red-rusted carcasses of antique cars and weather-worn bones of abandoned barns. In Rawlins, in a parking lot next to a McDonald's, a man from Game and Fish put Bam Bam in a different trailer, driven by a different man, headed for a different place.

At Sybille Wildlife Research and Conservation Unit, four hours and some 250 miles from Sinks Canyon, Bam Bam had 500 fenced-in acres in which to roam with elk, bison, and two other bighorn rams. The other rams ventured up from the flatlands into the facility's higher, rougher terrain. Early on, Bam Bam found a weak spot in the fence, slipping out. He started walking in a direction that suggested he was aiming for home. It took a tranquilizer dart to get him back. After his foiled escape attempt, he kept mostly to himself. He stayed by the fence. The fence was by the road. He butted gently at the posts, waiting for cars to stop. People came to see him, Bam Bam from YouTube. Matt Huizenga, the Sybille manager, would find in Bam Bam's feed bin scraps of snacks. Chips. Licorice. Hamburger halves.

Wise, from Sinks Canyon, checked in every January by phone. He was afraid the people at Sybille might forget the people from Sinks. If Bam Bam were to die, he wanted to make sure they remembered that they wanted him back.

One evening in January 2013, a few days after Wise's call, Huizenga heard from someone who had driven by. The person said a sheep at the far end of the pasture looked hurt or sick. Right around dark, down by a creek, Huizenga found Bam Bam, lying on his side, legs stretched out straight and stiff. He stared into space. He tried to get up, but he couldn't. The next morning, Huizenga went back to the spot, and Bam Bam was still there, not just listless now but lifeless.

The necropsy concluded that Bam Bam was seven, several years short of what would have been a typical lifespan, and had died of reticulorumenitis and complications, including acidosis, dehydration, and electrolyte disturbances. In plain language, what killed Bam Bam wasn't an eagle, or a coyote, or a bear or a mountain lion or a wolf, or pneumonia, or a winter storm finally too savagely cold, or even old age. What killed him were the peanuts and seeds found stuck in his rumen. What killed him was that he ate too much of too many things he shouldn't have eaten. What killed him was what people fed him.

Bam Bam the bighorn ram.

YouTube celebrity. Monarch of the mountains. The last surviving sheep from the Sinks Canyon herd. Symbol of wilderness in the American West.

Dead of bloat.

(Originally published June 2014)

YES, IT IS A LOVELY MORNING. NOW WHY DON'T YOU JUST GO TO HELL.

SARA CORBETT

No other workplace on the planet has a more finely calibrated recipe for disaster than the Amundsen-Scott South Pole Station. Drop 28 researchers—and virtual strangers—in Antarctica. Blend in eight months of mind-numbing darkness. Fold into extremely close quarters. Add a pinch of dysfunction. Stir.

Spend time with people who've spent time at the South Pole and you will hear tales about deprivation and longing—longing for friends and family, for a long hot bath, for sex, for sunlight, for the Red Sox—basically for anything that's 3,000 or more miles out of reach. But inevitably the war story that gets delivered most emphatically is one that involves an agonizing and primal lust for fresh produce. At the South Pole, any fruit or vegetable that doesn't come in a can or belong in the freezer is called a "freshy" and is treated with real reverence. Freshies are stored in the "freshy shack," which is one of only two places at the Pole, the other being a small commissary stocked with toothpaste and other sundries, that is kept under lock and key.

One might reasonably calculate the season at the South Pole simply by watching what happens when someone eats, say, a peach. If the peach is consumed without incident, then it's likely to be November, December, or January, one of three summer months when warmer air and 24-hour sunlight allow National Guard planes to fly in several times weekly from New Zealand. Yet if that peach provokes an argument, or a scuffle ensues, or, as is more likely, everyone sits around glowering at the peach-eater, then you could reasonably presume you've entered the colorless melancholy of a South Pole winter, when for eight months it's too cold and dark to land a plane at all.

During the safer summer months, as many as 185 people—scientists and support staff sponsored by the U.S. government—live at the Amundsen-Scott South Pole station. But when the light dims and winter descends, the masses depart, leaving behind a skeleton staff of only 28, what's known as the "winter-over" crew. From then on, the crew lives alone in four barrack-like wooden buildings beneath a windproof geodesic dome 164 feet in diameter, made of aluminum and buried almost entirely by drifting snow. The air gets so cold it will literally crack the enamel off your teeth. Ice grows on the inside walls of the cell-sized bedrooms in long, creeping stains. It takes longer to dress—to don three layers of long underwear, insulated Carhartt overalls, boots, and a government-issue parka—than it does to reach the point of hypothermia, to achieve Ice Cubeness. Not to mention that with almost two miles of solid ice beneath it, the Pole sits at an altitude of 9,450 feet, making breathing a chore. Thanks to the dry, frigid air, there are no natural smells at the South Pole. Nor, given the unending blankness of the ice, is there color. Nor, for more than half the year, light. When explorer Robert Swan pulled a sled to the Pole in 1986, he declared visiting the place to be "the cleanest and most isolated way of having a bad time ever devised."

If being thrown in with a group of relative strangers and cast to the exquisitely terrible edge of nothingness is humankind's deepest escape fantasy (see: *Moby Dick*, *Star Trek*, Joseph Conrad, *Gilligan's Island*), then the South Pole is probably its closest earthly embodiment. Not surprisingly, NASA, with an eye toward colonizing space, has followed life at the South Pole carefully in recent years, funding anthropologists to study the people who winter there, to chart the angels and beasts of Antarctic isolation and determine how, in a stripped-down, cut-off environment, we who belong to this overstuffed green world might manage to survive.

Wintering at the South Pole, those who've done it will tell you, isn't just about surviving physically. It's about opening one's mind to the unbroken darkness and minus-100-degree cold, to the fact that you've got 800 miles of empty ice on all sides and that, from February to October, there's no way out. It's about internalizing the blankness, the quiet. It's about letting the winter inside. This is when a person starts to change, they say. This is when, out on one of the Earth's last frontiers, surrounded by space-age paraphernalia and satellite technology, you meet your most primitive self.

Take, for example, one recent night in that most dreary of Antarctic months, August, when researchers discovered that the South Pole's hydroponic greenhouse, which thus far had produced no more than a few meager heads of lettuce each week, had miraculously mustered two ripe tomatoes. These were not prize tomatoes, not meaty softball-sized beauties, but rather sorry, stunted fruit, their skins a royal pink, their size reminiscent of a pair of slightly swollen cherry tomatoes. Nonetheless, they were freshies, arriving months after the freshy shack had been emptied, when no produce remained save for a few potatoes and some brittle garlic. Imagine it then—two pulpy sweet tomatoes, like twin chambers of the heart, quivering pregnantly on the vine! A meeting was called. People took turns parading into the narrow greenhouse to have a look. Then, finally, somebody suggested a lottery—everyone's name put into a hat, the tomatoes plucked and handed to the lucky winners.

The first guy immediately popped the tomato into his mouth and reflexively began to chew, a tide of horror seeming to wash over him at the precise instant he swallowed, understanding perhaps that like a brazen hedonist he'd squandered the moment, that his tomato, four months in the making, was already gone. The second fellow, who had clearly given the matter more thought, carried his tomato carefully on his palm to the South Pole galley, with a number of his crewmates following behind. He laid the tomato on the counter, located a knife, and began with utter deliberation to whittle the fruit down. He then produced a slice of toast, a strip of leftover bacon, a wilted lettuce leaf, and a jar of mayo, and, after a moment's furious work, triumphantly held aloft a Lilliputian BLT, which he consumed in small, mincing bites. Maybe in that instant he saw himself with his mouth around the most sumptuously oversized Carnegie Deli sandwich, or maybe his appetite was simply for a moment's dark pleasure, a Have lording it over the Have-nots. Whatever the case, the BLT disappeared quickly, and soon he was empty-handed again, a wild flicker in his eye, a touch of bacon grease on his chin.

"Sometimes," one of the bystanders that day says now, "you can tell a lot about a person by what he does with a tomato."

There are two potentially life-saving things a person should know before deploying to the South Pole for a winter: how to fight fire and how to get along with others. This gets explained to me by a fellow named Gumby, a native of Minnesota who over the past nine years has logged 76 months of Ice Time, as Antarctic experience is called, and is shortly to head back to the Pole as a maintenance specialist on the '98 winter-over crew.

"First of all, you can't exactly dial 9-1-1 down there," says Gumby. "And secondly, people tend to wig out on one another when it's dark that long."

It's a Saturday in early September. We're eating pork chops for lunch as sunlight slices through the dining hall windows at Camp La Foret, a facility set deep in the pines northwest of Colorado Springs. Twenty-two members of the 1998 South Pole crew have convened here for a weekend of group hugs and various team-building exercises before shipping off in October for the Pole. After this weekend, the group will move on to suburban Denver to attend five days of firefighting school. Gumby, who is six-foot-three and built like a Mack truck, wears Ben Franklin glasses and has a big brushy beard that smells like peat moss. I am acquainted with the smell of his beard because when, at the start of the meal, I asked the ten or so people at my table just how tight the living conditions are at the South Pole, Gumby immediately dropped his pork chop and hurled himself onto my lap to demonstrate.

The promise of this kind of claustrophobic intimacy—and the interpersonal meltdowns it can cause—is what inspired the La Foret weekend. The next 36 hours will offer a chance for this year's crop of deployees to dip their toes in the waters of emotional togetherness. It's also a last chance to back out. While the wintering-over Pole employees undergo a psychological screening prior to departure, purportedly to weed out anyone not fit, veterans will tell you that almost everyone passes, so the decision to go or not, to detach yourself from the rest of the world and throw your lot in with a bunch of possibly crazy strangers, is yours alone.

While roughly a third of the South Pole crew is made up of scientists—"Beakers," in Antarctic parlance—the rest consists of tradespeople sent to keep the Beakers alive. Together, they form a sort of vocational Noah's Ark—one doctor, one cook, one electrician, and so forth.

Even with the Beakers mixed in, the South Pole crew looks like a cross section of white America—folks you might find in line at the DMV in Traverse City, for example. Of the five women and 17 men who've made it to camp (six crew members were unable to come), nine have wintered at the Pole before. There are three married couples, five scientists from foreign countries, and three guys named Dave who, thanks to an earlier alliterative name game, are now distinguishable as Drinking Dave, Daring Dave, and Dangerous Dave. Ages run from 23 to 53, hairstyles from a military crew on Loud Larry the Navy communications specialist to a down-the-back snarl of early-dreadlock blond on Rabid Rodney, a young Aussie astronomer. Given that the women have named themselves things like Venomous Victoria and Dastardly Diana, I start to suspect that the male-female ratio causes them to feel defensive. This is mitigated, though, by a young woman who happens to be Gumby's bride of exactly one week. She has enthusiastically baptized herself Merry

Mary and is the first to speak up when our supercheery team-building facilitator, Leo, asks if we're having fun yet, blurting out, without irony, "Oodles!"

As Leo sees it, the more hugging everybody does this weekend the better. Already he's led us through a bevy of get-to-know-ya games, things like tag and human knots and "favorite worst smell." For this, the group sorted itself into the dueling body-odor people and the garbage-dump people, with several splinter factions, including "outhouse" and "dirty diapers" and, somewhat worryingly, a lone vote for "decomposing flesh" from Loud Larry. We now know who was born in what state (Minnesota prevailing), who's afraid of heights, and who gets squirmy about snakes. We've held hands and inched in opposite directions across a narrow log mounted several feet above the ground. Between activities, Leo has pulled everyone into a circle—what he calls the Circle of Comfort—and debriefed us.

"What did we learn up on that log just then?" Leo asks. "Did we notice anything about the group?"

Each time so far, the circle has fallen silent. Leo smiles expectantly and waits. Usually it's one of his two co-facilitators, Franco, the only guy here with a crystal around his neck, or Pat, a tanned and muscular woman, who then chimes in.

"I thought we did very well up there on the log," Pat says.

"I'm proud of the way everyone cooperated," Franco agrees.

A wind stirs the trees. More silence.

"Yes, cooperation will be important at the South Pole," Leo says finally. "But it's communication, people, that will get you through."

Silence again. It seems tacitly understood that Leo wouldn't last five minutes at the South Pole, a place where the psychology is hard-edged and of high consequence, where what seems at first like an amusing little idiosyncrasy can quickly become a frost-riven and divisive horror. The Pole, our group already seems to know, just isn't a touchy-feely kind of place.

Although the U.S. Navy has been phasing out its Antarctic operations for the past several years, the military has left enduring fingerprints on South Pole culture. Pole employees use military time, military slang such as "comms" (for communications), and eat in a galley. In keeping with the hard-drinking, foul-mouthed reputation of the Navy men who once staffed the base, Pole people as a rule log plenty of free hours at the station's bar. There's no chapel at the Pole, no counselor. "If you're in a bad mood, you drink, lift weights, or go sit in the greenhouse," says one veteran.

Or you embrace a kind of grim and swelling black comedy. Shortly after the last summer-season plane takes off in February, leaving the winter-over crew alone for the first time, everybody cracks open a beer and sits down for a ceremonial video presentation of *The Thing*, a 1982 movie that involves a crash-landed space alien who body-snatches the people living at an Antarctic base one by one, leaving a single survivor. Last winter, not long after the viewing, a prankster smeared ketchup on his shirt and went tearing into one of the Pole's outbuildings, wielding a cleaver and shouting at the station doctor, "You're the only one left! You're the last one!"

Isolation, after all, does strange things to people. Due to a lack of social and physical outlets, day-to-day life with one's fellow castaways can be like tiptoeing through a sociopathic minefield: You never know who might snap, and for what reasons. In a well-publicized case in October 1996, a cook at Antarctica's McMurdo station inexplicably turned on several of his coworkers, attacking one man with the claw end of a hammer. FBI agents had to fly in from New Zealand to arrest him. That same week—and this was during the early summer, when the sun actually shines in Antarctica—a rebellion reportedly broke out among 15 employees at the Australian Casey base, requiring a professional mediator to fly in from Sydney and babysit for a few months.

In *Moby Dick*, Melville describes the color white as "the intensifying agent in things the most appalling to mankind." Antarctic history would seem to prove him right. There are rumors at the Pole, most of them dating back to the 1970s when it was primarily a Naval operation, that crew members who posed a threat to the rest of the group were put in a wire cage for the winter. Similarly, during the 1950s, a resident of Australia's Mawson base supposedly grew so deranged and violent he spent the winter locked in a storage room. In 1983, when the sun began to set on the Argentinean Almirante Brown station, the staff doctor, apparently nursing second thoughts about the season ahead, evacuated himself as well as his peers by burning the station down. And in a legendary act of poor-loserism, a worker at a Soviet base one year ended a chess game by killing his opponent with an ax.

All of this makes it difficult to look around Leo's Circle of Comfort without wondering who might be an eventual candidate for the cage. At lunch, however, several experienced Antarcticans explain that it's difficult to know who to fear down there. "It's not always obvious who's going to make it and who won't," says Drooling Drew, a kindly, longhaired native of Maine and the person in charge of the Pole's extensive computer network. "Sometimes the real weirdos actually flourish down there and the more normal people get driven crazy."

"It's the little things that get to you," says another guy at the table, a young technician with a goatee named Creative Craig. "Like your room's close to the bathroom. I heard about some guy who couldn't stand listening to the tap-tap-tap of toothbrushes against the sink over and over and over again. I hear one day he just went ballistic...."

After lunch, as Leo marches us into the woods to do trust falls, pattering on about how we have a "full-value contract" between us, I start to catch bits of sideline dialogue that suggest that the exploration going on between future Polemates is, perhaps aptly, more practical than emotional. "You're not a country music fella, ah y'mate?" Rabid Rodney, the Aussie, is asking someone. The station physician is casting around for somebody who shares his interest in Buddhism. And quietly working the periphery is Daring Dave, who at 26 is one of the group's youngest members—a rangy, good-looking Colorado kid with shoulder-length blond hair and what's unanimously accepted as the highest-pressure job at the Pole. When darkness falls this winter, it will be Dave who ministers to the crew's deprived senses and otherwise beaconless internal clocks. Dave, you see, is the cook.

I can hear him now as we tromp through La Foret's forest, quietly polling people about the particulars of their appetites, identifying allergies, separating the vegetarians from the carnivores, working to discern who, in the deepest, loneliest part of winter, will crave what. In the next week, Dave will help put together the order for an entire year's worth of food to be shipped to the Pole. "Do you like curry?" he is asking. "How do you feel about beef?" The answers come in hushed, confessional tones until he reaches Loud Larry, who it turns out has named himself well. There is something obdurate and possibly a little frightening about Loud Larry, an ectomorph in black cowboy boots who commandeered most of the morning's group activities, impatiently bossing everyone across the log, pausing at one point to remove three knives from his belt.

"I like all meats," Larry is telling Dave as a breeze lifts the tree branches around us. "I like squirrel meat. I like horse meat. My friends in the service ate a puppy once...." The sun kaleidoscopes through the woods and the group stays in step behind Leo's cheery gait, every one of us studying the ground. Dave nods his head gently and then, with a diplomat's grace, moves on to the next person. "Do you like coffee or tea?" we can hear him saying as we press forward into the wind. "Would you mind a lot of potatoes?"

Sustaining human life at the South Pole comes at a high cost. With no native organic matter there, not even microbes, the Pole is nothingness built upon nothingness, a big, vacuumy, million-year pileup of ice and drifting snow. It's as dry as the Sahara and almost as cold as Mars. Yet for the last 40 years, the U.S. government has had a presence at the Pole. The South Pole station, set on an icy plateau beneath the world's cleanest and most vaporless air, allows atmospheric scientists to track pollution worldwide and to monitor the ozone hole overhead.

Astrophysicists, looking in the opposite direction, have drilled holes a mile deep into the ice to track the movement of neutrinos.

But as scientists have immersed themselves in the great mysteries of life and physics, their shelter has slowly fallen apart around them. A senior science foundation official has called the station a "firetrap," while a 1996 study concluded that half the station's systems—namely the water pipes and generator-operated power plant—have outlived their intended lifetimes and can be expected to fail soon. After some political haggling, Congress last year appropriated $70 million to dismantle the existing station and erect an improved one in its place by 2005.

All of this is a way of moving us one step closer to the cosmos. If the new station works as planned, its proponents claim, it can help prepare us for a future out in space, where clusters of people will eventually be living and working, much as they do now at the Pole. "You won't take just astronauts and Ph.D.s to the moon to build a spaceport," says Jeff Johnson, an Eastern Carolina University anthropologist who has spent several years studying the group dynamics of South Pole winter-overs. "You'll need steel workers up there, too."

To make their lives together bearable, Johnson says, these floating pools of humanity should remember the principal lesson of life at the Pole: Conflict is best faced openly and resolutely. "It's the crews that are able to go face to face with issues that are able to resolve them. The more socially engaged they are, the better," he says. Johnson would get along well with Leo.

Robert Hogan, an industrial psychologist at the University of Tulsa who studied Antarctic crews in the early eighties, firmly disagrees. "All this B.S. about teamwork!" he says. "You have to realize the people best suited for the South Pole make crappy team players. The Pole's not an exciting environment. You're basically staring at a cinder-block wall for six months. It's a plain-vanilla, tedious environment, and the last thing we need is people who crave stimulation and excitement down there. It drives them crazy."

~~~~~~

Our facilitator Pat is trying to put a good face on our performance. "There's a quiet strength in this group, a quiet strength," she is saying as we complete our final debriefing for the day.

"Yes there is," says Leo. "A quiet strength."

"I find it worrisome," Pat continues in a blunter tone. "There's something odd about how quiet it is."

Facilitator Franco is nodding his head vigorously.

The group is, of course, quiet.

"How are you going to communicate with each other if you're all so quiet?" asks Pat.

More silence. Pat will later confess that she's accustomed to team-building with groups of executives and high-schoolers—people whose trust-falling is fraught with office politics and teenage angst, the stuff of high drama.

Suddenly, though, Dangerous Dave, a 33-year-old telescope technician from Chicago, steps forward. "I don't get what you want from us," he says to the facilitators. "What kind of stuff do you think we're going to say to each other here? Do you think I'm gonna tell somebody I don't like the way he looks and then go live with him at the South Pole for a year? You gotta be kidding."

Now it's the facilitators' turn to be silent. It's moving into late afternoon. The woods are overrun with squirrels. The rest of us are studying the ground again. If Dangerous Dave is looking for backup, he's not going to get it. Nor, however, is anyone disagreeing.

Pat draws herself up. "I think that was very brave of David to say," she says, looking around the circle again.

"Yes, brave," says Franco. "Very brave."

They don't bother to ask if anyone else has something to add. Dangerous Dave looks deflated. Leo scores a last victory for the touchy-feelies: "Let's do one more activity today," he says. "We call this the cinnamon-roll hug." Soon we have joined hands in a line, falling in behind Dangerous Dave. Leo directs him to spin slowly in a circle, and so, looking disgruntled but too beat to fight, he begins to turn. Linked in a human chain, the rest of us get pulled along, spiraling slowly and wrapping around Dave until we are bound in a giant, swirled-up hug, body to body, giggling now like disciples of feel-good as we press in toward the middle, where the naysayer stands squashed at our core.

An Antarctic vocabulary primer: if you are new to the ice, you are a "Fingee," which stands for "FNG," which stands for "fucking new guy." If you are not a Fingee, if you have survived a winter down there, then you are an "OAE," which stands for "Old Antarctic Explorer." If you are an OAE and you are finishing up another year on the ice, you are probably, in the eyes of the Fingees, a little "toasty." Toasty, from what I understand, means that you're ghastly pale, translucent even, plus grumpy and maladjusted. Toasty is also something of a spiritual condition. It means you have finally figured out what it means to be alone.

Most of us can hardly conceive of this. We are, on a symbolic level, Fingees, able to understand isolation only from the outside. In our prelapsarian innocence, we might well spend our last days, like the Fingees at La Foret, planning the parties we'll be throwing in our new, tight quarters. Steffen, a 26-year-old German researcher, already has taken inventory of birthdays and various national holidays, adding in the traditional bashes thrown for sunset and again for sunrise, and concluding that the calendar will absolutely hold "one rager per month."

Asked if they feel the year ahead might chasten or otherwise change them, the Pole first-timers are dismissive. "Naaah," Rabid Rodney says nonchalantly. Steffen giggles. But Daring Dave is more thoughtful. "I'm sure it will," he says. "I'm a little afraid, like maybe I'll be messed up after this, but I don't think so. I think we'll all be fine. We'll just be good and toasty by the end."

It's hard to know, of course, how this enforced isolation will affect anyone. For those who've never experienced it, who know it only from a distance, it can seem so titillating, a potential party, or perhaps, most desirably, an escape—a big blind date with yourself and a bunch of new friends. But spend time with the people who've actually spent time at the Pole and you'll hear tales that are much deeper than this, tales not only of deprivation and madness but of euphoria and fulfillment, the glory of having one's senses restored after a long period of impoverishment. For the Old Antarctic Explorers, especially the ones who choose to return for a second, a third, or even a fourth winter at the Pole, isolation becomes a kind of religion. The Chinese Taoists believe that social withdrawal can lead to enlightenment. In Hindu thought, every human ideally matures into a hermit. Nearly every form of faith has its monks and ascetics—those who cast off material goods and retreat, those who believe it's good, even glorious, to be alone. For the people who fall in love with the Antarctic winter, it's much the same. "Sure we get depressed sometimes," says Drooling Drew, "but mostly we just get quieter, more thoughtful for a while."

The hungers and deprivations of this long winter make the return north almost overwhelmingly beautiful, as one's senses are inundated. Many South Pole veterans claim to have a permanently heightened sense of smell. Creative Craig has described to me in prolonged, sensual detail the first thing he rushed for once the plane deposited him in Christchurch, New Zealand: a cold tall glass of fresh milk. "Since then, I've never tasted milk the same way," he says. Others, however, claim to feel alienated and discombobulated back in the green world. "I never went back to the real world, really," says Lester, a Pole veteran who's now taking some time off. "What is the real world, anyway?"

Sitting at a bar with the other toasties on one of the last nights of camp, Paul, who tends the station's power plant, grows momentarily wistful. "Last time I came off the ice," he says, "I got to Christchurch and immediately went to sleep. The next morning I walked over to the botanical gardens. I found a bench and just sat there, getting acquainted with the trees. And then I heard this noise, which I didn't recognize for a second. It was the sound of schoolchildren playing somewhere close by. It was the most beautiful sound I think I'll ever hear."

~~~~~~

After camp ends, in the few weeks remaining before they board the National Guard LC-130 plane that will carry them to the ice, the Pole people rush to complete a litany of last things—last visits with elderly grandparents, last trips to the dentist, last trysts with lovers. They'll make pilgrimages to the places closest to their souls: the ballpark, the hometown pub, the ocean. Daring Dave will climb the greenest mountains he can find near his home in Denver. Dastardly Diana will spend hours in a Maine pasture feeding carrots to her horse.

Most have begun to feel trepidation, to have second thoughts. Merry Mary, whose first year of marriage to Gumby will be consumed by their service at the station, admits to me at one point that the prospect of the long bleak winter is unnerving, her only previous Antarctic experience having been at the relatively luxe Palmer base, accessible by ship all year. "The Pole is so different," she says with a frayed smile. "It's the real thing."

There's so much still that the group cannot know or control. When they finally do leave en masse in mid-October, they'll go, for instance, without Loud Larry, he of the authoritarian temperament and multiple knives, who was asked at the last minute to withdraw. Bad weather later will strand the entire group first in New Zealand and then at McMurdo station, 840 miles from their final destination. Flu will fell others for days at a time. But finally, in early November, for better or worse, the 1998 South Pole winter-over crew will reach the darkest, farthest place on earth.

And then, for the next several months, the group will watch the sunlight at the Pole weaken, diminish, and finally disappear. By now, in early February, the first winds of winter will have begun to howl. Within the next two weeks, the last plane will arrive, carrying in 27,000 pounds of perishables to supplement the kilo of sun-dried tomatoes and 800 pounds of French Roast Daring Dave has laid in. Then the plane will take off in the lengthening dusk, its cargo hold filled with the last of the summer people. The winter-over group, swaddled in parkas and face masks, will march onto the icy tarmac and watch the plane go, waving. After that, they will be irrevocably alone, left with only one another and memories of trust-falls as the long, dark season stretches on.

(Originally published February 1998)

CONTRIBUTORS

Jon Billman lives in a log cabin along the Chocolay River in Michigan's Upper Peninsula.

Taffy Brodesser-Akner is a staff writer at the *New York Times* and its Sunday magazine. She lives in New Jersey.

Tim Cahill, a National Magazine Award winning writer, is the author of nine books and co-writer of four IMAX documentaries, two of which were nominated for Academy Awards. He lives in Montana.

W. Hodding Carter has been writing for *Outside* for twenty years and is the author of six books. Nearly everything he's written has involved, or been about, water. He grew up in Greenville, Mississippi, but now lives in Camden, Maine, with his wife Lisa and their four children.

Sara Corbett is a contributing writer to the *New York Times Magazine* and a long-time correspondent for *Outside*. Her work has been widely anthologized, including in *The Best American Travel Writing* and *The Best American Sports Writing*. She lives in Portland, Maine.

Kevin Fedarko has written for *Esquire*, *National Geographic,* and the *New York Times*, among other publications. His first book, *The Emerald Mile: The Epic Story of the Fastest Ride in History Through the Heart of the Grand Canyon*, was a *New York Times* bestseller. It won the National Outdoor Book Award and the Reading the West Award. Fedarko lives in Flagstaff and works as a part-time guide in the Grand Canyon.

Joshua Foer is the author of the international bestseller *Moonwalking with Einstein: The Art and Science of Remembering Everything*, published in 34 languages, and co-author of the *New York Times* bestseller *Atlas Obscura: An Explorer's Guide to the World's Hidden Wonders*.

Ian Frazier writes humor, reporting pieces, and longer works of nonfiction. His books include *Great Plains, On the Rez,* and *Travels in Siberia.* He lives in Montclair, New Jersey.

McKenzie Funk's writing also appears in *Harper's, Rolling Stone, National Geographic,* and the *New York Times Magazine.* His first book, *Windfall* (2014), won a PEN Literary Award and was a finalist for the Orion and Rachel Carson awards. A former Knight Wallace and Open Society fellow, Mac is a story consultant for the Center for Investigative Reporting, a cofounder of the journalism cooperative Deca, and a board member at Amplifier. He speaks English, Spanish, German, Italian, and Russian.

Will Grant was born and raised in Littleton, Colorado. He earned a bachelor's degree in natural resources from a liberal arts college in Tennessee, and spent the following six years working as a cowboy and horse trainer in Colorado and Texas. After leaving Texas, he earned a master's degree in journalism from the University of Montana. He currently lives in Santa Fe, New Mexico, with a few horses and a border collie.

S. C. Gwynne is the author of two *New York Times* bestselling books, *Empire of the Summer Moon,* a finalist for the Pulitzer Prize, and *Rebel Yell,* a finalist for the National Book Critics Circle Award and the PEN Literary Award for Biography. He was executive editor at *Texas Monthly* and a national correspondent and senior editor at *Time,* where he won a number of national awards. He lives in Austin, Texas.

Eric Hansen is an award-winning senior writer at *Partners In Health* and a contributing editor at *Outside.* From 2006 to 2010, he wrote the magazine's "Out of Bounds" column.

Nick Heil is a contributing editor for *Outside* and the author of *Dark Summit: The True Story of Everest's Most Controversial Season.* His work has appeared in *Men's Health, Men's Journal, Backpacker, Skiing, Reader's Digest,* and many other publications. He lives in Santa Fe, New Mexico.

Rowan Jacobsen is a contributing editor to *Outside* magazine and the author of seven books. His *Outside* piece "Heart of Dark Chocolate" received the Lowell Thomas Award from the Society of American Travel Writers for best adventure story of the year, and "The Spill Seekers," another *Outside* piece, was selected for inclusion in *The Best American Science & Nature Writing*. In addition to *Outside*, he has written for *Harper's*, *Mother Jones*, *Forbes*, *Vice*, the *New York Times*, and many others.

Michael Kruse is a senior staff writer for POLITICO and POLITICO *Magazine*. Before POLITICO, he worked at the *Tampa Bay Times*, where he won the Paul Hansell Award for Distinguished Achievement in Florida Journalism and the American Society of News Editors' distinguished non-deadline writing award while also contributing to *Outside* and ESPN's Grantland. A graduate of Davidson College, he lives in Davidson, North Carolina, with his wife and two daughters.

Paul Kvinta is a Contributing Editor for *Outside* and has written for many other publications. His article on human-elephant conflict in India, "Stomping Grounds," won the Daniel Pearl Award, was a finalist for the National Magazine Award, and appeared in *The Best American Magazine Writing*. His awards and fellowships include the Knight Journalism Fellowship at Stanford University and the Templeton Journalism Fellowship in Science and Religion at Cambridge University. He lives in Atlanta, where his surfing options are extremely limited.

James Nestor is an award-winning author and journalist who has written for *Outside* magazine, *Men's Journal*, the *New York Times*, *Scientific American*, and more. His book, *DEEP: Freediving, Renegade Science, and What The Ocean Tells Us about Ourselves* (Houghton Mifflin Harcourt, 2014) was a Finalist for the PEN American Center Best Sports Book of the Year, a BBC Book of the Week, and more. *DEEP* has been translated into eight languages. Nestor lives and free dives in San Francisco.

Susan Orlean has been a staff writer for the *New Yorker* since 1992. She is the author of eight books, including *The Bullfighter Checks Her Makeup*, *My Kind of Place*, *Saturday Night*, and *Rin Tin Tin: The Life and the Legend*. In 1999, she published *The Orchid Thief*, which was made into an Academy Award-winning film, *Adaptation*, written by Charlie Kaufman and directed by Spike Jonze. She is currently writing a book about the Los Angeles Public Library.

Nick Paumgarten is a staff writer at the *New Yorker*. He lives in Manhattan.

Stephanie Pearson is a contributing editor to *Outside* magazine. After earning her master's degree from Northwestern University's Medill School of Journalism, she served on *Outside's* editorial staff for twelve years and has since logged many hours in the field, reporting stories from Bhutan to Colombia to the Falkland Islands and beyond. She recently came full circle and moved from Santa Fe back home to northern Minnesota.

David Quammen's fifteen books include *The Song of the Dodo* (1996), *Monster of God* (2003), and *Spillover* (2012). For fifteen years, he wrote the Natural Acts column in *Outside;* more recently, he is a Contributing Writer for *National Geographic.* He has three times received the National Magazine Award. Quammen's forthcoming book is *The Tangled Tree,* to be published in 2018 by Simon & Schuster. He lives in Montana with his wife, Betsy Gaines, and their family of other mammals.

Steven Rinella is the author of *The Scavenger's Guide to Haute Cuisine; American Buffalo: In Search of a Lost Icon; Meateater: Adventures from the Life of an American Hunter;* and the two-volume *Complete Guide to Hunting, Butchering, and Cooking Wild Game.* He is the host of the MeatEater TV show and the MeatEater Podcast. He published his first story in *Outside* in May, 2000.

Bob Shacochis Shacochis is the author of seven award-winning books of fiction and nonfiction. His most recent novel, *The Woman Who Lost Her Soul,* was a best book of the year in ten major publications and on NPR, winner of the Dayton Literary Peace Prize, and a finalist for the 2014 Pulitzer Prize for fiction. His latest book, *Kingdoms in the Air,* collects thirty years of his travel writing.

Henry Shukman has won many awards for his poetry and fiction, including Arts Council England Award, Arvon Prize, and Jerwood-Aldeburgh Prize. He lives in New Mexico where he teaches at the Mountain Cloud Zen Center. His latest book is the poetry collection *Archangel.*

Natasha Singer is a reporter at the *New York Times,* where she examines how tech companies are influencing education, health, and privacy. She is also an instructor at School of The New York Times, a pre-college program where she teaches tech ethics. Among other far-flung capers, *Outside* magazine variously sent her to track the traffic in endangered species in Myanmar; commune with Keiko the killer whale in Iceland's Westman islands; and traverse the Northwest Passage on a U.S. Coast Guard icebreaker.

Christopher Solomon is a contributing editor for *Outside* who has written about severed feet in the waters off Vancouver, British Columbia; hapless homemade boats in the Hudson River; Seattle's Bike Batman; Italy's tradition of making the world's best climbing boots; Utah's wilderness wars; and an Alaskan scientist who climbs inside whales, looking for what killed them. He lives in Washington State.

Patrick Symmes is a contributing editor at *Outside*, and the author of *The Day Fidel Died: Cuba in the Age of Raul, Obama, and the Rolling Stones*, published by Vintage/Random House in October of 2017. He became a small-town newspaper reporter at age twenty, a foreign correspondent at age twenty-five, and since then has specialized in conflict zones and environmental crises around the world.

Sarah A. Topol is a contributing writer for the *New York Times Magazine*. Her work has also been published in the *Atlantic*, *Businessweek*, *GQ*, *Harper's*, *Newsweek*, the *New Republic*, *Outside*, *Playboy*, and *Popular Science*, among others. She lives in Istanbul.

Wells Tower writes fiction and nonfiction. He lives in North Carolina.

Tom Vanderbilt is a contributing editor at *Outside*, and has written for many publications, ranging from the *New York Times Magazine* to *Wired* to the *New Yorker*. He is the author of numerous books, including *Traffic: Why We Drive the Way We Do* and *You May Also Like: Taste in an Age of Endless Choice*. He and his family live in Brooklyn, New York.

Elizabeth Weil is a contributing writer for the *New York Times Magazine*. She lives in San Francisco with her husband, the writer Daniel Duane, and their two daughters.

Florence Williams is a contributing editor at *Outside* magazine and a freelance writer for the *New York Times, National Geographic, Mother Jones*, and numerous other publications. She is the author of *The Nature Fix: Why Nature Makes us Happier, Healthier and More Creative* (W.W. Norton, 2017), and *Breasts: A Natural and Unnatural History* (W.W. Norton, 2012). She is also the host of 2017's The XX Factor podcast for *Outside* magazine. She lives with her family in Washington, D.C.